THE ONLY WOMAN IN THE ROOM

THE ONLY
WOMAN
IN THE ROOM

GOLDA MEIR AND HER
PATH TO POWER

PNINA LAHAV

PRINCETON UNIVERSITY PRESS

PRINCETON & OXFORD

Published by Princeton University Press
41 William Street, Princeton, New Jersey 08540
99 Banbury Road, Oxford OX2 6JX

press.princeton.edu

All Rights Reserved

Library of Congress Cataloging-in-Publication Data

Names: Lahav, Pnina, 1945– author.
Title: The only woman in the room : Golda Meir and her path to power / Pnina Lahav.
Description: First edition. | Princeton : Princeton University Press, 2022. | Includes bibliographical references and index.
Identifiers: LCCN 2021052572 (print) | LCCN 2021052573 (ebook) | ISBN 9780691201740 (hardback) | ISBN 9780691239316 (ebook)
Subjects: LCSH: Meir, Golda, 1898–1978. | Women prime ministers—Israel—Biography.
Classification: LCC DS126.6.M42 L34 2022 (print) | LCC DS126.6.M42 (ebook) | DDC 956.9405/3092 [B]—dc23/eng/20211028
LC record available at https://lccn.loc.gov/2021052572
LC ebook record available at https://lccn.loc.gov/2021052573

British Library Cataloging-in-Publication Data is available

Editorial: Fred Appel, James Collier
Jacket Design: Emily Weigel
Production: Erin Suydam
Publicity: Kate Hensley, Kathryn Stevens
Copyeditor: Therese Malhame

Jacket image: Golda Meir attending World Conference on Soviet Jewry, Brussels, Belgium, March 2, 1976. Everett Historical Collection / Alamy Stock Photo

This book has been composed in Arno Pro

Printed on acid-free paper. ∞

Printed in the United States of America

10 9 8 7 6 5 4 3 2 1

To Moshe Lahav, MD
1939–1998
In Loving Memory

CONTENTS

PART III. 1948–1964

PART IV. 1964–1978

INTRODUCTION

THIS BOOK tells the story of Golda Meir's evolution from the time she was a young girl in czarist Russia to her emergence as an internationally respected leader on the world stage. My aim is not, however, to retell a familiar cradle-to-grave story. Rather, I wish to reconsider Golda Meir and her accomplishments through the lens of gender and to offer a new perspective on a series of events that shaped her development. These events—from bitter struggles with a father, who threatened to drag her home by her hair if she dared speak in public, to her confession in 1974 that she resented being called the only man in the cabinet—reveal the womanly side of Golda's identity and will thus allow us to integrate this often-neglected dimension of her character with the outward persona we have come to know. What did "being a woman" have to do with the obstacles Golda encountered as she fought her way to the top? And what price did this insecure yet ambitious young woman pay for her perseverance? What, too, was she able to achieve?

The second woman in the world to serve as minister of foreign affairs, and the third as prime minister, Golda "broke the glass ceiling" long before the term was coined. Nevertheless, she was mindful of her alterity, or otherness, as a member of the second sex. Golda was quite familiar with feminist theories, which she had encountered as a teenager in the United States during the suffragists' struggle to ratify the Nineteenth Amendment, and later as a member of a kibbutz in 1930s Palestine. More directly, she faced discrimination at almost every turn in her life and frequently endured verbal ridicule because of her

Figure 1. Golda as a young girl. Photograph
taken in Pinsk, Bellarus, Russia, circa 1900s.
Courtesy of The Lavon Institute—Labor
Movement Archive—the *Davar* newspaper
photograph collection.

gender. Given these experiences, how should we understand Golda's
later decisions to distance herself from feminism and staff her cabinet
entirely with men?

To answer these questions, this book explores Golda's perspective—
how she understood and navigated her alterity and how she balanced her
womanhood with her political ambitions. It also examines the gendered
contexts in which she made her most important decisions as a politician.
How did she navigate fierce diplomatic battles in a thoroughly misogynistic United Nations? How did she handle the Yom Kippur War surrounded by generals who wore their biases against women as a badge of
honor? And how did she survive political commentators who insisted
that, as a woman, she was too emotional to lead the country?

Figure 2. Prime Minister Golda Meir visiting the White House 1969, hosted by President Richard Nixon and First Lady Pat Nixon. Courtesy of Israel Government Press Office. Credit: Moshe Milner.

A Journey from Object to Subject in Photographs

Golda is photographed at age three or four with bows in her hair, dark curls framing her pale face. Her dress is feminine, decorated with a shiny bib and big embroidered ribbons. She appears poised, somewhat wistful. Her parents hoped she would grow into an attractive woman and become a good housewife: the object of a man's desires and the fulfiller of his needs.

Seventy-one years later, Prime Minister Golda Meir is photographed in the company of President Richard Nixon and First Lady Pat Nixon. She appears comfortable with her advanced age, graceful and confident in her role as head of her state. In these photographs Golda is an agent shaping history, on a par with the president of the United States rather than the first lady.

The photos tell a striking story. Golda was raised to become an object. She willfully and deftly turned herself into a subject. How did she do it?[1]

Golda Meir, Mrs. Meir, or Simply Golda?

Born Golda Mabovitz, she took her husband's name, Myerson, at the age of nineteen. David Ben-Gurion, Israel's legendary founder, forced her to Hebraize her name when he appointed her minister of foreign affairs. He may or may not have noticed that Meir was not only the abridgment of Myerson (in Hebrew, Meirson) but also the first name of her estranged husband, who had adopted the name Morris upon immigrating to America. This "new" last name, which she kept for the rest of her life and by which she became famous, tied her irrevocably to the man who fathered her children but whom she had left in the late 1920s.

If we want to write about a woman in a way that honors her authentic personhood, is it appropriate to address her by her first name, Golda, or does respect for her professional achievements require that we call her Mrs. Meir, or at least Meir? Does the history of the name "Meir" matter in this context? The dilemma is not easy to resolve. In this book, I have chosen to address her simply as Golda for two reasons. First, I follow her own example. Her many memorandums and unofficial letters were always signed "Golda," not Meir or Golda Meir. If she experienced her essence as "Golda," why not respect her preference? Second, in Golda's social circle, name changes were expected. Hebraizing one's name signified the Zionist return to the roots of ancient Israel. David Ben-Gurion, for instance, was born David Grün; Golda Lishansky, a leader in the labor movement, changed her name to Rachel Yanait Ben-Zvi. It would have been natural for Golda to Hebraize her first name as others did, yet she did not. We do not know why Golda resisted changing her name, but we do know that already as an eight-year-old in Milwaukee she turned down the suggestion that she Americanize her name, accepting only the slight change from Golda to Goldie.

The clue to her resistance might be found in her namesake, her mythical grandmother Golda Naidich. Legend had it that in Jewish Pinsk, the family's hometown in czarist Russia, Bubbe Goldae, a strong and wise woman, was a pillar of the community. Both men and women arrived from near and far to seek her counsel. Perhaps young Golda's imagination was ignited by these stories. Perhaps she believed that the name served as a talisman whose magic would make her, too, a pillar of her community. Given Golda's lifelong attachment to the name, referring to Golda as "Golda" should be understood as an act of respect—respect for her preference and for the woman she had become. Meir, by contrast, is a name that was forced upon her, and although she did accept it, it is not organic to her personality. It is no exaggeration to say that there are many Meirs but only one Golda.

A Schoolteacher from Milwaukee?

Golda was always haunted by her deficient education. In public she would often refer, only half-jokingly, to her "primitive mind." She enrolled in but never completed her studies at the Wisconsin State Normal School for teachers in Milwaukee, as studying always took a back seat to political activities. Later in life, though, she listed herself as a schoolteacher and indeed taught in an afternoon Yiddish school, which did not require a license. The only course she took from start to finish, ending with a certificate, was a poultry raising course while in the kibbutz. That accomplishment never made it onto her resume.

Despite her lack of formal credentials, Golda was not "uneducated" or "intellectually lazy" as her critics claimed. She possessed sharp intelligence, tremendous energy, and a keen aptitude for absorbing and analyzing information, skills confirmed by the accomplished men who worked with her in the prime minister's office. Although it is true that she was neither much of a reader nor a writer (perhaps indicating an undiagnosed dyslexia), she always displayed a voracious curiosity, befriended intellectual men, and absorbed their knowledge and wisdom. Few outside her family circle knew, for example, about her love of classical music or her ability to sing some of Schubert's lieder with warmth and passion.[2]

Golda's decision to describe herself as a schoolteacher is telling. By aligning herself with a stereotypical female profession, she may have diverted attention from the fact that her very presence among political leaders (domestic as well as international) challenged their stereotypical expectation that women should be subservient to political men. Positioning herself as a schoolteacher sent a message of humility: "I am neither overly ambitious nor too accomplished," she said and disguised the fact that she was a professional politician accumulating power as she climbed up the party ladder.

Golda the Younger and Golda the Old Woman

As a young woman Golda was quite attractive. She had dark, wavy hair, nice features, and a prominent but unobtrusive nose. She dressed neatly, often wearing suits with a belt around her waist that emphasized her feminine figure. Like most women of her generation, she never wore pants. Photos of her from this era display a woman who cared about her looks and invested in her appearance, and some said that she would shop at Macy's during her many fund-raising trips to New York City. Even during her time in the ascetic kibbutz, Golda showed a fashionable flair, posing in the field in a cap and an all-white dress, as if she were a suffragist from the American Midwest, rather than a woman immersed in the working-class ethos of Zionist Palestine. To appreciate the boldness of Golda's decision to invest in an all-white outfit, one needs to recognize both her strong practical bent and the impracticality of wearing white in a place without washing machines, not to mention dry cleaners. Beyond her physical appearance, Golda had a magnetic presence, the elusive quality that turns one into the center of attention: her joy and quickness of spirit were accompanied by a "a marvelous laugh that left [men] tingling."[3]

Opinions differed about Golda's looks at an old age. Cartoons from the 1960s and 1970s depict a short, stocky woman, her big nose protruding forward, as if to emphasize a phallic quality to accompany the popular saying that "she was the only man in the cabinet." Men were often unflattering in their descriptions. The historian Avi Shlaim, for instance, described her as "a kindly Jewish grandmother, with her craggy face, baggy suits, orthopedic shoes and old-fashioned handbag."[4] Michael Bar-Zohar, another historian, opined that "she was far from good-looking, her taste in clothing was pathetic."[5] Some women agreed. Upon meeting Golda, the American feminist Letty Cottin Pogrebin said that she reminded her of a "lower East Side landlady." The journalist Oriana Fallaci, by contrast, saw Golda's inner qualities reflected in her appearance: "Sweet and energetic, the look of a housewife obsessed with

Figure 3. Golda in Kibbutz Merhavia. Courtesy
of The Lavon Institute—Labor Movement
Archive—the *Davar* newspaper photograph
collection.

cleanliness . . . [her] wealth consists in a disarming simplicity, an irritating modesty, a wisdom coming from having toiled all their lives in the
pain, discomfort, and trouble that leave no time for the superfluous."[6]
Israel's leading historian, Anita Shapira, in an essay titled "Golda: Femininity and Feminism," emphasized Golda's adherence to her authentic
self: she "did not play the game of the male world, did not imitate male
behavior but forced the men who interacted with her to accept her as
she was—a woman who plays in the male court as a woman."[7]

Golda's Maternal Appeal

The discerning Oriana Fallaci put her finger on an important secret: the
elder Golda reminded people of their mothers or grandmothers, and
they projected their attitudes toward her accordingly. Fallaci admitted
that Golda reminded her of her own mother Toska, whom Fallaci
adored. The opposite phenomenon also occurred: those who disliked

Golda drew from the wells of their own complicated emotions toward their mothers. Golda intuitively understood the magic inherent in the maternal image and, as she grew older and more powerful, increasingly presented the persona of a "Jewish matriarch"—a wizened woman with gray hair tied into a simple bun, dressed neatly but not extravagantly, often wearing a brooch or a string of pearls around her neck (the latter at the suggestion of her more sophisticated secretary, Lou Kaddar).

Golda's maternal image tapped into the deep sources of the popular imagination. One of the better-known songs in the Yiddish repertoire is "A Yiddishe Mame"—a Jewish mother. The lyrics wax eloquently about the stereotypical "Jewish Mother," "a blessed gift from God," who "through fire and water, runs to rescue her child."[8] In the state archives one finds many letters praising Golda as the mother or grandmother of the Jewish people. A letter from an Englishman who had served in Palestine in 1948 draws this comparison in unequivocal terms: "I said to myself 'There is one name for [Golda Meir] and that is "Mother Israel." If I had my way, I would place a large portrait of you [everywhere with] the words "MOTHER ISRAEL" in lights underneath for posterity.'"[9]

That Golda could evoke the stereotype of the perfect mother while also being considered "the only man in the cabinet" speaks to the complex and contradictory nature of her public image. She could be maternal and empathic but also tough and sometimes cruel. The significance of this achievement was not lost on people, and Golda served as a role model to many young girls. As a child in America, Ronitt Rubinfeld, an outstanding mathematician and professor of computer science at Massachusetts Institute of Technology, actively searched for books on Golda and looked up to her as a model of what she might become. So did Daphne Barak-Erez, a brilliant jurist and justice on Israel's Supreme Court. As a young girl, Barak-Erez considered Golda an example of the endless options that were open to women. Since the very inception of the Israeli state, Golda showed girls and women that a meaningful career beyond the home was possible and that women could be much more than mothers and wives. Standing on Golda's shoulders, these women became role models for the next generation of women, and they represent one of Golda's underappreciated achievements.

The Only Man in the Cabinet

The idea that "Golda was the only man in the cabinet" originally derived from a comment made by Ben-Gurion. While his motivations remain unclear—did he intend to shame other cabinet ministers by casting doubt on their masculinity, or to shame Golda whose gender was thereby inverted?—the public adopted the statement as an amusing but insightful pearl of wisdom. To this day, if you mention Golda to an Israeli, he or she will soon note, with an embarrassed, even sly smile, that "she was the only man in the cabinet." The phrase is ambiguous, connoting the exceptionality of Golda's strength, thereby attributing weakness to women in general. But it also reflects an Israeli failure to accept the simple fact that a woman, too, can lead in matters of security and defense. In a government made up almost exclusively of men and one in which the military is put on a pedestal, manhood remains the "natural" standard for leadership.

Golda generally kept silent about Ben-Gurion's statement, but when Oriana Fallaci raised the question, she admitted that she found it "irritating."[10] Given Golda's tough, uncompromising attitude in matters of defense and foreign affairs, to the person in the street, the notion that Golda was "the only man" quickly became the notion that Golda was "the only one with balls." The distortion of her female body offended Golda's self-image as a heterosexual woman. She had little problem with being tough and decisive, but she resented the notion that these qualities belonged exclusively to men.

Despite her general silence on the subject, Golda surreptitiously debunked the image of herself as "the only man" by reminding the public of her womanly qualities. While prime minister, for instance, she regularly held cabinet meetings at home, complete with coffee and cookies, which the press dubbed as meetings in "Golda's Kitchen." The kitchen was a place for housewives, not for generals and eminent statesmen, and yet when "kitchen" entered the political lexicon it somehow "kosherized" the fact that political deliberations could also be held in the sanctum sanctorum of a woman's space. Golda subtly reminded the public that she was a female prime minister, and that this too was natural.

Golda's Alterity

Throughout Golda's life, she inhabited environments that designated her as "other." Despite the differences between czarist Russia, the United States, and Palestine and Israel, that sense of "otherness" existed in each. In Pinsk, poor Jewish boys went to a cheder to study reading, writing, and Torah, while poor Jewish girls stayed at home to acquire homemaking skills. In Milwaukee, Golda's parents refused to let her enroll in high school, which became one of the formative traumas of her life. Golda's mother, a pragmatic woman, did not think much of her daughter's aspiration to become a teacher. Wisconsin law banned married women from the teaching profession, and for her mother marriage defined the good life. Her father concurred, telling Golda that "men don't like smart girls."[11] If she were a boy, her parents, like most Jews, would have done everything they could to enable her pursuit of higher education, but they believed such efforts would be wasted on a girl.

Golda experienced alterity in Palestine and Israel as well. Those experiences were more complicated and produced a tension within her that accompanied her for the rest of her life. Social life in the Yishuv (pre-1948 Jewish Palestine) and the young State of Israel extolled gender equality. From the rhetorical culture of the kibbutzim, to the women paratroopers sent behind the enemy lines during World War II, to the adoption of the Women's Equal Rights Law in 1951, the idea of gender equality played an undoubtedly valuable role in the self-image of Israeli society.[12] It was also mostly a myth. As Golda rose to power, men and the values of masculinity retained their hegemony on the ground.

In the early 1920s, as soon as Golda joined a kibbutz she realized that despite the egalitarian rhetoric, the traditional division of labor persisted intact. Women were excluded from guard duty and encouraged to pursue "feminine roles," such as kitchen and laundry work. She witnessed the Orthodox camp's fight to deny women the right to vote in Zionist institutions, and later, as a budding politician, she encountered rabbis who vetoed her candidacy for mayor of Tel Aviv. Later still, as an established politician, a prominent Orthodox member of the Knesset declined to support her nomination as prime minister on the grounds that according to the great medieval sage Maimonides, women were not eligible for political office.[13]

Israeli media also tended to apply stereotypical notions when they analyzed Golda's character. Joel Marcus, a senior commentator for the prestigious Israeli daily *Haaretz*, volunteered that far from Golda's being the only man in the cabinet, "with her hostilities, her jealousies, she is the ultimate woman. A woman with all her negative attributes."[14] Golda's alterity was reaffirmed and reinforced by Israeli culture. Succeeding in such a culture was an uphill battle, one that affected her developing selfhood and informed her choice of strategies for survival. As Golda later reflected, "to be successful, a woman has to be much more capable than a man. . . . When a woman does not want only to give birth, to raise children . . . when a woman also wants to work, to be somebody . . . well, it's hard. Hard. Hard."[15]

Golda's Alterity as a Jew among Gentiles

Golda experienced otherness (being different from the men surrounding her) not only as a woman but also as a Jew. Her Jewishness was the pillar of her identity, although this identity was cultural rather than religious. She grew up in a home where the rules of kashrut were observed, but she did not follow any of the central tenets of Jewish law; she observed the Sabbath as a day of rest, recreation, and meetings with family and friends but not as a "sacred" day; and she neither attended synagogue nor approved of the separation of men and women during services.

Golda was a secular Jew, and her highest priority was the existence of a Jewish state, where Jews would not be vulnerable to the power of gentiles. A Jewish identity and a Jewish state, both victims of alterity, were inseparable to her, which is why she insisted that territories conquered by Israel during the 1967 war would only be returned following face-to-face negotiations between the parties, thereby recognizing Israel as a legitimate partner. Her insistence bore fruit at the end of the Yom Kippur War, when Egypt's president Anwar al-Sadat agreed to negotiate with Israeli representatives, a process that culminated with Israel's 1979 peace treaty with Egypt. Toward the conclusion of her tenure as prime minister, as the Yom Kippur War was coming to an end, a heartbroken Golda summarized the major fear that shaped her political philosophy:

an Israel that is not strong will be devoured by its enemies. She was afraid that the Israeli people, overwhelmed by the hostility of the Arab states surrounding them, would give up: "One thing that leaves me anxious is the possibility that the people . . . feeling frustrated will lose the ability to determine what is the necessary minimum essential for survival."[16]

She foresaw for Israel a trajectory of continuous military struggle. This belief gave rise to a painful dilemma with respect to the question of gender equality. What would happen if the interests of the Jewish state and the demands of gender equality came into conflict? Did the reality of Jewish alterity mean that Jewish women would forever be asked to wait for "better times" when physical security allowed the leadership to address their needs?[17] Golda tried to reconcile the tension, known in the literature as the dilemma of intersectionality, but her compromises mostly gave short shrift to the values of women's rights.

Golda and the Socialist Agenda

Golda was committed to the progressive tenets of socialism, but in this commitment she again promoted the social priorities of men. From the time she joined the socialist party of Poalei Zion until she ended her career as head of Labor Zionism in Israel, Golda worked with men who were unmoved by feminist concerns. They were not necessarily misogynists or incurable patriarchs, but they did not believe that the lower status of women was a matter requiring urgent attention. They thought that time, not present action, would cure the inequalities of gender. Golda shared this view. She was a firm believer in human agency and wanted to see women demand more equal treatment. After all, she had done it, why shouldn't they? In her mind, if women preferred the traditional division of labor, so be it.

The Perils of Pragmatism

Between principle and pragmatism, Golda leaned toward pragmatism. Her wedding exemplifies her flexible approach. She and Morris wanted a civil ceremony but her parents insisted on a Jewish wedding. After many arguments and much emotional upheaval, the young couple yielded. As Golda saw things, "What damage would fifteen minutes under the chuppah do to our principles?"[18] In a more sober environment, the seventy-four-year-old Golda offered a less playful assessment of her flexible approach: "When you're doing the job I am doing, you always have to stoop to compromises, you can never let yourself remain one hundred percent faithful to your ideas."[19]

Even though she enjoyed repeating the maxim (attributed to Voltaire) that the "best is the enemy of the good," Golda also recognized that stooping and compromising could be harmful and, in hindsight, regretted some of her actions: "I stoop enough. And that's bad."[20] To give just one example, in order to secure industrial peace, Golda put the imperative of equal pay for the equal work of women on the back burner. One wonders whether this inner instinct "to stoop" was also a part of her gendered identity, an impulse that partly explains her poor record on the status of women during her long career.

Golda and Israel's Wars

Golda never served as a soldier in any of Israel's wars. From the 1940s onward she was nevertheless a central figure in the growing army of diplomats and fund-raisers promoting Israel's interests on the international stage. Golda's first direct encounter with war and diplomacy came in 1956. Prime Minister Ben-Gurion decided to join France and the United Kingdom in launching a preventive war against Egypt. He knew that doing so was illegal under international law but calculated that the European powers would veto any attempt to activate the United Nations Security Council against Israel. He needed a minister of foreign affairs who would lead the Israeli cabinet to approve the war and defend Israel before the United Nations, the United States, and world public opinion.

It remains unclear whether Golda approved of the collaboration with France and the United Kingdom, and she was clearly unhappy about acting behind President Eisenhower's back, but she put her trust in Ben-Gurion's judgment. Following the invasion, Israel was harshly condemned. Eisenhower insisted that Israel withdraw from the Sinai

Peninsula forthwith and, with the UN's secretary-general, Dag Hammarskjöld, called for severe sanctions on Israel. Golda found herself representing an isolated, practically friendless country. Although Golda insisted that the war was one of self-defense and she resisted the pressure to leave these territories, most nations viewed Israel as a lawless aggressor and sided with Egypt. In Washington and at the United Nations she crossed swords with several high and mighty men: Eisenhower, Hammarskjöld, and the U.S. secretary of state John Foster Dulles. Four months of harrowing diplomatic battle ended with a dire disappointment: Israel was forced to evacuate the Sinai Peninsula and Gaza Strip—the two territories it had conquered during the war. The diplomatic conflicts left deep scars on Golda's soul and surely influenced her decision to avoid a preemptive strike at the beginning of the Yom Kippur War.[21]

The consensus among historians, however, is that despite an initial string of disappointments, the Suez War ended quite well for Israel. The Sinai Peninsula and the Gaza Strip were returned to Egyptian control, but secret agreements between the countries terminated the guerrilla warfare against Israel. The Straits of Tiran, another point of contention, were opened to Israeli navigation. Israel's army, now relatively well equipped, gained prestige as a swift and highly competent military force. Between 1957 and 1967 Israel experienced ten years of calm that it used for construction and development.

Shortly after the end of this decade, Golda, now prime minister, navigated the ship of state during the Yom Kippur War.[22] Between 1969 and 1973, she negotiated with Anwar al-Sadat about peace prospects between Israel and Egypt. Several proposals were considered and, to reach a deal, the U.S secretary of state Henry Kissinger pressured Golda to soften her positions. Many commentators criticized Golda for being stubborn, even capricious. However, documents in Israel's State Archives show that Golda presented several proposals for territorial compromise and was willing to accommodate the other side.[23] On October 6, 1973, Yom Kippur on the Jewish calendar, Egypt and Syria launched simultaneous surprise attacks on Israel. Golda received confirmation of the planned invasion that morning and decided against launching a preemptive strike. Her decision has been bitterly criticized, though it is impossible to know what would have happened had Israel attacked first. A few days into the war, rumors spread that a panicked Moshe Dayan, the legendary minister of defense, had declared an imminent Israeli defeat. The seventy-five-year-old Golda, ill with non-Hodgkin's lymphoma, again proved her remarkable backbone.[24] Just as she had done in 1956, she refused to accept defeat and spurred the military onward. She spent days and nights in the bunker of the central military command consulting with the officers, examining maps of battle, and helping to make strategic decisions. At the same time, she kept a close eye on the diplomatic scene. Her good working relationships with Nixon and Kissinger paid dividends, as she obtained Nixon's approval for a much-needed American airlift of essential weapons. Reading through the cabinet deliberations during those dark days one cannot fail to note the reliance, trust, and dependency desperate ministers directed toward Golda. She was their pillar of strength.

The traumatized and grieving public thought otherwise. A wave of criticism grew louder and angrier in the following weeks, with several critics attributing the malfunction of the government to Golda's gender.[25] In a book published shortly after the war concluded, Y. Ben-Porat, the widely respected political commentator of the popular daily *Yediot Ahronoth*, targeted Golda's womanhood directly: "As an emotional woman Golda leads the state in accordance with her private loves and hatreds." On the preceding page, Ben-Porat also offered detailed criticism of a well-known general—Aharon Yariv—the prime minister's adviser on the war against terrorism. However, the description of Yariv, while critical, included terms such as "very knowledgeable, possessing a brilliant analytical mind and a strong personality."[26] The bias could not have been starker. Both Golda and Yariv were denounced harshly, but the man (Yariv) was painted as analytical and clearheaded whereas the woman (Golda) was described as emotional, a slave of her "loves and hatreds," a popular stereotype of a woman under stress.[27]

The time has arrived to reconstruct a less one-dimensional portrait of Golda.

PART I

GROWING UP

CHAPTER 1

IN IMPERIAL RUSSIA

1898–1905: Kiev, Pinsk, and the Formation of Gendered Identity

Golda Mabovitz was born in 1898 in Kiev, then part of the Russian Empire. With good reason her parents, Bluma and Moshe-Itzhak, treated her as a particularly precious daughter. Child mortality among poor Jews was high, and in the nine years that had passed between the birth of their first daughter Sheyna and Golda's arrival, they had lost five infants to various illnesses. Golda's father was a carpenter, though mostly unemployed, leaving it to her mother, the daughter of a Pinsk pub owner, to provide for the family through a variety of odd jobs.[1]

From birth, Golda was marked as an "other," Jewish and female. She learned very quickly that the world was divided between gentiles and Jews, and that Jews were the czar's second-class subjects, unwelcomed by Russian society. The Jews of Pinsk, a small town with muddy streets in the Pale of Settlement, were mostly poor and unemployed. Work was available in the major Russian urban centers, but law banned Jews from these areas. Kiev, for instance, with its proud ancient history and cathedrals glittering in gold, allowed Jews to enter its gates only if they had obtained a work permit. When the czar's government embarked on a project to provide public education, it needed carpenters to build the schools' libraries. Golda's father was among those fortunate to obtain a permit, and the family moved from Pinsk to Kiev. Golda was born the following year.

Life in Kiev did not bring the anticipated prosperity. Moshe was a failing entrepreneur and any business he started soon collapsed, leaving him frustrated and deeper in debt. The family moved often, penniless, consumed by the anxiety of losing the precious permit, and intimidated by antisemitism. Later in life, Sheyna still remembered the frightening searches by the Kiev police, who arrived unannounced and demanded proof of the permit's validity. Golda, by 1972, could only recall three memories from Kiev: the death of her grandmother who shared their dilapidated one-room home, the gnawing hunger, and the frightening rumor of an impending pogrom.[2]

Jewish Identity and the Pogrom That Wasn't

Pogroms were a periodic part of Russian Jewish life. Gentiles would violently attack their Jewish neighbors, destroy and loot property, murder, maim, and often rape. If the government did not cooperate with the perpetrators, it turned a blind eye. The most famous pogrom, in the town of Kishinev in 1905, wrought such devastation that it "cemented the feeling that Russia was unsafe for Jews."[3] This fear of antisemitic violence became a cardinal justification for the Zionist movement, which sought to establish a state for the Jewish people where they could rule themselves, free of persecution and abuse.

A single pogrom, one that did not in fact materialize, remained etched in Golda's memory of her childhood. When she was five years old, a rumor spread across town that a pogrom was imminent. She was sent to the neighbors upstairs, while her father secured the main door with wooden boards. Sheyna armed herself with a kitchen knife and their mother with boiling water, although Sheyna would later describe these tools of self-defense as "tragicomic." In the event of an attack, the family was defenseless.

In the end there was no pogrom—most of the early twentieth-century pogroms erupted later, when Golda was already on her way to America—but Golda's memory is important for two reasons. First, the fear piercing the child's heart as she awaited an invasion by a group of rowdy, drunken thugs must have been staggering, and must have become even more poignant as she told the story over and over again throughout her life. Second, Golda's experience of the pogrom helped construct her Jewish identity and prepared her embrace of Zionism as the only solution to the Jewish predicament. In Kiev, Sheyna studied in a Jewish socialist school, where she absorbed a theory that fused working-class consciousness with Zionism and in turn instilled it in her young sister. Golda, five or six years old, was captivated by socialist Zionism and turned her concern for the welfare of the Jewish people into her life project.

Golda's recounting of the pogrom scare also captured the Zionist perception of Jewish masculinity in exile. To Golda, "it was typical of father that he made no plans to take his family and hide some place."[4] The Jewish males in "galut"—exile—were bitterly criticized by Zionists as passive and cowardly, incapable of defending their wives and children. Self-rule, they argued, would revive the heroic spirit of biblical Israel, and transform the Jews of galut into Maccabees. As an Israeli leader, Golda never missed an opportunity to shower praise on brave Israeli "Sabras" (authentic Israeli-born people) defending their land and their people.

What about Golda's identity as a woman? Speaking of the "pogrom that wasn't," Golda did not blame her mother for not seeking appropriate shelter. It was her father's duty to provide defense. During her early childhood, Golda accepted the gendered division of labor as God-given. She was standing at the intersection between antisemitism and sex discrimination, but whereas her exposure to Zionism provided a theory to challenge the Jewish condition, neither Sheyna nor Golda had been exposed to feminist theories that challenged sex-based discrimination. They could not comprehend the double burden Jewish women were carrying.[5]

Gender Identity and the Luxury of Schooling for Little Girls

Golda was born into a traditional patriarchal society. From birth Jewish women were initiated into alterity. In their synagogues—the central institution of their community—they were separated from men and treated as passive observers. They were not counted as a part of the quorum needed for prayer, did not partake in an initiation rite to become members of the Jewish people (Bar Mitzvah), and were pro-hibited from saying kaddish (the final prayer at burial) for their loved ones. Stereotyped as dangerously alluring, women were required to cover themselves, shave their heads upon getting married, and wear a homely head cover. They were also expected to marry young—Sheyna, for example, pejoratively described her unmarried aunts as "rotting in their virginity for many years."[6]

Jewish Russian society was, however, beginning to experience mo-dernity. Girls in previous generations did not even attend cheder (the traditional Jewish school), but by the time Golda reached school-age, parents were sending their daughters to secular schools for young Jews.[7] In Kiev, Golda's mother, being practical and focusing on survival, planned to have nine-year-old Sheyna apprentice with a seamstress or a milliner. After several heart-wrenching arguments, however, Sheyna persuaded her mother to let her attend school and even took the initia-tive to locate a free Jewish school aimed at educating children of the proletariat. She loved school, writing in her memoirs, "If I did not turn into a misanthrope, it is due to that school."[8] Golda looked up to Sheyna and internalized the message. She too hoped to be seated in a classroom, but this did not come to pass.

The family's financial situation soon worsened, and the future looked grim. A third daughter had arrived, Tzipke, and Moshe and Bluma de-cided that he should join the flood of migrants searching for better luck in America. When Moshe migrated, the family lost its permit to stay in Kiev, so Bluma and her daughters returned to Pinsk. Money was scarce and the option of enrolling in school evaporated. Sheyna, already a teen-ager, devoted most of her time to a Zionist revolutionary group, deter-mined to topple the czar and improve the lot of her fellow Jews. Young Golda felt abandoned and lonely. Perhaps this is the reason that throughout her adult life she was known to crave company. She found solitude hard to endure.

If Golda were a boy, cheder education would have been mandatory. Either her grandparents or the community would have seen to it that she received basic Jewish learning. But the education of a girl was a luxury, one her mother did not prioritize. Lonely and bored, Golda was determined to teach herself the basic skills of literacy, an early sign of agency. Occasionally Sheyna would help, but Golda mostly copied the letters of the Hebrew alphabet from the Jewish Prayer Book (probably the only book in her home). Even if Golda was too young to process her experience, she was internalizing her identity as a member of the second sex. Her lot was a woman's lot—based on the traditional gendered division of labor. Her destiny was to become a good "balabusta" (Yiddish for homemaker) and thereby attract a husband who would provide her with a good life. No one expected her to have a life of the mind.

While Bluma never valued education, she did value appearances and encouraged Golda's femininity; maybe she saw her ideal self in the pretty little girl. Bluma focused on Golda's bright, thick and curly hair, often ornamenting her daughter's head with ribbons or even a crown braid that made her look particularly regal. Sheyna recalls Golda basking in her mother's attention and delighting in her own reflection in the mirror. Here was another layer of Golda's alterity, her otherness, as a woman. She was groomed to be an object of desire and attention, not a person of independent mind and will. At the same time, this aspect of her identity probably nurtured in Golda that self-confident, dignified appearance for which she became famous in her later years.

Four Strong Women Who Shaped Young Golda's Gender Identity

Jewish society in czarist Russia accepted patriarchal values as a part of God's will and the natural order. But there were also strong, able women whose energy and resolve made a difference in the lives of their families and community. These women, who defied stereotypes of femininity by exercising power, were also a part of young Golda's environment.

First and foremost, there was her mythical great-grandmother, Bubbe Goldae, after whom Golda was named. Bubbe Goldae, who died before Golda was born, was reputed to be tough, clever, and wise and an authority among the Jews of Pinsk. Family lore had it that men and women from near and far would seek her advice about their business transactions. Golda's mother never tired of telling the story of how Bubbe

Goldae gave the green light to her marriage to Golda's father. Bluma first saw Moshe at Pinsk's public square, where young recruits for the czar's army were assembled: "I saw a handsome young man, a giant, and I said to myself this is the one I want for a husband." It was love at first sight. But in Russia in the 1880s marriage was a family transaction, and love counted for little. Typically, a matchmaker would be hired to bring a couple together, and it was imperative that the father consent to the marriage. Bluma's father, Menachem Neiditch, a pub owner, was not sure that Moshe was a good match for his daughter, as his social status was lower than Bluma's, in virtue of his being merely a carpenter. A yeshiva education could have compensated for his humble origins, and there were hints that he had spent some time in a yeshiva, but not enough to make a mark. It fell to Bubbe Goldae to make the decision. The old woman's analysis shied away from principles and focused instead on practical matters. Rather than suggest that an uneducated carpenter was a good match for her granddaughter, she opined that "even a carpenter may be turned into an entrepreneur," and gave young Bluma the nod of approval.[9] If there was a silver lining in Golda's upbringing, which was mired in trouble and conflict, it was the genuine affection her parents felt for each other.

From the legend of Bubbe Goldae, Golda harvested the confidence that women could be valued decision makers, that they could be strong and wise, exert authority, and earn respect. She learned that even if women had no access to education, they could still effect change. It stands to reason that, regardless of the deep misogyny surrounding her, little Golda would have intuited that female power was possible. In all likelihood, Golda felt that Bubbe Goldae bestowed a special privilege on her—in later years she came to wear her name like an amulet that armed her with the strength she needed to make a mark in society. Both in the United States and in Israel, the name Golda was considered old-fashioned, a relic of the disparaged Jewish life in exile—galut. While other members of the family Americanized their names upon arrival in Wisconsin, and many of her friends in Palestine Hebraized their names in keeping with Zionist ideology, Golda staunchly resisted changing her name, ultimately making it internationally iconic.

Another role model in Golda's life was Mrs. Janovsky, though Golda did not know her personally. Mrs. Janovsky represented the emerging Jewish middle class. According to Sheyna, Mrs. Janovsky was the only member of the middle class the family had "known." Mrs. Janovsky was educated, spoke Russian in addition to Yiddish, and lived in a comfortable house. Her relationship with Golda's family began when Bluma was hired as a wet nurse to one of Mrs. Janovsky's eleven children.[10] There, for the first time, Bluma learned basic hygiene and the progressive principles of child-rearing—bathing the babies, changing their diapers frequently, letting them move their limbs freely rather than keeping them tightly wrapped like mummies. Whereas Bluma did not bathe Sheyna until she reached the age of one, baby Golda not only enjoyed the pleasure of baths but often delighted in bathing with the neighbor's puppy.

The two women who had the most influence on the life of young Golda undoubtedly were her mother and her sister. Both Bluma and Sheyna had controlling natures, but they were polar opposites in their approaches to the world. Whatever earned the respect of one would soon become the focus of scorn from the other. Golda was always torn between them, and yet each had a decisive influence on her development.

Mother Bluma's Disappointments

The harsh reality of everyday life shattered many of Bluma's hopes and expectations. Bubbe Goldae's speculation that "even a carpenter may be turned into an entrepreneur" failed to materialize. Moshe Mabovitz was unable to find steady work, so the task of providing for the family fell to Bluma, who turned bitter, critical, and quarrelsome. She was particularly hard on Sheyna. As was customary, Bluma used Sheyna as a mother's helper and assigned her chores that the young child was not always capable of performing. Failure was met with mockery and sarcastic comments (today we would call it shaming, perhaps even emotional abuse) that scarred the young child.

Yet Bluma was also an energetic woman who took seriously her responsibility toward her family. When Moshe migrated to America,

Bluma became a single mother who had three mouths to feed and little to no means to do so. She returned to Pinsk with her daughters and frantically searched for work. Mostly, she baked goods to sell in the market or deliver to "rich women's" homes. On the side, she would peel potatoes at a nearby restaurant in return for a glass of milk with which she made porridge for her daughters. Bluma was an agentive woman. Her family depended on her ability to pull herself up by her bootstraps and, while she did not always succeed, she certainly showed Golda the meaning of self-empowerment.

Sheyna, a Burgeoning Revolutionary

Sheyna, who turned fourteen when the family returned to Pinsk, was opinionated and self-motivated like her mother. When they left Kiev further education became moot. Even if Bluma could have afforded it for her elder daughter—which she could not—Pinsk's schools did not welcome Jews. So Sheyna turned her attention to political activism. Like many young Jews during this time of political upheaval and social unrest, she joined a social-Zionist revolutionary movement and discovered the basic principles of political organization. She read banned literature, distributed propaganda leaflets, and stood guard during forbidden meetings. If Bluma communicated an unequivocal commitment to family values, Sheyna communicated the excitement of the coming political change, the fight for social justice, and the belief that Jewish redemption lay in a social-Zionist agenda. Young Golda absorbed both.

Originally, Moshe was hoping to make some money in America and return to Russia. But as the social turmoil in Russia intensified, Bluma became increasingly afraid for her family. With the collapse of the 1905 revolution, Pinsk became the site of massive repression. Day and night, Bluma and Golda heard the screams of the tortured prisoners from the neighboring police station and worried that Sheyna was among them. Bluma grew desperate, and her letters to Moshe became more alarmist. She even spent precious money on a family photograph, which captured herself and the girls as particularly feminine, and mailed it to Moshe. For this occasion, Bluma borrowed a lovely dress for Golda and placed paper ribbons in her hair. She even washed her hair in sugar water to make it curlier and shinier.[11] Bluma was probably hoping that the sight of his lovely women would prompt Moshe to take the decisive steps needed to unite them in America.

CHAPTER 2

TO AMERICA

The Long Journey

After deciding to flee to America with her daughters, Bluma faced yet another "woman's problem." By law, only men possessed the right to a passport, and women were required to travel under their husband's documents. To make some extra money, Golda's father had previously registered another woman and her children in his passport, thereby forfeiting Bluma and the girls' official identity. Yet again, young Golda witnessed the patriarchal world declare women unfit for agency. Without a passport, Bluma's only choice was to smuggle her family across the border. The fear of being at the mercy of smugglers, however, paled in comparison to the larger unknown, "America." As Golda later recalled, America felt like the moon, inaccessible and mysterious. Hope and trepidation swirled in Golda's soul as she watched her mother, frightened and bereft, sob uncontrollably as they prepared to leave behind all that was solid and familiar.

They left following the Passover Seder, perhaps thinking of the exodus to freedom. At their first stop, waiting to cross the Russian border into Galicia, an "agitated Jew" arrived with bad news. The government had received word that they were leaving illegally, so they needed to avoid the train and take a wagon through the forest. He also asked for more money. Bluma, savvy enough to recognize this trap, demanded that the smuggler take them back to Pinsk or put them on the train. The argument was contentious, but Bluma prevailed. The family embarked on the train to Antwerp, Belgium.

Like the train, the boat crossing the ocean overflowed with poor, anxious, and uprooted passengers, nursing hope for a better life. Traveling on the cheapest tickets available, Bluma and her girls were directed to the lowest level, where they shared a dark, tiny cell with another family. For meals, they waited for the bells to ring and then stood by their cell's door until their portions were distributed. Soon, however, they felt that the food was inedible. It was time again for Bluma to display her resourcefulness. She begged the kitchen to give her onions and potatoes, with which she cooked a meal in their cell. Sheyna later recalled that the dish her mother produced tasted like fish soup and gave off the aroma of home. Bluma was not an affectionate woman, but her resilience and care shone through in moments like these.

Milwaukee, 1906

After fourteen days at sea, they arrived in Quebec. From there, they took a train to Milwaukee, Wisconsin, and, at long last, reunited with Moshe. Golda ached to see him. Three lonely years had passed since she had last seen him, and for Golda, "the idea that he would come back to us made our [time] without him easier to bear."[1] Despite such high hopes, the sweet scene of "falling into each other's arms" did not come to pass. When they arrived, chill and alienation enveloped the family. Bluma and her daughters were self-conscious about looking like beggars: unclean, unkempt, and exhausted. Overwhelmed by the excess of novel sensations, an eight-year-old Golda looked at her father and saw a stranger. The father she longed for had a Jewish Russian look: an untrimmed beard, a yarmulke, and black clothing. The father who greeted them at the station looked "American": smooth shaven, his head uncovered, and his clothes peculiarly "western." Three years in America had transformed him. Moshe, however, had little patience for nostalgia. He had easily adjusted to his "new" American identity—he had become a member of a synagogue, joined a trade union, and made friends—and wanted his family to follow his example. In his mind, a "mensch" (human being) was one who dressed and acted like the locals. The "old-country look" had to go.[2]

The very next morning, he marched his family downtown (an unfamiliar concept) to the Schuster department store (another novel concept) with its awesome five floors. For his daughters, Moshe chose frilly blouses, white "flying" dresses, and lovely hats, the ultimate symbol of Americanization. It is telling that it was Moshe, not Bluma, who was determined that the family Americanize, and that he was the one to decide what appearances such a transformation required. Family conflict started immediately. While Golda was delighted to conform, Sheyna was sour. She missed Russia, and the American attire appeared clownish to her. A rebellious and frustrated teenager, Sheyna's confrontations with her parents became intense, and home became a place of yelling, crying, and endless arguments. Golda was miserable.

Despite Moshe's embrace of American customs and dress, the American entrepreneurial spirit did not change his passive streak. Well aware of his family's imminent arrival, he had not rented an apartment to welcome them, so the first car ride of Golda's life was to Moshe's rented room. Bluma yet again displayed her practicality. From fellow migrants she had learned she could rent an apartment with a grocery store adjacent to it, allowing her to fulfill her homemaker's duties while simultaneously earning a living. She adhered to the stereotype that the wife was merely "helping" the husband, who was the primary breadwinner, even though in her case the roles of helper and provider were reversed.

Throughout this rough period of adjustment and the endless confrontations between her parents and Sheyna, Golda found herself growing into a new role: family mediator. She would later remark, "Even as a little girl I had some persuasive power and often I would sit on my father's lap and try to soften his heart and make him change his mind about one or another sanction he was imposing on the rebellious Sheyna, and in other matters as well."[3] Golda was learning the way to a man's heart: be nonconfrontational, be pleasant, and gently massage his ego—all acts Sheyna could never bring herself to perform.

An Unwilling Shopkeeper's Apprentice

The first apartment her parents rented in Milwaukee's Jewish ghetto had no bathroom and no electricity. Yet Golda thought it was a palace and, compared to her dwelling in Pinsk, it probably was. Bluma valued the adjacent grocery store and was determined to become a shopkeeper. The neighborhood women offered advice and suggestions about "American expectations," such as wrapping salted fish before handing it to the customer. Bluma was a fast learner, yet she needed a helping hand, someone to open the store and serve the customers while she took the bus to the market to purchase the goods.

Moshe, not holding a steady job, did not mind the extra income, but the idea of performing such a "woman's job" offended his manly dignity. Bluma did not argue. She accepted the gendered division of labor as if it were ordained by the laws of nature. Accustomed to the nineteenth-century understanding that children constituted a labor force at the disposal of their parents, she expected Sheyna to help. Sheyna, however, was steeped in Marxist ideology. She saw shopkeepers as "social parasites" who engaged in bourgeois activity and she refused to compromise her principles. Their daughter Tzipke, only five, was still too young to help, so the task fell to eight-year-old Golda. Working in the store meant that Golda was chronically late for school, and sometimes missed it altogether. For Golda, who loved everything about school—the fortress-like building, the teacher, her classmates—this set off a new round of rancorous arguments at home. "We have to live," Bluma yelled at her complaining daughter, "what do you want me to do?" Her sarcasm was sharp and humiliating: "So it will take you a little longer to become a rebbetzin" (a learned woman in the Jewish tradition). As perceived by Golda, Bluma did not focus on education but rather on material survival. She did not think of education as a value that would justify sacrifices, certainly if it applied to girls rather than to boys.

One wonders: Was Moshe Mabovitz a male peacock, a man in love with his appearance and perhaps other comforts, charming but somewhat lazy? Was he in denial of his role as paterfamilias, his obligation to fulfill the deeply established expectation of the male, to serve as primary breadwinner of the family? Without a regular job, couldn't he have given his wife a hand and let his daughter go to school? The family followed the age-old rules of patriarchy, according to which the man, even if he were not earning a living or making critical decisions, retained his appearance as the dominant figure in the household. From what we know about her life at this time, Golda did not seem critical of this dynamic.

Golda's career as a shopkeeper's apprentice ended when a policeman visited the home, explaining to Bluma that her daughter's truancy was a violation of Wisconsin law. It was yet another departure from the communitarian and traditional culture of the shtetel. American individualism held that basic education was necessary to provide children with the tools to pursue their individual dreams. The needs of the family were of secondary significance.

School

Being forced to work at the store and missing school could have turned into the most traumatic event of Golda's childhood. "The bane of my life," she called it, which "almost ruined the years I spent in Milwaukee."[4] In fact, Golda had a complicated relationship with learning. She was a good student and earned good grades as a child, but as we shall see she was less diligent in high school and never completed her studies at the teachers' seminary. What she loved so much about school must have been the social milieu. School was an escape from home life, a place where she was sheltered from her mother's acerbic tongue. School nurtured her emerging charisma and honed her budding skills as a mover and shaker. In addition, it delivered another enormous benefit: it was where the eight-year-old, Yiddish-speaking Jewish immigrant from Russia acquired an American identity.

American Identity, as Golda Becomes Goldie

In Moshe's eager effort to blend in, he took an American name, Morris, and—as the patriarch of the family—encouraged the rest of his family to follow suit. Bluma became Bella, Sheyna became Jenny, and the school principal changed Tzipke's name to Clara. Golda became Goldie.

Why didn't Golda, like her sisters, receive a name that would further distance her from her foreign roots? One reason is that the English word "gold" was already present in her name, and the Yiddish pronunciation of her name "Goldae" invited a slight shift to make it sound like an American name, Goldie. Perhaps Mr. Finn, the school principal who advised the family in their choice of new names, thought the name fit well with Golda's lovely curls, given the popularity of the fairy tale "Goldilocks and the Three Bears." It is also likely that Golda resisted a more radical change and may have felt that Bubbe Goldae's name was a talisman she must keep. "Goldie" was an acceptable compromise. Later, upon their arrival in Palestine, both Golda and Sheyna restored their Yiddish names, yet to her American friends Golda always remained "Goldie."

Wisconsin elementary schools at the turn of the century were well aware of the need to assimilate the massive immigrant population. Patriotism was woven into the curriculum, including an emphasis on learning English and reciting the U.S. Pledge of Allegiance daily. Children studied the history of the American Civil War and learned about the valiant contribution of the State of Wisconsin to the Union forces. President Abraham Lincoln's speeches about the United States' commitment to freedom, justice, and equality must have been impressed upon Goldie's young mind, along with his pledge to help the "widow and the orphan" in his second inaugural address. Goldie's developing socialist principles, initially engendered by Sheyna's Marxist theories, were modified and cultivated by Wisconsin's commitment to the idea of progress. Goldie's love for American values continued to permeate her soul long after she arrived in Palestine.

The momentous American trauma, slavery, was also burned into her mind. In her memoirs she recalls getting free tickets from her school to attend a performance of Uncle Tom's Cabin, during which she jumped "to her feet with uncontrollable hatred for Simon Legree, the sadistic slaveholder who tormented Uncle Tom." She also notes the excitement of repeating the story at home, over and over again. Like millions of Jewish children across America, she identified Uncle Tom's suffering at the hands of slaveholders with the suffering of Jews under the czar.[5] This formative experience may also explain her decision, years later, to welcome her daughter Sarah's dark-skinned Yemenite husband into the family. At that time, the late 1940s, Golda was already a central figure among the Israeli Ashkenazi elite, a group that was decidedly prejudiced against Middle Eastern Jews. It could be that her deep empathy for the humanity of African Americans and belief in their right to equal treatment, nurtured in Milwaukee, paid dividends a generation later in Tel Aviv.

During this period of her life the Jewish lifestyle her family brought from Russia dominated, but it was modified to fit the lifestyle of their adopted homeland. They attended synagogue, celebrated Jewish holidays, and obeyed the laws of kashrut (keeping kosher), but they also made the necessary concessions demanded of them by the American business culture, such as working on the Sabbath—a practice that would have been unacceptable in Pinsk. The need to make a living overrode Jewish law. It did not, however, prevent them from celebrating the Sabbath in other ways. Like other members of her family, Goldie loved to sing. The family often sang Yiddish songs at home during Friday night dinners and in Lincoln Park on weekends and holidays. Decades later, her grandson Gideon recalled how Golda taught him the lyrics to the famous Yiddish song "Oifen Pripitchick."[6]

The best proof of Goldie's immersion in American culture was her accent. Yiddish was her mother tongue and the language she loved. She spoke Yiddish with her boyfriend, whom she later married, and with her children when they were born in Jerusalem. Yet in Milwaukee she taught herself to shed her Jewish accent in English, with its German-sounding "r," and for the rest of her life spoke with that unmistakable American Midwestern lilt, with only a faint hint of Yiddish woven into it. To American ears it could sound Jewish, but to Israeli ears it sounded perfectly American.

A Crisis at Home

In Bluma's eyes, elementary school endowed Goldie with all the education she needed. Goldie had blossomed into a good-looking teenager, bright, energetic, and charming, and well trained by her mother in homemaking skills. Bluma was eager to see her daughter married. One may imagine that Bluma, traumatized by her husband's chronic failure to provide for the family, was determined to spare her daughters the same fate. Now an experienced woman, she saw romantic love as a cruel ideal. Bluma also had a patriarchal worldview: the destiny of women was domesticity—homemaking and children—and a woman should find a provider capable of sparing her the trouble and worry of putting food on the table. If she succeeded in this endeavor, she should consider herself lucky. Self-fulfillment and its sibling, individualism, were childish concerns. Bluma also believed that her daughters should marry American-born men who could bestow some "native" status on them.

Goldie witnessed the bitter arguments Bluma had with Jenny-Sheyna. "Marry a man who would allow you to live in opulence" (*leben far im in "roskosh"*), she implored Jenny-Sheyna.[7] The Yiddish phrase Bluma used reveals the dilemma of the downtrodden. "Roskosh"—a Russian word meaning luxury or opulence—contained a reference to the biblical fleshpots that the Jews left behind in Egypt. Freedom without good food, the Jews complained to Moses, was not satisfying. Similarly, love without an economic base could only bring want and hunger; it was not a recipe for a good marriage. But Jenny-Sheyna followed her mother's example, rather than her advice, and married Shamai Korngold, a comrade in the Russian revolutionary movement who had joined her in America. Being revolutionaries and eager to defy Bluma, the two married in a civil ceremony in Denver, Colorado (where Jenny-Sheyna was recovering from tuberculosis), far from Milwaukee, which only added to Bluma's misery.

Bluma was now even more eager to see Goldie marry well. She had even found the right man. Mr. Goodstein, a man in his early thirties, was pleasant, friendly, and financially secure. He would engage Goldie in conversation when he frequented the store. Goldie was horrified by Bluma's suggestion. It was one thing to exchange pleasantries with Mr. Goodstein as he was purchasing milk and honey, and quite another to become his wife. From Golda's perspective as a fourteen-year-old, Mr. Goodstein was very old and, in any event, she could not picture herself as a married woman. Goldie dreamed of becoming a teacher. She liked the idea of shaping young minds, leading them in the "right" direction, and she felt the urge to engage in something bigger than herself. Her teachers—powerful, authoritative, confidently shepherding a class of youngsters—were probably the only women serving as role models in her life at that time. Had working-class Milwaukee offered other role models she would perhaps have thought differently, but like most girls of her generation this was the only female position of power she had known.

The squabbles at home intensified, and Bluma offered a practical compromise: a secretarial school. Goldie would learn typing, shorthand, and other skills useful for a secretary. Such were the horizons of a working-class woman like her mother. Golda later recalled, "I sobbed, I would rather die than spend my life—or even part of it—hunched over a typewriter in some dingy office."[8] Teaching, she believed, would give her the power and dignity for which she yearned. She wanted to graduate high school and enroll in Wisconsin State Normal School for teachers. Goldie's horizons were broader than her mother's, but still limited. She did not dream of becoming a lawyer or a doctor, the favored emerging professions (for men) among Jews. Nor did she aspire to elected office. Her expectations were those of an ordinary woman.

Bluma, the epitome of practicality, would have none of this "nonsense." Goldie's plan required too many years of study. Furthermore, Wisconsin law prohibited the employment of married women as teachers.[9] Goldie would either have studied "for nothing" or remained unmarried—both unappetizing options. For Bluma, the prospects of an unmarried daughter threatened disgrace, a blemish on the reputation of the family, not to mention a ruined life for Goldie herself. In her own way, Bluma displayed plenty of agency and shrewdness, but always within the patriarchal model of working-class womanhood. She did not have the imagination to foresee that her daughters could break the iron chains of this paradigm and flourish.

The resulting struggle between Goldie and her parents severely scarred her. Having already experienced so much trauma in life—poverty, cold, hunger, and migration—she had difficulty handling these fights. Her beloved father, while expressing pride in his studious daughter, was of no help. "It doesn't pay to be too clever" he declared. "Men don't like smart girls."[10] Whether Moshe merely wished to side with his wife in order to avoid a conflict or felt threatened by the chance that his daughter might outshine him, Golda was never able to forget her father's warning. Even when confidently dictating policy as prime minister, she would often drop statements about her "primitive mind" and "stupidity." She was neither stupid nor primitive, but as the "only woman in the room," she followed Moshe's warning not to appear too smart.

The pressure at home was unbearable and Goldie shared her agony with her sister. Jenny-Sheyna was being treated for tuberculosis at a Jewish community hospital hundreds of miles away in Denver, Colorado. Tuberculosis often afflicted new immigrants, as the disease thrived in sweatshop conditions, and Jenny-Sheyna may have caught it while working in the sweatshops of Milwaukee and Chicago.[11] As happened often, Jenny-Sheyna and her parents were estranged from each other, and Goldie was instructed to refrain from corresponding with her sister. But Goldie loved her sister too much to obey. She wrote to Jenny-Sheyna regularly, even sending her a few pennies and stamps to continue the correspondence, and she reported her struggles at home in detail. Making good use of the skills they had acquired as members of the underground, Jenny-Sheyna and Shamai told Goldie to conceal their correspondence from their parents by collecting their letters at a friend's address.

Jenny-Sheyna urged Goldie to leave home and come to Denver. She promised her food, shelter, "the necessary clothes that a person ought to have," and, most importantly, the freedom to go to school.[12] Jenny-Sheyna also instructed Goldie to keep the plan secret, which put her in the unhappy situation of acting behind her parents' back and further distancing herself from them. It is not impossible that, in addition to feeling the need to help her sister, Jenny-Sheyna may have been motivated by the urge to take revenge on her parents for their abusive behavior toward her.

Goldie's escape from home and travel to Denver was planned like a meticulous military campaign. First, she needed an accomplice to help her carry out her secret plan, so she enlisted her devoted friend Regina Hamburger. Determined not to depend on anyone for her expenses, Goldie taught new immigrants basic English for ten cents an hour and saved her earnings for the train ticket. Regina, though not financially comfortable herself, offered to share some of her own meager savings. The girls transferred Goldie's clothes to Regina's house, so they could pack them without raising suspicions. The night before her departure, Goldie packed another small bag with her remaining belongings and, like Rapunzel locked up in the tower by the witch, dropped the package down to the yard below her window. Regina dutifully collected the bag and deposited it at the train station. The next morning, Goldie went through the motions of leaving for school but headed to the train station instead. On her way, she dropped a postcard in the mail, informing her parents of her departure. Goldie clung to her sister's advice, which echoed an underground activity manual: "The main thing is never to be excited: always be calm and act coolly. This course of action will always bring you good results. Be brave." This piece of advice, Golda later recalled, stood her in good stead many times during her political career. Even if she did not explicitly recall it during the Yom Kippur War, she nevertheless acted on its basis.[13]

It took more than twenty-five hours to travel from Milwaukee to Denver by train, including a very long, frightening night. The cheap, overcrowded emigrant train cars of 1912 had a grim environment and, for the first time in her life, Golda was all alone. Surrounded by strangers, she was likely hungry and thirsty, probably sickened by the overused bathrooms (she was always sensitive to hygiene), and was feeling guilty, worried, and anxious. Cut off from her family, she had only herself to rely on.

What should be made of this unsettling event in Golda's young life? It is no simple matter for a fourteen-year-old girl to defy her parents and ride penniless and alone across state lines. Golda was rebelling against the diminished destiny prescribed to women by the prevailing patriarchal paradigm. It was a formidable, audacious act of personal agency. She envisioned a life that would be devoted to social change and refused to accept defeat. She wanted to acquire knowledge and thereby free herself from the shackles that fettered women of her class in centuries-old traditions. She also wanted to transmit this knowledge to others. Golda was a soldier in the fight to challenge the gender paradigm that confined women to home and marriage.

It did not occur to her that she was a heroic trailblazer; far from it. She was torn and tormented by her decision to leave. Despite the raging waves of anger that she felt toward her parents, she loved them. She felt guilty about her stealthy disappearance and missed the sounds and smells of home. Throughout her political career, she was often faced with the choice of slamming the door behind her or patiently negotiating a solution. In 1974, for instance, she slammed the door at the final Labor Party meeting she attended, when the party that was "her home" let her nemesis, Shulamit Aloni, join the Rabin cabinet. (See parts III and IV for additional discussion.) In the end, she saw no alternative. One wonders if, in that moment, she was reliving this earlier trauma.

Denver, Colorado, Where Goldie Discovers Politics

Jenny-Sheyna welcomed Goldie with open arms. Goldie enrolled in high school and worked in Shamai's dry-cleaning shop in the afternoons, which allowed him to take a second job. She ironed clothes and waited on customers while trying to find time to do her homework. As always, she was energetic and diligent and, feeling unentitled, never complained. In the evenings, she gained a different kind of education by observing Jenny-Sheyna and Shamai's political gatherings.

The young couple held a proletarian salon composed of an assortment of Russian and Jewish immigrants, all bright and self-taught aspiring intellectuals. For the first time in her life, Goldie was introduced to high-level, vibrant intellectual discussions. These young immigrants discussed a whole range of subjects, including "the anarchist philosophy of Emma Goldman and Peter Kropotkin . . . President Wilson and the European situation . . . pacifism, the role of women in society, [and] the future of the Jewish people."[14] At these meetings, Goldie kept quiet, absorbing every word. She loved the milieu of the intelligentsia and their informed and passionate discussions about public matters.

Meeting Morris Myerson

One of Jenny-Sheyna's less talkative guests was Morris Myerson, a young immigrant from Lithuania, five years Goldie's senior, whose family had moved from Philadelphia to Denver to facilitate his sister Sarah's treatment for TB. Like many young Jewish men of his generation, his circumstances did not permit formal education, but he was passionate about art, music, and poetry, as well as being a voracious reader. Goldie called him by his Yiddish (also Hebrew) name Meirke. Besides sharing a first name with Goldie's father, her young suitor had similarly lost his father at a young age and lived with his mother and sisters, supporting the family. Also, like her father, he'd only been able to find sporadic work, in his case as a sign painter. Growing up in the company of women—the only boy and youngest of six children—Morris was sensitive to women's needs. This sensitivity helped him carve a path to young Goldie's heart.

In Morris's company Goldie felt the warmth and validation she craved. He introduced her to poetry, and together they read "Byron, Shelley, Keats, and the *Rubaiyat of Omar Khayyam*." He took her to public lectures on literature, history, and philosophy and to concerts in the park. He gave her "terrifyingly long reading lists."[15] Enchanted by the new horizons before her and eager to learn about the treasures of Western civilization, Goldie felt energized, impressed, and grateful.

She was equally hungry for affirmation of her intelligence and looks, which Morris satisfied by generously showering her with compliments. From both Sheyna's and Golda's memoirs, one learns that while their parents provided their children with the best material conditions they could afford, they were neither affectionate nor attuned to their daughters' emotional worlds. They were also largely indifferent to the "life of the mind." Shamai and the young Morris offered a different perspective and attitude, which the sisters found attractive. For the first time in her life Goldie had a male cheerleader by her side. She could confide her innermost fears and adolescent insecurities to him: that she was unattractive, that she wished she could have "black hair and big lustrous eyes," that, alas, she was neither lovable nor smart. Morris enveloped her with affirmation and bolstered her sense of self-worth.

By defying her parents and moving to Denver, Goldie rebelled against the patriarchal paradigm of a woman's destiny, yet she did not wish to sacrifice her femininity. In her memoirs, she recounts a tender moment when, having accepted Morris's invitation to go to a concert in the park, she spent her precious pennies on the "frivolous act" of buying a cheap red hat (whose color she feared "would trickle all over me" if it rained) because she yearned to look attractive.[16] From this early age, she refused to see a contradiction between femininity and self-fulfillment in the public sphere. Sacrificing her looks, she might have reasoned, would be a capitulation to the patriarchy, as it would amount to accepting the prejudice that good looks signaled spiritual emptiness. As she grew older, she gradually did neglect her appearance, but in her youth, she paid close attention to her looks and saw no contradiction between good looks and character.

Crisis Redux as She Rents a Room of Her Own

The honeymoon at Jenny-Sheyna's was short-lived. Jenny-Sheyna and Shamai took their responsibility as her guardians seriously, and they worried that Goldie—lively, charming, and good-looking—neglected her studies and attracted too much male attention. Some men were also likely attracted to her insecurity. As a restless and traumatized teenager working at the shop every afternoon, Goldie may not have had the energy or peace of mind to concentrate on her studies. In her memoirs, she notes that high school "would have to wait after all."[17]

Jenny-Sheyna soon proved to be a controlling disciplinarian, unconsciously stepping into her mother's shoes. One night, incensed by her sister's "bossiness," Goldie walked out, slamming the door behind her. She never returned, and the sisters would not speak to each other for several months. This was the first serious display of what Goldie would later recognize as one of her major character flaws. When hurt, she tended to act impulsively and found it tremendously difficult to make a gesture of repair, even if she wished to mend the relationship. Instead, she would hide her insecurity by building walls between herself and the person who hurt her.[18]

Two young women who frequented Jenny-Sheyna's home rented Goldie a small room. Unfortunately, they were both sick with tuberculosis. Listening to their coughing through the wall, Golda grew anxious about catching the disease. Only her stubborn streak prevented her from returning to her sister. She quickly found a job at a department store, taking measurements for custom-made skirt linings, one of the few jobs available to an uneducated immigrant. Unlike Jenny-Sheyna, Goldie quickly mastered manual skills. For the rest of her life, she observed, "I find myself automatically giving a quick glance at the hems of skirts and can run one up with total confidence."[19]

One detects in this period of Golda's life several emerging characteristics for which she would later become famous: stubbornness, dexterity, keen attention to detail, and perhaps most importantly, resilience. At the age of fourteen, estranged from her family, Goldie was "learning to cope with life alone." She comforted herself with a principle often repeated by her father: "When you chop wood, you get splinters." As soon as she had saved some money, she moved into a "germ-free room of my own."[20] She braced herself to survive the splinters, but living alone left its scars. She had already experienced loneliness as a young child in Pinsk, and she knew how dreadful it felt. For the rest of her life, she experienced this sadness when alone, particularly at night, and even at the age of seventy, as a very busy prime minister, she would summon friends to her home to keep her company.[21]

Shortly after Golda left Jenny-Sheyna's apartment, her life took a surprising turn. The girl who had run away from home so that she could enroll in high school dropped out. "High school can wait," she assured herself. While she remained as ambitious as ever, she no longer saw education as essential for her future. Perhaps the intellectual discussions at Jenny-Sheyna's had convinced her that self-education was both possible and sufficient. Or perhaps her parents' insistence that girls did not need an education had found a niche in her soul. Given her social milieu, however, her decision was in some ways unsurprising. No one in her circle was highly educated or aware of the long-term benefits that education might bring, and many shared her parents' view that a woman did not need formal education.

After seven years in America, almost half of her life, Goldie had internalized the American ethos of individualism. The freedom to do as you will and the obligation to pull yourself up by your bootstraps— these became the governing principles of her life.

CHAPTER 3

GOLDIE AND MORRIS GET MARRIED

Back in Milwaukee

By the time Goldie celebrated her fifteenth birthday, living alone and far from her parents was wearing her down. When her father wrote to her, tersely stating, "If you value your mother's life you should come back home at once," she seized the opportunity and returned.[1]

In Milwaukee her parents no longer objected to high school education but she soon discovered that education was not her true vocation. Her father had already joined the Poalei Zion party, and Goldie happily followed suit. As Rachel Rojanski has documented comprehensively, Poalei Zion (Workers of Zion) was a tiny left-leaning party with Russian roots.[2] Its platform rested on the theory that Jews were a nation in exile, entitled to a collective life in their restored, ancient homeland. Their goal was to gather the exiles in Palestine (the biblical Eretz Yisrael) and form a sovereign nation. Unlike other Zionist ideologies, Golda's party did not see the revival of Hebrew as a part of the overall revival project—Yiddish was to be the national Jewish language—which explains why Golda would later arrive in Palestine without knowledge of Hebrew. Another cardinal precept of Poalei Zion was socialism. The party emphasized the needs of the impoverished Jewish masses and aimed to improve their welfare. Members imitated the communist practice of calling each other comrades. Comradeship, an echo of the French revolutionary commitment to "fraternité," was meant to erase differences of class, age, status, and gender. For the rest of her life, party members in Israel addressed Golda as "Comrade Golda"—"Ha-haverah Golda."

Goldie found the idea of a Jewish utopia electrifying, and the ideological platform of the American Poalei Zion shaped her understanding of politics and informed her lifelong commitment to Zionism. In the beginning, however, there was an impediment. The party's bylaws required that members be at least eighteen years old. Goldie could not wait, so she launched her second political campaign (her first, which she had undertaken shortly after she arrived in America, was a successful fundraiser to support poor children who could not afford school textbooks). Despite facing older men who considered the requirement of age reasonable and were disinclined to let a teenaged woman change their rules, Goldie succeeded and was allowed to join the party. For the first time in her life, she experienced the power of her persuasive skills in the company of adult men.

Although she was "the only woman in the room," the party soon became her home. She felt welcomed and excited as never before. Perhaps the company of like-minded men was sufficiently different from her family's constant bickering; perhaps escaping the company of women allowed her to present her better self; or perhaps the opportunity to act alongside her father brought a measure of peace to her tormented soul. Through her party activity she gained self-esteem and recognition, and until nearly the end of her life, the party was that home away from home where she felt congeniality and purpose.

Morris and Romance

Morris remained in Denver with his mother and sisters, but his letters showered Goldie with warmth and affection. He called her "my very dearest Goldie," Goldele, Gogo, and Gogole; he invariably signed them "with deep love."[3] And he insisted that she was beautiful: "I have repeatedly asked you not to contradict me on the question of your beauty. You pop up every now and then with these same timid and self-deprecating remarks which I cannot bear."[4]

He also praised her quick intelligence and emphasized her potential: "I am very glad that you like school. . . . I wonder what will be forthcoming after you'll be graduated. You'll take the world by storm." Goldie was accustomed to the lashing winds of criticism, and his zephyrs of genuine fondness were healing. Morris's letters also show his awareness that gender stereotypes were changing before his very eyes. He criticized the sexist attitude of Goldie's brother-in-law: "Radical as he [Shamai] would have people believe he is, he couldn't digest the idea of a modern, sensible girl striking for her independence." Yet he too could be a male chauvinist at times, such as when he declared, "Only my opinion of you shall prevail." Little did he know that the moment would soon arrive when she would reject his opinion as well.[5]

Morris was learning the hard way that despite her professed love, Goldie would not return to Denver. He implored her to understand his constraints—his mother and sick sister needed him to remain close. He even offered to fund her studies if she returned, but she declined. Why was that? Many have thought that by declining she was defending her decision to remain financially independent. But given the speed at which their marriage unraveled, her best friend Regina's statement that this was not a "marriage made in heaven" seems prescient.[6] When they met, she was a troubled teenager, confused and certainly romantically inexperienced. A year later she may have been unsure whether Morris was the one and only. Because Morris was her savior in Denver, and because of her great affection for him, she may have felt hesitant to articulate such doubts, even to herself. Her actions, however, clearly communicated hesitancy. The story she loved to repeat throughout her life, that she conditioned their marriage on immigration to Palestine, is revealing. Half consciously, she may have been gambling that Morris would refuse to go, and so it would be up to him end their relationship.

The Emergence of Sexuality

Was Goldie bothered by the fact that she did not feel swept off her feet by Morris? Did she long for the excitement of romance? Her mother frequently told Goldie the story of how she fell in love with Goldie's father, at first sight, and her sister Jenny-Sheyna did not hide her passion for Shamai. Goldie, however, never felt entitled to such amorous love, and this could be the reason that she stayed with Morris and decided to accept what good he had to offer, rather than hold out for more.

During the months Goldie spent in Denver, her mother, like all traditional mothers, was beside herself with worries about her teenage daughter. One particular concern was Goldie's emerging sexuality. A traditional woman, Bluma accepted life without birth control as the bitter lot of women (she had recently suffered a bad miscarriage following her ninth pregnancy). She knew about venereal diseases and was all too familiar with the unpredictable consequences of sexual relations. She feared for Goldie, unsupervised in faraway, unknown Denver. Also, the reputation of the family was at stake. What will the neighbors say? It is not surprising, therefore, that Moshe warned his daughter that she was putting her mother's life at risk.

Indeed, Golda was well aware of the worry she was causing her parents, and these dynamics played a role in shaping her perception of gender. Both Regina and Clara, Goldie's younger sister, reported in letters to Goldie about spreading rumors that she had "eloped with an Italian." In one letter Regina mentioned, "I met Franck, your old-time sweetheart" and Franck was sending a "KISS." Regina also referred to Goldie's circumstances living alone in Denver, the dangers of being "free to do as you wish," and "the temptations in a girl's way" that might lead to a "loss of self-respect"—veiled warnings about the dangers posed by sex to the adolescent girl. Regina also hinted of the "safe," legal way to channel sexual desire—marriage. In 1914 Regina wrote from Milwaukee to Goldie in Denver: "Goldie, do you intend to come back to Milwaukee next June and resume your normal course or did you give up the teaching proposition? The matrimonial course appeals to you better with the man you love. I do not blame you."[7]

This was the milieu in which Goldie was coming to terms with her sexuality. When she was back in Milwaukee, a letter from Morris reminded her that he was "waiting anxiously" for her photo.[8]

The photo she most likely sent in response is one of the more famous photos of her youth. It appears to have been taken by a professional

photographer and shows Goldie in profile, a beautiful teenager, her formidable hair loose and lightly brushed, light shining through it. It
reminds one of Rossetti's *Lady Lilith*, which evokes erotic female powers.
Goldie's decision to display her hair as an attractive feminine asset in
this photograph stands in stark contrast to the approach she would take
later in life, during which time she wore her hair pulled back into a traditional bun, projecting an austere, matter-of-fact appearance, perhaps
more fitting for a politician. If sexy hair was a part of her feminine identity, she chose to hide it from the public eye.

Abortion

Shortly before Morris and nineteen-year-old Goldie married, Jenny-
Sheyna (now reconciled with Goldie) added an almost casual postscript
to one of her letters:

> Forgot to tell you about preventives. There are many of them in the
> market. Some it helps, some it does not, the only think [*sic*] I know
> of and that is more or less certain, is that the man should take care. It
> is very hard, and it is an extreme nervous strain on both, but was the
> only thing that kept us safe. Anyways try not to get in trouble again
> for too often operations is going to ruin you in no time.[9]

Jenny-Sheyna's language is opaque, but it makes plain that Goldie
was sexually active before her wedding. While abortion was illegal in
Wisconsin, as well as in Illinois, Goldie's friends helped her get one in
Chicago.[10] The letter testifies to the vast changes in Jewish life at the
turn of the twentieth century. In America, young Jewish women, feeling
liberated, did not see sex as necessarily restricted to marriage. Patriarchy's hold on their lives was weakening and, for a while, it appeared as
if reproductive freedom loomed in the future.

This episode signals another phase in Goldie's maturation. She neither
followed conventional morality nor let an accidental pregnancy determine
the course of her life. Instead, she exercised her right to choose. There is no
information about Morris's feelings, but from what we know about him,

one would expect that he respected her autonomy and went along. The abortion must have prompted her to use contraception, as her son was not born until six years after her wedding. Golda valued family and children, but she also valued the freedom to make her life choices by herself.

When Israel became a state, abortion was prohibited by law, but an edict of the attorney general allowed prosecutions only if the doctor performing the procedure was negligent. By the 1970s, when Golda was prime minister, and perhaps as a result of the agitations of the women's movement, the minister of religion began a campaign to restrict abortion. In an interview with the minister, he reports, "Golda Meir got mad at me as prime minister and said, 'why do you want to control my body?' and she said it as a woman."[11]

A Jewish Wedding for Mrs. Goldie Myerson

Golda was content to return home while Morris stayed in Denver. They agreed to continue their relationship and postponed the idea of marriage until she graduated from high school. As expected, Bluma found Morris unfit as a husband. He was another no-good greenhorn without money or prospects. Nor was she impressed by his erudition. Once Morris moved to Milwaukee, however, Golda's parents reluctantly acquiesced.

Experimentation in romantic relationships was not a welcomed practice in traditional immigrant society, so there must have been pressure on the couple to set a wedding date promptly. Yet Goldie remained unsure. In her memoirs, she recalled that "we parted for a while," that she moved to Chicago where she worked as a librarian, and that she was unhappy. She did not report whether she tried to date other men. Rather, she distracted herself with political activity. Politics as a distraction from personal problems, she candidly confessed, would become her modus operandi. Political activity, too, may have persuaded her that having a ring on her finger could be useful. She was surrounded by men, and one can expect that many made passes at the attractive young woman. Men, she once observed, "cannot be mere friends."[12] Being married made it easier to fend off unwanted suitors and ensured enough space for unadulterated political activity. At age nineteen, after Morris promised her that he would accompany her to Palestine, Goldie agreed to tie the knot.

Despite the expectations of Goldie's parents, the young couple had their own ideas about the marriage ceremony. Golda was teaching at the Yiddishe Folks Schule, the party's school for Jewish children, where the curriculum emphasized cultural Judaism, as distinct from religious Judaism. As good party members (to please Golda, Morris had joined the party earlier), the two disdained religion and planned a secular wedding. For modern, secular Jews, religion was perceived as a relic of the past, and the old Jewish wedding was replete with the ancient marks of gender inequality, including the groom formally "buying" the bride and the bride circling her husband seven times before she stands under the chuppah. Goldie had no use for these customs.

Bluma was furious. Writing about the event more than fifty years later, Golda presented Bluma more as a caricature of the Jewish mother: "Mother" said that "a civil wedding would kill her . . . she would have to leave Milwaukee at once, that I would be shaming the entire family, to say nothing of the Jewish people."[13] How much Golda was replicating popular stereotypes for the amusement of her audience and how much she was recalling her mother's actual reaction, we will never know. What we do know is that, in the end, Goldie agreed to her mother's terms, and Milwaukee's prominent rabbi, Solomon Scheineld, a progressive Orthodox Jew, officiated at a ceremony at Goldie's parents' home.

In her memoirs, Golda offered a practical rationalization for her acquiescence to a religious ceremony, which reveals the state of mind of the seasoned politician: "What damage would fifteen minutes under the chuppah . . . do to our principles?"[14] In this episode, Golda's mother taught her a lesson about the power of Jewish peoplehood and continuity, a lesson that echoed in her soul and helps explain her willingness to bend her secular principles when she came to power. As prime minister, for example, she once blasted a gentile woman for refusing to convert. You could almost hear her ask "What damage would it do your principles?"[15] Similarly, this event perhaps helps explain why, as a cabinet minister, Golda raised her hand in support of giving Israeli rabbis a monopoly on matters of marriage and divorce.

Very few women of her generation kept their maiden names after marriage, and Goldie was not among them. Becoming Goldie Myerson felt right, and she would rise to fame with this name until 1956, when a powerful man, Prime Minister David Ben-Gurion, forced her to Hebraize it to "Meir" (coincidentally, Morris's Hebrew name). By then, Morris was dead, and she, an estranged widow.

CHAPTER 4

FINDING HER VOCATION
Political Activism

GOLDIE AND MORRIS settled into a small apartment in Milwaukee. Her star was rising in the tiny party of Poalei Zion, and she tirelessly attended meetings, raised funds, and traveled near and far. Morris, often unemployed, used some of his free time to turn their apartment into a love nest. Golda later recalled that when she returned from her travels "there were always a few flowers" around.[1] This pattern—the young wife building a career and earning a modest but steady income, her husband doing house chores and waiting for his beloved's return—inverted conventional gender roles and upset her family. By contrast, Jenny's husband, who now adopted the American name Sam, was industriously building a future for himself and his family, taking evening classes and honing his business skills. One thus sees the different types of masculinity that surrounded Goldie: active male party members, an ambitious brother-in-law, and a father and husband who were gentle yet passive.

Golda was also different from most women in her circle. Whereas Jenny-Sheyna, the old revolutionary, chose to stay home and care for her children, Goldie decided to postpone having children in order to pursue her career. It struck her as natural and reasonable to place the party's needs and her ambitions ahead of her wifely duties. In an interview with Oriana Fallaci decades later, she said: "Domestic bliss wasn't enough for me. I had to be doing what I was doing."[2]

Patriarchy, Alterity, and Politics

Secure in her relationship with Morris, Goldie grew closer to her father. Fond of organizations, Moshe joined a carpenters' union, the local chapter of B'nai B'rith, and a synagogue, but he never aspired to leadership positions. Goldie, however, was like a young whale in the ocean of political activism. She never articulated her goal of turning the traditional gendered division of labor on its head—maybe not even to herself—but turn it she did. Significantly, there were no female party members to take her under their wings or offer inspiration. Bluma's skills as a cook, homemaker, and hostess were useful to Goldie and her father's networking, but they were secondary to the political skills Goldie sought to develop. Goldie was carving her path on her own.[3]

She was beginning to understand, if only implicitly, that politics was her vocation and that politics was the world of men—party comrades who were vigorous, confident, occasionally aggressive, and oblivious to domesticity.

Goldie also discovered the allure of nationwide American politics. As 1918 approached, plans began in earnest to hold a national Zionist convention in Philadelphia. At the age of twenty she was included in the delegation from Milwaukee, and the experience of meeting delegates from all parts of the United States, arguing and deliberating policy, was exhilarating. "This is the good life," she wrote to her friend Regina, "it was the most wonderful thing imaginable."[4]

She grew accustomed to being the only woman in the room and honed her interpersonal skills, learning how to succeed in the company of men: a woman must "play nice," avoid confrontation, seek accommodation, take care not to offend the male ego, and above all, be helpful. If coffee was to be served—serve it; if papers had to be distributed—volunteer to distribute them. It was probably around this time that she took up smoking, further signaling a departure from the traditional feminine stereotype. Perhaps the ritual of smoking— lighting up a cigarette, tapping the ash off, crushing the butt—played a role in building her self-confidence and added some authority to her youthful appearance.

To understand Golda, the mature politician, one must consider her level of comfort with male political culture from an early age. This is not to say that she did not value women or enjoy their company. Far from it. She was a quite competent cook and could run an efficient household, skills her mother made sure she possessed. She had dear and loyal friends like Regina Hamburger and Sara Feder, and over the years formed deep bonds with several more women.[5] And she valued the contribution of women to society and to her personal welfare. But all this was background music to the main theme: political work essential to promoting a cause. The world of men offered this opportunity, and she was determined to join it.

Goldie also learned during this time that if promoting the cause of socialism for the Jewish people was going to be her life project, she should not dwell too much on her alterity as a woman or on the hegemony of the patriarchy. Between women's equality and Jewish sovereignty, she wagered, the latter cause was more likely to succeed, and it was more urgent. An anecdote from her memoirs succinctly captures the gender discrimination she experienced in her young political career. During World War I, David Ben-Gurion was touring American Jewish communities, trying to spread support for Zionist labor ideology. At that time, he was an insignificant leader of an insignificant movement, exiled from Palestine by the Ottoman government. Goldie took part in arranging his visit to Milwaukee:

> My first recollection [of Ben-Gurion] was actually not [of] meeting him. He was due to visit Milwaukee, and it had been arranged for him to give a speech on Saturday night and to have lunch at our home on Sunday. But Saturday night the Chicago Philharmonic was in town, and Morris . . . had invited me to the concert weeks earlier, and I felt duty bound to go with him.[6]

Goldie's decision to attend the concert with Morris, instead of the leader's speech, incited immediate backlash.[7] Her comrades interpreted her absence as signaling a lack of "serious commitment" (what can you expect of a young woman?) and canceled Ben-Gurion's planned lunch at her parents' home. The message was loud and clear: if you put your family duties ahead of your political commitments, you will not count as "one of the guys." Goldie understood. In 1956, just before the Suez War, when Ben-Gurion asked her to move from her beloved labor ministry to head the Ministry of Foreign Affairs, she accepted the job and stated: "If Ben-Gurion asked me to jump from the fifth floor, I would."[8] The party's needs came first.

A Zionist-Socialist Activist and an Independent Young Woman

Once she became a full-fledged member of Poalei Zion, her work began in earnest. There were fundraising campaigns, efforts to increase party membership, and animated ideological discussions in which she was increasingly active, thereby sharpening her debating skills. People often observed that she was "the only girl in the room."[9]

A well-known story about Goldie volunteering to speak from a soapbox in Milwaukee's Jewish ghetto testifies to her increasing sense of self-worth as well as the gender discrimination she had to overcome. Because only men were traditionally permitted to speak in synagogues, a synagogue in her neighborhood denied her request to address the congregation about the merits of labor Zionism. In response, she and her comrades decided that she would deliver her speech outside the synagogue. Her father was incensed. It was the only time Golda mentioned her father being outraged: "He was red in the face: Moshe Mabovitz's daughter was not going to stand on a box in the street and make a spectacle of herself."[10] It was a classic assertion of patriarchal privilege. He "owned" his daughter, and she was making a spectacle of herself, but more importantly, of him. Women were supposed to stay quietly in the margins, not attract public attention. The rather gentle man now threatened violence: he would come to the meeting, pull her by her braid and drag her home. Whether he would have followed through on the threat is less important than the fact that, confronted with an offense to his honor as a man, this was his fantasy. He wished to humiliate Goldie in front of the community. Dragging her by the hair, the very manifestation of her femininity of which she was so proud, would show everyone who was "boss."

Goldie was full of trepidation, but she went ahead anyway. To his credit, her father stood in the crowd, listening. He watched her message go right into people's hearts, including his own. He experienced what many later observed: Goldie had presence and charisma. Rage gave way to awe. "I don't know where she got it from," he returned home to tell his wife. The rite of passage had been completed.

Zionism's Preferred Language, Yiddish or Hebrew?

In addition to the conflict between Poalei Zion and local religious authorities, a fierce ideological battle was raging within the party about the appropriate language to be used in the Zionist revival. Should the new believers adhere to Yiddish, the warm and familiar tongue of Eastern European Jews, or should national revival discard Yiddish in favor of Hebrew, the language of the Bible, spoken by Jews before they were exiled? At the time, Hebrew was a sacred language limited to religious rituals, its modern grammar and vocabulary only recently invented.

No one in Goldie's family spoke Hebrew, and she instinctively sided with Yiddish. Ever the pragmatist, she was not swayed by the symbolic aspects of revival. Yiddish was a "Jewish" language, a pillar of Jewish civilization and, therefore, good enough for her. She did not bother to study Hebrew and ignored news from Palestine that Hebrew was quickly spreading as the preferred language. Later in her life Mizrahi Jews would accuse her of identifying Yiddish as the authentic language of the Jews.[11] Indeed, she worked to bring to life the new Poalei Zion newspaper, Die Zeit, a medium that affirmed the affinity between Jewish revival and Yiddish. She even joined the teaching staff of the party's supplementary school in Milwaukee—the Yiddishe Folks Schule—where she taught Yiddish, history, literature, and folk songs.

The Folks Schule, an initiative of Poalei Zion, offered a socialist, nonreligious, secular curriculum, which aimed to develop working-class consciousness and enhance Jewish culture. However, because the party school did not offer preparation for a Bar Mitzvah, parents tended to enroll only their daughters (the idea that girls, too, should have a religious Bat Mitzvah was not yet widely accepted). As a "secular Jew," Golda saw religious ritual and the gender-based discrimination it entailed as relics of the past. She remained a secularist to the end of her life.[12]

Golda's indifference to Hebrew may have been partly rooted in her lack of proper Jewish education. Reading and writing in Hebrew (as preparation for participation in religious life) was not part of her up-bringing. Nor did she share Ben-Gurion's passion for the beauty of the biblical text and its potential to enrich the cultural revival. Only when she arrived in Palestine did she begin to study Hebrew in earnest, but her heart never warmed up to the language. Her handwriting always reflected her lack of training and contained more than the occasional misspelling. She eventually spoke Hebrew well, but never eloquently, and many Israelis turned up their noses at her unadorned vocabulary and unimaginative prose. Throughout her life, she continued to weave Yiddish idioms into her speeches and arguments, whether in the public arena or in cabinet deliberations.

Socialism

For Goldie, Zionist ideology was more about Jewish political power than about a cultural renaissance. From this perspective, she was very different from the Labor Party leadership in Palestine that she would shortly join. And yet she shared their passion for socialism. The idea that the state had a responsibility to care for the poor and the under-privileged had always been dear to her heart, and she was determined that it should prevail in Palestine.

During Golda's teenage years socialism attracted a modest following in the United States. Milwaukee, in particular, leaned toward socialist principles. Victor L. Berger, the founder of the American Socialist Party, served as Milwaukee's representative in Congress. The party's newspa-per was published in Milwaukee, and employed Regina Hamburger, Goldie's best friend, as a secretary.[13] The attorney Robert Hess, on a cassette in the Jewish Archives at Hebrew Union College, refers to Goldie as a cofounder of the chapter of the Socialist Party in Milwau-kee's Jewish district and states that the two of them often addressed crowds in the streets of Milwaukee's Jewish ghetto.[14]

The nascent success of socialism faded quickly, as it would soon be targeted as "un-American," and its adherents painted as "disloyal." Golda first experienced antisocialist hostility during the war years, and then again as the Red Scare and the Palmer Raids, a federal campaign to locate and deport immigrants suspected of socialist leanings, swept the land. With the encouragement of the Wilson administration, Americans grew to identify communism with socialism, anarchism, and lawlessness, and persecution became widespread. Under Attorney General Mitchell Palmer scores were arrested and deported because of alleged disloyalty. Eastern European Jews were particularly targeted and the threat to Golda's family (known for their socialist leanings) felt very real indeed.

Years later, Golda watched the senator of her own state of Wisconsin, Joseph McCarthy, terrorize communists and fellow travelers in the period that came to bear his name. With good reason, Golda did not include the chapter of her life as an American socialist in her autobiography. Her rise to prominence in the United States, first as a major fundraiser and later as Israel's representative in matters of foreign affairs, would have been compromised had she been "exposed" as a socialist, and she took care to avoid being identified as such in America.

Gender Identity

When Goldie arrived in New York City to prepare for the trip to Palestine, she came to the Poalei Zion headquarters on the Lower East Side and offered her services as a volunteer. A "comrade" later recounted the moment: "[I remembered] the despair on her face when [I] gave her the broom and asked her to clean up the floor. She 'did a very good job.'"[15] The man remembered despair, not indignance or resentment. Goldie could have refused, lectured him on the basics of equality, and informed the comrade of her past activity and party connections. Instead, perhaps believing that the male instinct to "put a young woman in her place" would never go away, she took the broom and complied with his request. Intuitively, she knew that self-assertion might backfire.

While living with Morris in New York City and planning to emigrate to Palestine, Goldie held a temporary job as a librarian. By the turn of the twentieth century, librarianship was accepted as a woman's job, which reflected an understanding of women as agents of change who would bring culture and refinement to the masses. Female librarians made less money than female teachers and worked within a hierarchy that kept men in senior, better-paying positions, even if women performed comparable work. The profession of a librarian offered an opening to women who sought work but were mostly turned away by employers.[16] There is no indication, however, that Golda worried about the gender-based discrimination that she must have encountered in the profession. Perhaps she thought that all this would disappear once socialism came to prevail.

Golda had worked previously at libraries in Milwaukee and Chicago and proved to be quite adept at the work. In New York she was encouraged to stay on staff, which must have been a tempting opportunity. Golda was at a crossroads. The job offered a comfortable life, and she was a practical woman, but already at the age of twenty, she knew a comfortable life was not for her. Her gaze was set upon the horizon of political activism.

In New York City her diligence and energy as a party volunteer soon earned her recognition. She was embraced by the party's New York leadership and regularly visited the homes of Baruch Zuckerman, one of Poalei Zion's founders, and Jacob Goodman, the editor in chief of the Yiddish socialist daily *Die Zeit*. As was her practice throughout her life, she cultivated relationships with their wives and daughters as well, effortlessly mixing private and public life. Golda aspired to hold a man's job but was drawn to the warm ambience offered by women, and felt equally comfortable in both domains.

In their official literature Poalei Zion upheld the principle of gender equality, but as a fellow woman comrade Sophie Udin recalled: "The 'female comrades' were expected to prepare food for the meetings and stay home with the children when [the men] ran late. The women did not partake in discussions or make suggestions in the presence of the men." The standard answer to anyone inquiring about the discrepancy between theory and practice was that with the spread of socialism, society would gradually eradicate gender discrimination. Goldie developed her own approach to this problem: she focused on her own integration, content to be the only woman in the room and leave the resolution of deeper problems to the future.[17]

The Suffragists and the Nineteenth Amendment

While Golda generally turned a blind eye to gender discrimination within the party, it would have been difficult to ignore the broader suffragist movement, which was gaining strength as Golda was growing up. During 1911–1912, for instance, the suffragists launched a grassroots campaign directed at the ethnic enclaves of Milwaukee. In 1916, the planners of a suffragist parade offered women yellow regalia and coordinated hats, "emblazoned with 'On Wisconsin,'" and as Goldie entered the Wisconsin State Normal School for teachers, a massive petition drive circulated in favor of the right to vote. Indeed, the Nineteenth Amendment to the U.S. Constitution was ratified one month before she and Morris arrived in New York City. Being intimately involved in politics, she must have been following the fight.[18]

Yet in her memoirs Golda mentioned the movement only twice: first, as one of the subjects discussed in Sheyna's salons in Denver; and second, in a brief comparison of the U.S. suffragists and their sisters in Palestine: "It seemed to me that [Rachel Yanait Ben-Zvi, a feminist and labor leader] and women like her, were doing more—without the benefit of publicity—to further the cause of our sex than even the most militant of suffragists in the United States or England."[19]

Should one conclude that Golda was blind, indifferent, or even hostile to those fighting for women's right to vote? This is a tempting conclusion, especially in light of Golda's frostiness toward second-wave feminism. But again, one must remember that Golda's memoirs reflect a savvy prime minister rewriting her history to fit events that took place much later. Her reference to the possibility of supporting gender equality without "publicity" was likely directed at 1970s feminists who were disappointed in her for not taking more visible action. Moreover, Golda never viewed publicity as a bad tool for promoting policy; it was only bad when deployed against her policies. Had she supported their cause, she would not have denounced the suffragists as "publicity hungry." We are thus left with the question: Did she reject their cause in the 1920s, or only in the 1970s?

A rejection of the suffragists' campaign would be hard to reconcile with her experiences—her fight to be admitted as a member of Poalei Zion despite her young age, her defiance when she was denied the right to speak at her synagogue, and her being crushed when she learned that she was barred from the Jewish Legion because of her gender. Furthermore, given her aspirations to make a career in party politics, it seems implausible that she would oppose expanding the right to vote to her own gender.[20] We also know that both Victor L. Berger and Eugene V. Debs, the two socialist leaders Golda adored, strongly supported women's right to vote, and that Meta Schlichting Berger, Victor's wife and an activist in her own right, energetically campaigned for both the national and local involvement of women in politics.[21]

The circumstantial evidence thus supports the conclusion that Golda favored women's suffrage. And yet, as a member of the Jewish immigrant working class, she might have been conflicted. Her immigrant community respected the traditional gender-based division of labor: in Wisconsin, the brewery industry, in which her brother-in-law worked, opposed the suffragists for fear that women would vote in favor of prohibition. Moreover, the predominantly middle-class Protestant suffragists were not her people. Some of them opposed immigration and believed immigrants should not be eligible to vote. Some even accused the suffragists of antisemitism. She might have felt reluctant to support them, let alone act on their behalf.[22]

The suffragists' attitude toward socialists in general and Jewish socialists in particular might also have chilled Goldie's enthusiasm for their cause. The New York Socialist Party actively supported the Nineteenth Amendment. Its members included union activists and workers—among them many Jews—all Goldie's people. Amid the political climate of the Red Scare, antisuffragist conservatives weaponized this support. Dreading the possibility that they would be labeled un-American, the suffragists distanced themselves from the "radical" socialists.[23] Golda was one of those "radicals" (pejoratively branded Miss Bolsheviki), and perhaps this is why she felt that they did not deserve her support.[24] Over time, as she buried her American socialist past, she might also have buried the reasons for her condemnation of the American suffragists.

These factors, however, do not indicate that she did not value the effort to give women an equal say in democratic decision making. At most, one can conclude that for Golda, the rights of women took second place to the nationwide oppression of progressives.

World War I, Xenophobia, and Antisocialist Propaganda

Golda's memoirs do not dwell on the dark clouds of propaganda and animosity during World War I. Here again, her silence is significant. One must consider the possibility that, given the suffocating climate during World War I and the postwar years, Golda may not have felt that America was much better for Jews than Russia, and that the only solution was a land of their own. Palestine offered an increasingly attractive alternative.

The likelihood of a world war had been a topic of discussion three years earlier in Denver in Jenny-Sheyna's salons, where the debate concerned pacifism, American neutrality toward the European belligerents, and President Wilson.[25] The war broke out as Goldie returned to Milwaukee from Denver, and although the United States would not declare war against Germany for three years (1917), Goldie must have been aware of the social upheaval around her well before then. Milwaukee was known as a "socialist town" and had a large population of Americans of German descent.[26] Both socialists and German Americans were harassed as "others"—people who were not considered bona fide Americans. Political dissidents suffered the same fate. Criticizing government policy equaled disloyalty.

On December 7, 1915, President Woodrow Wilson denounced the growing number of Americans who disagreed with his policies: "There are citizens of the United States . . . who have poured the poison of disloyalty into the very arteries of our national life . . . and . . . debase our politics to the uses of foreign intrigue. . . . Such creatures of passion, disloyalty, and anarchy must be crushed out."[27] In the wake of Wilson's call to arms, many Jews were persecuted, intimidated and branded as "un-American." A volunteer organization, the American Protective League, was established with the blessing of the government. Thousands of volunteers, spread across the country, sought to identify and root out "disloyal persons." In Milwaukee alone, the league fingered 19,783 suspected un-Americans.[28]

Soon after the United States entered the war, the Espionage Act of 1917, further strengthened by Congress in 1918, led to the prosecution of several allegedly disloyal persons.[29] Both Eugene V. Debs and Victor L. Berger were prosecuted. During 1919–1920, the wave of domestic persecution reached its peak under Wilson's two attorney generals, Thomas Gregory and A. Mitchell Palmer, known for the Palmer Raids. Congress was also aggressively considering an end to the open-door policy, which had allowed Golda's family to immigrate to America. It aimed to shut the gates of America to Eastern European Jews at the very moment they were being subjected to new waves of violence following the Russian Revolution.[30]

People in Golda's circle were angry and depressed. A letter to Golda from an acquaintance in 1919 states:

> Was shocked to read in this morning['s] paper of the killing of the brave Liebknecht and Rosa Luxemburg. It's about high time . . . that the tables were turned in other countries as completely, if necessary, as they have been in Russia, so as to allow the development of a social order and a dominant social psychology that would make insecure the lives and thwart the liberties, not of our Liebknechts, Debs', and other spokesmen of the laboring "'many,' but rather those of the . . ." liberals "who champion the exploiting interests of the 'few.'"[31]

The tone of the letter strongly suggested that its writer felt he was writing to a kindred soul. Everyone in Goldie's circle was a "hyphenated American" and a socialist. It defies reason to imagine that she did not feel herself a target of the propaganda assault.

In her memoirs the mature Golda mentioned the war only in the context of her activities on behalf of Eastern European Jewry. She

volunteered with the People's Relief Committee, an organization established by Poalei Zion to help Eastern European Jews, which involved
walking door-to-door and requesting small contributions, a cent here
and a nickel there. Her involvement heightened her awareness of the
internal divisions inside the Jewish community, as the organization was
shunned by mainstream Jewish organizations—such as the American
Jewish Relief Committee and the Central Committee for the Relief of
Jews Suffering through the War—because it was identified as socialist
and hence potentially "subversive."[32]

When Goldie organized a march to protest the spreading pogroms in
Russia, she drew the ire of some community leaders. A wealthy Jewish
businessman summoned her to his office and asked her to cancel the
march, which, he expected, would embarrass the Jewish community and
invite hostility. As Golda proudly recalled later, she answered with a mix
of commitment to the cause and youthful chutzpah: "I told him I had
every intention of going on with the plans. . . . I wasn't at all worried
about what people would think or say. There was nothing for us [Jews]
to be ashamed of."[33] Here were the first signs of Golda, the proud Jew.
The march was, in fact, well received and garnered Poalei Zion nationwide publicity.

During this time, Golda came to the realization that Milwaukee was
a "provincial town" (pejoratively referred to as "Beerwaukee" by her
friend Regina), too small for one aspiring to become "somebody." She
began spending more time in Chicago, where Jenny-Sheyna and Regina
had already moved. But even in Chicago, she recognized that her party
had few prospects of appealing to large numbers of American Jews and
that women of her political persuasion were targeted as "undesirable."
Regina captured the climate:

> I am very much wrought up over what is going on here. A few days
> ago a sailor shot a man, in [illegible] park, because he did not stand
> up when the Star-Spangled Banner was played. The sailor was at once
> released and many people applauded his act and shook hands with
> him. I tell you it's disgusting. It is impossible to walk on the street
> unless you loudly proclaim your patriotism. A woman was beaten up

for wearing an E. V. Debs button. I just wonder how much longer the workers of this U.S. of A. will stand for [illegible]. I wish the time would already come when we can get out of here.[34]

For Golda and Regina, getting out could only mean one thing: heading to the "promised land": Palestine.

The Allure of the Promised Land

Beyond being favored by Zionist ideology, Palestine was also a pragmatic choice as a place to found a new society. While the United States was shutting its gates to Jewish immigrants, the British Empire issued the Balfour Declaration, which opened Palestine as the "Jewish national home." Goldie and her friends began talking of Palestine as their true home, a land waiting to be developed for the entire Jewish people and promising Jews the opportunity to rebuild themselves.[35]

During the tumultuous postwar years the American Socialist Party collapsed. Poalei Zion was similarly devastated. *Die Zeit*, the newspaper Goldie had worked so hard to establish, was struggling to survive and would permanently close its doors in 1922. If Goldie stayed in America, what could her future be? Her biographer, Meron Medzini, noted: "It is not clear when and how she came to the conclusion that she would not have a glorious future in America. She thought carefully, alone or perhaps with her sister and friends, what could be the chances of a poor Jewish girl in America? And especially if she were married to a poor painter, who, like her, had no university education and both living on the fringes of society."[36]

Palestine as the American Frontier

The history of the frontier, in which the state of Wisconsin itself played a part, was a pillar of American consciousness. The frontier—that wild and "empty" territory, waiting to be tamed and cultivated by white settlers—ignited the imagination. American settlers heading west were pioneers: hardworking, industrious, and self-sufficient. They were liberated from the ties of the old world and bent on the construction of an authentic American identity. Noted Wisconsin historian Frederick Jackson Turner thought that the period of the frontier ended in 1890, eight years before Golda was born, but the idea remained potent well into the early twentieth century and must have fed Goldie's imagination. It is not farfetched to assume that she saw similarities between the American frontier and Labor Zionism. Not knowing much about contemporary Palestine, she may have imagined Zion as an empty land waiting to be redeemed by idealistic Jewish pioneers, and have seen herself as one such Palestinian pioneer: hardy, strong, self-reliant. Like their American counterparts, they would shed the bonds of the old country and construct a better society. The American frontier may have come to an end, but a new horizon had opened in Palestine. For Golda, what could have been more inspiring than the chance to devote herself to the creation of a Jewish state? She could save her people and, in doing so, save herself as well.

The decision to leave America and go to Palestine was, then, rooted in both personal and political reasons, as decisions to immigrate often are. As time went by Goldie tended to highlight only the Zionist motive— her desire to partake in building a state for the Jewish people—and let other motivations fade away and be forgotten. Whatever her true motivations, once she made her decision she characteristically displayed leadership qualities and quickly assembled a group, including Regina, Sheyna, and Shamai, that would together set sail for Palestine. Her parents, along with Tzipke, would travel later.

PART II

PALESTINE, 1921–1948

CHAPTER 5

THE USS *POCAHONTAS*

EVERYTHING ABOUT THE USS *POCAHONTAS*, the ocean liner that ferried Golda's party to Italy and then to Palestine, evidenced the upheaval that the world had recently experienced. Originally built in Germany as a passenger ship named *Prinzess Irene*, it was commandeered by the U.S. Navy during World War I and turned into a transport ship for delivering soldiers to the European front. The ship had known old-world elegance as well as ruthless war. Meanwhile, the world around it had fundamentally changed. The empires of Russia, Germany, and Austro-Hungary had been dismantled, as had the Ottoman Empire, which reigned over the Middle East. Great Britain now ruled in Palestine, which gave legal force to the Balfour Declaration, promising Jews a national home in the promised land.

Golda was likely familiar with the new ship's name, as the legends of the seventeenth-century Native American princess were widely known by the time Golda attended school in Wisconsin. It is not clear, however, whether anyone in Golda's group recognized the irony of their traveling on the *Pocahontas*, given its connection to the struggle between natives and newcomers and the natives' ambivalence toward the "white man." The month that Golda and her companions set sail, May 1921, the Palestinians had just begun their own protest of the "new world order." Palestinian Arabs, like Pocahontas's tribe, resented the new immigrants and, in a series of riots, murdered forty-seven Jews. This was the first signal that the great Zionist dream of "returning to the homeland" would not be fulfilled easily. Fear crept into the hearts of the group, exacerbated by news that their ship was in such bad condition that it might not survive the journey.

To make matters worse, mutiny erupted as soon as the passengers embarked. The disgruntled crew often resorted to sabotage, stopping the supply of electricity, breaking the refrigerators so that food supplies were spoiled, and flooding the engine room.[1] Under normal conditions, the ship would have reached Italy within two weeks, but on this trip, the *Pocahontas* took forty-three days to arrive in Naples. Throughout that time, Golda's friend Regina later remembered, Golda received private lessons in Hebrew from one of the passengers. She had finally accepted the Zionist rejection of Yiddish as the language of exile. (The new language, however, proved difficult to master and even a year later Golda had to obtain special permission to address the Labor Convention in Yiddish.) In Naples, the group discovered that all trips to Jaffa had been canceled because Arab boatmen had discontinued service to Jewish immigrants. The abstract conflict between Arabs and Israelis became painfully concrete.

These obstacles only fed Jewish indignation and strengthened their resolve: Why should Jews be singled out and denied entry to Palestine? Besides, in their minds, they were not ordinary immigrants. They were "olim," people returning home from exile. They had a right to settle in Palestine. They decided to sail to Egypt and from there take a train to Tel Aviv.

In Brindisi, as they prepared to embark on the boat to Egypt, they received exciting news: a group of pioneers from Lithuania (called Chaluzim—the Hebrew term for "trailblazers") would be joining them. Glumness gave way to joy. By all accounts, Golda was ecstatic and immediately sprang into action. She wanted to merge her group with the Lithuanians: eat with them, sleep by their sides, and hope their good fortune rubbed off on her and her companions. She persuaded her group to give up the modest "luxury" of their cabins and move their belongings to the deck, where the penniless pioneers were parked for the two-day trip.

These Lithuanian pioneers epitomized the Zionist project. Young, idealistic, determined, and well built, they were fluent in Hebrew and had already received training in agriculture. They were ready to toil the land and "make the desert bloom." For the first time, Golda encountered the "new Hebrews," those young people Ben-Gurion and Ben-Zvi had spoken of years earlier in Milwaukee. One particularly observant member of Golda's group noticed the masculinity exuded by these Lithuanians: they were all muscle and toughness—Clint Eastwood rather than Woody Allen.[2]

Was this another, less ideological, reason for the strong attraction Golda felt toward the Lithuanian pioneers? "I could hardly take my eyes off them," she is reported to have said.[3] Did it occur to Morris, watching his wife, that he was an old-world Jew, effeminate and soft, hopelessly committed to music and the arts, and unfit for the hard labor necessary to work the land? Could he see the looming threat that the new Hebrew sexuality posed to his marriage?

Despite Golda's efforts, the Lithuanians did not welcome her group with open arms. They had no use for "Americans," they declared, even if they were socialist Jews. All of a sudden, even before setting foot in Palestine, Golda understood that although she had left America, she was still unmistakably American. Making a nation out of exiles meant creating compatriots of people whose lives had been shaped in different homelands, and this early encounter made evident to Golda the difficulty of such a task. It is worth noting that, in their memoirs, neither Golda nor Sheyna referred to the Lithuanians as "pioneers," perhaps an indication that simply being Zionist was not enough to overcome marked ethnic differences. Notwithstanding the shared aims of the two groups, they remained Americans and Lithuanians.

Golda exerted considerable charm in attempting to ingratiate herself with the Lithuanians. She offered food, emphasized commonalities, and joined them in singing songs they all knew. But the trip was too short— only two days—to create the bond she coveted. One wonders how she decoded the gender expectations of this new group. Did they expect their women to be traditional and deferential, or, as "new Hebrew men," did they expect an assertive "new Hebrew woman?" Golda was accustomed to dealing with Morris's vulnerability, but could it be that these pioneers had another sort of vulnerability, the need to assert their manhood and receive the validation and support provided by traditional femininity? These questions were still in the depths of Golda's unconscious mind, but they would surface in a few months, as she was confronted with the assertive feminism of the kibbutz and the Women Workers Council.

Golda yearned for a happy ending to her encounter with the Lithuanians, and in her memoirs, recorded as much: "We told . . . [them] about life in America, they told us about how they had lived in Eastern Europe, and as the stars came out, we sang Hebrew and Yiddish songs together and danced the hora." That tableau of idyllic fraternity must have been her fantasy. Neither Sheyna nor Golda's biographer Marie Syrkin corroborate it.[4] It is more likely that, through this experience, Golda came to recognize that conditions on the ground would probably refute her fantasy of coming home and to appreciate the hardships inherent in immigration.

CHAPTER 6

A SOJOURN IN TEL AVIV

GOLDA'S ARRIVAL in Tel Aviv "was an anticlimax."[1] Twelve years into its existence, Tel Aviv was not the vibrant, cosmopolitan city it would become in later decades, and Golda had never been exposed to heat or the white, blazing light of the Middle East, so different from Pinsk, Milwaukee, and New York. But Sheyna and Golda did not have time to dwell on these differences. They had to perform their traditional roles as homemakers, which included fetching food from the market to feed the group.

Tel Aviv aspired to be a European town, but its market was and remains an oriental bazaar, the likes of which Golda had never seen. Here is the historian Anat Helman's description: "Butchers threw bones on the ground and fishmongers tossed rotten fish into the street. Poultry was slaughtered on the spot; the birds' blood dried on the sand and, carried by the wind, feathers wafted through windows of nearby homes. The marketplace was full of flies. . . . Rats and mice were everywhere."[2] After arriving in Milwaukee from Russia, Bluma had learned that Americans liked their food purchases wrapped and she adjusted her practices at the store accordingly. Her daughters, having left America, now encountered the opposite problem. Tel Aviv's vendors, if they offered any wrapping at all, offered old, stained newspapers, picked from the mucky ground. For Golda, a woman so sensitive to hygiene, it was terribly off-putting.

Golda and Sheyna rented a small two-bedroom apartment on the edge of town, with no electricity and a communal bathroom in the yard.

The situation must have reminded them of Pinsk, or their first years in Milwaukee. Golda intuitively understood that a well-decorated space could combat depression and, adept at sewing, busied herself making bedspreads and curtains, trying desperately to make the place more livable. Morris, also sensitive to aesthetics, painted the walls and turned their unpacked crates into furniture.

Morris quickly found a job as a bookkeeper, and Golda's friend Regina a job as a typist. The secretarial skills she had acquired in Milwaukee proved useful, and soon enough Regina landed a high-paying job with the World Zionist Organization and moved to Jerusalem. The contrast between Golda and Regina is instructive. Regina integrated easily into the labor market, slack as it was, in part because her skills were precisely what the market expected of women. Golda, on the other hand, had rejected her mother's suggestion that she enroll in secretarial school and was not so easily employable. It was a struggle for her to find a teaching job, partly because she had never obtained her teaching certificate. She could offer private English lessons, but this pursuit felt like a failure. "I did not come to Palestine to spread American culture," she recalled in her memoirs. But how would she earn a living in her new country? That was not clear.[3]

Concerns about Morris added to her frustration. Morris was no Zionist ideologue, and he did not look upon Tel Aviv as the miraculous beginning of a new age. There was no radio service in Palestine, and Tel Aviv had few, if any, cultural events (it would be more than a decade before the Palestine Philharmonic Orchestra was established). Tel Aviv, for Morris, was hot, provincial, and disappointing. Worse yet, the books he had sent from American arrived torn and water-damaged.[4] Golda worried that Morris might decide that enough was enough and return to America, the only home he remembered fondly.

Golda was dispirited. As she dryly summed it up, the summer of 1921 "was no treat." As despair filled her heart, she responded by exercising agency: "We knew that it was up to each one of us personally to make our life in Palestine easier . . . and that we had no alternative other than . . . settle down as quickly as we possibly could."[5] Zionism was burning in her heart, but one should not underestimate the powerful influence of American individualism on Golda—her unwavering belief in self-sufficiency and self-help. Unlike many of her fellow immigrants, Golda accepted that it was her responsibility to act and blaze the path.

She decided that they should join a kibbutz and take part in creating an authentic Zionist-socialist culture. The philosophy of the kibbutz— radical egalitarianism and a commitment to revive the homeland (to make the desert bloom, as they said)—epitomized Golda's aspirations, which Sheyna, who remained in Tel Aviv with Shamai, did not share. She even identified the kibbutz she wished to join—Merhavia—a kib- butz in the Yezreel Valley, close to Mount Tabor, where veterans of the American Jewish Legion had already settled. Notwithstanding her de- termination to turn over a new leaf, she gravitated toward the familiar and comforting—American acquaintances. Surely, she felt, they would be more sympathetic to her and to Morris than the Lithuanians had been. The fact that Meir Dubinsky, a young man from Milwaukee who had courted her in the past, was one of the founders probably contrib- uted to this feeling. We do not know what Morris thought of her choice, but as always, he went along.

CHAPTER 7

COMRADE GOLDA AND COMRADE MORRIS IN KIBBUTZ MERHAVIA

GOLDA SOON DISCOVERED that the mere desire to join a kibbutz was not enough. Kibbutz members were free to accept or reject new members as they saw fit, which presented a paradox at the heart of the project. The kibbutz was established on the principle of utopian social justice—from each according to his abilities, to each according to his needs—and was conceived as a collective based on solidarity. As a result of these commitments, the collective felt obliged to be self-sustaining, and therefore the ideal member was one able to perform hard labor. This dynamic generated a strong preference for men, and a majority of the kibbutz members rejected the Myersons' application.

Golda was stunned. The statement they received did not even provide a reason for their rejection. Her American upbringing—a culture committed to due process in both law and custom—likely guided Golda's response. She demanded to know why they had been rejected and made three long, strenuous bus trips to the kibbutz to insist on a hearing and her right to advocate on her behalf. The prejudices they had encountered on their voyage reappeared: Americans like the Myersons had a reputation for being soft and bourgeois, accustomed to a comfortable life. It was indeed ironic. Golda had been raised in a tough working-class neighborhood and embodied the values of the American frontier, yet here she was tarred with the gross generalization that all Americans were weak and pampered. For the current members of the kibbutz, an American girl (as they referred to Golda) could not possibly meet the strict standards of hard labor. Besides, being married, she was likely to get pregnant soon. Who then would support the child? The same comrades who proudly wrote the principle of gender equality on the kibbutz's banner were openly discriminating against Golda, oblivious to the contradiction between word and deed. But Golda fought like a tigress. She refused to take no for an answer, and after several meetings, she won her battle. The Myersons were admitted for a trial period. Golda was determined to come and stay.

Merhavia bore several marks of Zionist ideology, the theory that the Jews are not colonizers, but a people rightfully reclaiming its ancient national home. The name itself means "divine wide space" and comes from Psalm 118: "I called on the Lord in distress; the Lord answered me in a wide space."[1] Before Merhavia was established in 1910, this place was a Palestinian village called Foulae. The Jewish National Fund had purchased the land from its Arab landlord. The purchase itself was considered a sacred act: redeeming the land after years of exile. The purchase of Merhavia was also rooted in strategic considerations, as it was set on a geographic crossroads between Egypt in the south, Greater Syria in the north, the Mediterranean Sea to the west, and Iraq to the east.

Given its location, Merhavia offered awe-inspiring views. Yet the land was stony, marshy, and infested with malaria mosquitoes. There were only a few small buildings and very few trees. As it was nearly everywhere in Palestine, shade was hard to find. "It looked not at all as I had imagined," Golda later recalled.[2] Golda and Morris were given a tiny room of their own, with two cots, a chair, and a lamp. Privacy, however, was in short supply. The showers, the toilets, and the dining room were all communal, and a cup of tea could not even be had in the privacy of one's room. Morris found these conditions insufferable.

The young couple immediately went to work, determined to prove that they were worthy new comrades. One of Golda's first tasks was to dig "endless holes in the soil between the rocks and then carefully plant saplings." Beautifying the land, bringing it back to life, was a central part of the noble dream, and hard labor was a cornerstone of pioneering. On her first day, she worked so long and hard that she collapsed when she finished, unable to "lift a finger."[3] With steely determination, she dragged herself to the collective dining room only to find that supper consisted of a chickpea mush "not worth the effort of bringing the fork to my mouth."[4] Her comrades were carefully eyeing her, awaiting confirmation that "this American girl" was unfit for kibbutz life. She was determined to deny them the satisfaction.

Is the Woman's Place in the Kitchen?

> It is a curious fact that novelists have a way of making us believe that luncheon parties are invariably memorable for something very witty that was said, or for something very wise that was done. But they seldom spare a word for what was eaten.
>
> —VIRGINIA WOOLF, *A ROOM OF ONE'S OWN*

Seven years before Virginia Woolf published her literary feminist critique of male hegemony, Golda encountered the connection between food and the "woman question" at the kibbutz. The chickpea mush, which Golda felt was not worth lifting a fork for, was emblematic of the quality of food served in the early kibbutzim. The kibbutzniks were austere and ascetic. They thought of "good, tasty food" as a bourgeois whim that should be crushed under the feet of the "new Hebrew revolution." Food was a necessity, meant only to help one continue doing work. Chickpeas were inexpensive, and boiling them until they practically lost all flavor was easy and efficient. This was sufficient for the collective's purpose. The mush that Golda first encountered, it is worth noting, would have been light years from present day hummus, with its olive oil, garlic, tahini, lemon juice, and an occasional pinch of paprika.

Notwithstanding their egalitarian principles, the kibbutzim regularly assigned kitchen duty to their female members. The justification was familiar: women were "naturally" endowed with cooking skills, so they were better suited to kitchen work than to hard manual labor in the fields. Even though many male comrades were sophisticated in their

understanding of the social construction of reality—they were well acquainted, for example, with the construction of the "greedy Jew"—they
could not see that gender roles were similarly constructed and that,
therefore, not all females were "born to cook."

The women, however, were unhappy with the replication of the old
social order and expected a more radical effort to effect change. Feminism was an important part of their Zionism. Furthermore, most of the
women were clueless about how to cook for a thirty-person group. Their
clumsy efforts, coupled with the cheap, unfamiliar ingredients, yielded
unappetizing dishes. Their male comrades, presumably remembering
fondly their mothers' food, expressed their frustration with ridicule and
torrents of insults. In one humiliation ceremony, called "the train," the
comrades would pass the "inedible" food from plate to plate, each man
emptying his plate onto his neighbor's until all but the last plate were
empty.

This was the situation Golda encountered when she arrived in Merhavia. In contrast to her female comrades, however, she sided with the
men and supported increased kitchen duty for women, a decision that
has contributed to the claim that she was an antifeminist. In reflecting
on this decision, however, one can see the possibilty of several different
underlying reasons at work, some more and some less hostile to feminism. Golda was already a political person with some experience in
group dynamics and she had likely calculated her stand.

First and foremost, Golda was aware of the demographics. Men
formed a majority in Merhavia, and taking their side would distinguish
her as "sensible" in their eyes. Golda also took pride in her skills as a
cook and this opportunity to show them off could only increase her
prestige among her male comrades. Gaining the support of the male
majority would work to Golda's advantage when other matters arose
that necessitated a vote in the kibbutz, such as designating delegates to
the nationwide socialist convention. Furthermore, Golda may have in-
ferred that her male comrades were struggling to meet the ideal of that
"new Hebrew man." Assigning men to the kitchen and asking them to
engage in activities they associated with their mothers and sisters would
undermine their struggle to turn into "real men."[5] For Morris, in

particular, Golda may have thought that preparing edible food reminiscent of home would mollify his resentment of kibbutz life. Last but not least, Golda may simply have felt more empathy toward men. The voices of women arguing about what is right and just in the kibbutz may have reminded her of the never-ending squabbles between Bluma and Sheyna.

To her credit, Golda led by example. The minutes of the kibbutz's general meetings record her requests to be placed on kitchen duty, and she declared repeatedly that kitchen work was as noble as any other task on the kibbutz and that (female) comrades should be proud to feed the collective. Golda soon proved that the kitchen, too, could be a place for reform. Her first target was the herring. Typically, cans of herring in tomato sauce were served for breakfast. The unskinned herring would be cut into small pieces and placed on a plate. Golda, however, peeled the fish before cutting it. Why make the kitchen staff engage in this tedious task? She explained that the kibbutz did not have enough utensils for all members and, therefore, some members did not have the appropriate fork to pick the fish themselves. Furthermore, because the kibbutz could not afford napkins, the comrades would wipe their oily fingers on their clothes or on the table, thereby making the task of cleaning, which also mostly fell to the women, more difficult. The rest of the women were unhappy with this change and worried that the men would grow accustomed to being spoiled. But Golda refused to budge: this is our home, and we should serve the meal as if we were serving it to our family, she insisted.

She also introduced a more festive atmosphere on Shabbat. In keeping with the Zionist-socialist credo, the kibbutz mostly ignored religious restrictions on activity on the Sabbath. However, it did observe the Friday night ceremony, recognizing the beginning of Shabbat. Golda proudly introduced a new aesthetic to go with the day of rest: she spread sheets on the dining room tables and decorated them with flowers. Some denounced the innovation as "bourgeois," but many appreciated it, so it stayed. She also increased the volume of cookies baked on Shabbat and offered another treat: fried onion rings sprinkled with bits of hard-boiled egg. In her own way, Golda was making a mark on the culture of the community.

Dress, the Anti-Fashion of Fashion

For a penniless comrade Golda made sure to dress as best she could. The kibbutz provided a work uniform: a sackcloth into which three holes were cut, one for the head and two for the arms. It was shapeless and it wrinkled instantly, making the wearer look unkempt and unappealing. That, too, was part of the socialist ideology. Intentional anti-fashion was adopted to achieve uniformity of dress and signal a rejection of materialism, part of the broader effort to standardize the social body.[6] Using a coal iron, Golda spent hours pressing her sacks. She also used her personal allowance to purchase a white swathe of cloth and a white kerchief, which added to her appeal on special occasions.[7] A photograph from this period shows her doing agricultural work, smiling and content, decked out in white, which we should recall, was the trademark of the American suffragists. Perhaps Golda was thinking of them as she ascended the hierarchy of the kibbutz.

A Valued Comrade, Her Presence and Leadership

If Golda vexed some of the women with her remarks about kitchen duty or with the attention she received from her male comrades, it was a small price to pay. Golda was in her element drinking delicious water from the well of an active life. Work during the day made her feel she was fulfilling the Zionist dream, and she spent many a night at the kibbutz's distant stations where the men were doing guard duty. She would then join them in the communal dining room for a late night snack. All the while, she eagerly listened to their stories about battles, sieges, and fortunes (many of the men were veterans of World War I). They, in turn, received a boost to their egos from this attentive and charming listener.

An important part of the egalitarian ethos of the kibbutz was the comrades' assembly, the equivalent of a town hall meeting, in which they discussed collective problems and voted on policy. Golda was rapidly becoming important in kibbutz organization and politics. The minutes of the meetings show that she was no longer "Goldie" but "Comrade Golda," and they mention her name often; Morris, by contrast, was referred to as Meirson (the Hebrew spelling of Myerson) and appears in the minutes only once. Shortly after her arrival, Golda was elected to the prestigious steering committee of the kibbutz, the central executive body in charge of policy and vision.

Golda also secured a resolution to attend a training school to acquire skills in poultry farming. Her considerable success in establishing a poultry component added to the kibbutz's struggling economy. The kibbutz began to harvest eggs and chickens to feed its members and it sold what was left over for profit. Golda even began to raise geese. This was an achievement for Golda, not only because it was the first and probably only skill she ever acquired through formal training, nor because she succeeded so handsomely, but because she forced herself to overcome her childhood fear of animals. Here again, her perseverance in the face of obstacles—this time, clucking chickens and aggressive roosters—displays her resolve and strong will. It also shows Golda's desire to move away from the "general chores" of the kibbutz (digging, picking almonds, and even kitchen duty) to a field that required training and expertise. This could be interpreted as an attempt to prove her worth in order to stay in the kibbutz, but it might also indicate that she was already beginning to plan her long-term political career.

The minutes of Merhavia's general assembly showcase Golda as a policymaker. She cared for the women and proposed that the kibbutz send a few female comrades to receive training in various fields of specialized work. "It is important that they be experienced workers," she reasoned. The resolution passed. By the end of her first year in Merhavia, she had gained enough confidence and stature to demand a generous policy in matters of childcare:

> Comrade Golda raised the question of our policy about the issue of raising a family, and demands that we reach a clear policy about this. The question of child expenses is raised, who will pay and will there be a limit to the expenses paid. Confirm and decide that the child's expenses will fall upon the collective, without any limits.[8]

It is worth noting that this topic was controversial, and that Golda insisted on the principle that childcare be provided by the collective "without limits." This victory marked an important turning point, for until then the kibbutz had been ambivalent about children and worried about the expense associated with their care. At Golda's prompting, Merhavia accepted the idea that "it takes a village" to raise a family.

Stepping Into National Politics at the Second General Socialist Convention

Golda's ambitions soon expanded beyond the kibbutz. Her comrades recognized her for her energetic talents and, one year after they had initially rejected her as a member of the kibbutz, appointed her as their delegate to the Second General Socialist Convention. That convention created the building blocks of socialism in Palestine, including the Federation of Labor (Histadrut), the "Workers' Corporation" (Hevrat H-ovdim), and a daily newspaper. Golda, although an unknown delegate, was present at what later became known as "the State in the making."

Her maiden speech, delivered in Yiddish, was cleverly calculated to impress the leadership of the social-Zionists in Palestine. She criticized her comrades in the United States, thereby both reminding the delegates that she came from America and asserting that she was now one of them. More important, she addressed the question of whether women needed their own political organization. Having had some experience with the Women Workers Council as a kibbutz delegate, she argued that, while the needs of women workers—particularly the tension between work and family as well as gender discrimination—deserved attention, the Federation of Labor itself was capable of handling them. There was no need for a special women's organization. Golda's opinion was honey to the convention leaders and vinegar to the feminists. The head of the Women Workers Council, Ada Fishman Maimon, fiercely believed that discrimination against women was rampant and that only women's advocacy would remedy the situation. Maimon was a thorn in the side of the male leadership, as was the organization she led, and Golda provided them with an alternative approach, one that would allow the federation to discard the special interests council.

Golda's view, that the male leadership would be willing to serve all workers regardless of gender, must have been at least partially genuine. After all, the whole leadership expressly supported the principle of gender equality. But one should not underestimate her willingness to curry favor with Ben-Gurion and his lieutenants. Golda understood where her bread was buttered, and this speech boosted her climb up to the top of the political leadership. Stepping upward, however, would coincide with the unraveling of her marriage.

CHAPTER 8

LOVE AND MARRIAGE
Not a Fairy Tale

FOR MORRIS, kibbutz life was hell. He found the communal way of life ugly, intrusive, and overbearing. He hated the shared showers, he hated the stinking squat toilets, and he hated receiving a different set of clothing, including underwear, from the communal laundromat every week. Morris found the kibbutz's assault on the "bourgeois way of life" and its experimentation with radical egalitarianism offensive. Most unbearable to Morris, however, was the anti-intellectual climate.

In their zeal to create a new and revolutionary way of life, the early kibbutz ideologues rejected much of Western liberal culture. Avraham Shlonsky, one of Israel's canonic poets, recalled his days in the nearby Kibbutz Ein Charod in the early 1920s:

> Reading a book, thinking of a concert, was shameful . . . writing poems, playing the piano, these were cosmetics (fluff) . . . one day one of my poems was published in a [workers' magazine] and the news reached the Kibbutz . . . "What? a traitor among us? . . . Writing poems? Throw him out! Boycott him!" . . . I was cosmetics and unworthy of their company.[1]

Shlonsky was fortunate to have the inner strength to continue writing. Morris lacked such strength. Shortly after their arrival, he contracted malaria and sank into a deep depression. He was a gentle soul, in possession of "feminine virtues"—thoughtful, delicate, and sensitive to the aesthetic presentation of everyday life—and unfit for the rough and tough pioneer culture. It did not help matters that he was skeptical of nationalism, collectivism, and the intrinsic value of hard labor—the core tenets of the Zionist project.

Meanwhile, Golda bloomed. She was like a flower following the sun, lightly turning this way and that, bestowing her smiles and good humor upon her comrades, who responded with appreciation and affection. She spent a fair amount of time with her male comrades, visiting the guard stations, preparing snacks for the midnight meal, and dancing the hora on Friday nights. This could not have improved Morris's sullen mood. Nor did it help that Golda was beginning to make a name for herself in the labor movement, which included frequent travel. Morris's suspicion that she might be having an affair added to his sense of desolation.[2]

Golda tried to alleviate his burdens. Her attempts to provide better food and a more aesthetic presentation of the kibbutz meals, for instance, must have been in part an effort to make Morris feel better. She also took the bus to Tel Aviv to fetch Morris's gramophone, which along with his books, defined Morris's identity and nurtured his soul. Sheyna, who had kept the gramophone when the young couple moved to Merhavia, was upset by this change of events. There was no radio station in Palestine, and the American and Yiddish songs coming from the gramophone were a vital source of entertainment and moral support for her and her children. But Golda decided to sacrifice her sister's welfare for that of her husband's, hoping the music would boost his morale.

Morris's state of mind, however, only grew darker, and his crisis began a vicious downward spiral. The more melancholy Morris became, the more Golda sought the company of others. The more alone and abandoned he felt, the more compulsively he buried his misery in music, replaying certain pieces again and again. Their relationship was failing.[3] Golda's biographer Meron Medzini judged each party to be at fault for the situation: "They were both self-centered. They systematically destroyed each other and did not have the courage to take the drastic step."[4]

Golda's remedy was to start a family. Like many spouses in failing marriages, she convinced herself that children would somehow change the dynamic of the marriage. Although, at Golda's earlier insistence, the kibbutz had agreed to bear the financial burden of raising children, Morris's dislike for Merhavia and his aversion to raising children communally were strongly felt. (See chapter 7 in this volume.) Now came his turn to issue an ultimatum: kibbutz or children. He may have hoped that, as had happened with her sister Sheyna, children and urban family life would tame Golda's ambition, and her political drive would slowly fizzle out.

Any psychologist could have told the young couple that the prospects of saving the marriage in this way were meager. But even though Golda had already recognized the driving force of her ambition—that she could not do without politics—neither could she envision herself as a woman without children. She also wanted Morris to be the father. Ultimately, with a heavy heart, she agreed to leave the kibbutz.

Her resentment toward Morris subsided as soon as they left the kibbutz. They moved first to Sheyna's home in Tel Aviv before settling in Jerusalem. Their children, Menachem and Sarah, were born in the following two years, perhaps a sign that Golda wanted to expedite the cycle of childbearing, so she could free herself for other activities. The children's names confirmed Golda's traditional values. Unlike her more ideological comrades, who chose biblical or Hebrew names (Ben-Gurion, for instance, gave his elder daughter the name Renana, Hebrew for song, and his son the name Amos, after the biblical prophet), Golda and Morris chose to affirm family tradition. Menachem, born in 1924, was named after his grandfather. Sarah, born in 1926, was named after Morris's sister. (Golda, too, had an older sister named Sarah, who died in infancy in Kiev.) Their decision to speak Yiddish with the children at home, which would have been verboten among faithful Zionists, was another sign of their "non-Zionist" traditionalism.

Motherhood alone, however, was not satisfying. Feelings of suffocation and resentment soon took over. The chilling realization that Golda had trapped herself in a prison of her own creation made her increasingly miserable. A stable, solid life with nothing else had never been Golda's ideal. But life with Morris in Jerusalem was not even solid. They lived in wretched poverty, unable to make ends meet. And she was tormented by the emptiness of everyday life. She needed more, and her experience at Merhavia had confirmed for her that there was an alternative life, satisfying and full of excitement.[5]

Golda, in later years, would emphasize that when confronted by a choice one should always choose life. While she would never explicitly refer to marital strife as an instance in which one must choose life, her failed marriage may have been at the bottom of her deep conviction that one should always be guided by the light of life. We do not know whether Golda incidentally bumped into David Remez during this rocky patch in her life or whether she reached out to him to let him know about her agony. What we do know is that he would soon become both her mentor and her lover. With her marriage in shambles, she accepted his offer to serve on the secretariat of the Women Workers Council and move to Tel Aviv. A traditional mother despite her desire for freedom, she took the children with her. Morris remained in Jerusalem.

She was now a single woman with two young children and a job that offered upward mobility. She did not yet tell the children that she and Morris were separating, but her sister and mother were aware of the situation. As Golda frequently disappeared during the night or would have a nighttime visitor to her apartment, her family soon learned that Golda had a lover, a married man. For very traditional Jews, it must have been perceived as a ghastly scandal, tarnishing the family's honor and likely to ruin their daughter's and their grandchildren's lives. What would the neighbors say? How can a woman live without a man? How would the children survive without a father?

Golda's parents arrived in Palestine shortly after she left the kibbutz. There is no information about the confrontation between Golda and her parents when they received the news of her separation. But it would not be farfetched to let Elena Ferrante's rendition of a similar confrontation feed the imagination as we reflect on Golda's confrontation with her mother. The similarity between Ferrante's heroine and Golda is striking: a traditional working-class background; an uncultivated mother who could not understand her daughter's aspirations; an able, ambitious daughter, married with children, estranged from her husband

and in love with another man; and a mother–daughter relationship boiling with tension and conflict:

> Once we got home [mother] ... made me a long speech. ... She praised my husband in an exaggerated fashion, she ordered me to ask his forgiveness immediately. When I didn't she began to beg him herself to forgive me and swore ... that she would not go home if the two of us did not make peace. ... She urged us to think of the [children]. ...
>
> I drew back, I was aloof. The whole time I thought: I can't bear her. ... When she grabbed me for the hundredth time, insisting I admit that I made a serious mistake, I couldn't take it anymore. ... I said something like: "Enough, Ma ... I can't stay ... anymore, I love someone else. It was a mistake." ... She slapped me violently, shouting nonstop: "Shut up, you whore, shut up, shut up."[6]

Golda in Love with David Remez

David Remez was a powerhouse, one of the handful of men who constructed the hegemony of the labor movement in Palestine and facilitated the establishment of the state. Born in Belarus, Russia, in 1886, he was an avid Zionist and immigrated to Palestine before World War I. As a labor leader, he participated in the 1922 socialist convention, where he heard Golda give her maiden speech. One of his jobs at that convention was to assist the comrades in choosing Hebrew names, so that they could be transformed into "new Hebrews." As discussed previously, such a transformation did not catch Golda's fancy. Still, he noticed her. It may not have been love at first sight, yet there must have been chemistry between the two. They kept in touch, and Remez even helped Morris find a job in Jerusalem.

Golda was still married, but she was emotionally available, and there were many reasons for her to be attracted to Remez, twelve years her senior. Bald, not too tall, and slightly heavy, he sported a chevron mustache and looked like the CEO of a major corporation. Brilliant, analytical, and rational, he embodied the ideals to which she was attracted—he was, as Golda hoped to be, a mover and a shaker. As one of the founders of the Histadrut as well as one responsible for the socialist camp's economic expansion, Remez was self-confident and well-connected. In addition, he wrote and published poetry and was known as a gifted linguist (he gave El Al, Israel's airline company, its name).

If her relationship with Morris provided any clue to her romantic inclinations, Golda sought men who would validate her self-worth and soothe her deep insecurity. Remez, like Morris, valued her, guided and mentored her, and helped her grow emotionally and intellectually. He gave her the confidence she needed to hold the ladder steady as she continued her climb. The fact that he was well-connected may have served as an additional aphrodisiac. Remez had studied law in Constantinople with Ben-Gurion and Ben-Zvi, the two men who had electrified her imagination in Milwaukee at the age of sixteen, and Golda might have felt that his friendship with them enabled her to reach out and touch the stars.

There are several love letters from Golda to Remez, mostly from the late 1930s to the mid-1940s. The letters use a "coded language," indicating that the lovers wanted to hide their relationship. The code word for their love and relations was "antiquities." Golda wrote, for instance, "With great pleasure I read the letter on antiquities. In general, anything related to antiquities gives me a warm feeling." And on one New Year's Eve, she wrote:

> My hand in your hand. Do you know how dear you are to me, can you imagine the things in my heart. If I could see you now I would say everything—despite the fact that we forbade ourselves to use the certain word. . . . I so much want you to know. I thought that maybe the book of poems will tell you this.
>
> Today I cannot but think of another holiday, the eve of Passover. How good I felt then. We were together, every day, every hour, every night. I look forward to it (to more?).

And, wishing him a happy New Year, she signed: "*We*, in the full meaning of the word." In another letter, she elaborated on how much he meant to her:

Figure 4. Golda and David Remez at the convening of the first Israeli Knesset.
Courtesy of Israel Government Press Office. Credit: Hans Pinn.

I got used (is it so bad?), for many years, wonderful years, to do[ing]
substantial things together. . . . I could not have done it with
others—meaning you created this precious feeling . . . every day,
every action without you is for me a high mountain that I climb with
great difficulty. . . . If I could speak to you, you know that there could
be nothing greater for me than the opportunity to tell you everything, from the moment I leave to the moment I return . . . and now,
only one word that in the days of antiquities I did not say! . . . If you
were at home now, I would have, despite the tacit agreement, called
you and asked you to come over for a cup of tea at this table where I
write. Greetings from a full heart.[7]

Golda was not a good writer. Her vocabulary was basic, and she used
the word "thing" for any concept she needed to name, a tendency exacerbated by the couple's decision not to express their love in writing. And
yet the depth of her emotions, the love that blossomed into a lifelong
friendship, cannot be missed.

As his affair with Golda flourished, Remez's relationship with his wife Liuba turned icy. In an undated letter to him, Liuba wrote: "We received your letter from London, after you returned from Paris, a long time ago. Since then there has been no letter. It seems that you have no wish to write to us—maybe you prefer not to receive any letters."[8] Did Remez contemplate a divorce? He may not have. Many Zionist leaders had extramarital affairs, and their wives came to accept that reality.

Golda, it appears, decided that single life suited her better than stable attachments and never, despite her writings, sought a formal relationship with Remez. Golda settling down with another man would have devastated Morris, who was still hoping that she would return to him. It also would have made their children's lives more difficult, as they would have to share what little time Golda had for them with another person. Most important from Golda's perspective, had she remarried, she would have shackled herself again. She would have had to perform wifely duties that were much more demanding, given that her spouse would have been an important political actor. One can imagine her asking herself, "Who needs it?" Why not remain single and take advantage of the freedom to pursue a career? Life as a single woman would not be easy and people would talk, but it was still the least bad option.

Golda's relationship with Remez continued until he passed away in 1951. For decades, he supported, advised, and coached her as she ascended the political ranks, which raises the question: Was Remez a feminist? In the mid-1920s, when Golda was trying desperately to resign herself to life as a wife and mother, Remez actively fought for women's right to vote in the constituent assembly of the Jewish community in Palestine. Remez insisted that "an assembly without the women would have a male rather than a human identity and that men, too, are insulted when women are denied the right."[9] And yet Remez was also a political and pragmatic thinker. His relationship with the Women Workers Council indicates that he found their version of gender equality too radical and may have favored the ideal of gender neutrality—that decisions should not take gender into account. Thus, he gave no concessions to Golda because of her family responsibilities, and she would have to work twice as hard at her job to prove herself—a major factor in her neglect of her family life.

One might also wonder whether Golda's meteoric career depended on her decision to have a relationship with this powerful man. The evidence indicates, however, that Golda is largely responsible for her own success. As a rising but low level functionary, Golda excelled in the tasks assigned to her and she was very dependable—following instructions carefully and dutifully. She was a highly intelligent, able and loyal team member, and it is these attributes that best explain her brilliant ascent. In fact, her talents were such that by the early 1950s, her status in Israel's cabinet was higher than Remez's. When Prime Minister Ben-Gurion considered reshuffling the first Israeli cabinet, it was Golda's turn to help Remez, and she prevailed upon the prime minister to keep Remez in the cabinet as minister of education. Remez's politics was too dovish for Ben-Gurion and he was quickly phased out. Golda, on the other hand, made good use of the opening offered to her by Remez and soon consolidated her power as a Ben-Gurion ally.

The sexist culture of the Yishuv, and later Israel, would condemn Golda's character in the decades to come. People looked at this daring, good-looking, ambitious woman, neither married nor divorced, with a mixture of astonishment, jealousy, and anxiety. Her status as a single mother with an apartment of her own spawned rumors that she was promiscuous. People whispered that she was "available"—that anyone could take her to bed. Some even went as low as to call her a "mattress."[10] Her affair with Remez generated the joke that "Golda understands a hint" (the Hebrew word Remez means "hint"), which some cheerfully repeat to this day. No such mean-spirited and self-righteous barbs were directed at Remez or any other Zionist leader. Men who indulged in extramarital affairs were normal and virile, easy to forgive, and perhaps even to be admired.

Liberated from Morris at the age of thirty, Golda may well have experienced her erotic self-awakening during this period; she was not averse to tasting some "forbidden fruit." The Yishuv culture of the late 1920s contained a contradiction: it was morally puritanical, clinging to Victorian values, but also rebellious, challenging conservative conventions and often approving of "free love." Golda's actions boldly declared, even if she never said so, that what was permitted of men should be permitted of women and that she had the right to satisfy her sexual desires and cultivate romantic relationships.[11]

Whether there were, indeed, some one-night stands, we do not know. All that is known is that she had more than one significant lover. Zalman Rubashov, a close friend of Remez's who would eventually serve as Israel's third president, was among those smitten with her charms.

Golda in Love with Zalman Rubashov (Shazar)

Rubashov (later Shazar) was the quintessential eastern European intellectual—charismatic, vivacious, erudite, and always ready to tell an apt anecdote. He had a fiery intellect and would soon become the editor in chief of Mapai's leading daily newspaper, *Davar*. Born in Russia and educated in Russian and German universities, he was a gifted poet, commentator, and orator. Some say his speaking style imitated Jean Jaurès, the famous leader who reshaped the French Left. If Remez represented the brain of the movement, Rubashov was its soul. His love for Golda brought excitement and passion into her life, and in his company, as in Remez's company, Golda felt she was walking on Mount Olympus.

Rubashov was married to none other than Rachel Katznelson, the intellectual voice of Palestine's Zionist women's movement, and he actively supported women's right to vote. He was well-known, however, for having many extramarital affairs, and in Palestine, people could not stop talking about his affair with the legendary poet Rachel. Katznelson appears to have known about Rubashov's escapades and probably accepted his romance with Golda.[12]

One letter from Rubashov bears testimony to the depth of his feelings toward Golda:

> Goldi-nyu [a term of endearment], precious of precious: Your voice suddenly reached me from the podium, and felt like a special prize. . . . If you only knew how my soul is stirred when I think of you. . . . How shall I convey to you how we missed you here in Paris? . . . and how much I have missed you—I have never known if you know it truly, how can I tell if you know it today?[13]

Surely, such a confession of love would never be written to a mattress.

A Liberated Woman?

Some of Golda's biographers have thought that her relationship with Rubashov preceded her relationship with Remez. There is, for instance, an angry letter from Remez, in which he denounces Golda as selfish and morally flawed for conducting an extramarital affair with his friend.[14] However, could it be that along with abandoning her marriage she was also rethinking the value of monogamy and had decided it was quite all right to conduct two affairs simultaneously? If this was a period of sexual liberation for Golda, she might well have embraced the idea of taking pleasure when she wanted it, in the same way that most of her male acquaintances did. Remez had another lover, who would bear him a child in 1931, so why should she bow to convention and restrain herself?[15]

Golda's frantic lifestyle during this period took a heavy toll on her physical well-being. She suffered from frightening migraines, which were exacerbated by her reliance on cigarettes and coffee for energy. She also had heart and kidney problems, for which she was hospitalized more than once. Her son Menachem recounts his grandmother's repetitive question: "Goldie, why so many cigarettes? Have a piece of chocolate instead."[16] One can imagine Golda shrugging her shoulders and reaching for another cigarette. Golda justified her hyperactive lifestyle as a necessary means to an end—advancing the cause of "the state in the making." There is no question that she enjoyed being in the thick of the maelstrom, taking part in everyday politics. From her perspective, this was an end worthy of the physical and emotional toll she endured.

Over time, she developed her own version of her personal history: she loved Morris dearly, but they were simply incompatible. Laying the blame on herself, she all but stated that he had married the wrong person. "It was a tragedy ... with a different woman he could have been very happy."[17] While Golda stopped wearing her wedding ring, the two never legally divorced, and Morris kept a key to her apartment, where he could stay while she was traveling. In addition, as Golda rose to prominence after his death, she placed his photograph on her nightstand. It was her way of making amends and reconstructing herself as a widow. It was also a signal that she was not available for a formal relationship, even as rumors continued to circulate about affairs into her sixties and even seventies.

Golda's romantic self, like many women of her generation, was contradictory. She wanted and experienced freedom but could not unmoor herself from traditional stereotypes. It was never her intention to present a different model of the career woman: single, with children, free to act as she wants. And yet in practice this is exactly what she did. Perhaps this fact, buried deep in the societal unconscious, underneath the misogyny and the resentment, explains why so many people in her later life put her on a pedestal. She could be conventional and conservative at times, but when it came to living a full life, she was not inclined to sacrifice without a fight.

Naqba down the Road

Could it possibly be that Golda had a Palestinian Arab lover? As the history of Palestine progressed, the divide between Arab and Jew grew so wide and the mutual hostility so deep that relationships, let alone romances, between the two became unthinkable. For Golda, whose Jewish and Zionist identity seemed so fixed, the prospect seems particularly unlikely. To understand what it would have been like for Golda to have broken this taboo, one should imagine an affair between an Orthodox Jew and a devout Catholic in the early twentieth century, or between a white person and an African American in the American South before the 1960s. Such relationships may have happened, but they were uncommon. A fictionalized novel published in France in 2004, however, imagines just such a relationship.

The Palestinian Lover, written by Selim Nassib, a Lebanese journalist living in France, centers on a relationship between Golda and an aristocratic Palestinian banker.[18] When Golda's son, Menachem, at age eighty, was asked to comment on the just-published novel, he dismissed it angrily as "trash." He must have seen it as yet another poisonous arrow in the quiver of those determined to besmirch his mother's good name.[19] The book itself explicitly disclaims veracity, maintaining that it is a work of fiction and that "any references to historical events, real people, or real locales are used fictitiously."[20]

Nevertheless, the novel is worthy of our attention, as it speaks to the Arab fascination with Golda as a woman, even as she represented the "woman of the enemy," and the power she had to ignite the imagination. The novel also echoes the literary myth of a family feud (as in Shakespeare's *Romeo and Juliet*) between Arabs and Jews—the biblical cousins—whose love is destined to fail. According to Nassib's story, which he claims to have heard from the lover's niece, the thirty-year-old Golda met Albert Pharaon, the scion of a wealthy Lebanese Palestinian family, at a party in Jerusalem thrown by the British High Commissioner to honor King George V's birthday. Golda was serving there as an interpreter for the Labor Party leadership. At the party, David Remez overheard that Pharaon owned a bank, and through Golda, he approached Pharaon about a loan for the Public Works Company that Remez was heading. Remez spoke Yiddish to Golda, who translated his questions into English for Pharaon.

There was instant chemistry between the two. Pharaon reminded Golda of her first flame, a young Jewish man in Milwaukee who had drowned in an accident. As Golda introduces herself, "the confidence in her voice, her gestures and her gaze confirm Albert's first impression. While he is holding her hand in his own, he feels her tremble slightly, a shadow passes over her face, and she seems for a split second to lose her poise. And then immediately regains her composure."[21] Pharaon found her mixture of confidence and vulnerability irresistible. For her part, Golda was confounded by the resemblance between Pharaon, who was light-skinned, and her dead friend. A few nocturnal meetings at her apartment in Tel Aviv followed. However, their clandestine relationship, which always reflected the rising and abating tension between the Arabs and the Jews, did not last long according to Nassib's account.

While this story may well have been fiction from beginning to end, it helps us understand the Golda who lives in people's imaginations—the Palestinian and Arab imagination in particular—as well as the more general tension between desire and ideology. Had Golda, the most visible female in the Zionist pantheon, allowed herself to follow her heart, who knows how the Palestinian story would have unfolded? Perhaps the idea that there is a spark of love between the two peoples, a spark that can be located and ignited, underlies the fable.

The novel also deserves our attention for recounting the history of Palestine not from the perspective of the victors but from that of the vanquished. A broken Palestinian heart is thus an appropriate interruption in the soaring epic of the Zionist century. We learn of Pharaon's surprise at seeing Jews arrive in Palestine and experience his growing resentment as he realizes that the coveted Zionist state ignores the needs and aspirations of his people. In the exchange between Pharaon and Remez, in which Golda acts as a translator, Pharaon informs Remez that he would not give the Public Works Company a loan:

> "I will not lend you any money," says [Pharaon] in a calm and confident tone, "any more than I will sell you one single dunom [a quarter acre] of my land."
> "Why not?" asks Golda briskly.
> "Because I am, as a matter of principle, opposed to any company which aims to develop Jewish society alone in Palestine."[22]

Pharaon, like most members of the Palestinian upper class, is pleased to see progress brought to Palestine, yet he is anxious. He wants the blessings of modernity to extend to all and fears that his own people are about to pay a drastic price. In his mind, the grand Zionist project is built on the demise of his people. He cannot fathom, however, that this small minority of Eastern European Jews could prevail. At every turn in the saga, he believes that the Jews will lose, and each time he is proven wrong. Near the end of the novel, Pharaon witnesses Haifa, his hometown, fall into Zionist hands. Golda, long estranged from him, arrives to warn him of the upcoming mayhem and begs him to stay. As a member of the elite, Pharaon is able to avoid the refugee camps by fleeing to his home in Beirut, Lebanon, but like all Palestinians carries with him the scars of his society's demise.

The novel thus presents us with two sides of the same coin: the Zionist epic of a people rising to claim its right to self-determination, and the Palestinian Naqba (catastrophe) of a people's loss of sovereignty and descent into misery. Again we encounter in Golda's life a strong woman who eventually wins the struggle, and a gentle man who is doomed to lose; the male lover condemned to obscurity, while the female lover is elevated to international fame. Their paths would never cross again.

Haifa, 1948

In early May of 1948, Golda was dispatched to Haifa to persuade its Arab residents to remain in town. Ben-Gurion feared that the American public would be appalled by the spectacle of tens of thousands fleeing their homes in panic and despair. While touring the Arab section of Haifa, Golda arrived at a house half-ruined in the recent shelling of Jewish paramilitary forces, the Haganah. According to one of her biographers, "Suddenly an old Arab woman came toward them, holding her meager bundles. When she saw Golda, she burst out sobbing. Golda looked at her and tears began to stream down her face."[23]

This story is not included in the novel, which ends in the midst of that same pandemonium. Pharaon looks at Golda: "She is looking through him, he has become transparent. He is afraid, she is so real. She is still talking, he cannot concentrate anymore, but who is she talking to?"[24] Was that old Arab woman similarly transparent to Golda? Were the Palestinians as a people? Or do Golda's tears testify to her capacity for empathy?[25] In the coming months, she would defend the government of Israel as it steadfastly refused to take responsibility for the Palestinian refugee problem. Here we confront another contradiction in Golda's character: she could be emotional, yet she was made of steel.

Postscript

In the 1970s Golda became known for her staunch refusal to entertain the idea of a Palestinian state between Israel and Jordan.[26] To Golda, rather than a distinct national group Palestinians were Arabs, no different from those living in the Arab countries surrounding Israel. Therefore, she believed, the Palestinian refugees should be settled in existing Arab countries, rather than given a national home in Palestine. She sometimes claimed that she, too, was a Palestinian, because she held a Palestinian passport issued by the Mandatory government, a maneuver that demonstrated her capacity to engage in the very casuistry she generally despised. Near the very end of her tenure there were signs that her views began to soften slightly, such as her declaration in 1973 that the question of the existence of a Palestinian entity must be decided by the Palestinians themselves. That said, she remained generally unsympathetic to the idea.[27] Her resistance to a Palestinian state may be partially explained by the fact that until the Yom Kippur War, Arab leaders steadfastly refused to negotiate with Israel, as well as by the rise of Palestinian terrorism against Israel. But the central and deepest explanation for her resistance must have been her fierce loyalty to her own people, the Jewish people. She clung to the narrative that Jews were returning home after two thousand years of exile and she could not overcome her fear of her people's demise. That fear made her increasingly blind to reality, even when she retained empathy for the plight of individuals.

CHAPTER 9

THE ATTRACTION OF SOCIALIST POLITICS

ONE REASON THAT ZIONISTS conceived of Palestine as a potential homeland waiting to be reclaimed and rebuilt is that they saw it as blank slate on which the ideal society could be constructed. Palestine in the 1920s was not only underpopulated but also economically underdeveloped. There was no Jewish middle class, Jewish political party, or capitalist system against which to struggle.[1] Unlike the just defeated Ottomans, the British, who were new in the area and committed to the Balfour Declaration, initially welcomed Jewish immigration (that would change later) and were committed to economic development. This provided a golden opportunity for socialist activists—mostly Russian immigrants—to create a model society in Palestine. As we have already seen, kibbutz life itself rested on these premises, at least as far as men were concerned.

In 1920, two years before Golda's arrival, the pioneers of Palestine gathered together and founded the Histadrut—the Federation of Labor. The goal of the Histadrut was to organize Jewish workers under one roof and provide a safety net, including everything from health insurance to employment guidance, professional training, and even education for themselves and their families. It aimed to become the umbrella organization in charge of developing a socialist economy for Palestine, by and for the Jewish worker. Over the next few years, the Histadrut, with David Remez as its mastermind, would actively develop agriculture,

construction, and industry. Within a decade, the Histadrut would become Golda's political home, a platform for the promotion of political
ideas and a ladder to higher positions of political powers.

The Women Workers Council

The women who arrived in Palestine between 1904 and 1914 came
mostly from revolutionary Russia.[2] They were educated, zealous Zionists like their male comrades, but they harbored an expectation that the
Zionist revolution would also remake gender relations. In their minds,
the project included the creation of a New Hebrew woman as well as the
liberation of both men and women. These dreams were soon shattered.
Their male comrades were not ready for a fundamental change in gender
roles, which would require a deep reconstruction of masculinity and a
commitment to sharing tasks they perceived as strictly female. Such
changes threatened their self-image as liberated (male) pioneers.[3]

In response to the intransigence the women encountered in their
new homeland they developed several strategies to improve their situation. Among them was the identification of fields of work appropriate
for women, such as laundry, poultry farming, and collective kitchens
serving persons working in town. They also set up training programs to
enable women to join the labor force. Since agriculture, seen as mixing
one's labor with the soil of the homeland, was considered the epitome
of Zionism, they established agricultural training farms, where women
were taught how to grow vegetables and tree seedlings.

In pursuit of gender equality, they also founded the Women Workers
Council, an organization open only to women.[4] The purpose behind
this separate organization was, in part, to provide women with a space
where they could assert their agency. Many women complained that in
public meetings their efforts were ridiculed and their voices silenced,
which encouraged an "inferiority complex" in them and made them
timid and unlikely to participate. Yet these women also recognized the
need for unity with their brother pioneers. They therefore organized the
council under the broader umbrella of the Histadrut. At least, this is
where things stood when Golda entered the picture.

As her kibbutz's delegate to the second socialist convention in 1922, Golda had already declared that a separate organization for women was unnecessary: "As for the question of the woman worker—it is a sad and abominable fact that we were forced to create a special organization. . . . This convention should create the appropriate conditions for the woman worker, such that we shall not need this special organization anymore and may abolish it."[5] Golda was well aware of the sorry state of the woman worker, but she thought that their problems could be addressed without a special women-only organization.

Fifty years later, when as prime minister Golda would clash with feminists, it was convenient for her opponents to use this statement as proof of her long opposition to gender-based organizations. Placed in its proper context, however, her original statement was more nuanced: if the convention (led by men) would address the needs of women, then there would be no need for a separate, segregated organization. So interpreted, Golda set a condition under which a separate organization would become unnecessary, rather than conceding that such organizations would never be necessary.

Be that as it may, the gap between theory and practice at the Histadrut left little doubt about its male-centered worldview. This gap, which did not diminish in the coming decades, is crucial in understanding Golda's intellectual development. From the start, she inhabited an environment that was steeped in gender discrimination. At every step in her political career, whether she articulated it or not, she had to account for male discomfort with having assertive women in the public square. To illustrate the persistence and depth of the sexist attitudes held by members of the organization, consider an event that occurred fifteen years after Golda's speech. At that time, the Histadrut issued only one membership card to the head of the household, generally a man, and listed his wife on that card. The Women Workers Council requested that wives of Histadrut members be issued their own membership cards in order to nurture their agency and self-worth. The Histadrut agreed but required additional dues, the payment of which would be confirmed by a special stamp. Members were stunned to learn that the new stamp, meant to show that the cardholder was a "wife," displayed a drawing of a bucket and a broom.[6] The new stamps were destroyed once the plan became public. Nevertheless, the incident makes clear that some Histadrut decision makers saw a wife's role as little more than buckets and brooms.

Such was the sea of misogyny surrounding Golda as she ascended the Histadrut hierarchy. Unsurprisingly, she never felt that her political career stood on firm foundations.

Golda at the Women Workers Council

The secretariat of the Women Workers Council was not Golda's dream job, but it was one for which she was undoubtedly qualified. Given her experience in Jerusalem, she understood the needs of the poor urban mother, whether for warm clothing for her child in winter or medicine when illness struck.[7] She felt the bitter resentment of a stay-at-home mom, asking herself "was this what it was all about—poverty, drudgery and worry?"[8] She was also familiar with the more comfortable but still inferior status of women in the kibbutzim. And yet her heart was elsewhere. To paraphrase one of her earlier statements, she did not come to Palestine to advocate for women.[9] "I yearned for a purposeful, interesting life," she wrote in her memoirs, and fighting for women's rights did not constitute such a life.[10]

Why, then, did she take the job? The simple reason is that nothing else was available. This was the only offer she received and, being vulnerable and needy, she did not feel confident about asking for another. Work at the council's secretariat was her one opportunity to escape her Jerusalem prison, earn enough money to be independent of Morris and care for her children, and place herself near the center of the action. If she did well in the eyes of her patrons, she must have reasoned, perhaps she would get better jobs. Thus understood, Golda's acceptance of work at the council expressed her will to survive rather than a genuine political interest in women's concerns.

Her patrons (Remez, and perhaps Ben-Gurion) had obvious reasons for wanting Golda at the council. The male leadership of the Histadrut viewed Golda as a trusted ally who would keep them abreast of the council's activities and perhaps deflect policy decisions that might not be to their liking. This is likely one reason that the women on the council did not embrace Golda with open arms. In light of this inauspicious start to Golda's career, we should read with appropriate skepticism Golda's later statement to Oriana Fallaci that "being a woman [had] never hindered her in any way at all."[11] The men who helped her, while seeing her as clearly capable, apparently did not think she should fill any job that a man could take.

Golda and Ada Maimon

Golda was already acquainted with the leaders of the council from her earlier activities. The undisputed leader of the council was Ada Maimon.[12] Maimon was a towering figure of socialist feminism, active on behalf of women since the beginning of the century.[13] Ada's relationship with the Histadrut leadership, including Ben-Gurion and Remez, was tense because she refused to compromise her feminist principles. A few years before Golda joined the council, Ada had been ousted from her position on the Histadrut immigration committee because she insisted that 50 percent of the immigration visas be granted to women. Everyone agreed with her that the immigration policy discriminated against women, but most justified it on utilitarian grounds and turned a blind eye.[14]

Ada felt passionately about Zionism's duty to elevate the status of women and never tired of pointing out that women in Palestine remained shackled by tradition and patriarchal values. A heavy, feisty, religiously observant woman, she was born five years before Golda to a family of learned rabbis in czarist Russia and immigrated to Palestine before World War I, earning the pedigreed "Mayflower" status of the second Aliyah (immigration). Unlike Golda, Ada was highly educated and familiar with Jewish law, which allowed her to argue that discrimination against women reflected deep-seated stereotypes nurtured over generations, rather than the dictates of scripture. And unlike some other founders of the council, she was not an orthodox anticapitalist. She was willing to collaborate with industry and capital if collaboration would advance the rights of women. For her, the sanctity of the party's principles and the party's unity were second to the cause of gender equality.

Ada's older brother, Yehuda Leib Fishman (later Maimon), was a rabbi and, by the 1920s, a rising star in Palestinian Jewish politics. The founder of the Mizrahi (religious Zionist) movement, Rabbi Maimon would eventually engineer the famous compact between secular and religious circles in Israel that kept the interdependence between church and state intact.[15] He was also high in the political hierarchy of the Zionist leadership, eventually sitting alongside Golda in Ben-Gurion's cabinet. Ada, by contrast, never received the recognition she deserved, and today is practically forgotten.[16] There are some indications that by witnessing Ada's fate, Golda learned an important political lesson that informed her own approach to politics: the male leadership of the party did not approve of principled, assertive feminists and did not hesitate to undermine their power and derail their promotion.

The power holders in the Histadrut viewed the council as a nuisance and perhaps expected Golda to take some of the wind out of its sails. Both personally and politically then, Ada could not have been too enthusiastic about Golda's arrival. Additionally, one must remember that while Golda and Ada were on the left, they belonged to different political factions with different agendas and policies.[17] On substantive matters, though, the two had a lot in common. They both believed that communal childcare was the right path out of the conundrum of motherhood and work, that full gender equality meant not only equal rights but also equal share of duties, and that it was imperative to encourage women to develop agency and feel empowered. But when it came to prioritizing their goals, the gap between them was vast. For Golda, the unity of the labor movement was supreme. She believed that once the movement achieved hegemony and secured its place as leader of the Zionist effort to establish a Jewish state, women's equality would follow. Ada viewed calls for unity as an excuse to keep women at the back of the line. She believed that true liberation could be achieved only if women and men worked toward the Zionist goal hand in hand as equals. This fundamental difference alone was enough to doom their relationship.

But there were other differences as well. Ada, opinionated and easily offended, had a tendency to dominate the group and expect others to follow. Her fluency in Hebrew and educated arguments may have intimidated or alienated Golda, while Golda's decision to leave her husband and pursue romantic affairs with powerful, married men may have irritated Ada, who was not known to have relationships with men. The ill-wishers in Tel Aviv who referred to Golda as a "mattress" referred to Ada as "Ada Ma-Fishman," Arabic for "Ada who has no man," which goes to show that a stereotype was always available to humiliate the woman who challenged the patriarchy no matter how she lived her life.[18]

Further Complications at the Council

Other women on the council might also have frowned upon Golda's appointment. Golda was an outsider, an American who did not share their common roots in revolutionary Russia. Moreover, some of these women were married to leaders in the labor movement, and they may have looked suspiciously upon this young woman conducting affairs with their married friends. Indeed, soon after joining the council, Golda was rumored to have started her affair with Zalman Shazar, whose wife Rachel Katznelson-Shazar was second only to Ada on the council. The personal and the political, as feminists have often noted, are never neatly segregated.

From the beginning, then, Golda's situation spelled trouble. To make matters worse, the women at the council tended to engage in heated arguments. For Golda, the constant bickering perhaps felt too close to home—reminding her of her mother and sister—and she may have been looking forward to finding a more peaceful environment, one filled with men. The problems that Golda encountered on the council were mirrored by the problems the council itself faced. Despite the council's good intentions and astute understanding of the needs of women, it failed to thrive. As its historian Bat-Sheva Margalit Stern observed, "it had wings but could not fly."[19]

A First Trip to Europe

Shortly after Golda joined the council, a ray of sunlight shone on her burgeoning career. In 1928 the labor leadership was contemplating two trips to Europe. Ada Maimon was planning to attend the board meeting of the Women's International Zionist Organization (WIZO) in Berlin, and Ben-Gurion, Remez, Shazar, and others were planning to attend the Third Congress of the Labour and Socialist International (LSI) in Brussels. A plan was hatched at the Histadrut headquarters to send Golda with both delegations, first to Berlin and then to Brussels. Although she was young and inexperienced, she was a good speaker and fluent in English, and the trip would provide an opportunity to assess her performance as an emissary abroad. Besides, Golda and her lover Shazar could finally enjoy some intimate time together, away from the peering eyes of Tel Aviv. Ada fought the plan tooth and nail, but the trip proved to be a great success.

After a few days in Berlin, with Shazar at her side guiding her through the city he knew well from his student days, Golda proceeded to Brussels, which she loved. She later recounted the trip, "I could hardly believe the trees, the trams, the flower and fruit stands, the cool, gray weather . . . so unlike Tel Aviv."[20] At the convention, she listened to world-famous socialists (such as Leon Blum, the French leader), rubbed shoulders with established and emerging leaders, and endeavored to persuade as many delegates as possible that the Zionist project must be supported. As the junior member of her delegation, Golda was also excited to be in the company of Ben-Gurion, Ben-Zvi, and other Zionist leaders, and by the chance to impress them with her political skills.[21]

Golda returned home with a modest achievement: she was appointed to the Congress's advisory committee on the status of women. The Zionist delegation aimed for participation in as many of the Congress's committees as possible, and Golda's appointment added to their tally. The job also brought together women's rights activists, thereby exposing her to ideas and policies that deepened her understanding of the issues women faced. This experience would benefit her both as a high-level official of the Histadrut in the 1940s and as the minister of labor in the 1950s.

With Shazar in Brussels as well, the trip was not entirely business. According to Golda's biographer, Meron Medzini, the romantic affairs of the leadership were facilitated by shared travel, hotels, and meals—all paid for by the Histadrut. These were men of humble means, and travel

Figure 5. Golda and her young family (with husband Morris and children Menachem and Sarah). Courtesy of Shaul Rahabi Private collection.

allowed them to evade family and enjoy relative privacy.[22] Golda felt guilty about this situation, as she admitted in her memoirs. In Tel Aviv, her two-year-old daughter Sarah was quite ill, and Morris, Bluma, and Sheyna were fuming, accusing Golda of "selfishness" and being a bad mother.[23] She knew that they were right. Golda returned with gifts, music albums, and luxury items not available in Palestine, but doing so hardly alleviated her guilt.

Once again, we see Golda acting decisively when faced with hard choices. Without explicitly articulating her preferences, she decided to behave like her male colleagues, leaving others to take care of the family as she went away on party business. No one would credit her as a role model for acting this way, but she was a true pioneer in this regard. The feminist leaders at the council were too dominated by traditional values to see that her actions could be celebrated rather than condemned. Golda refused to give up her right to drink from the cup of a full life, which included sexual satisfaction and political activity. She was, in short, acting like a man.

Motherhood

Is there something wrong with me?

—GOLDA MEIR, "BORROWED MOTHERS"

Golda was not a good mother to her young children.[24] Living in Jerusalem with Morris, in the mid-1920s, Golda likely bestowed on Menachem and Sarah the motherly love and attention of which she was certainly capable. But between the mid-1920s and late 1940s, motherhood did not feature on her list of priorities.

When Golda arrived in Tel Aviv she was a traumatized young woman, separated from her husband and facing an uncertain future. Menachem was four, and Sarah two years old. For the children, the move from Jerusalem to Tel Aviv was like being transferred to another planet. Tel Aviv was the urban bastion of the labor movement, bustling with secular modernity, and light years from the traditional, religious, poor Jerusalem milieu to which they were accustomed. In Tel Aviv, Hebrew was spoken everywhere, instead of the Yiddish the children spoke at home. The climate was hot and humid, and an overpowering sun illuminated the bright blue sky. Menachem and Sarah missed their father, who would only visit on the weekends, and were frustrated by the constant disappearance of their mother and, one can imagine, by the presence of strangers hired to take care of them. They slowly came to realize that their parents' marriage had ended.

Golda dove headfirst into the maze of party and council politics. She went far beyond the call of duty, attending meetings, volunteering to run any meeting into the small hours of the night and offering to undertake additional tasks anytime they were mentioned. As a result, she would return home exhausted and could only offer a minimum of motherly care.[25] This situation was made worse by the fact that Golda was not blessed with healthy children. Sarah suffered from a kidney disease and had been sickly since birth. Even when Sarah was bedridden with a high fever, her mother was unable to place a reassuring hand on her forehead or comfort her as she swallowed her medications. Menachem, too, was "underweight, supposedly afflicted by a heart murmur" and yearning for his mother.[26]

Golda was living proof that motherhood and a political career were nearly impossible to juggle. Her solution, like that of millions of women the world over, was to hire help. Housekeepers and nannies took care of the children in sickness and in health.[27] A newspaper article from 1988 described their home routine:

> In general she was not at home. Nannies and persons who rented the third room managed the apartment. [Golda slept on a folding bed in the living room.] Tehilla Shapira was one of the nannies. Tehilla washed, did the laundry and cooked for Sarah and Menachem. While Golda busied herself with the ideals and values of the state in the making, Tehilla . . . slept on a folding bed in the children's room, taking their temperatures when necessary, making sure the medication was taken on time. Leah Biskin, a friend who rented the third room, helped with the homework. From time to time the pedantic sister Sheyna would appear, to keep an eye on the nanny, make sure the correct amount of vitamins is put in the oatmeal cereal and argue about the amount of protein the children needed. She would then return home to write another grim letter to Golda, asking why the Party always wins over the children.[28]

When she was an adult with children of her own, Golda's daughter Sarah recalled: "She would travel and leave a very sick girl behind for many months. Today I cannot understand how she did it. I would have never left my children." Sarah also recalled that, even when Golda was around, she was less attentive than a parent ought to be. One afternoon, for instance, she and Menachem wanted to go to the movies. Golda agreed, but stressed for time, asked that they walk to the theater by themselves and wait for her. The two were left twisting in the wind: "Mamma will come, will not come." "Mamma will be late, will not be late."[29] They knew that they were not her first priority.

Golda's letters from abroad nevertheless show a mother aware of her children's needs and concerned for their welfare. From London, she wrote: "Morris, dear, please see that Menachem's teeth are taken care of, also see about his Hebrew classes. We must help him get thru this year. It will be terrible for him if he doesn't make it." To Sarah, who had recently turned twelve: "Sarah'le: write to me how was your birthday, what did you do? When I return home, and if only it is quiet in the land, we shall arrange a big party and invite all the children. Tell me what to bring, I really do not know." And to Menachem: "Of course I shall get for you the Brahms symphony . . . what have you done about raincoats?" Later, to a sixteen-year-old Sarah, she wrote with affection, although hinting that she understood a teenager's embarrassment at parental affection: "Many kisses to you (Shsh, don't tell). Shalom Shalom, Mother."[30]

Decades later, as prime minister, she told the journalist Oriana Fallaci that to succeed a woman must work twice as hard as a man. In the late 1920s Golda must have experienced that truth acutely. The workplace environment did not welcome a woman with children, and working women understood not to discuss their children at work, particularly if the children were sick or otherwise needy. The norm was that a mother's place was at home, with her children. If she chose a career, she was better off avoiding any mention of her personal life, thereby enabling men to evaluate her "on the merits," that is, as if she were a man. The fact that men had a wife at home to take care of the children was a truth no one mentioned.

Golda was awash in guilt. Her feelings of inadequacy were exacerbated by Morris—who was melancholic and often demeaned her political activities as vulgar and shallow—as well as by her sister and mother, who were fiercely critical of her choices.[31] "Only my father understood" she wrote in her memoirs, but there is no indication that he stepped forward to take on family chores. Everyone in the family was applying the conventional double standard. In the letter to Sheyna quoted above, Golda pleaded for empathy, adding a cry of despair: "One thing is clear: I have only two alternatives; to cut off my connections with all outside interests as I once did at Morris' insistence, or to go to [Kibbutz] Ein Charod. I have no further strength for my present life. My sole problem is what is better for the children."[32] One sees here an early example of Golda's strategy of presenting two paths, one of which was unacceptable, thus leaving her no choice but to embrace the other. Her "solution" therefore ignored any relevant alternatives. She could have asked Morris to take custody of the children; she could have low-ered her political ambitions and spent more time at home; or she could have pursued, like most women, a variation on what came to be known as "the mommy track." These were real options, but to Golda they were all unacceptable. She would not even contemplate slowing down her career, nor would she ask Morris or anyone else to take custody of the children.

Her letter to Sheyna shows that Golda did not confront the nub of the problem of a mother with a career. Instead, she fell back on the fa-miliar cliché that she only cared "for what was better for the children," even though it does not appear she ever seriously considered what, in fact, would be better for her children. In her article "Borrowed Mothers," Golda asked defensively: "Who is to say that the stay-at-home Mom is more devoted than the career Mom?"[33] This response, however, was a digression from the problem at hand. The level of a mother's devotion does not provide any answer to the concrete question of what is good for the children. As Sheyna insisted, Golda's understanding of what was best for the children was flawed and self-serving.

Golda certainly understood that she was the victim of a double stan-dard. No one, for instance, applied the same level of scrutiny to the parenting decisions made by Ben-Gurion or Remez. According to con-vention, fatherhood had superior prerogatives. But even though, or perhaps because, she was a member of the Women Workers Council, whose leaders both understood and experienced similar problems, she knew that if she wanted to pursue a career she would need to pretend that the standards were fair and fairly applied. Men did not want to face the reality that their careers depended on an unfair system.

By 1929 when Virginia Woolf published *A Room of One's Own*, Golda already had an apartment and a salary of her own in Tel Aviv. At that time Pioneer Women USA, a left-wing Zionist organization committed to women's equality, asked Rachel Katznelson-Shazar to edit a volume recording the reflections and experiences of women workers of Pales-tine. The goal was to document their experiences and thereby draw at-tention to women's issues. It would be the first feminist volume emerg-ing from Zionist Palestine. Golda was not much of a writer, yet she decided to contribute a short commentary, which is in part a mea culpa and in part a defense of her feelings and actions as a woman. It was titled "Borrowed Mothers" and signed only by her initials, G. M., indicating perhaps that she felt uncomfortable with the exposure of intimate feelings or understood that drawing attention to her intimate feelings would not help her career.[34]

A cri de coeur of a young woman violently torn between maternal love and a desire to pursue her political ambitions, Golda's commentary opens by noting the unique circumstances she occupied: the "inner struggles and the despairs of [the working mother] are without parallel in human experience."[35] Even if she did not think of herself as a true feminist, she understood that a mother wishing to branch out of her traditional roles was a new phenomenon, part of modernity. She also avoided generalizations. Not all work and not all women were the same, she observed, so she presented a typology of three mothers. The first worked out of necessity, obliged to support her family. This configuration adhered to traditional family roles except that the husband was unavailable or incapable of supporting his family. The third was the stay-at-home mother, who preferred the vocation of homemaking to a career. The second, however, was a woman like Golda, who rejected traditional gender roles and was involved in a "unique struggle." For this woman, work was the activity through which she achieved the self-realization— she was fighting to preserve no less than her very selfhood.

The first type of mother, a woman whose life conditions forced her to work to support her family, did not receive much elaboration in the essay. This was a mother without a choice. Her struggle, Golda said, was well-known in history. Even though Golda did not mention her own mother, Bluma must have served as her model. Bluma always worked hard, because she had to, and her endless fights with her daughters stemmed from her wish to spare them this lot. If they did not insist on love but married the perfectly acceptable men that she had found for them, they would be able to stay home, comfortable and happy. At the other end of the spectrum was the mother who could chose not to pursue a career. Golda identified this type as suffering from an "incapacity," a psychological defect. Such a woman spoke of "duty to family, devotion or love" as justifications for preferring motherhood to a career. Golda viewed these reasons as mere rationalizations. The woman who chose to stay home was psychologically weak: "Her soul is not able to take into itself the many-sidedness of life, with its sufferings, but also with its joys."[36] The prototype she might have had in mind was her greatest inspiration and fiercest critic—her sister Sheyna, whose revolutionary zeal fizzled once she started a family.[37]

Golda's essay reveals that she thought carefully about the choice to stay home. She offered an inventory of the benefits enjoyed by the stay-at-home mom: she educates the child by example, teaching the values and practices that she, rather than the hired help, considers important. She bears witness to the child's development and hears firsthand "the clever things" the child says. And she comforts the child, as only the mother's kiss can communicate the "magic healing when the child falls and has a bruise." After paying homage to those significant benefits, she then reviewed the cost paid by mothers who opted for a career. A working mother was a victim of estrangement: when she returned from her travels, "a feeling of alienation from her nearest and dearest steals into her heart."[38] Often the children are unhappy and let her know it:

> One look of reproach from the little one . . . is enough to throw down the whole structure of vindication. That look, that plea to the mother to stay, can be withstood only by an almost superhuman effort of the will.

As a result, guilt is her companion:

> The modern woman asks herself: Is there something wrong with me if my children don't fill up my life? Am I at fault if . . . there is something left over which has to be filled by things outside the . . . home?

Golda also listed the difficulties the career woman faced in the workplace:

> She feels the drive to prove herself. She "always" . . . has the feeling that her work is not as productive as that of a man, or even of an unmarried woman.[39]

Combining career and motherhood, her essay made plain, required Herculean powers. A career leads to heartache, guilt at home, and stress in the workplace.

After tallying up the benefits forfeited and the costs incurred by the working woman, Golda finally came to the core of her argument: the human need to self-actualize. A woman has a right not to be forced to suppress her own humanity. In Golda's words, "Her nature and being demand something more; she cannot divorce herself from the larger social life. She cannot let her children narrow down her horizon." Golda was not trained in philosophy, but this emphasis on her right to selfhood raised the torch of the Enlightenment and, in particular, its commitment to individualism. She was totally dedicated to the party and its communal ethos, yet she still insisted on the equal moral worth of every individual man and woman. The essay rejected her own fondness for neatly polarized options (motherhood or career), insisting that a woman had a right to both. Succeeding at both, she knew, required superhuman will power, which she felt she had. What she hoped for, perhaps the primary reason for having written the article, was understanding and support in this endeavor.

"Borrowed Mothers" was Golda's answer to the question she posed in the middle of her article: "Is there something wrong with me?" Her answer was an emphatic no. There was nothing wrong with wishing to be a full human being. The pain and suffering inherent in it are to be endured as a part of the human condition. Some who observed the sorry state of Golda's family life—the sad eyes of the children, Golda's migraines and precarious health, Morris's melancholy and bitterness—commented that it might have been better if she had never had children, thus falling back on the age-old dichotomy that a woman had only two choices: become a housewife and have children or remain a spinster.

Golda did share at least some of the conventional worldview. To her, a woman had to have children, and her yearning was so powerful that she accepted Morris's conditions to leave the kibbutz and abandon politics. She tried to fit the traditional mold of a housewife who cooks, cleans, and cares for the children. Yet once she began raising a family she felt like a prisoner. The misery of poverty certainly made things worse, and one wonders whether material comfort could have changed her feelings. As it was, however, family life felt like punishment rather than a reward.[40]

Tikkun

As Golda's career stabilized and she became more confident in her place in the political world, she made what Jewish culture calls *tikkun* (amends). By choice or necessity, Golda let her children decide for themselves what kind of life they wished to lead, and both grew to be responsible, productive adults. Menachem became an accomplished cellist and the father of three; Sarah dropped out of high school before graduation, founded a kibbutz in the Negev, married a fellow socialist, and raised two children. Had Sarah not been shy and reclusive, she could have served as a poster child for the ideals of the labor movement. Golda visited them often, hosted them in her apartments, showered them with love and attention, and never failed to display her pride in their accomplishments. During the last decades of her life, she lived next door to her son Menachem, and considered Sarah's kibbutz as her second home.

The children, it appears, understood and forgave. As they were growing up their mother must have been an object of longing and resentment. But they also knew that Golda's neglect reflected the demands of ambition rather than a lack of love. She just needed more than family life. Her wish to fulfill her selfhood and her devotion to Zionism went hand in hand and, for these dreams, she willingly sacrificed a traditional family life.

A Grandchild with Disabilities

One cannot complete the story of Golda's family life without mentioning her granddaughter who had intellectual disabilities. Meira (named after Morris, whose Hebrew name was Meir) was born to Menachem and his first wife. Her disability aggrieved her young parents and likely contributed to the unraveling of their marriage. Meira was later placed in a home for people with intellectual disabilities, and Golda helped cover the expenses to support her. While Golda's granddaughter was rarely mentioned by the press, it is not clear whether Golda took any steps to hide this information from public view or whether the public silence reflected the culture of the time, which viewed children with disabilities at best as an embarrassment and at worst a shame on the family.

After Menachem and his first wife divorced, the relationship between the two families soured. Chana Weinberg, Meira's mother, complained that Golda and Menachem had turned their back on the child. Menachem denied it vehemently, while Golda, as was her custom, kept silent. Menachem and his family insisted that they loved Meira, hosted her whenever they could, and saw her as one of them.[41] It is hard to know whose version is closer to the truth, although we know that Golda did continue to contribute toward Meira's care and that, as prime minister, she signed legislation to protect the rights of people with disabilities.

CHAPTER 10

PIONEER WOMEN

A Platform of Her Own

PIONEER WOMEN, established in 1924 in New York City by the women of Poalei Zion, was already up and running when it welcomed Golda as its new emissary from Palestine. Arriving in late 1928, she expected to spend eight months in the United States and Canada. Her tasks included expanding the membership, increasing the level of contributions, and, in particular, strengthening the ties between the organization and the Histadrut.[1]

It must have been painful to leave the children in the care of Morris and Sheyna, both critical of her "reckless behavior." But the party's wish was her command. In addition, Golda knew that the movement was testing her skills, and the assignment would offer a valuable opportunity for her to prove herself. The chance to return to the United States must have been quite tempting as well. Seven years after leaving there penniless, her hopes mixed with trepidation, Golda was returning as a "somebody." Here she was, a member of the mythical pioneer class, a woman who had fulfilled her dream, now proudly returning to persuade others to follow her example or to help make the Zionist dream come true with their financial contributions. When she had first arrived at Poalei Zion offices in 1920 and offered to volunteer, she was given a broom and asked to clean the floors. Now she was representing Palestine and collaborating with the top echelons of the party leadership in America. Indeed, just two years earlier, Morris's mother, in Philadelphia, begged the young couple to accept a return ticket to America after reading about their destitute condition. Now Golda no longer depended on family members to pay for her expenses. The party was supporting her. Golda must have taken tremendous satisfaction in the way things had unfolded. Even if the children missed her, they would be all right.

Pioneer Women had been established because its founders were fed up with the shabby treatment that they received from their male brethren. The men at Poalei Zion accepted the traditional division of labor and took for granted that a woman's destiny was to become a wife and mother. As already discussed, their comrades in Palestine shared this understanding. Taking the initiative the American sisters showed their commitment to help the Women Workers Council fulfill its mission of protecting and advancing women's rights. They organized as a separate group and, through hard work and abundant energy, managed to raise a decent amount of money for the council. Pioneer Women supported women's agricultural training farms, sponsored courses to train women as skilled workers, and provided the equipment necessary to mechanize kibbutz work. They also funded temporary shelters for women who arrived in Palestine without family or support.

The organization's success caught the eye of the male leaders of the Histadrut, and they wanted Golda to convince Pioneer Women to share some of their bounty with them. Sharing, they argued, would benefit all, but it was quite clear that the funds thereby diverted would benefit mostly men. Pioneer Women were not easily swayed. Their experience had taught them that men would not hurry to support women's needs, and they insisted that their money go directly to the council—that is, to women's causes. Golda's tactic was to blur the distinction between the council and the Histadrut. Wasn't it a fact that policies benefiting their husbands would benefit women as well? She urged Pioneer Women to see "the bigger picture"—that of nation building—and the need to support all workers, men included.

Golda's approach displayed her moderate feminist philosophy: empowering men would also empower women. Zionism needed to focus on male power because they were the ones most likely to pull the train forward. In the process, women too would benefit. Ultimately, Golda prevailed and Pioneer Women added their funds to the general pool as she had requested. How did she manage to persuade her American sisters? By emphasizing their commonalities. They all shared an Eastern European background, the Yiddish language, experiences of immigration, and a commitment to socialism. They bonded almost instantly and Golda, with her charisma, managed to win their support. She also worked tirelessly. She traveled the land by bus and train, stayed at members' homes (to save money), and regaled them with stories demonstrating the pioneers' courage in the face of a harsh climate, disease, and the Palestinian Arab resistance. She made much of the jewel of socialist Zionism, the kibbutz. Of course, she knew very well that she was embellishing the truth, but that was standard practice among the emissaries from Palestine, and it was not clear who needed that "embellishment" more—the speaker or the audience.[2]

Golda displayed a clever ability to deploy the various angles of her identity in order to fit changing contexts. In America she was Goldie, the Yiddish-speaking immigrant from Milwaukee. But she was also a "Palestinian"—the wonder woman making the desert bloom. They fell in love with her and, in the process, opened their hearts and pockets. The relationship was not entirely one-sided. While Golda prevailed upon her American sisters to support the Histadrut, she also slowly came around to empathizing with their point of view. Her resistance to a separate gender-based organization faded and her comprehension of the particular problems facing women in the public sphere deepened. She no longer accepted the simplistic principle of gender neutrality. Golda was undergoing a transformation.

Golda's Reflections on Feminism

On May 25, 1932, midway through her sojourn in America, Golda published an article in Mapai's daily, *Davar*, reflecting on her travels. Pioneer Women were not mentioned by name, but the article discussed the organization's ideology and its conflict with the Histadrut.[3] Golda called for reconciliation, pleading that both sides needed to recognize the kernel of truth in the other's message. Each needed to embrace the value of equality and recognize equal rights and obligations for men and women.[4] The implication was that unless the Histadrut and its male leadership revised their perspective about women's role in society the goal of cooperation might be doomed.

Golda's argument traveled a winding path to reach this conclusion, yet her article powerfully delivered a feminist message, criticized prevailing gender stereotypes, and emphasized the intrinsic value of women-only organizations. Golda's *Davar* article opened with an unqualified recognition of the pervasiveness of patriarchy:

> Many women harbor a prejudice toward single-sex organizations regardless of the objectives of these organizations. Women do not always liberate themselves from their personal and social subordination, they do not always use their powers to reach the perfect liberation. To the contrary, their very opposition to the women-only organization reflects their own backwardness as well as their desire to deny their backwardness from themselves.[5]

The statement could not be more explicit. Prejudice against women was rampant and resulted in personal and social subordination. Gender-based stereotypes had shaped the consciousness not only of men but also of women, and women, just like men, nurtured false consciousness about the second sex being second: "[They] turn a blind eye to their backwardness," which is why they develop a resistance to feminist ideas and feminist organizations.[6]

Golda was declaring herself a feminist. One would expect the next paragraph to elaborate further, perhaps to insist on the need to spread the feminist agenda, or at least to praise Pioneer Women and the council for carrying the torch. Instead, Golda immediately deployed the rhetorical move known as "on the other hand": "On the other hand, it is hard to view positively the feminist trend [where] gender-based segregation is portrayed as a great achievement. The hostility against men among feminists may sometimes take very obnoxious forms: they don't let men participate in their deliberations and they always stand guard against this nemesis."[7] Within one page, Golda joined together a bold feminist statement with a condemnation of those "extreme" feminists who viewed men as their enemy. In decrying "hostility against men," Golda was referring to the very few incidents in Palestine and America, where women, weary of male domination, refused to allow men to attend their meetings.[8] Those incidents were real, albeit infrequent, and Golda's article used them to distance herself from feminism. Yet, immediately after issuing this disclaimer, Golda reasserted the quintessential feminist grievance: "Truth to tell, I should note that maybe there indeed were many male members who could not fathom how women could manage and organize serious issues by themselves."[9] Sexism was a problem, she seemed to be saying, and feminism was based on sound empirical evidence regarding the prevalence of negative male attitudes. Golda must have been torn. She recognized the powerful patriarchal hegemony. Yet she felt uncomfortable with what she called "extreme" feminism that would openly point a finger at male chauvinism. Her goal was to build bridges with the male establishment, not burn them.

After paying tribute to the Pioneer Women, who were "extremely devoted and work incessantly," she assured her readership that despite the bold claims with which she had opened the article, progress toward gender equality was already being made.[10] Women who had acquired gender consciousness found it easier to cooperate with men at the Histadrut, and many men, she said, "have discarded the stereotype that the woman is less intelligent and less talented than the man, etc." She seemed to be saying that bridges were already built and that cooperation was now possible on egalitarian grounds. Golda closed the article with her signature rhetorical style: "Can anyone deny that the liberation of the woman does, finally, liberate the man as well?"

Golda's rhetoric could almost be described as "cute." Even if everyone agreed that the liberation from oppressive stereotypes would free both sexes to pursue the pressing task of nation building, she knew that mere agreement about this fact would not by itself bring about equality. Hence, the radical principle lying underneath the pacifying rhetoric: men too would be much better off once they acknowledged their male chauvinist prejudices, stopped blaming women's insecurity for the evils of the social structure, and earnestly worked to dismantle gender stereotypes.[11] In Golda's view, "massive reform and improvements are needed." There is hope for change, she wrote, but it will not be accomplished through "superficial ploughing," which is easier, indeed, but likely to yield "low quality gains. What is needed is fundamental work, deep ploughing."[12] As ever, Golda was a political activist, a woman in search not of high theory but practical solutions. Apparently only two solutions were on the table: declaring that a reconciliation was on its way (the superficial gain) or launching a project of deep ploughing. She knew well that the second was the necessary policy, but she was reluctant to take it upon herself. That is where her feminism stopped.

Golda's article reflected an unwillingness to walk a straight path. Why was that? One simple answer is that the article resembled a stream of consciousness, an unfiltered representation of the ideas wrestling in her mind. Here, one may argue, her lack of formal education showed. She had not been trained in the art of essay writing, which perhaps explains the disordered zigzagging. But the article's ambivalence also raises deeper questions. First, did Golda's views about gender equality and the value of women-only organizations in fact undergo a transformation? Second, who or what could be responsible for this fundamental change in perspective? Third, once she came to terms with this transformation, what did she do?[13]

The key to answering these questions is provided in the second paragraph of her article, following her bold feminist statement: "There were many women who, because they have joined a Party were doubting or even opposing . . . women's organizations. They thought that the Party offered them full satisfaction. And then, after working for a few years with Pioneer Women, they found that they became more active members of the party."[14] One woman in particular fit this description— Golda Meir. When she joined Poalei Zion, first in the United States and then in Palestine (later called Achdut Haavoda, then Mapai), she explicitly avoided women's problems. Living in a society saturated with patriarchal stereotypes, she had internalized their message. She had accepted her job with the Women Workers Council because it was an offer she could not refuse, not because she was interested in promoting women's rights.[15] Back in America, her interactions with admiring and empathic American women accelerated a transformation that, following her separation from Morris and the move to Tel Aviv, had already been in the making. In Golda's words, "The gender exclusive organization *served as a school, where they learned to act independently, take responsibility and gain self-confidence.*"[16] Indeed, while the sentence employs the third person pronoun "they," pointing to her American sisters, it can easily be replaced with "we" or "I." Golda was recounting the trajectory of her own emotional and intellectual development and paying tribute to the members of Pioneer Women who shaped her understanding of gender roles.

Golda attributed this transformation in thought to her work with women's organizations: both Pioneer Women and the council, the feminist organization in Tel Aviv that sponsored her mission in America. Surely, her own recent experiences also played an important role. Her poverty and loneliness in Jerusalem, financial dependence, and tormented realization that motherhood was an obstacle to a brilliant career made her intimately familiar with the issues that concerned her comrades on the council.[17] It is also possible that one man in particular played a part in effecting this transformation: Zalman Rubashov (Shazar).[18]

In the history of the labor movement Shazar was a leading intellectual and supporter of women's rights. While not an active feminist, he would have been privy to the thoughts and concerns of his wife, Rachel Katznelson, one of the most prominent and active feminist leaders in Palestine.[19] It is not fanciful to imagine that while Golda and Shazar were together in New York, conversations between the lovers touched on precisely these issues.[20] Shazar thus may have served as the conduit through which Rachel Katznelson's ideas reached Golda, and he may have offered legitimacy to the feminist theories now percolating in her mind. Ironically, Shazar lent the required male authority to the views of Pioneer Women. Admiring and sympathetic, these women showered Golda with love and approval and, at the same time, focused her attention on feminist theory and the special needs of women, women like herself. Golda's heart opened in ways it could not under the critical disapproval and didactic lecturing of council meetings in Tel Aviv. Pioneer Women was the right kind of women's organization to convert Golda, and convert her it did.

Why then the ambivalence? Why the resistance to join the feminist wave? Golda absorbed ideas from others like a sponge but she never relinquished her independence of thought. Golda was an ambitious young politician, eager to succeed, and the Histadrut was already rapidly consolidating its hegemony in Palestine. Given her desire to play a meaningful part in nation building (even in a nation based on patriarchal principles), the temptation to remain in the good graces of the organization would have been immensely seductive. By contrast, working with women and for women was difficult and might well lead nowhere. She had witnessed the tightfisted policy toward women's needs by both the World Zionist Organization and the Histadrut. Moreover, conditions in Europe at the time generated tremendous pressure on the Zionist institutions in Palestine to expand their capacity to absorb immigrants, especially men.[21]

The atmosphere at the council was another impediment.[22] It was known for bitter internal fights and divisive bickering which, again, must have reminded Golda of her home life as a child.[23] The truth is that Golda mostly experienced harmony in the company of men, including her father, her lovers, and her coworkers. Further still, there were economic considerations that spoke against embracing "radical feminism." Golda was a single mother with two children to support. Her salary at the council was thirteen pounds per month—a substantial sum compared to anything she had ever made and higher than many white-collar workers at that time.[24] If she acted like a radical feminist—that is, fighting the vestiges of gender-based discrimination wherever she saw them—she might find herself marginalized as Ada Maimon was. If she modified her feminism and chose her battles carefully, she could continue not only to benefit from Remez's support but also to receive the perks offered to high-level officers at the Histadrut. Perhaps the experience of poverty and helplessness as an adult made her less inclined to take unnecessary risks.

Golda probably concluded that for all these reasons it was best to discontinue her activities with Pioneer Women and return home, both literally and figuratively.[25] As she stated in her article, "it was time to become a more active member of the Party."

Golda, a Member of the Top Echelons of the Party

As she had hoped, the bosses of the Histadrut rewarded her hard work in America. Upon her return, Golda was promoted to serve on the powerful Executive Committee of the Histadrut.[26] Additionally, in 1935 when Remez, now the general secretary of the Histadrut, decided to expand its economic portfolio by developing a shipping company, he asked Golda to undertake parts of this project. He believed that the company, to be called Nachshon, would bring about "the conquest of the sea." Golda was thrilled to join—enticed by the vision of ships operated by Jewish sailors and sailing under a Zionist flag.[27] In a few years Nachshon would become the conduit through which the World Jewish Organization purchased vessels to transfer Jewish refugees from Europe to Palestine.

From wells, tree nurseries, and plowshares operated by and for women, Golda moved into shipping and sailing, a field dominated by men and associated with masculinity. The road to political success required male-centered projects and, in any event, she felt most comfortable working with men. She did not, however, remain with this project for long. Soon enough, she moved farther up the ladder, earning her position in the inner circle of the political leadership that within fourteen years would lead the Yishuv to statehood.

For the rest of her life she had a warm spot in her heart for Pioneer Women. However, moving forward, she left active feminism by the wayside. She understood that the party was less than enthusiastic about such work and that if she persisted her career might be derailed. She was not willing to pay that price for gender equality. She might have thought that, in any event, she was treated as an equal and there simply were not enough women willing to fight the traditional gender-based division of labor for the cause to prevail. It was another fight for another day.

CHAPTER 11

WORLD WAR II

The Ground Is Burning

When one hears the stories from Germany . . . one feels that he has no right to live at all.

—UNDATED LETTER TO MORRIS, FROM LONDON

AS THE 1930S PROGRESSED, news out of Europe became increasingly ominous. Right-wing movements waved the flag of fascist ethnonationalism, an idea that would soon translate into widespread antisemitic persecution. Not only were the Jews of Germany and Austria in need of refuge, but Jews all over Europe felt unsafe in countries they had called home for centuries. At the same time anti-immigration policies were intensifying everywhere. Chaim Weizmann, then president of the World Jewish Congress, observed wryly that "the world seemed to be divided into two parts—those places where the Jews could not live and those where they could not enter."[1]

Meanwhile, in light of the eruption of the 1936 Arab revolt in Palestine and the looming prospect of war with Germany, British decision makers were changing their minds about the status of Palestine. Pacification of the Arab majority emerged as a priority, and it came at the expense of the Jewish minority. Despite the grand promise of the Balfour Declaration, the policy ending Jewish immigration to Palestine was begun just as the ground began burning under the feet of European Jewry.[2] As a result of this international unrest Golda was catapulted into the maelstrom of national and international politics. As head of the political department (foreign secretary) of the Histadrut she traveled extensively and took part in deliberations affecting British foreign policy. In 1938, for instance, she attended the Evian Conference in France as a spectator—she was not allowed to speak because she did not represent a state—and experienced firsthand the indifference of the nations of the world to the Jewish plight.

Golda's letters from Europe reflect anxiety about the utter helplessness of her people at this moment of dire peril. Because they did not have a state of their own, Jews as a collective, were utterly without a voice in matters affecting their survival. Reading between the lines of her letters one feels her rage toward world leaders who refused to acknowledge the rumblings of the approaching tsunami. Golda's deepseated pragmatism never permitted her to become an idealist in matters of foreign affairs, but she was coming to believe that diplomacy was a hollow hope as a means of ensuring Jewish survival. She soon adopted the view known as Catastrophe Zionism: the belief that Jewish history has been full of catastrophes and that only a state backed by military power would prevent further calamities. This belief shaped her understanding of foreign policy in the decades to come and partly explains her willingness to apply force to many of the crises she would later encounter, including the Yom Kippur War. For Golda, the failure of the international community meant that to survive Jews could rely only on themselves, and survival justified a wide range of means.

Most of her letters from this period are undated, which may reflect the state of her anxiety when she wrote them, but the letters refer to events both before and after Kristallnacht. Golda was in London on November 9, 1938, when antisemitic riots encouraged by Hitler's government erupted throughout Germany.[3] Jewish homes, hospitals, and schools were ransacked as the attackers demolished buildings with sledgehammers. Over one thousand synagogues were burned and more than seven thousand Jewish businesses were either destroyed or damaged. Jews were murdered and the wounded went untreated. No government offered assistance. Golda was horrified. From London, she wrote Morris:

> Dear Morris . . . Meetings all day and night and the heart breaking with all that is happening. When one hears the stories from Germany from people who have just come from there one feels that he has no right to live at all. . . . As one walks in the street all you see are newspaper posters about Jews in Germany. . . . Everybody is writing about us.[4]

She was upset by the extensive British media coverage, which was full of dreadful description but contained no calls for action. The Jews, she observed in her letter to Morris, were "benefiting" from extensive publicity and little material help, like Motl, the boy in Sholem Aleichem's iconic Yiddish story. She used the Yiddish refrain: "S'is mich gut ich be a Yatom" (I am an orphan: lucky me).[5]

Golda witnessed Chaim Weizmann—the legendary head of the World Zionist Organization and the man who midwifed the Balfour Declaration—plead for help, to no avail. Golda did not see the crisis through the eyes of a politician, nor did she apply the sober analysis expected of men. Her reaction was personal to the core. She felt responsible for finding a solution, and guilty that none was available. It is worth quoting one of her letters at length to understand the extent to which she was speaking in a different voice. Whereas Ben-Gurion reflected on the political meaning of the crisis and its impact on the Zionist project, Golda felt the pain of the persecuted:

> Weizmann is scampering from one ministry to the next and asks that something be done and cannot succeed. Everyone says that indeed this is awful but he cannot do anything. . . . We buy [an] endless number of newspapers and each newspaper tells more horrible news. . . .
>
> You have probably read the news, tens of thousands of Jews were detained, a man from Germany told me about what was going on at the concentration camps, one can lose one's mind listening to this. Now they have taken *everything* from the Jews, they are left without the means of survival.

And here just during these days came the report that wishes to cut down on the opportunity for immigration to Palestine. And we sat in the meetings of the Zionist Executive Council and were thinking that the entire world abandoned us, and we only had ourselves to rely on.

Yes, dear ones, we live in a horrible time in a bad world, and I only hope that in your lifetime you will still see a better world and that our place in the world will also be more humane.[6]

Five months before Kristallnacht, from Chicago she voiced similar disappointment in American Jewry. Poor Jews made donations, but the more prosperous held back:

Conditions in the US are quite difficult now and the Jews are not willing to give under any circumstances. . . . Only the poor Jews give and the rest are too busy having fun and cannot think of the status of Jews elsewhere and about Palestine. The trouble is that they are so distanced from the suffering Jewry that it is hard to move them. But never mind, we built many things in Palestine without them.[7]

Golda's mood in these letters shifted from utter despair ("one feels that he has no right to live at all") to bitter sarcasm ("I am an orphan: lucky me") to reaffirmation of the need to fight back and build for the future. As she returned to Tel Aviv, devastated, she regained her resolve to fight the British Mandate government with every ounce of her strength in order to reopen the gates of Palestine to Jewish immigration.

During the war years Golda was recognized as a member of the top leadership of both the labor camp and the Jewish community in Palestine. She also became an active participant in several arguments concerning social and economic policy: how to deal with rising unemployment, how to respond to right-wing acts of terror, how to solve the Arab-Palestinian conflict, and whether such a solution might include a partition of the land. On this last question, she took a firm and consistent stand against the creation of two states, one Jewish and one Palestinian. Perhaps Golda's American education, with its focus on the American Civil War and morning pledge to "one nation, indivisible," played an unconscious role in forming her intuitive opposition to partition.

When the war ended the British policy restricting Jewish immigration to Palestine became the subject of renewed conflict. Jewish survivors of the Holocaust concentrated in displaced persons camps needed homes. The Arab Palestinian majority, backed by the Arab countries of the Middle East, adamantly rejected the idea that survivors should be allowed to resettle in Palestine. In their view the refugees ought to return to their home states, even if these were sites of recent carnage, or immigrate elsewhere. Palestine was not their home. The Zionist leadership by contrast felt that these refugees belonged in Palestine. These survivors needed a land to call their own and their presence would strengthen the cause of the Jewish state. Claims for a state, the leadership believed, necessitated a Jewish majority. This belief, however, depended on how one answered perhaps the most difficult question faced by the Zionist leadership: Is a Jewish majority a precondition to a Jewish state, or could a Jewish state without a Jewish majority be legitimate? As we shall see, Golda played an important role in resolving this question.

The Black Sabbath

In mid-June 1946 Haganah forces (of which Golda was a member) authorized by the Zionist executive in Palestine bombed eleven bridges across Palestine. The extravagant terrorist acts were meant to send a message to the British: the gloves were off. Dismayed and impatient, the British retaliated. In Israeli historiography, Saturday, June 29, came to be known as "Black Saturday." British troops searched and detained 2,700 Yishuv leaders, among them David Remez, head of the Yishuv National Council.

Golda, however, remained free. To this day it remains a mystery why she was not detained, but some have suggested it was due to her status as an American. Mindful of America's ascent, the British were hoping for help from Washington, DC, in finding a solution to the conflict in Palestine. Detaining an "American" would only exacerbate the already negative American public opinion concerning British policy.[8] Whatever

the reason, the situation worked to Golda's advantage. Among the de-
tainees was Moshe Sharett (then Shertok), head of the political department of the Jewish Agency. His detention allowed Golda to climb another rung up the political ladder. Sixteen years after arriving in Tel Aviv
as a young, idealistic, married woman, full of dreams but with little
actual knowledge about the homeland or its politics, Golda became
Ben-Gurion's de facto deputy and one of the few steering the ship of
state in the making.[9] Her father, who had died a few months earlier, did
not live to see this new feather in his daughter's cap. Nor did her mother,
who was now in the last stages of advanced dementia.

There was no time for Golda to rest on her laurels. Calamity was at
the gate. How could the small Jewish community resist the mighty British Empire? With her newfound political power Golda was standing at
a fateful crossroads that might determine the destiny of Zionism for
decades to come. Should the leadership escalate the struggle in the hope
of driving the British out of Palestine, or should it choose moderation
in the hope of negotiating an acceptable compromise? Ben-Gurion
summed up the dilemma succinctly: "If we choose activism and fight
the British tooth and nail, including through terrorist means, we would
risk another Massada. If we choose peaceful negotiations, we might
beget the fate of Vichy."[10]

A Visit to King Abdullah of Jordan

A few days before the expiration of the British Mandate, Ben-Gurion sent
a message to Golda in Jerusalem instructing her to travel to Transjordan
for a meeting with King Abdullah. Palestinian forces were blocking the
roads from Jerusalem so she would need to fly to Tel Aviv and from there
drive to the meeting spot. In this last stab at diplomacy Golda would pro-
pose a deal: the king would annex parts of Palestine in exchange for letting
the Zionists keep the territory assigned to them under UN Resolution 181.
Ben-Gurion chose Golda because she had previously discussed the matter
with King Abdullah, and she was a persuasive and reliable negotiator. He
knew she would carry out his mission to the letter.

The flight to Tel Aviv was nerve-wracking. The nascent state possessed only small, worn-out aircraft that fierce winds batted about like feathers. To make matters worse, Golda was still recovering from her recent hospital stay and her doctors thought she might have had a heart attack. But the first leg of the journey was the least of Golda's worries. Traveling by road in enemy territory was considerably more dangerous. The battle over Palestine was raging, and Palestinian refugees, experiencing the mayhem of war, were streaming across the river. If captured, both Golda and Ezra Danin—her security escort and translator—could be killed, so the two disguised their appearances. Danin sat in the back of the car, dressed in a suit and a kulfac, a hat worn by the members of the Ottoman police. His dress signaled the identity of a middle-class merchant, a Middle Eastern man of unspecified origin. Golda sat next to him, pretending to be his wife. Wrapped in a hijab with a veil hiding her face, the proud Jew had assumed the role of a docile companion. Later that night she would engage in negotiations affecting the fate of the region, but for now she kept her mouth shut and her eyes modestly averted. Golda did not speak Arabic and any word from her would betray her identity and endanger both the mission and her life.

Once they arrived at the arranged meeting spot, the king sent a car driven by his confidant to bring them to Amman. This final leg involved ten checkpoints staffed by soldiers of the Arab Legion, but the car's windows had thick blinds and upon recognizing the driver the soldiers let them pass. Three hours later they arrived at the capital. The journey was emblematic of the fundamental transformation of the Middle East during the years since Golda had set foot in Palestine at the end of World War I. Before then the entire area was part of one country, the Ottoman Empire. Now Golda and Danin were crossing a border separating Palestine from the Kingdom of Transjordan; the establishment of Jewish and Palestinian states would bring yet more borders. Freedom to travel throughout the region was coming to an end.

In Amman they were driven to the home of another of King Abdullah's confidants where Golda waited for the king in the women's quarters. The hostess, a Turkish woman, complained bitterly of the monotony of life in Transjordan. Given the circumstances, Golda thought to herself that a bit of monotony didn't sound half bad. When the king arrived he looked pale and distraught. Golda looked him straight in the eye and wasted no time. "You reneged on your promise to honor the partition resolution," she stated boldly but calmly. Even though they had not signed any formal agreement at their 1947 meeting, Golda believed that they had reached a mutual understanding. Things have changed, the king replied. A massive refugee problem was emerging and his army insisted that he join the Arab states in seeking revenge against the Jews. We intend to take all of Palestine, he told her, but we will honor our Jewish subjects by giving them representation in Parliament and recognizing their civil rights. She had heard these promises before. She responded with the chutzpah befitting a twentieth-century woman: "We have not waited for 2,000 years to implement such a plan."

Golda proceeded to explain that if he rescinded his promise, the Yishuv might take more than the land allocated it by the United Nations. She also alluded to the needless lives that would be lost on both sides by war. The king agreed but said there was nothing he could do. Well then, she responded, we shall meet after the war. It is worth noting that there are conflicting understandings of this final exchange. No one disputes what Golda said, but questions remain about *how* she said it. Did she say it arrogantly, matter-of-factly, or despondently? And how did he respond? Did he say "yes, after the war" with a measure of confidence that his Arab Legion would defeat the Jews, or did he gloomily say "inshallah" (God willing), as some have reported?

After the meeting ended, food was served in the glorious Arab tradition. The spread comprised the best of Middle Eastern cuisine, a world away from the chickpea mush that Golda ate on her first night in the kibbutz. Golda, however, had no appetite. Her mission complete, she wanted to leave. Years later, Golda and Danin would joke about his frustrated desire to sample the royal spread, but even though she was disguised as his wife Golda was still the boss. Important business awaited.[11]

The king and Golda were anything but transparent with one another. Each possessed an agenda and neither was willing to reveal their true intentions. Each desired to expand their territory: the king dreamed of annexing Syria in addition to Palestine; the Yishuv, worried about the small territorial space allocated by the United Nations, hoped for more. In hindsight many have considered the meeting to be a missed opportunity, and critics have claimed that the war could have been averted if only a man had been sent in Golda's place. Golda, in their view, was too arrogant and forceful during the meeting. The king, not accustomed to such behavior and certainly not from a woman, felt alienated. Moreover, they have argued, the king was a Bedouin and therefore bound to find the negotiations with a woman awkward. Golda's failure, these critics assert, was the inevitable result of sending a woman to do a man's job.

Ezra Danin, Golda's translator and an experienced member of the security forces, denied that she was arrogant. In his recollection she was quite respectful. "We are your best friend in the region," he remembered her saying; "avoid war and let us reach a modus vivendi."[12] Despite what her critics claim, the failure of diplomacy cannot be attributed to Golda's gender. Before this meeting, the king never indicated any discomfort about negotiating with a woman, nor had he behaved in accordance with the orientalist stereotype of a "Bedouin." Had he felt uncomfortable, he easily could have made known his preference that Ben-Gurion send a man. Moreover, King Abdullah was an experienced politician who would hardly allow the gender of his opponent to influence his plans. In her memoirs Golda recalled that the king assured her he would keep his initial promise to her "because she was a woman."[13] But both Golda and the king knew well that in politics promises are often broken.

Golda and Danin drove back under cover of night. As the faint signs of sunrise emerged on the horizon the car stopped. The driver, an Arab man in Jewish territory, recognized the danger and refused to drive farther. They had to continue by foot, a journey that made clear to Golda how the socially functional, traditional long-flowing dress might restrict her movement and thereby prevent her escape. Throughout the walk Golda feared that she would trip and fall. She later recalled, "We didn't even dare breathe too loudly . . . not at all sure that we were going in the right direction and [I was] unable to shake off my depression and sense of failure."[14]

A State of Her Own

The state of Israel will ensure complete equality of social and political
rights to all its inhabitants irrespective of religion, race or sex.

—ISRAEL'S DECLARATION OF INDEPENDENCE

The British Mandate was set to expire on Saturday, May 15, 1948. While
the secular majority of the People's Council cared little for religion they
were nevertheless reluctant to proclaim a Jewish State on Shabbat,
which would have been a flagrant violation of Jewish law, so they decided to hold the ceremony on the Friday afternoon. For the site, the
organizers, concerned about security, chose Beit Dizengoff, a small
building on Rothschild Boulevard belonging to the first mayor of Tel
Aviv. They blackened the windows in anticipation of an air raid (which
came the following day) and, above the table, they hung a big picture of
Theodor Herzl, the visionary who decades earlier had prophesized a
Jewish state. Thirteen members of the provisional executive branch
faced the audience, David Remez among them.

In preparation for the ceremony, Golda had washed her long, thick
hair, as was her custom before special occasions. She donned a little
black dress in the French style, a stark contrast to the oriental Arab dress
she had just shed. We do not know if she wore makeup but she probably
powdered her nose in anticipation of the presence of cameras. By virtue
of being one of the thirty-seven members of the People's Council, Golda
was invited to sign her name on the declaration. Standing in line, waiting for her turn, she became overwhelmed by emotion. Tears streamed
down her cheeks uncontrollably.

She was crying in awe. This moment justified everything that had
come before: the pain she had inflicted on her family, the physical toll
on her health, the abuse and humiliation to which she had often been
subjected. Watching the state come into being, she realized that it had
all been worth it. When her turn came, she signed the declaration "Golda
Myerson," a departure from her regular practice of simply signing "Golda."
Perhaps she did so in appreciation of the historic moment, or perhaps
she remembered Morris as the primary victim of her political career.

In her memoirs, Golda devoted several pages to the details of the ceremony, noting who was there and who was absent due to premature death. She also discussed the declaration's recognition of the struggle for free Jewish immigration: a Jewish state meant a home for displaced Jews. Notably absent, however, is any mention of the struggle for women's equality. Even though the declaration held that the new state would honor gender equality, Golda's memoirs do not point to this fact as an achievement worthy of celebration. One reason for this silence, perhaps, is that actions spoke louder than words. Despite the formal pledge to honor gender equality, only two of the thirty-seven signatories were women: Golda and Rachel Kagan. Together, they constituted 5.4 percent of the signatories.

While those who planned the list of signatories explicitly attempted to reflect the diversity of the Jewish Yishuv, they ignored the second sex. Ada Maimon was left off the list, while her brother Rabbi Fishman Maimon was invited to sign. Other formidable women were also ignored. Implicitly, Israeli women were asked to be content with 5.4 percent even though they constituted 50 percent of the population. Given the limited number of signatories, someone had to sacrifice—and as nearly always happened, this sacrifice fell to the women.

Like Golda, Rachel Kagan was thrilled to sign. Providing balance to Golda's left-wing politics, Kagan represented the center. The chairwoman of WIZO, the Women's International Zionist Organization, she was also a leader in promoting women rights. Ten years after the event, the signatories were asked to share what they had felt on that awesome day. Golda's reflections centered on the security risks and the legalization of Jewish immigration. Kagan, to paraphrase Abigail Adams, remembered the ladies.[15] She wrote: "At this fateful hour, when I added my name to the scroll, I felt that I was signing in the name of all Jewish women."[16]

The Jewish women's organizations in Palestine, primarily but not only the Women Workers Council, fought mightily to advance the Zionist cause. They believed that Zionism meant the liberation of women as well as of men. But the men of the Yishuv, quite simply, could not understand the concept of liberation through the lens of gender. The fact that only two women were invited to sign the declaration and that one of them—Golda—was not associated with the struggle to advance the status of women is illustrative of the sorry status of women at the founding of Israel. Golda, however, had internalized the preferences of the party establishment long before this moment had arrived, which explains her silence on the matter.

PART III

1948–1964

CHAPTER 12

FROM ISRAEL'S FIRST EMISSARY TO THE SOVIET UNION TO MINISTER OF LABOR

IN MAY 1948 the provisional government came into power. Ben-Gurion was eager to show his commitment to the principle of gender equality proclaimed by the Declaration of Independence and spoke openly about his hope to include a woman in the cabinet. Golda, however, was not included in the list submitted by the Mapai committee designated to recommend who would be invited to serve as ministers. Nor was any other woman asked to serve. One theory to explain Golda's exclusion was that the two powerful Mapai members on the committee, Moshe Sharett (designated minister of foreign affairs) and Eliezer Kaplan (designated minister of the treasury) were not keen on including her. They either did not approve of her "hawkish" views, fearing that she was too close to Ben-Gurion and therefore would strengthen his power in the cabinet, or simply did not think that the inclusion of a woman was important. It may also be that they felt competitive with her, resentful of her speedy rise to power in Mapai, and therefore identified her with the stereotype of "women who did not know their place" in the hierarchy.[1] Instead of inviting Golda to join the first cabinet, Ben-Gurion, at Sharett's recommendation, sent Golda to Moscow to serve as Israel's first emissary to the Soviet Union.[2] Gender equality prevailed here as well since

Golda was the only woman in the entire Israeli diplomatic corps. Indeed, eighteen years would pass before Israel appointed another woman ambassador.[3]

Golda felt defeated and bitter. While she was born in Kiev and had lived in Russia until the age of eight she had no love for Russia, did not speak the language, and harbored an aversion to Bolshevism. For Golda, service in Moscow was tantamount to exile.[4] She yearned for a job that would enable her to implement the Zionist-socialist vision to which she had devoted nearly her entire life. But Golda was first and foremost a party soldier. Her willingness to do whatever the party demanded, even sacrificing life and limb, was made evident by the circumstances under which her appointment to Russia began.

Golda received the news while stationed in New York doing what she did better than anyone else—raising money. Earlier that day a car accident had severely injured her foot, and when she heard about the appointment she cabled the minister of foreign affairs from her hospital bed to inform him that her doctors had counseled against travel. Fearing international complications with the Soviets, the foreign minister pressed the urgency of the mission. The Soviet government, he believed, might misinterpret the failure of an emissary to appear in Moscow as a sign of disrespect, and Israel was eager for Soviet support. Golda left New York immediately, still in great physical pain. As a result her foot never properly healed, she developed phlebitis, and had to wear orthopedic shoes until the end of her life.[5]

Back in Israel she began to make preparations for Moscow. As a Jewish woman operating in a man's world, this involved making some complex decisions about dress. Conventionally only men served as top diplomats, and the tuxedo served as their standard uniform. There was no protocol and no uniform for a woman diplomat. Golda toyed with the idea of wearing something simple to symbolize the humble ideology of Labor Zionism, but decided against it. A top Israeli seamstress sewed a long black gown for the occasion, probably the fanciest dress Golda had ever worn. Additionally Golda requested that members of her staff, mostly secular men, learn the tropes of the Jewish ritual and be ready to chant a blessing during the customary *aliya* (reading from the scripture). Golda expected her delegation to attend the upcoming High Holiday services at the central Moscow synagogue and insisted that they arrive prepared. As a woman she knew that she was absolved from this responsibility, insofar as in the late 1940s, even Jewish Reform women were not considered equal to men in the performance of the Jewish ritual.

Golda had abandoned religious Jewish practice long ago and viewed the various limitations on women, such as the requirement that during services women be segregated from men, as relics of the past. Religion, however, was useful for the purpose of connecting with Russian Jewry. To be a Jew in Moscow meant to go to the synagogue, primarily on the High Holidays. If the synagogue practiced the traditional segregation of women, so be it. It was a small price to pay to recruit more Jews to the cause of Zionism, and she might have thought that once they "returned" to Israel, their religious practices would fade away.

Golda spent seven miserable months in Moscow. She had never admired Soviet society and her stay only reinforced her views. Later in her political career she would occasionally lash out at the communist members of the Knesset for supporting Moscow. In the heat of a debate about legal protections for working women, for instance, she observed: "I have a lot to say about some of the jobs that women take in those socialist countries, under what conditions they work and how they are dressed for the jobs."[6] In Moscow she had seen cleaning women on streets in the middle of winter with rags tied around their feet instead of shoes.[7] She knew well that the Soviet Union was no bastion of gender equality, despite what her colleagues might claim.

There were, however, a few rays of light during her Moscow sojourn. First, her daughter Sarah officially joined the delegation as a radio operator. It was probably the first time that Golda had spent intimate time with her daughter, and by all accounts this experience helped heal their relationship. Second, Lou Kaddar, a Paris-born secretary, was assigned to her by the Ministry of Foreign Affairs. Lou would become Golda's lifelong confidante and serve as her assistant until her last days as prime minister. The chemistry between the two was evident from the start. Golda wrote: "I liked her the moment I set eyes on her . . . for the better part of the next twenty-seven years Lou was my close friend, my indispensable assistant and, more often than not, my travel companion."[8] Something about Lou and Golda clicked. They shared a biting sense of humor and understood each other without the need for much elaboration. Lou was also a woman who "knew her place." Their relationship, while not romantic, illustrates the complexity of gender: Golda needed a companion in precisely the way that a career man needs a wife. Lou, a woman with bourgeois sensibilities who cared about feminine appearance, fit perfectly with Golda, a woman with proletarian sensibilities and love of cooking. Lou gently encouraged Golda to pay attention to herself, something Golda had neglected as she tirelessly climbed the political ladder. Golda, who was accustomed to doing everything for herself, submitted her nails to manicure and agreed to wear a string of pearls to formal occasions.

Golda also willingly stepped into her role as "mother of the delegation." Israel sent its diplomats to Moscow on a shoestring budget and asked the members of the delegation to forgo a salary. To remain within the limits of that budget Golda imitated her mother Bluma. She bought basic cooking utensils, which she distributed to the members, and at seven o'clock every morning she would go to the market to purchase bread, cheese, and other produce. She allowed the members only one meal a day in the hotel dining room and forced them to make do with the produce she had acquired for their remaining meals. On Saturdays she turned her bathroom into a kitchen and prepared brunch ("Yidishist food," as Lou recalled) to serve to the entire delegation.[9]

Despite these silver linings, Golda was frustrated and felt she was languishing in exile. Her anger showed in several ways. Lou Kaddar, acting as her official interpreter, reported that Golda often responded with hostility when other diplomats attempted to engage her in "small talk." For example

AMBASSADOR: How did you arrive in Moscow?
GOLDA: [TO LOU]: What, you don't know how?
LOU [TO GOLDA]: I know, but he wants to know.
GOLDA: So tell him, by airplane.

AMBASSADOR: Where do you stay?
GOLDA [TO LOU]: What, you don't know where we live?
LOU [TO GOLDA]: I know; he doesn't.
GOLDA: So tell him, in the Metropole Hotel.

After being subjected to the same questions over and over again, Golda finally snapped: "Tell his highness the ambassador that we arrived here riding donkeys" and "tell him that we live in a big tent."[10]

Golda's rebuke was, in part, pent up resentment at the image of Israel held by the diplomatic corps. The young state was viewed as an under-developed orientalist country that used donkeys for transportation and tents for dwellings, a far cry from the vibrant, modern city of Tel Aviv. But it also expressed her swelling anger at being stranded in Russia. Golda was a savvy politician who knew how to engage in polite small talk and could be charming if she wished. She resented the fact that while her comrades in Israel were building their new state she was obliged to engage in empty talk in Moscow.

This resentment boiled over during the Jewish High Holidays, which took place shortly after she had arrived in Moscow. Golda quickly came to realize that although Stalin's government was willing to lend inter-national support to the Jewish state, it was decidedly hostile to any re-lationship between Israeli officials and Soviet Jews. Soviet Jews were expected to be exclusively Soviet without any allegiance to the Jewish state. In her youth, Americans, too, were hostile to "hyphenated Ameri-cans," so Golda identified with the plight of Soviet Jews. She hoped to awaken Jewish national pride in Russia, convince Soviet Jews to immi-grate to Israel, and share with them the splendor of the dream come true. Golda was no longer acting as the mother of the delegation but as the prophetess Deborah, its fearless leader.

On the morning of Rosh Hashana, the Jewish New Year, Golda and her delegation walked to the synagogue to publicly express their bond with local Jews. When they arrived at the synagogue they divided along gender lines. The women climbed the stairs to the balcony to join the women's section while the men wrapped themselves in prayer shawls and prepared to partake in the traditional ritual. The event was cataclysmic.

Crowds arrived to welcome her and demonstrate their solidarity with the Jewish state and its female representative. "Goldele," they shouted, with the same accent as her parents. The overwhelming reception caught her by surprise and she was elated.[11] Her audacious behavior had broadcast to both Soviet Jews and Stalin the resolve of the New Hebrew Jew. In the only photo taken at the event, one sees Golda with a fur hat on her head and a tight-lipped smile on her face amid a sea of excited well-wishers.

As Golda herself recounted in her memoirs, there was considerable fallout from the stunt. Stalin's government accelerated its suppression of Jewish activity, including Yiddish newspapers, the Yiddish theater, and other ethnic institutions designed to promote Soviet Jewish culture. One might argue that given the significant costs of this symbolic event, Golda's behavior was reckless and ill-conceived. But what remains is a story about a determined woman who dared speak truth to power and the tens of thousands of oppressed Jews who, for a brief moment, were able to recognize their Jewish identity in the context of the Jewish state.

CHAPTER 13

IN ISRAEL'S FIRST CABINET

Golda Is Appointed
Minister of Labor

GOLDA WAS EAGER to end her "exile" in Moscow and return to the active political environment in Israel. Ben-Gurion promised her to do all he could to add her to his cabinet and made good on his promise. The first Israeli elections were a landslide victory to Mapai and Ben-Gurion immediately cabled Golda an invitation to join the cabinet.[1] Golda returned to Israel, pledged allegiance as a member of the Knesset, and met with Ben-Gurion. He offered her the position of deputy prime minister, but she declined. She wanted the ministry of labor. The ministry fit her active temperament and her vast experience with matters related to labor as a high-level executive in the Histadrut. It also reflected her socialist worldview. On March 10, 1949, she took the oath of office and entered the ministry she coveted.[2] In an early group photograph of the cabinet, Golda, the only woman in the picture, is seated at the far end of the table, with Ben-Gurion at its head. Zalman Shazar, the man who had been her lover earlier, is sitting to her left, and David Remez, another lover, is across from Shazar. While both were instrumental in her rise to power, their ministries in the first cabinet were less powerful than hers, and neither lasted long in the government. After a disappointing diversion to the Soviet Union, Golda now held the prestigious portfolio of the minister of labor and social security.

Figure 6. Golda at the first Israeli cabinet meeting, May 1, 1949. Courtesy of
Israel Government Press Office. Credit: Hugo Mendelson.

Golda's responsibilities in her new position included immigrant settlement, housing, job creation and employment, transportation, and other
matters connected to the post. This was a herculean undertaking given
the hundreds of thousands of immigrants coming to Israeli shores, and
it came with a substantial budget. With the passage of time, the policies
her office implemented during these years have generated considerable
controversy, but these cannot all be addressed in this book. By and large
the mostly Mizrahi immigrants (natives of Arab countries) were sent to
the south of Israel and were expected to become farmers. Their wishes
and qualifications were mostly ignored, which nurtured resentment and
trauma. Many mistakes were made in these early days. Yet it is also true
that, by and large, new immigrants were successfully integrated into the
country.[3]

As Israel coped with a massive influx of immigrants, it was chronically
on the verge of bankruptcy. Golda had to travel to the United States

again and again, begging American Jews to open their wallets. "We cannot do it without you," she implored, and generally they did as she asked.[4] As if these tasks were not enough, Golda took it upon herself to overhaul the codification of Israel's labor laws. The Mandate government, in consultation with the Histadrut, had already taken steps in the direction of progressive labor legislation. Golda, however, wished to push the project further, in keeping with the recommendations of the International Labor Organization and the progressive countries of the West. In addition to the remarkable range of policy decisions Golda made as a minister, she had to make a different, no less novel decision: How should a woman be addressed in the political arena?

A Female Minister in Search of a Title

Whatever emphasizes the male gender gives him a slight advantage, a plus. Whatever emphasizes the female gender creates a slight disadvantage for her, a minus.

—DAFNA N. IZRAELI

For the first time in two thousand years, the Jewish people had a state, a government, and cabinet ministers.[5] New terminology was needed to meet this new reality. What would a prime minister be called? A cabinet member? The ministers decided to follow the Bible. In the ancient kingdom of Israel, a man in charge of government policies was called a "Sar." In addition to its biblical pedigree, the monosyllabic word had an authoritative and pleasing ring to it.

Consequently, nearly every political appointment was called a "sar," a male designation, since men were in control of nearly everything in the emerging state of Israel. Of the 120 members first elected to parliament, only 12 were women (9 percent of the legislative body), and only 1 chaired a Knesset committee (not surprisingly, she chaired the "education committee"). In the newly constructed judicial branch no woman was appointed to the Supreme Court; only one woman was appointed as a lower court judge.[6] Israelis were proud of their commitment to gender equality in the Declaration of Independence and of the fact that women served in the military, but few noticed the gap between theory and practice when it came time to distribute political offices.

Golda faced the choice of whether she should be addressed as Sar, or, instead, by the female conjugation of the term, "sara"—a "she-minister." To give non-Hebrew speakers a sense of the linguistic stakes of this decision, they are invited to imagine the Queen of England being addressed as King Elizabeth.[7] That was a historic choice. Had she chosen sara, she could have influenced the culture makers to come to terms with the fact that women, too, were bearers of power and perhaps have indicated that more women would soon be arriving in government. But this was not a fight she cared to pick. One can think of many sound reasons for her choice: her plate was already full, and using a female term would attract more attention to the fact of her gender, giving her foes an easy opportunity to mix the poison of misogyny with substantive criticism of her programs. In the end, Golda decided that she needed the symbolic power that the male term suggested. The cabinet protocols listed her as "the Sar, Mrs. Golda Meyerson," and Israel's only radio station called her a sar. Israeli women were thereby invited to leave their gender at home when they stepped into the public arena, and Israeli girls received the message that to hold power you must pretend to be a man.[8]

And yet if Golda had wanted to wipe out her gender identity entirely, she could have insisted on being called "Myerson" and later "Meir." Instead, she insisted on being called Golda, an unmistakably female name, and for the most part Golda remained Golda in politics and in the media. Most people did not, maybe could not, perform the necessary switch and address her as a he-minister, a sar. During deliberations in the cabinet and Knesset she was sometimes referred to as a sar but most often as a sara.

A quarter of a century later, Shulamit Aloni, the leader of the civil rights party whose career Golda tried to torpedo repeatedly, was appointed to Rabin's cabinet (see part IV in this volume). She requested to be addressed as "sara" and so it was. Israelis took to the change very quickly and with little fuss. There is little doubt that had Golda decided to insist on being addressed as sara, Israelis would have embraced her choice.[9]

Czarina of Israel's New Deal: Contradictions in Golda's Feminist Philosophy

The State of Israel will not tolerate within it poverty that shames human life.

—GOLDA MEIR

Golda arrived at the Ministry of Labor as the czarina of Israel's new deal, determined to provide the state with forward-thinking labor legislation.[10] A lifelong socialist and labor activist in the Histadrut, Golda now had the power and opportunity to implement her ideas about employment and welfare policy. She surrounded herself with men, all well-known experts in labor and welfare policy who assisted her in overcoming the opposition of those who preferred a more liberal approach based on the ideology of a free market.[11] It was a team of dedicated, like-minded men who encouraged each other, planned carefully, and drove the program to fruition. The project proved Golda's capacity to focus on the target at hand. It also proved her preference to work with men, not with women.

Under her leadership the Knesset passed ten statutes that, together, created fair labor standards and ensured a central role for organized labor in the new state. Her achievements included an eight-hour workday, a weekly day of rest, mandatory annual vacation with pay, vocational training, the regulation of child labor, and rights and benefits for working women and pregnant women in particular.[12] The crown jewel, however, was the Social Security Act (known in Hebrew as National Insurance). Utterly novel throughout the entire Middle East, the statute provided benefits to the elderly, workers' compensation, disability benefits, unemployment benefits, and benefits related to birth and maternity leave. The plan encountered fierce opposition both within her own party—Mapai—and from the private sector. Many felt that considering the poor resources of the state, the benefits were simply too extravagant. The minister of finance thought the plan irresponsible.[13] When Golda left Israel on one of her fundraising missions abroad, her opponents in the cabinet shrunk her bill. Angry, she appealed to

Mapai's caucus in the Knesset, called the move to curtail her initiative unfriendly and added, "From now on I shall not leave the country when an important matter is under discussion . . . this Knesset . . . [better pass the entire bill]."[14] A fellow minister, the German-born economist Peretz Naftali, helped her develop the argument that in fact the burden on the state budget would not be too heavy. They provided two arguments. First, they omitted spending items from the bill that were already covered elsewhere (such as health insurance provided for Histadrut members); and second, the bill was an anti-inflationary measure because it was drawing on funds supplied by members of the public now covered by the law and required to pay the insurance. To these Golda added intense lobbying with Ben-Gurion and threatened to resign if the cabinet did not approve the bill. By drawing upon her political experience and acumen, she was able to overcome the opposition, and the legislation prevailed.[15]

Golda first encountered the idea of social security as a teenager in Milwaukee, when Victor Berger—the founder of the American Socialist Party and a congressman from her own district—introduced a bill in Congress to provide old-age pensions. The bill failed, but it attracted significant attention. Later, during Golda's several-months' visit to the United States in the 1930s, she was exposed to the activity of another great American woman: Frances Perkins, FDR's secretary of labor. With FDR's help, Perkins pushed through the American Social Security Act, which became the law of the land in 1936.[16] While similar social security programs had already been implemented in Germany and Great Britain, it is quite likely that in Golda's case the American influence was decisive because it resonated with her history as a young socialist from Milwaukee.

Today most Israelis are surprised to learn that Golda, the woman they blame for the Yom Kippur War, was the mother of a program they consider to be their natural right. They tend to credit Ben-Gurion, and yet, without Golda's vision and determination, the act would not have been adopted. The Social Security Act was Golda's law.

Golda's Dilemma, the Conception of
Women in the Workforce

The greatest conundrum Golda confronted during this period concerned the question of women's employment: Should labor law encourage women to join the workforce, or should it support the traditional institution of the family?

As a child Golda experienced the ravages of her father's unemployment and she never forgot the days of gnawing hunger and shivering cold in Russia. In Milwaukee she described being forced to forgo school in order to work in the family's grocery store as "the bane of my life." These deep, personal traumas fed her fight for social justice and determination to protect workers. At the same time Golda vehemently protested the fate of mothers who were expected to sacrifice their dreams in order to perform their traditional motherly duties.[17] As minister of labor, she was tasked with shaping legislation that would take these difficulties into consideration.

Golda was well aware of the arguments between gender-sensitive feminists (who believed that a set of rights should explicitly protect working women) and gender-blind feminists (who insisted that the law should treat men and women impartially, overlooking their gender). Golda's own views on women's role in the labor force were contradictory and complex. On the one hand, she was quite aware that sexism was ubiquitous, shared throughout Israel from its elite to the hoi polloi, from young to old, left to right, and rich to poor. Israeli society treated the patriarchal hierarchy as a part of the natural order. On the other hand, Golda was familiar with those pockets of Israeli society that sought to break down the existing gender hierarchy. She endorsed such efforts, but as a politician knew that she had to be careful not to alienate traditionalists; if she lost their support, her legislative agenda would be doomed.

Despite the need to walk this political tightrope, Golda did not hesitate to expose the rampant sexism among the decision makers. In a 1952 speech delivered to the Women Workers Council concerning the Employment of Women Bill, Golda pointed to the tendency to treat women's issues as matters of secondary concern:

Female members of the Histadrut will recall, that for many years . . . whenever we arrived at a discussion concerning women, the agenda was set in a way that attached the subject to several other items proposed for discussion. In general, the combination [was]: women, youth and Mizrahi Jews. Very seldom did we get a discussion solely addressing the female member. Apparently, it was not a subject sufficiently respectable to justify a special discussion. When we brought before the Knesset the three bills—working youth, apprenticeship and employment of women—the presidium of the Knesset expected, following tradition, that we introduce all three bills together. But we said that the Employment of Women Bill will be introduced on its own, and we managed to get a special time and place for it in the Knesset agenda.[18]

Golda clearly understood that women were a marginalized group and their interests were expected to be lumped together with other vulnerable groups (Mizrahim, children) and dealt with in one package as befits marginal issues. Society tended to overlook the diverse needs of women, and the idea of serious reform regarding women's employment remained low on the nation's agenda.

Golda hoped that by demanding a separate Knesset discussion of women's employment, she would put women center stage and raise awareness of their needs. During the ensuing discussion she presented a wide range of astonishing data: since the 1920s the number of unemployed women had risen by 131 percent, while the total number of women in the population had grown by only 61 percent; before World War II most working women were single, but in recent years the presence of married women in the workforce was rising. She also pointed out that less than a quarter—only 22 percent—of Israeli women were gainfully employed. Of the 4,950 job seekers, only 650 were women.[19]

Golda understood that more fundamentally the Israeli attitude toward labor itself had changed. The ethos of labor, so dear to the hearts of the pioneering generation, grew weaker with each passing year. Agricultural work was no longer viewed as the quintessential means of self-fulfillment, and the appeal of middle-class culture, so despised in the early kibbutzim, was also on the rise.[20] In this new middle-class environment, women did not want to be forced to work two jobs, one at home and one outside the home. Following the devastations of the war years and the Holocaust, most Israeli women wanted a traditional family in which the husband went to work and the wife raised the children and ran the household. Most married women, if compelled to work, preferred a part-time job that would allow them to attend to their familial responsibilities. Golda also knew well that traditional men, both Ashkenazi and Mizrahi, were unhappy to see their wives work outside the home. A working wife in their view diminished their manhood. Married women, Golda's statistics made clear, primarily worked because doing so was a financial necessity rather than as a means of "fulfilling their inner self," as Golda had put it in her essay "Borrowed Mothers."[21] Golda also had to acknowledge the increasingly central place that motherhood and childbearing occupied in Israeli culture. The Israeli people longed for renewal, which children provided, and the government had political reasons for encouraging the birthrate of Jews.

Golda was dismayed by the situation. Her conviction that every woman possessed an "inner need to go to work" remained firm, and she believed it was up to the state "to do propaganda among women to encourage them to go to work."[22] The question of which policies would accomplish this goal, however, remained a thorny issue. Golda called for a major campaign: "The women's workers movement should embark on a systematic campaign that would go back to fundamentals and explain anew to the female immigrants as well as to the female veterans the ABC of the honor of the women workers in Israel."[23] Golda knew that a mere campaign was insufficient to solve the massive problems that women faced, but she believed that if more women joined the workforce they would come to recognize the benefits of autonomy and agency and with time support a more progressive agenda that would improve women's lives in general.[24]

The unarticulated premise of Golda's labor program, at least at this time, upheld the patriarchal family. She enacted laws that protected mothers who wished to join the workforce, but these laws also expected women to participate in the traditional institution of the family, exactly what Golda had refused to accept for herself. There were several different reasons underlying Golda's decision to chart this more conservative path. While Mapai was committed to the principles of social justice emblematic of the left, it also accepted that governance required compromise and accommodation. Israel had a large public sector with strong unions and vast assets owned by public corporations. But it also had a burgeoning private sector represented by right-wing and centrist parties. Guided by Prime Minister Ben-Gurion, Golda's legislation aimed to recognize these private interests in her labor agenda. She also had to be careful not to alienate members of her own camp who thought of themselves as progressive yet still implicitly believed the view that women were in need of paternalistic legislation. Last but not least, Golda was a woman of contradictions. While she did not lead a traditional family life, she nevertheless retained a soft spot for the ideal.

By enshrining the traditional family in labor law, Golda parted company with Israeli feminists such as Rachel Kagan or Ada Fishman Maimon. The goal of the Zionist revolution was to create a New Hebrew man. The New Hebrew woman and the New Hebrew family were again placed on the back burner.[25]

CHAPTER 14

GOLDA'S CONCEPTION OF THE FAMILY

AS EARLY AS MAY 23, 1949, Golda publicly made clear her underlying conception of the family. Responding to a member of the Communist Party who ridiculed her plan to attach a small garden to each of the units built for the incoming immigrants, Golda set forth a vision of the ideal family: "To the ordinary person a garden is valuable. A garden with a few flowers next to the home, for the children, for the wife and even for the head of the family, who may be unemployed . . . is a very important thing."[1] In this description of the ordinary family Golda assumes that the head of the household will be a man, with a wife, children, and a small garden—the precise definition of the patriarchal family.[2] In 1955 with her proposed labor agenda nearly complete, Golda reiterated her patriarchal view of the family when she introduced a workers' compensation law: "The purpose of this law is to give the worker . . . his main right, to live, to make a living for himself and his family and not to become disabled or make his wife a widow and his children orphans."[3]

The central thread running through the labor laws was unmistakable: the family was a traditional unit made up of the head of household—inevitably a man—and his wife and children. Even if she worked outside the home, the wife remained the primary caretaker as well as the one in charge of household chores, everything from cooking and cleaning to attending to the children's education. As head of the household, the man had little to do with any domestic tasks. This traditional family model was

Figure 7. Golda Meir, Minister of Labor, 1949–1956. Courtesy of Israel Government Press Office. Credit: Teddy Brauner.

prevalent among middle- and lower-class workers in Israel, whose interest and culture the labor camp proudly championed. Golda's social security act, one of the last statutes on her labor agenda as well as her defining achievement, cemented this vision of the family by enacting different retirement ages for men and women: sixty for women and sixty-five for men.[4] This arrangement followed English law and ignored the situation of women who needed to continue working because they were heads of families or because their husbands had failed to provide sufficient support for them—in short, women like Golda. It is worth noting that men, too, suffered the tyranny of stereotypes embodied in these laws. They were expected to act as breadwinners and alone bear the burden of supporting their family. Under the same social security statute, for instance, widows were entitled to compensation, but widowers were not.[5]

Golda understood the woman's predicament, yet chose to embrace the conventional model of a family. Should one conclude that she was blind to the many varieties of the family or to the specific needs of women, or even to the lessons of her own experience? Or does the explanation lie in the art of politics—her recognition that the majority of the public was unsympathetic to the complex needs of women and that it would be better not to risk antagonism? Golda's strategy on family issues was to proceed incrementally rather than suddenly, in the hope that time was on her side. There was, however, one exception to this modus operandi: the prohibition on child labor.

For Golda the issue of child labor touched a nerve. Recall that when Golda was merely eight years old and eager to attend school her parents decided that she would stay home and help her mother in the store. Golda was miserable and resentful but had no choice in the matter.[6] As a teenager, moreover, she witnessed the failed campaign to amend the U.S. Constitution to prohibit child labor, a policy that would not be enacted until FDR's New Deal.[7] Golda's child labor law derived from, but went beyond, the British Mandatory law, which had already prohibited children from working until the age of twelve. Golda raised the bar to fourteen. She also expressed the hope that the bar would be raised further yet in the future and that teenagers would be required to attend school rather than work. Her justification for the policy was grounded in the communitarian philosophy of Zionism: "Just as the future of the nation is in its youth, so the future of youth is in its occupational training."[8]

During the Knesset debate on the law, she encountered opposition from the left. Hanna Lamdan, a member of the left-wing Mapam Party, wondered how a poor family who relied on their child's labor could survive. Lamdan was thinking of the many Israelis whose culture of origin viewed child labor as a normal part of life. Lamdan asked: "What will happen to the family if the boy cannot work?" Golda answered:

They should behave as if this source of work is non-existent. As if the family did not have this child. As if he never went to work. This is the only way to approach this legislation. The choice is either complete freedom for exploitation and everything evil, or a law that indeed creates a temporary obstacle, but in the long term safeguards the interests of youth and brings benefits.[9]

How could Golda justify her stark deviation from pragmatism in the matter of child labor? To do so she deployed her favorite rhetorical move: articulate the matter as a choice between two stark options, one obviously unacceptable. It was classic Golda. Given a choice between "exploitation and everything evil" on the one hand, and a temporary sacrifice on the other, it was obvious which road one must take. Ironically both Golda and Lamdan, two experienced politicians, referred to the working children as boys. Girls, who often served as domestic workers, remained invisible.[10]

Golda's bill concerning women's work, the Employment of Women Law, addressed one topic that was entirely unique to women: pregnancy. The general aim of the law was to provide women with certain privileges that would make it easier for them to join the workforce. With respect to pregnancy, this meant the provision of maternity leave.

The basic arrangement already provided in the statute passed by the government of the British Mandate gave pregnant women the right to eight weeks of maternity leave and required that employers pay 75 percent of an employee's salary during her leave. Golda's bill was significantly more generous. In keeping with the recommendations of the International Labor Organization, her bill extended the guaranteed leave to twelve weeks and shifted the financial responsibility for the leave from the employer to the government.[11] The National Insurance Institute, Golda's proud creation, was to administer the program. In Parliament she said: "We are not enthusiastic about placing the burden on the employer. Some employers have many women workers and some don't."[12] By placing the responsibility on the state and thereby redistributing the burden of maternity leave from the individual employer to the entire society, the law made certain that employers were not penalized for employing women. It was, she believed, fairer to both women and employers. In time Israeli women would internalize the right to maternity leave so fully that, like social security, they would consider it a birthright, a part of natural law. Indeed, to this day Israeli women are puzzled by the fact that Golda's beloved United States remains so resistant to the idea.

The law also gave women the right to decide whether or not to take maternity leave. Many in the Knesset suggested that a woman should not be allowed to make such a decision by herself. On the legislative committee, Elimelech Rimalt, a member of the centrist liberal party (General Zionists) and a prominent educator, offered a straightforwardly paternalistic amendment: "The purpose of the law is to protect the woman even against her will; we must hold that the employee should consult a doctor, and he will decide."[13] The fact that Rimalt was acquainted with several women doctors including the wife of the minister of treasury did not prevent him from referring to the doctor as a "he." Nor did it bother him that female employees would depend on the (male) doctor's determination, thereby giving men the power to decide what was in women's best interests. Rimalt successfully persuaded the committee to adopt his amendment to the bill. Golda objected, and during the Knesset deliberations insisted on the woman's agency: "A reasonably healthy woman, who does not engage in exceptionally difficult physical work, generally works until almost the last day before she gives birth. And she is better off this way, because it helps her psychologically, and I think—also is good for her health . . . let her make the decision."[14]

In addition to providing twelve weeks paid maternity leave, Golda's law allowed women to prolong their leave and return to work later. If the woman was fully employed by the same employer for a period of two years prior to giving birth, she could take an additional year of leave without pay and return to her same job. During the debate over this provision, a representative of the liberal party speaking for the middle class asked Golda why only one year? Why not two years of leave without pay? Golda's answer disclosed her preference for keeping women in the workforce. She repeated that too many privileges would only backfire:

> To replace the mother another woman may be hired. Why is it just that the new mother will sit at home for two years and the woman

replacing her will only be a temporary worker? She too is a woman and maybe she also has children, why should she be discriminated against? . . . I cannot accept this. They are both equal and they have equal rights"[15]

While Golda was intent on protecting women's rights in the workplace she refused to idealize them. During the debate about protecting pregnant women from being discharged, for instance, she defended her power as minister of labor to permit a worker's dismissal under certain circumstances:

Is it reasonable to hold that because of pregnancy it would be impossible [to fire the employee]? And what if the pregnancy is purposeful [the woman had conceived a child in order to prevent being laid off] or the woman was fraudulent, dishonest or even purposefully harmful to the employer? Indeed, pregnancy and motherhood are great but they do not atone for all sins.[16]

In addition to protections for pregnant women, which served to enhance women's autonomy, the bill also provided women with privileges meant to encourage traditional family life. For example, the bill enacted a prohibition on night shifts under the patriarchal assumption that a wife and mother should be at home with her family during the night. During the debate over this prohibition, Golda allowed her true feelings about the sexist nature of the law to surface. Hanna Lamdan proposed to regulate the night shifts so that the shifts ended at 10:00 P.M. rather than at 11:00 P.M., thereby allowing women to return home before midnight. This suggestion triggered Golda's most memorable line in the debate:

I wish to tell [MK Lamdan], and she will understand. Women, especially, should not view the woman as a *nebechil* [Yiddish for pitifully ineffectual]. A working woman is a working person. If the transportation to and back from work is difficult, it is also hard for the man. It will undermine the working woman if we insist on special conditions that do not apply across the board. The law should treat men and women equally.[17]

Many of Golda's labor policies were similarly conflicted about women's autonomy. She wanted to help the Israeli woman fend for herself and develop agency, but her agenda struggled to come to terms with the concept of the liberated woman, or in some cases with her own rather traditional understanding of family. The resulting program incorporated into law many gross generalizations about women reflecting traditional gender stereotypes. Moreover, significant structural barriers facing women remained untouched. Golda refused to address the issue of equal pay for equal work, even though she was well aware that women were making much less than men for comparable work and that this disadvantage affected their willingness to enter the workforce. Nor did she face the fact that most women in Israel at the time took jobs as seamstresses, waitresses, secretaries, and nurses rather than striving to enter more lucrative fields. It is not clear whether Golda thought she would be able to address these issues later in her career once the fundamental labor program had been adopted, or whether she would have done so had the opportunity presented itself. However, before succumbing to the urge to criticize her too harshly, one must recall the patriarchal environment of the early 1950s.

Golda was surrounded by men. She knew that to retain her position she must not challenge their worldview too aggressively. Her advisers in the ministry of labor were all traditional men who led traditional family lives, even if their wives were professionals or worked outside the home. The same applied to most members of her party and most members of the Knesset. Even had she wanted to push forward a radical view of the role that women should play in society, the political support for such a program simply did not exist. As for the Israeli feminists of the 1950s, they were knowledgeable but powerless. If Golda wanted to keep her job she could not afford to adopt their agenda. Hence her willingness to compromise.

Golda was nevertheless influenced by her fellow feminists. For example, Ada Maimon's principle—that women make up 50 percent of the population and are thus entitled to the same rights as the other 50 percent—was not entirely lost on her. Here is Golda speaking to the Knesset in her feminist voice, a voice she often minimized but never entirely ignored:

Whoever writes our history in this country, the settlement and construction, the defense, the struggle and the war of liberation, the projects concerning health and education, the revival of the Hebrew language—will be obliged to emphasize the role of the woman in our achievements . . . it is inconceivable that the state could give up on the productive power of fifty percent of the population.[18]

With the revival of the women's liberation movement in Israel from the late 1970s onward, labor policy took some major steps toward gender equality. The prohibition on night shifts was repealed, and maternity leave became parental leave, giving parents the power to decide which parent would care for the newborn. Most significantly, in 1988 the government enacted a law requiring equal employment opportunities for women and prohibiting gender-based discrimination, and in 1996 it adopted a law requiring equal pay for equal work regardless of gender. In practice, gender-based discrimination is still widespread, but progress has been made, much of it built on the foundations erected by Golda's initial labor agenda.

CHAPTER 15

ENTER THE "OTHER WOMAN"

Shabbat, the "Sacred Queen," and the Secular Minister of Labor

The state should use its power, as much as possible, to impose the eternal rule of the Shabbat [as decreed by God].

—RABBI YITZHAK MEIR LEVIN

ISRAEL'S DECLARATION of Independence promised freedom of conscience and implied the separation of church and state. This separation was not, for the most part, particularly controversial since in the early 1950s the majority of Israelis were, like Golda, staunch secularists. The version of Zionism embraced by the majority held that Jewish religious practices were archaic, unfit for modern life, and had weakened the community: the myriad system of rules required by Jewish law had created a Jewish consciousness that was meek and subservient and that directly contributed to Jewish misery in the Diaspora.[1] A sovereign state of Israel, many believed, would rid the people of the shackles of religion and thereby encourage their freedom to grow as New Hebrews. To be sure, Zionists did not wish to leave behind the cultural legacy of Judaism. What they wished for was a spiritual transformation, to pour modern content into the old institutions and loosen the traditional constraints. The public expected a cultural revolution and looked to Ben-Gurion and Golda to bring it about.[2] However, one early conflict between the religious and secular elements of the country would result in a series of political crises that ultimately forced the government to call new general elections: the controversy over Shabbat.

The Controversy over the Meaning of Shabbat

In keeping with the recommendations of the International Labor Organization and Theodor Herzl's vision for a progressive Jewish state, the Hours of Work and Day of Rest Bill enshrined in law the eight-hour workday and provided that the Sabbath would be a mandatory day of rest for Jews.[3] A furious religious camp denounced the bill, leveling three criticisms against it: first, they claimed, only an absolute prohibition on the violation of the Sabbath (subject only to exceptions permitted by the Rabbis) would protect the sanctity of the Sabbath; second, they found some of the exceptions to the rule prohibiting work on the Sabbath to be offensive, such as exceptions for transportation and entertainment during the Sabbath, matters particularly irksome to the Orthodox; third, the bill vested the power to issue permits in the minister of labor—a secular authority—which they found unacceptable because it allowed the state to encroach on matters of religion. The fact that the minister happened to be a secular woman—Golda—only added insult to injury.

In the cabinet three male ministers served as representatives of the United Religious Front, a coalition party that brought together the three religious political factions. Of the ministers, Rabbi Leib Fishman Maimon, the minister of religions, was the most prominent and influential. In the Knesset and elsewhere he regularly clashed with his sister, Ada Fishman Maimon, the uncontested leader of Israel's feminist movement.[4] Rabbi Meir Yitzhak Levin, the minister of welfare, was head of the ultra-Orthodox Agudath Yisrael and the esteemed son of the legendary Hassidic Ger dynasty.[5] The Ger Hassidim were sympathetic to Zionism but opposed women's activity in the public sphere. The third religious minister, Moshe Shapira, was a modern Orthodox man who favored the modest adjustments of Jewish practice to the conditions of modernity. These men supported many aspects of the new labor legislation that they saw as promoting values embedded in Jewish law. They were even willing to accept Golda as a cabinet minister—not an easy pill to swallow by any means.[6] But they were uncompromising when it came to the Sabbath. Their speeches in the cabinet and the Knesset revealed the looming presence of that woman of royal pedigree, invisible yet ever present in Jewish consciousness, whom they had to safeguard: Queen Sabbath.

In secular parlance the "day of rest" to which the law referred simply required that employers give workers a day off to recharge their batteries. The Hebrew term, however, also carried deep religious meaning. In religious sources, rest—"menuha"—designates the special spirituality and tranquility associated with the Sabbath, a directive included among the Ten Commandments, a gift God gave to the Jewish people.[7] In order to safeguard that sacred tranquility, the rabbis had created elaborate structures over many generations to prevent human activity on Shabbat. The rabbis had also appointed themselves guardians of these arrangements, the only people with the power to permit exceptions or deviations from rest on the holy day. In the Middle Ages they personified the Sabbath as God's consort, or the Shekhina: God was the King of Kings, and the Sabbath was his "queen."[8] As time passed the arrival of the Sabbath on Friday evening became associated with a marriage ceremony and the Sabbath increasingly resembled a "bride." The rabbis heaped words of praise upon "her": she was radiant, beautiful, pure, a paragon of virtues. No one could mistake the male-centered nature of the devotion to Shabbat. She came to signify patriarchy, tradition, and the inviolability of Jewish law as interpreted by the rabbis.[9] Ahad Ha'am, one of cultural Zionism's most prominent theoreticians, once proclaimed, "More than Jews have safeguarded the Sabbath—the Sabbath has safeguarded them."[10] The Rabbis promised that if only the entire Jewish people observed all the rules of Shabbat for two Saturdays in a row, the messiah would come.[11] By proposing a secular law to regulate the Shabbat, Golda was a woman who failed to know her place and aimed to injure the sacred queen.

Shabbat, Religion, and Golda

The representatives of the United Religious Front insisted that the cabinet discard Golda's bill and adopt a Shabbat law that would dictate strict adherence to the religious requirements of the Sabbath. It was not enough merely to declare that there would be a day of rest and that for Jews it will occur on Saturday; the state needed to honor the Sabbath.[12] Golda and the secular camp remained skeptical. As Zionists they firmly believed that Jewish survival depended on having a sovereign Jewish state whose power did not derive from religious sources. What one camp viewed as a Jewish renaissance the other decried as desecration and profanity.

In Golda's approach to the Sabbath she yet again showed her pragmatic colors. She did not wish to uproot tradition. She valued the institution of Shabbat and merely wanted to transform it to meet the new reality of a progressive Jewish state and its contemporary sensibilities. In her mind a day of rest was associated with culture and the intellectual enrichment of ordinary people, particularly members of the working class. On Shabbat they could attend lectures, concerts, and public meetings, or spend time with family and friends. Such activities would expand their horizons and contribute to their well-being.

Golda, the immigrant child, experienced the impact of the industrial age on both working hours and the day of rest as she moved from Pinsk to the Milwaukee ghetto. In Pinsk the Sabbath was strictly observed. In Milwaukee, by contrast, working-class Jews hungry for employment had no choice but to work for very long hours, day after day, including Saturday. On Friday nights fellow immigrants would assemble in Golda's parents' home, sing Shabbat songs, and feast on her mother's dishes. The next morning, instead of going to synagogue as they did in the old country, they went to work. No one in her community felt it made them less Jewish. Through this experience Golda developed a more flexible understanding of religious requirements as well as compassion for improving the lot of working people.

In addition to her experiences in Milwaukee, another reason Golda favored a flexible approach to the Sabbath is that travel on Shabbat was necessary for her to see family. Since their arrival in Palestine, Golda's family had dispersed to different cities. Sheyna settled in Holon, a town south of Tel Aviv; her parents in Herzlia, north of Tel Aviv; and her daughter Sarah founded Kibbutz Revivim in the Negev. Shabbat was the only day they could visit with each other, and for this they had to travel. No less significant, Golda was a heavy smoker for whom lighting a cigarette on Shabbat was at once a necessity and a pleasure. Why turn the Sabbath into a day of self-deprivation? While Golda did not feel that the law should be tailored to her own needs, she could easily empathize with the average Israeli Jew who was happy to see Shabbat as a day of rest but was unenthusiastic about following its rabbinical constraints.

The Legislative Struggle

In the cabinet and during Knesset deliberations Golda defended her statute. She pointed out that her bill respected Shabbat as well as previous commitments made by the Zionist government to the religious parties. The bill did nothing to disrupt the famous "status quo" compact between Ben-Gurion and Rabbi Fishman Maimon, which committed the government to preserve those arrangements concerning Shabbat that were obtained under the British Mandate.[13] In fact, Golda observed, her bill went even further in accommodating the Sabbath. For example, the bill provided for a day of rest lasting thirty-six hours rather than the conventional twenty-four hours. Work on Friday was drastically curtailed so that workers could return home early to prepare for the Sabbath. She complained repeatedly that the religious ministers were twisting the meaning of the statute, willfully turning it upside down: "One may get the impression" from the rabbis' arguments that at present, "on Shabbat everything comes to a halt, everything is closed, there is no traffic and everyone stays at home; . . . But *vas tut Got* [Yiddish: what did God do?] everything is exactly the opposite." She argued that a significant number of businesses at present remained open on Shabbat but would be required to close under the terms of her bill.[14] She emphasized that only the minister of labor had the power to issue work permits and warned that the religious camp's adherence to dogma would alienate the majority of Israelis and deepen the gap between religious and secular Jews: "I want to say to the religious members of the cabinet: until now the non-religious public was divided. . . . One camp raise[d] the banner of war against religion; now the (anti-religion) camp is growing."[15]

Golda thought that strict enforcement of the Sabbath rules was bad politics because ordinary people would find it hard to accept. But the religious ministers had their own constituency to worry about. Religious groups, increasingly frustrated by the secular advances made by the new state, began to engage in illegal activities. Violent protests, including car burnings, became frequent in Jerusalem. The political fever was reaching a dangerous level and each side felt indignant and misunderstood.

As indicated above, beyond their insistence on a special law that would recognize the full sanctity of Shabbat and thereby officially recognize religion as the law of the land, the United Religious Front also objected to the specific arrangements set by the bill. First, they objected to the list of permits offered by the law.[16] They accepted some justifications for working on Shabbat, such as "danger to the national security," but other exceptions caused an uproar. In particular they were livid that events related to "culture, entertainment, and sport" would be permitted on the Sabbath. Golda rejected the notion that entertainment was necessarily low or vulgar. In keeping with the intellectual thinkers of cultural Zionism, she believed that entertainment could be both highbrow and spiritual. She also took exception to the legal fiction the rabbis had developed that designated some forms of work as "not work" and therefore exempt from prohibition under rabbinical law. Golda challenged the fiction by observing, "You can't rest without someone working to facilitate your rest." For example, she argued, in the synagogue, "Doesn't the Shamash [serviceman at the synagogue] work on Shabbat?" Didn't someone have to move chairs and clean up after the prayer? People were already working on the Sabbath, she argued, and the rabbis were simply turning a blind eye to it.

The United Religious Front was unpersuaded by Golda's objection. To the rabbis, once Jewish law designated "work" as "non-work" that "work" was thereby exempt from the prohibition. The bill was returned to the committee. A political crisis was brewing and Ben-Gurion, trying to keep his coalition together, looked for a compromise. Ultimately, the list of permitted exceptions was discarded and the minister of labor was vested with the authority to issue permits for "needs that the Minister of Labor deems essential to the public or a part of the public."[17]

This proposal, however, only raised the stakes of the religious ministers' other main objection—that the minister of labor as a secular authority should not oversee the issuing of permits. Only a religious authority should be allowed to authorize a violation of the Sabbath. While the religious ministers did not directly mention their discomfort with the fact that the bill gave this power to a woman, their counterproposal revealed their gender bias. The United Religious Front demanded that the Chief Rabbinate alone be put in charge: each request for a permit would be submitted to the chief rabbis who would evaluate the circumstances and pronounce a verdict. No Jewish denomination in the world at this time entertained the idea that a woman could be a rabbi. The replacement of a cabinet minister with a group of rabbis would therefore necessarily result in the exclusion of women, thereby leaving the question of who was allowed to work on the Sabbath entirely in the hands of men.

Golda kept searching for a compromise that would satisfy all parties. She proposed that the minister of labor, while retaining the authority to issue permits, should be legally required to consult with the minister of religions. The United Religious Front rejected her compromise. What if the cabinet had a minister of religions who happened to be a woman? Worse, what if it went to a woman who was a feminist? They even named names, and of all the women in the Knesset, they focused on Rachel Kagan. Their choice was telling. Kagan, the only woman apart from Golda to sign the Declaration of Independence as well as the only representative of the WIZO (Women's International Zionist Organization) Party, personified the agenda of women's rights. Unlike Golda, Kagan was a woman's woman. In the political reality of early 1950s Israel, the hypothetical worry put forward by the religious camp was ludicrous: there was no chance that Kagan would be appointed to the cabinet, let alone as minister of religions. But Kagan's name was a dog whistle. The United Religious Front was signaling discomfort with the very idea of autonomous women acting as high-level decision makers.[18]

The negotiations continued. Ultimately, the bill created a committee of three to handle the matter of permits: the prime minister, the minister of religions, and the minister of labor. Golda was demoted to being only one of three equal votes, her judgment subjected to the approval of at least one man. Patriarchy prevailed. But Golda could still be comforted by the fact that she had held onto some power despite the rabbis' objections. Moreover, Golda and Ben-Gurion saw eye to eye on most issues, so under this arrangement she could expect to have the power to issue the permits she thought appropriate.

As the bill was progressing toward the Knesset vote, each camp drew upon the biblical story of the wood gatherer to challenge its opponent. In laconic fashion the Bible reports that while in the desert on the way to the Promised Land a man was found gathering wood on Shabbat. Moses brought him before God, and the divine verdict was declared: take him outside the camp and have the entire community stone him.[19] The members of the Knesset engaged in a lively debate concerning the proper interpretation of this parable. MK Meir Argov of Mapai, known for his attachment to religious tradition, sparred with Avraham Goldrat of the United Religious Front. Argov asked if Goldrat could "find one verse in the Torah proving that the power of decree concerning Shabbat was delegated to the Rabbis?" To which Goldrat replied, "It says in the Torah that they found a man desecrating the Shabbat by gathering wood, and they came before Moses, not before Golda Meyerson." Another secular member of the Knesset jumped in to point out that God spoke to Moses, the political leader, rather than to Aaron, the priest.[20] The implication was that even in biblical times power rested in the hands of the secular government (the kings) rather than with the rabbis.

It was an age-old controversy. Zionism sought to restore Jewish political leadership as distinct from rabbinical leadership. Hence all laws, including those concerning Shabbat, should be made by the people's representatives and not by unelected rabbis. Another senior member of Mapai, the future president Itzhak Ben-Zvi, took the floor and used the story of the wood gatherer to highlight another lesson. Ben-Zvi admonished the religious members of the Knesset: "You no longer practice the punishment of stoning because you yourselves concede that life has changed. The Knesset is merely taking this lesson one step further. We want to keep the Shabbat as a day of rest, and merely adjust it to contemporary conditions." There is a cardinal principle guiding Jewish law,

Ben-Zvi insisted—the purpose of law is to enhance life. Transformation, not stagnation, should be their guide. Therefore, Ben-Zvi concluded, the United Religious Front should support rather than oppose the flexibility displayed in the new bill.[21]

During the heat of battle and probably realizing that ad hominem attacks might help in the upcoming elections, the members of the opposition escalated their attacks, targeting Golda in particular. A member of the right-wing Herut Party lamented: "How sad it is that the Shabbat will be desecrated in so many areas, and who will decide? The labor minister (Sara) whose attachment to Shabbat Malkata is known to us, and she is very far from having the spirit of understanding and love of the traditional Jewish sacred assets. . . . Shabbat will be mortally wounded."[22] Avraham Shag of the United Religious Front went so far as to fault Golda for being ashamed of being Jewish. The minister of labor, he said, was correct to point out that the Jewish Nation was the first to introduce a day of rest as well as fair labor standards. But why did she fail to mention that the source of these principles is the Torah? Why did she merely refer to "ancient [Jewish] texts"? He surmised that Golda's need to deploy such a euphemism indicated that she must have felt uncomfortable with her Jewish heritage.[23] Golda was stung, which might explain why she took the bait. A veteran of political debates, she was generally quite careful in choosing her arguments. In this moment, however, she unleashed her old contentious self, that of Goldie the teenager arguing with her mother. She responded that no one could doubt her Jewish pride: "Rabbi Shag unfairly hurt my feelings. . . . I want to tell him that indeed I have many faults, but I do not fear my Jewishness. I do not have this fault."[24]

As the disagreement grew more contentious, metaphorical talk of violence became increasingly common. Minister Moshe Shapira of the United Religious Front observed, "We are entering a very dangerous field, full of landmines"; Ben-Gurion warned, "Your demands will blow up this cabinet"; and the minister of religions accused the secularists of intending to "blow up the Shabbat." None of these men realized that as they were throwing these metaphors at each other, a small underground movement of religious men and women calling themselves "The Covenant of the Zealots" (Brit Ha-Kanaim) were plotting a terrorist attack on the Knesset itself. On May 14, 1951, one day before the third anniversary of Israel's independence, two controversial laws were brought before the Knesset for final approval: the Women's Draft bill and the Hours of Work and Day of Rest bill. That same day two ultra-Orthodox men were arrested as they entered the Knesset with homemade incendiary devices. Fortunately, they were caught before they were able to detonate the bombs.[25]

The Hours of Work and Rest Act passed by a small majority the following day. In the struggle between Golda and Queen Shabbat, the minister of labor had gained the upper hand. One would like to think that in that moment Golda realized that she too was a queen. At age fifty-four she was a rising political figure with considerable power. She stood her ground against Orthodox men and, in this round at least, she prevailed. Golda would encounter opposition from religious parties time and again during her long career, most notably with respect to the question of Jewish identity.[26]

Soon after these events Ben-Gurion asked Golda to take a leave from her beloved ministry of labor in order to run as Mapai's candidate for mayor of Tel Aviv. Always putting the interests of the party ahead of her own, Golda acquiesced. In that race the religious parties had the advantage and they would not tolerate the idea of a woman running Tel Aviv. In her memoirs Golda lamented that the religious parties' deep opposition to her "because I was a woman was a political tactic for which I had great contempt. . . . Suffice it to say that no easy way was ever found of getting around the place of religion in the Jewish State. It bedeviled us then, and to some degree it bedevils us now."[27]

Golda returned to the ministry of labor where she remained until Prime Minister Ben-Gurion decided to sack the independent-minded minister of foreign affairs, Moshe Sharett. Beyond a mere clash of personalities there was a more pressing reason for this move: war was at the gate and Ben-Gurion needed someone who would implement his policy. Golda was the ideal fit for the position although it was not easy for her to leave a position she had enjoyed like no other. Reflecting on this period, Golda wrote, "My seven years in the Ministry of Labor were, without doubt, the most satisfying and the happiest in my life."[28]

CHAPTER 16

GOLDA'S APPOINTMENT AS MINISTER OF FOREIGN AFFAIRS, 1956

A Crazy Vessel Riding on Wicked Waves in a Stormy Sea

One would need considerable long-term vision, courage and deep understanding of the real . . . circumstances of foreign affairs—in order to lead this crazy ship through the wicked waves of a stormy sea towards the safe harbor.

—DAVID BEN-GURION

In June 1956 Golda's life profoundly changed. Her appointment as the minister of foreign affairs catapulted her onto the world stage where she was responsible for representing her country's affairs. The new role brought Golda international attention, enhanced her status within the government, and shifted the focus of her political activity from utopian Zionism to the complex realm of foreign affairs. If her work so far had required balancing the ideals of social justice with the constraints of practicality, such as the state budget or the needs of the private sector, her new work required the hardheaded principles of realpolitik. She would need to befriend leaders who endorsed values and practices different from and even antithetical to her own: authoritarian dictators, religious fundamentalists, and American political hawks who had very little use for Israel except as an instrument in fighting the Cold War.

Still only in her mid-fifties, Golda began cultivating the image of the "grandmother of the Jewish people," an image that became her trademark for the remainder of her life. Ben-Gurion asked Golda to make another striking change to her identity: he wanted her to change her name from Myerson to Meir. In keeping with Zionist ideology, he believed that the Ministry of Foreign Affairs should symbolize the New Hebrew people who had revived their ancient homeland, a revival that included the adoption of Hebrew names. Golda had resisted the pressure to Hebraize her name since she had arrived in Palestine more than thirty years earlier, but at Ben-Gurion's request she acquiesced. Meir was a short version of Myerson, or Meirson as it was spelled in Hebrew. But Meir was also Morris's Hebrew name, and at home she called him Meirke (a term of endearment for Meir). The irony was sublime: a man (her boss) gave her the name of another man (her husband), whom she had left to pursue her career.

The Road to War

Israel was tiny, fledgling, insecure, and poor. It was a state yearning for peace, yet hesitant to make any painful concessions to the surrounding Arab states.[1] In order to send a message that the new kid on the block would not be intimidated, Ben-Gurion and his military command were determined to meet every violent attack on Israel with a swift and punitive response. Doing so, they believed, was the only way its Arab neighbors would come to accept the new state. The United Nations Security Council repeatedly condemned the Israeli reprisals. At the same time that the Cold War was raging, the Soviet Union completed its radical shift from being one of Israel's earliest supporters—the third country to recognize Israel's statehood—to being a close ally of the Arab world.

In 1955 Egypt and Czechoslovakia, with the blessing of the Soviet Union, signed an arms deal supplying offensive weapons to Egypt. The deal violated the Tripartite Agreement entered into by the United States, Britain, and France, which barred arms sales to the warring parties in the Middle East. To complicate matters, a new international group led by India—known as the Non-Aligned Nations—was also courting favor with the Arab world and remained frosty toward Israel. Few nations were willing to join Israel in denouncing the deal.[2] These were the wicked waves to which Ben-Gurion referred when he called for a savvy minister of foreign affairs to lead the "crazy ship" toward a safe harbor. And he was convinced that Moshe Sharett, the current minister of foreign affairs, was not the right man for the job.

Sharett, Golda's predecessor, was a founding father of the state as well as the author of its declaration of independence. A gentle, educated man, he emphasized diplomacy in the realm of foreign policy and advocated in favor of a restrained military posture. Sharett was no naive pacifist but thought Israel should exhaust all diplomatic avenues before choosing aggression. The cabinet deliberations between 1955 and 1956 included intense internal debate over these matters. Twice Sharett led a majority of the cabinet to oppose Ben-Gurion's proposals for military action. The cabinet also took Sharett's recommendation that cabinet approval be required prior to major military attacks.[3] These developments did not sit well with Ben-Gurion, who felt that the circumstances justified centralizing war powers in his office.

Against this background and with Sharett's full support, Israel was frantically searching for a country willing to sell it weapons. France had emerged as a potential trading partner and, by 1955, had agreed to sell Israel substantial quantities of arms, including state-of-the art combat airplanes and tanks. As the French and Israeli defense establishments grew closer to one another, the French asked the Israelis for a favor— help its effort to keep Algeria under French rule. The war in Algeria was intensifying and France was trying to maintain control over its beloved colony. Egypt's charismatic president, Gamal Abdel Nasser, was causing France trouble. Nasser encouraged the Algerian rebels, and once his military received Soviet arms, he even supplied the rebels with Egypt's former weapons. If Israel helped France neutralize Nasser, the Algerian rebels would have a harder time fighting the French.

Nasser was also Israel's enemy. His inflammatory speeches, which promised the swift and decisive elimination of the Jewish state, electrified Arab crowds and put a chill in the hearts of Israelis. Frequent violent raids across Israel's borders amplified the fear of an Arab invasion.[4]

This dynamic made the French and Israelis natural allies, yet only a few top decision makers in Israel were aware of a tantalizing opportunity. France indicated that it would assist Israel in building a nuclear plant. Ben-Gurion, afraid that Sharett might gather a majority of the cabinet to undermine the emerging deal with France, concluded that Sharett had to go. Golda became his choice for minister of foreign affairs.[5]

Why Golda?

When she was offered the job Golda felt conflicted. She enjoyed her work as minister of labor and was fully aware that many would view her willingness to take Sharett's place as an opportunistic betrayal. She must also have had personal misgivings about Sharett's dismissal. She and Sharett had worked side by side as midwives delivering the State of Israel. If Mapai was her home and family, as she had always stated, how could she justify the rather brutal banishment of a senior relative? She knew that just as the Ministry of Labor was her creation, so the Ministry of Foreign Affairs was Sharett's. How could she do this to him?

In addition to feeling conflicted, Golda also stated that the decision had taken her by surprise. "I couldn't believe my ears," she wrote. However, it is unlikely that the appointment caught Golda unaware, insofar as she and Ben-Gurion almost certainly discussed the possibility behind closed doors before any decision was announced. Her reported feelings of "conflict and surprise" were a cover for the political maneuvers as well as for her burning ambition.

Here again one sees Golda's gender come into play. The higher up the political ladder Golda ascended, the more difficult it became for others to accept her as a bona fide leader; the harder it became for others to accept her, the more she tried to cloak herself in self-effacement and humility, going so far as to deny knowledge of the events that brought her to her position. Golda's inner self-doubt exacerbated the problem. Because of her poor childhood, lack of education, and highly critical mother, Golda remained conflicted about her abilities. On the one hand, she wanted the job and felt she had the wherewithal to master it. On the other hand, she feared she lacked the necessary talents and knew that many shared this feeling. Golda must have felt that given these circumstances it was best to hide her ambition.

Golda was proving herself to be an "alpha woman." A few months prior she graciously accepted the nomination to run for mayor of Tel Aviv for the good of the party. Now that she had been offered a job she actually wanted, she was willing to do what was unpleasant but necessary to obtain it—turn her back on an old colleague. Golda knew that some would think a woman did not belong in foreign affairs, a rather masculine domain in politics, so she retained the modest posture of a woman suddenly pushed into position. To her comrades she gave the ultimate feminine excuse gilded in self-sacrifice: "If Ben-Gurion asked me to jump from the fifth floor—I would."[6] Though perhaps unaware of the fact, she was also making a prescient prediction about her political future: as the minister of foreign affairs, she would blindly follow Ben-Gurion's preferences.

Gender, Those "Wicked Waves"

When Ben-Gurion appointed Golda he never explicitly considered whether the appointment would inflame misogynistic attitudes. The myth of gender equality promoted by Israel's founding documents perhaps covered up stereotypes lurking beneath the surface. But those stereotypes were pervasive and they shaped the political atmosphere during Golda's tenure as Israel's top diplomat.

A few months into her service as minister of foreign affairs, as Golda was in New York leading a desperate battle to prevent U.S. and UN sanctions against Israel for invading Egypt, she received news that back in Israel none other than Ben-Gurion had publicly shamed her:

> I am sure that Golda will not be angry and will not disagree with me if I say that the comrade who preceded her [Sharett] . . . was superior to her in his extensive experience in Israeli and international affairs, in his general and Jewish education as well as in several other talents. But Golda, in addition to her unique talent, had one advantage . . . she had no experience in foreign affairs.[7]

Ben-Gurion's hurtful speech echoed reflections that Sharett recorded in his private diary:

> It is impossible to understand this great woman, neither from the perspective of her own self-interest nor from the perspective of her duty towards a friend. She knows well that this task is above her head, my experience and acquaintance of years lead me to the conclusion that she suffers from a deep inferiority complex for being only half educated—she is very sensitive to her limitations rooted in lack of education, inability to articulate her thoughts in writing, her incapacity to prepare a proper speech ... [and] define a political position.[8]

While Ben-Gurion refrained from mentioning Golda's gender, Sharett's reflection went straight for the jugular when he sarcastically referred to her as "this great woman." Some of Sharett's descriptions were, however, accurate. Golda always felt ashamed about her lack of education, the source of a lifelong inferiority complex, and struggled to express herself in writing, perhaps because she never studied it methodically. Sharett later leaked that during a three-day briefing session in his office Golda listened carefully but did not put pen to paper even once.

The press was equally unfavorable. In *Davar*, a well-known columnist denounced Sharett's dismissal as bad for party and country, adding that "she who replaced him must know this." The refusal to recognize Golda by name was dripping with contempt, perhaps for all women who sought power.[9] In the right-wing media, Isaac Remba, a noted columnist, offered a devastating appraisal of Golda's faults: "The political cargo she brings to the foreign office does not attest to broad horizons, to an ability to foresee the future, to vision and energetic leverage, to intuition and an expansive spirit." He also drew upon popular stereotypes of women: "Is it true that women can hate more than men? If it is true, Golda is the classic example to prove this thesis."[10] Remba's speculative observation about the capacity of women to hate struck a chord with the patriarchal Israeli public. It would reappear in different variations in future years.

Both Ben-Gurion and Sharett should have known better than to say that Golda lacked foreign affairs experience. She had worked alongside

Sharett throughout the period preceding the creation of the state and often served on the Israeli delegation to the United Nations. She was fluent in English, chosen to negotiate with King Abdullah in 1948, served as Israel's emissary to Moscow, and was frequently sent on missions to galvanize American Jews. She was anything but an inexperienced woman.

Meanwhile turmoil descended on the Ministry of Foreign Affairs. The senior staff remained committed to Sharett and his style of governance. Many felt that Golda was not the right candidate for the job, and some even threatened to resign. The ministry had long resisted the integration of women into its diplomatic staff and in its eyes Golda should not even have been considered for the post. The year after Golda's appointment, Walter Eytan, the director general of the Ministry of Foreign Affairs, wrote: "There is no rule against sending women to responsible posts abroad. . . . If in practice women are now sent to such posts but rarely, it is for their own sakes." He continued in this vein: "Women do, however, play an important part in the Foreign Service—as their husbands' wives."[11] Golda was aware of this culture when she accepted the position. Yet she did not make any effort to break the prevailing bias against women. She was preoccupied with her own survival. As she wrote of her arrival at the ministry: "I made my appearance at the ministry . . . all by myself, feeling and probably looking miserable."[12]

The Ordeal of Transition

Sharett was convinced that Golda had betrayed him. His dismissal could never have happened, he believed, without her maneuvering behind the scenes. Perhaps this feeling, too, can be traced to their respective genders. Had a man been selected to replace him would Sharett have felt equally "betrayed"? Would he have attributed the man's actions to low moral character or rather to a shrewd political sense?

A man proud of his sensitivity to protocol, Sharett publicly shamed Golda by refusing to participate in the formal transfer of power. Golda arrived at the ministry feeling lonely and dejected. She felt like an alien, unwanted and undervalued by the senior staff, who were all Oxford and

Cambridge graduates. Their English accents differed from her Midwestern accent, and her lack of "refinement" contrasted with their polished style. One must marvel at her courage and tenacity as Golda was forced to master complex issues of diplomacy and foreign affairs without having the benefit of a staff she could trust. Despite the considerable obstacles in her path, Golda was determined to prove that she could succeed in the job.

CHAPTER 17

GOLDA'S FIRST INTERNATIONAL CRISIS

The Nationalization of the Suez Shipping Company

GOLDA HAD barely settled into office when Gamal Abdel Nasser, Egypt's charismatic president, shook the international order by announcing the nationalization of the Suez Shipping Company. Before nationalization the company had been owned primarily by France and England, and it built and managed the vital shipping line between Europe and Asia. The two declining colonial powers viewed the move as a serious threat to their hegemony.[1]

In her public speeches Golda tried to advise the public that war was imminent. Her rhetoric was neither nuanced nor complex. In what came to be known as "Golda's style," she painted a world with wicked and just actors. Israel, of course, was on the side of the just. Egypt, she explained, intended to annihilate Israel; a war of survival was nearing. Using clever rhetoric—calling Nasser "Colonel" (his military rank before the officers' coup) and referring to him as "the dictator"—she implied that Israel was not only defending its self-interests but also leading the democratic fight against tyranny.[2] Golda was quite capable of nuanced analysis and did not herself see the world as divided between bad guys and good guys. But in these speeches she saw it as her obligation to persuade the public that the upcoming war was not only inevitable, but also just.

The fact that Ben-Gurion sent Golda as the head of the delegation to Paris to discuss joining France and Britain's alliance against Egypt is telling. The delegation included his confidante at the ministry of defense, Shimon Peres, and his chief of staff, Moshe Dayan. Both men aggressively advocated war. Ben-Gurion expected Golda to reach an objective evaluation of the ramifications of the alliance for Israel. And so it was that less than three months after her appointment, with a detailed memorandum of "dos and don'ts" in her bag, Golda boarded a worn World War II French military naval aircraft destined for Paris.

The French Connection

Golda later described the aircraft as "rickety" and "very badly lit."[3] Designed to carry antisubmarine bombs, it was sparsely furnished with small stools instead of chairs. The passengers were forced to sit on top of pipes or on the floor. Golda, however, was seated next to the pilot. Seven and a half uncomfortable hours later they had a brief layover at a French military base located in Bizerte, Tunisia. In her autobiography Golda dedicated only one paragraph to the trip, in which she noted the utter astonishment among those assembled to greet them when an elderly woman emerged from the belly of the old aircraft. Golda was again otherized, perceived as an alien because of her gender.

Once the shabby bomber had completed its journey to France, the small delegation was treated like royalty. They were driven to the sumptuous royal chateau of Saint-Germain-en-Laye and their hosts, mostly high-ranking generals, attempted to seduce their provincial guests with gourmet meals, superb wines, and beautiful presentations and table settings the likes of which the Israelis had never before encountered. It appears, however, that Golda was not swayed by their flattery. The memorandum Ben-Gurion had given to Golda before her departure was clear: Israel would not start the war; further, it was imperative to inform the United States of any plans against Egypt.[4] He wanted Golda to ask questions: If Israel joined the alliance, what kind of relationship would

Israel have with France? What role would the British play? In addition to Moshe Dayan and Shimon Peres, both set on war, the only other Israeli delegate in attendance was Moshe Carmel, a hard-line former military leader who leaned in their direction. Golda headed the delegation, yet she was alone.

During the discussion, Golda's views were mostly ignored. In a last-minute attempt to win her over, the French prime minister, Guy Mollet, joined the meeting. But Golda was unmoved by ceremonious gestures and she stuck to the instructions in Ben-Gurion's memo. Her speech to the assembled guests emphasized that no course of action had yet been decided and that the political complexity of the matters at hand must be addressed before concrete plans were made. She voiced Israel's concerns, particularly the fear that acting behind Eisenhower's back would cause a backlash and might even result in sanctions against Israel. She also expressed worries that the Soviet Union would rise to defend its Arab partners and punish Israel.

The "weirdness" of having a woman in their midst was a recurrent topic during the meeting. Mordechai Bar-On, a handsome young Israeli officer who recorded the minutes of the meetings (and later became the foremost chronicler of the Suez War) confided in his diary: "Lovely atmosphere . . . The French keep making fun of their ministry of foreign affairs . . . and . . . do not spare jibes, kindly and full of humor towards Golda. The fact that she is a woman holding such high office does not square with their modus operandi."[5]

Upon her return to Israel, Golda submitted a report that strengthened Ben-Gurion's initial hesitations. The defense establishment was furious. Dayan, Peres, and their entourage were eager to go to war, perhaps viewing the promise of another shipment of sophisticated weapons or assistance with a nuclear plant as too good to refuse, or perhaps itching to display Israeli prowess with the weapons they had just received.[6]

Dayan and Peres persuaded Ben-Gurion to exclude Golda from the next round of talks with the French, so Golda remained in Jerusalem when Ben-Gurion, notwithstanding his grave misgivings, signed what later came to be known as the "collusion" agreement.[7] The agreement stipulated that Israel, using its newly acquired military might, would be the first to attack Egypt and thereby the first to violate the UN Charter prohibition on preventive wars. Britain and France were to follow shortly, using Israel's invasion as an excuse to protect the disrupted international shipping in the canal.

Even though these developments went against Golda's better judgment she did not use her considerable political power to oppose them. To the contrary, in the cabinet meeting on October 28, 1956, she voted in favor of launching the attack. Ben-Gurion's decision to appoint Golda in Sharett's place had worked out just as he had hoped.

October 28, the Cabinet Authorizes a Preventive War

After flying to France to sign the Sevre Agreement, Ben-Gurion was running a high fever when he arrived at the fateful cabinet meeting of October 28 to approve the war.[8] Following the authorization vote, Golda demonstrated organizational skill as well as maternal concern by suggesting that Ben-Gurion appoint an advisory committee to assist him. Ben-Gurion, in a weak and irritable state, snapped: "I can't do it and I don't want to do it. Golda, you can't imagine the size of the moral mountains weighing on me. . . . I feel that all the responsibility is on me." Golda remained calm. "Perhaps you leave . . . [and] in your absence we shall choose several members to stand by you." He was fretting like a boy rather than acting like a leader ready for war, whereas she kept her cool and adopted a caring and supportive attitude toward the prime minister. Perhaps that is one reason he wanted her by his side and why there was always such a high level of trust between them.

Golda's arguments in support of a preventive war hewed to the party line and ignored the crucial fact that Israel would be the first to violate the UN Charter. Gone were her grave doubts concerning the "deal" with the Western powers, her insistence that Israel could not afford to act behind the back of the United States, and her sophisticated analysis of the international scene that so impressed Christian Pineau, France's minister of foreign affairs. Golda was now speaking like a party hack, blindly supporting her prime minister. While she admitted to the cabinet that "we are sailing into uncharted water," she maintained, using a justification that abided by the UN Charter, that "our lives are in danger and we must choose life."[9] She thus transformed the war of choice into a war of self-defense. As to the consequences of Israel's invasion she conceded that the Security Council might condemn Israel, but she advised that it was a price worth paying. No one on the Israeli team nor at the prime minister's office anticipated the clever trick that Secretary of State John Foster Dulles would deploy in wresting power from the Security Council and vesting it in the volatile, anti-Israel General Assembly.

Even though Golda was the minister of foreign affairs, she offered not a word about the expected American objections and other predictable international complications of which she was clearly aware. Whereas other cabinet ministers argued vigorously about the legality of the war as well as its merits and pitfalls, Golda merely marshaled arguments in its favor, dodging her duty to give her fellow ministers her expert advice. Loyalty to Ben-Gurion trumped her better judgment as well as the responsibilities of her office. She even told the cabinet that two days earlier she had visited the troops with the chief of staff and found them enthusiastic and battle ready. (She did not disclose that she had used the trip to visit her daughter's kibbutz where, prompted by her maternal instincts, she breached the strict secrecy surrounding the war and advised the kibbutzniks to "dig a few more trenches" around the settlement.)[10] Golda knew that many of the soldiers would be sent to their deaths. Switching to Yiddish, as she always did when she spoke spontaneously, she shared her agony: "Hat mir gegeben a riss im hertzen" (I have a tear in my heart). Golda and Ben-Gurion were working hand in hand but they were speaking in different voices. Ben-Gurion, speaking of the "moral mountains" on his shoulders, adopted a cerebral approach, while Golda spoke straight from her heart.

From a military standpoint, the Sinai Campaign (as Israelis called the Suez War) was executed gloriously. In seven days Israel conquered the entire Sinai Peninsula, the Gaza Strip, and the Straits of Tiran. Ben-Gurion was so thrilled that in his speech to the Knesset he drew a direct line between the campaign and the biblical stories recorded in the Book of Exodus. The ecstasy was short-lived. An intense international crisis quickly unfolded and Golda, unprepared and developing a kidney problem, was thrown into the deep end of the pool.

New York, Winter 1956

As Golda feared, the decision to launch a war behind President Eisenhower's back and in defiance of his explicit messages provoked significant backlash. Feeling betrayed, Eisenhower was unforgiving, perhaps driven by a desire to take revenge. He demanded an immediate cease-fire and withdrawal of troops from Egyptian territory. Within a week, the prime minister of the Soviet Union, Nikolai Bulganin, followed suit. Not only did the Soviets recall their ambassador from Tel Aviv, but they also threatened Israel's very existence if it did not immediately withdraw. In New York, Dag Hammarskjöld, the UN secretary-general, argued that the Suez War was a direct threat to the rule of international law as envisioned by the United Nations Charter. Britain and France immediately complied as they were unwilling to withstand the severe results of U.S. sanctions.[11] Israel also began a withdrawal, but it did so incrementally in hope of retaining some of the conquered territory.

United They Stood

Britain, France, and Israel expected business as usual: the Security Council would convene, a harshly worded resolution might be drafted, and the resolution would instantly be killed by a French or British veto. However, Secretary of State John Foster Dulles had a trick up his sleeve: the United We Stand Resolution. Six years earlier, during the Korean War, the UN found itself in a similar situation as the Soviets attempted to derail the Security Council's powers. To remedy the situation, the UN and the U.S. crafted the United We Stand Resolution. The resolution empowered a majority of the members of the Security Council to delegate powers to the General Assembly, thereby making the transfer immune to veto.

Israel and its allies were astonished to see the resolution revived.[12] Had Ben-Gurion, Golda, or their British and French counterparts consulted with their international lawyers they might have anticipated this possibility. But given their commitment to secrecy they had not brought their legal experts into the fold. The assembly had formidable powers to deal with a disobedient member. It could impose sanctions that would threaten a country's economic survival, it could suspend a recalcitrant country's membership in the UN, or it could even expel the member entirely. These were measures that Israel—eight years old, poor, and thirsty for recognition—could hardly afford to face.

Golda entered this storm only months into her tenure as minister of foreign affairs. She anxiously arrived in New York where she found a demoralized Israeli delegation. They had been subjected to overt hostility from Hammarskjöld, the press, and their fellow delegates. Displaying her characteristic firmness in the face of adversity, a trait for which she would soon become famous, she urged the delegation (and perhaps herself) to resist demoralization: "It is imperative that we do not create the impression that we are depressed and that we do not speak to people. To the contrary, we must launch a campaign to spread our position in an emphatically firm manner."[13] In consultation with Ben-Gurion and her staff, she devised a strategy of action. Israel would fight along four fronts: American public opinion, Congress, the Eisenhower administration (Secretary of State John Foster Dulles, in particular), and finally the American Jewish Community. Golda was familiar with Hammarskjöld and considered him hopelessly hostile to the Israeli point of view. She therefore felt that it would be best for Israel to concentrate its battle outside the walls of the United Nations. She calculated that if the American public would stand behind Israel, then Eisenhower and his administration would abandon the idea of unilateral sanctions and prevail upon the United Nations to tone down its aggressive stance.

Life as a Humble Female Minister of Foreign Affairs

Golda arrived in New York carrying with her a variety of ailments, from kidney stones to low blood pressure to lung and heart problems. She smoked more than two packs of cigarettes a day, drank too much coffee, and slept far too little. When Ben-Gurion was sick his wife Paula watched over him, making sure he rested and limiting his visitors. But Golda had no spouse to look after her and even if she did, it is unlikely that a man would have taken on such responsibilities in the 1950s. Moreover, she had never considered her personal well-being a priority and perceived her needs to be subordinate to the needs of the state. Near the end of January 1957, for example, Golda was hospitalized in New York City and "the doctor ordered a week's complete rest."[14] She ignored her condition and attended to her political responsibilities.

She also "suffered" from a "proletarian mentality." She was accustomed to a frugal, ascetic existence and was reluctant to take advantage of amenities that would burden the state budget. When she traveled she had to be persuaded to bring a secretary with her or to check into a comfortable hotel.[15] According to Esther Herlitz, the Israeli consul in New York at the time, Golda did not frequent hairdressing salons. Washing her hair had always been a ritual but one she performed in the hotel room, by herself.[16] As head of the Israeli delegation to the UN, she stayed in a suite in the Essex House close to Central Park and insisted that the suite include a kitchenette. She would buy food, tea and coffee, and prepare snacks, sometimes even meals in that suite, and entertain friends and officials. Unlike the Israeli diplomat Abba Eban, whose sophisticated wife Suzy presided over an extensive social network, Golda acted as both the "official" and the "official's wife." Many times, she jokingly observed that life would be much easier if she had a wife.[17]

In an article in *Good Housekeeping* magazine published in July 1957, Golda described her lifestyle during the long weeks away from home: "Room service usually seems unnecessarily complicated and elaborate. So I often have an arrangement for light cooking in my suite. Sometimes we even have spur-of-the-moment dinner parties, and in New York I've found very useful those little chickens you can buy already roasted." Golda's decision to forgo room service was in part simply a matter of her humble and thrifty nature. But it was also a calculated political move: she was presenting herself as a plain housewife in addition to being a minister of foreign affairs.

From Housewife to Grandmother of the Jewish People

Golda was aware that she had an "image problem." Following World War II, American women were expected to get married, settle down, and enjoy domestic life. A woman serving as minister of foreign affairs and particularly one leading a public relations campaign on behalf of her beleaguered country defied conventional expectations.[18] With this problem in mind, some of Golda's decisions regarding her self-presentation can be seen as canny maneuvers, several of which proved quite successful.

First she began to take advantage of her middle age. As an "older woman" Golda was not expected to meet any exacting beauty standard and she became less threatening to both men and women. Her children were now raising their own families and she began to make public use of the fact that she was a grandmother. She talked lovingly about her grandchildren and released photographs of herself in their company. Americans loved the entire package. They ignored the history of her marital status, never inquired about whether she had a companion or lover, and in due course came to ignore her sexuality entirely. Golda had successfully transformed herself into "the grandmother of the Jewish people."

She also made a point of proving to her American audience that while she was a very busy minister of foreign affairs she did not neglect her housekeeping duties. *Life* magazine published a series of photos of Golda in her kitchen, taken by gifted Israeli photographer David Rubinger. The photos were certainly contrived: they show Golda standing in the kitchen of her official ministry apartment in Jerusalem preparing for a diplomatic dinner. Dressed in a large apron and high-heeled shoes, she was shown tasting her creation like a dutiful chef. In another photograph she is standing by the dinner table like a good housewife checking on name tags and other details before the guests arrive. One assumes that as a busy public official Golda most likely had her staff perform these chores, but the photographs endeared her to the American public. Golda knew that conforming to the image that people hoped to see would work to her advantage, so she put vanity aside and embraced the role of the good woman.

While Golda presented the image of the "woman who could do it all" to the public, official duties often forced her to neglect her family's needs. In January 1957, for example, Golda flew to Israel to brief Ben-Gurion and the cabinet on Israel's precarious international situation. Flying was bad for her health, but in addition to her political obligations she had personal reasons for undertaking the arduous journey. Her daughter Sarah, living on her kibbutz in Negev, was about to give birth to her second child. Sarah's medical history was complicated and Golda was worried. She ached to be with her daughter. At a cabinet meeting in Jerusalem on January 12, she announced, "I cannot fly back." But her work in the United States was essential and Ben-Gurion and the ministers, all men, had little sympathy for Golda's obligations as a mother and grandmother. Her plea to remain in Israel fell on deaf ears as family matters faded in comparison with reasons of state. Her daughter Sarah delivered a healthy baby boy, but mother and daughter again had to forgo the joy of bonding. Nevertheless, the public image of Golda as the loving grandmother continued to work its magic.

The Battle of the Diplomats

In New York Golda presented Israel's diplomatic defense: if Israel were to withdraw from Gaza it needed assurances that Egypt would stop its guerrilla warfare along Israel's southern border, which inflicted violence on Israel's population in the Negev. Moreover, any withdrawal from the Straits of Tiran must be accompanied by international guarantees that Israel would have continued access to shipping routes.[19]

At her side during the negotiations was the formidable Israeli ambassador to the United States and to the United Nations, Abba Eban, a former Cambridge don who was an expert in history and international law, versed in ten languages, and a bon vivant.[20] The two diplomats were like oil and water. Golda knew that Ben-Gurion admired Eban's abilities and resented the fact that following her appointment as minister of foreign affairs Ben-Gurion appointed Eban to be her personal adviser at the ministry. Eban, too, did not harbor much affection or admiration for Golda. Their public attitudes toward one another generally remained cool and aloof. In private, however, neither hesitated to take a swipe at the other. It may well be that Ben-Gurion had adopted a deliberate "divide and conquer" policy, exacerbating the tension between them. Be that as it may, the two rose to the occasion and put the interests of the state ahead of self-interested calculations.

In addition to the staff at the Ministry of Foreign Affairs, Golda and Eban had a variety of reinforcements in New York: two public relations firms—Kenmore Associates and Edward Gottlieb and Associates—and scores of friends in high circles, including journalists, media leaders, senators, and members of the House of Representatives. Clearly, "it took a village" to fend off Israel's many detractors and reverse the anti-Israel climate.

The Strategy, "Assurances and Guarantees"

The Jewish community in America was initially flabbergasted by the invasion. "How dare you?" blasted Rose Halprin, then acting chairwoman of the Jewish Agency and one of the Zionist leaders of the 1950s, to Israel's New York consul Esther Herlitz.[21] Israel's invasion had taken place eight days before the U.S. presidential election, which appeared like sheer chutzpah on the part of tiny, needy Israel as well as a great embarrassment to American Jews, many of whom voted for Eisenhower. The Jewish community was torn between its growing devotion to the State of Israel and its desire to stand with the president and hero of the Allied victory in World War II, whose declared mission was to protect world peace.

Golda deserves credit for uniting the broad spectrum of the Jewish organizations behind a demand for a tempered U.S. policy toward Israel. She cast a wide net, building a coalition that included everyone from prominent opinion makers to labor leaders to ordinary American Jews. In her memoirs, Herlitz recalled that one day the union of the bagel bakers in New York (Local 338) called the consulate to find out if they should discontinue the baking of bagels with onions because the onions were imported from Egypt.[22] American Jews, while initially dismayed by the decision to go to war, stood firmly behind Israel. Golda also used her connections with other centers of society. Because of her long-term activism in the international labor movement she had close contacts with the AFL-CIO (American Federation of Labor and Congress of Industrial Organizations). American labor leaders listened to her pleas and urged President Eisenhower to take a more nuanced position. The support of these groups affected the U.S. response.

In the beginning, most major papers along with national radio and television stations were critical of the Suez War. Golda exploited those "opinion makers" at the top, including Walter Lippmann and the *New York Times* Washington bureau chief James Reston, by appealing to their hawkish support of the Cold War. These cold warriors were already casting doubt on the policy of punishing Britain and France, long-standing U.S. allies and NATO members, a policy they believed strengthened not only Egypt but also the Soviet Union. Their analysis helped bring others into the fold, such as the Republican leader Henry Luce, owner of the *Time–Life* magazine empire and his wife Claire Booth Luce, a savvy and well-known politician in her own right who undoubtedly had a say in giving Golda widespread exposure in the pages of *Life*. Golda also reached across the aisle to Eleanor Roosevelt—a pillar of American liberalism and mother of the Universal Declaration of Human Rights. Golda particularly appreciated the assistance of the women who came around to support Israel's position, which was in keeping with her general inclination over the years to value the companionship of women.[23]

With public opinion increasingly in Israel's favor, Golda trained her gaze on the United States government. She aimed to persuade the administration to abandon its insistence on full and unconditional Israeli withdrawal and to adopt a policy that would allow Israel to preserve some of its territorial gains. Her strategy of attack involved reaching out to members of Congress who would, in turn, put pressure on the administration. Not all of her targets were attractive bedfellows for progressive, socialist Israelis, but Golda was practicing realpolitik and she had no room for moral scruples. She was making new friends and moving in unfamiliar circles. It was one thing to befriend people like Abba Hillel Silver (the Republican Jewish leader who often criticized

Ben-Gurion's policies), George Meany (the powerful president of the AFL-CIO), and Lyndon B. Johnson (the Senate Democratic majority whip). It was quite another to keep company with William Knowland and others on the right wing of the Republican Party, many of whom were extremists, isolationists, perhaps even antisemites.[24]

Given Golda's commitment to socialist principles as well as her deep connection to the U.S. labor movement, how did she feel about ingratiating herself with such reactionary men? Did she feel she was betraying her conscience or did she simply tell herself that beggars can't be choosers? In her public speeches Golda continued to emphasize that Israel was striving for social justice and individual liberty. To the discerning ear this was an effort made in public to hint that the two concepts, social justice and individual liberty, could be reconciled and, moreover, that her State of Israel was doing so.

The pressure campaign worked to the extent that Congress began to protest Eisenhower's Middle East policy. On February 6, 1957, forty-one congressional Republicans and seventy-five congressional Democrats called on the administration to be more lenient toward Israel. They also discussed holding hostage Eisenhower's pending proposal aimed at preventing further Soviet influence in the Middle East until the administration displayed a more supportive position toward Israel.[25] Slowly Golda and her team began to see the tide turning in Israel's favor. Meanwhile, at the Department of State John Foster Dulles was recovering from cancer surgery and searching for a compromise.

Golda Meets with John Foster Dulles

Golda was already a celebrity by the time she met with Dulles in New York on December 29, 1956. The American media was fascinated by this woman "of a certain age." She walked humbly with her handbag hanging from her arm and her hair in an old-fashioned bun, yet she challenged the president of the United States, a heroic general, in tough and straightforward language. When she arrived at the meeting place, scores of journalists were waiting outside, their cameras and microphones at the ready as they expected breaking news.

Golda was accompanied by the two men who had so far handled negotiations with Dulles on behalf of Israel, Abba Eban and his deputy at the Israeli Embassy, Reuven Shiloah. If Eban was the intellectual who viewed diplomacy through the lens of world history and international law, Shiloah, the founder of the Mossad, was the spymaster. In sending both men, Ben-Gurion may have hoped to employ a "good cop, bad cop" strategy. Golda arrived at the meeting armed with documents and maps. Her aim was to walk Dulles through the countless Israeli grievances over the years, the extreme vulnerability of the Israeli settlements in the south, and Egypt's continued belligerence. The meeting took place on Friday afternoon, just before the start of the Jewish Sabbath. Eighteen minutes into the meeting, when Jewish women all over the world were lighting the Sabbath candles, Golda was busy making her country's case to perhaps the most powerful diplomat in the world.

The meeting lasted an hour and a half. Dulles was quite familiar with the subject matter and spoke at length. There was no chemistry between him and Golda, no meeting of the minds. It also became clear that for the United States there were only two contentious points: the status of Gaza and the matter of unencumbered shipping through the Straits of Tiran. With regard to Gaza, Dulles insisted that the United States saw no alternative to withdrawal and the restoration of Egyptian jurisdiction. With regard to the Straits of Tiran, he stated that Israel had a valid point. Egypt had violated international law, an action that called for redress.

Dulles was a tall man, "muscular, lean with broad shoulders," and exuded the confidence of status, power, and success. Eight years Golda's senior, he was well dressed, highly articulate, and had the look of a "stern church elder."[26] Born into a wealthy upper-class family of clergy and statesmen, he had decades of experience as a top-level corporate lawyer, and his international experience stretched from the Treaty of Versailles to the establishment of the United Nations. Like many in the State Department during that era he was likely pro-Arab and thus skeptical of that new state called Israel. Most important, Eisenhower trusted him, and if Golda wanted to change the president's view she had to convince Dulles first.

Prior to this meeting Dulles and Golda had rarely interacted and they had never had a serious conversation. Responding to the lack of contact between the two, one of Israel's prominent leaders on the left commented:

> The U.S. president and its secretary of state receive kings, counselors, counts, ministers of foreign affairs . . . while Israel's minister of foreign affairs is boycotted. . . . I do not understand the marginalization of her name, her image and her place in the current political drama. . . . How can you understand this matter?—[the] minister of foreign affairs is present and available—and the minister of foreign affairs is the government—and she is not privy to the developments. I am not worried about the status or value of Mrs. Meir, this is not relevant, but politically this is bizarre.[27]

To say that Golda had been "boycotted" was an overstatement. Eban's cables to Ben-Gurion were peppered with statements that "the minister has been consulted and given her consent." Nevertheless, it was true that Dulles primarily negotiated with Eban rather than Golda, the absentee decision maker.

One likely explanation for this unconventional arrangement is that Dulles was a male chauvinist who felt uncomfortable with women in high-ranking public office. He was reportedly offended when his daughter Lilian wished to attend college because, just like Golda's father, he believed that "education spoiled women." A conservative man, he took traditional gender roles for granted and neither Sullivan and Cromwell, the powerful law firm at which he worked, nor the State Department, hired women unless they were secretaries. The hiring of his sister, Eleanor Lansing Dulles, was an exception that took place against his will.[28] As the very first female minister of foreign affairs in the West, Golda may have represented an innovation that Dulles felt disinclined to encourage.[29] This would at least accord with the experiences of Dulles's sister.

John Foster Dulles's Sister

Eleanor Lansing Dulles, a gifted economist, pursued a career in foreign affairs. Her older brother discouraged her career every step of the way. In her memoirs Eleanor directly stated that her problems at the State Department "were rooted in sex discrimination," and she devoted an entire chapter to the various ways in which the department discriminated against women. When Dulles arrived at the State Department his sister was already a mid-level officer. He initially asked her to resign and only agreed to let her stay after she begged him to relent. His cable expressing his consent was painfully short: "All right, Good-bye." Eleanor observed that women were rarely appointed to "serious committee assignments or negotiating positions" because it was widely believed that "they would make dangerous intuitive, even emotional, decisions."[30] Given this culture as well as his own biases, it is unsurprising that Dulles chose to ignore Golda.

Golda may not have known about Dulles's sister but Eleanor knew about Golda. "We have no Golda Meir," she lamented in her memoir.[31] Otherness heightens the sensitivity to one's identity, and women everywhere find comfort in role models. Golda was rising to the position of an icon and Eleanor's choice to mention her proves that she drew strength from Golda's example.

An Aide-Memoire from the Department of State

On February 11, 1957, Dulles presented to Eban "an Aide-Memoire."[32] The document, stating the official position of the United States government, favorably noted the considerable withdrawal of Israeli troops and focused on the remaining issues of Gaza and the Straits of Tiran. It rejected Israel's position that Gaza should remain under Israeli control and asserted that "it is the position of the United States that Israeli withdrawal should be prompt and unconditional." For Golda this was a devastating defeat. With regard to the Straits of Tiran it offered Israel a victory. The United States recognized the waterways as part of international waters and therefore held that all nations were entitled to "free and innocent passage" through them. Israel would have preferred to maintain exclusive control over the waterway but the statement nevertheless recognized Israel's initial grievance.

A firm escalation of the rhetoric accompanied this compromise. Dulles expressed impatience at Israel's recalcitrance and hinted that the price of resistance to his offer might include sanctions or even the withdrawal of the U.S. diplomatic delegation from Israel.

A Political Sword Hanging over Israel

While Israel's government was fretting about the ramifications of these developments, President Eisenhower stepped into the fray with an address to the nation. He told his fellow Americans that the Suez crisis put the very existence of the United Nations in jeopardy and that world peace could not be maintained if nations that violated the UN Charter by invading other countries were allowed to set prior conditions before agreeing to withdraw. He said he believed that the UN should pressure Israel to withdraw immediately and that the United States should support this move.

In Jerusalem, Ben-Gurion and his cabinet felt that the wolf was at the door. In New York, Golda was similarly devastated. All her hard work amounted to one minor gain: the prospects of free Israeli passage through the Red Sea. If Dulles followed through on his threats—and Golda had no reason to think he would not—the status of Israel as a pariah state would be official. Israel would not be eligible to receive any international loans, donations from the American Jewish community would be blocked, and want and demoralization would spread over the land.

Golda was conflicted. Should she advise the cabinet to push further and perhaps expose the Aide-Memoire as a ploy to sacrifice Israel's security on the altar of Arab interests, urging the Jewish community and Israel's friends in Congress to defy Eisenhower? Or should she encourage the cabinet to accept Dulles's offer? Eban had already made clear that he leaned toward acceptance, and her staff at the foreign ministry expressed concern about a possible showdown. A worried cable from

Reuven Shiloah indicated that both congressional and Jewish leaders expressed discomfort about escalating the conflict with the American president.[33]

In addition to her concerns about the terms of the deal, Golda had a competitive spirit and hated the idea of losing. Furthermore, not even a year had passed since her appointment as minister of foreign affairs. Giving in could signal her ill handling of Israel's foreign affairs. It might prove that her detractors were right in saying she was not cut out for the job. From New York Golda informed Ben-Gurion that if the cabinet were willing to tighten its belt and face immense hardships, Israel might ultimately prevail and keep the territories. Nevertheless, feeling utterly defeated, Golda concluded that there was no way to avoid the deal proposed in the Aide-Memoire. In Jerusalem, Ben-Gurion and the cabinet soon voted to accept Dulles's offer. The traumatic experience provided Golda with a lesson about the imbalance of power. Acts of defiance against the express will of the president of the United States would result in dire consequences. It was a lesson she would remember when the Yom Kippur War threatened.

Showdown? March 1, 1957

On February 27, Golda arrived at the Waldorf Astoria Hotel in New York for the final and fateful consultation with Dulles. The Americans were preparing for the conclusion of the Suez crisis. The record of her meeting with Dulles shows that she implored, almost begged, for a few more days, but Dulles was adamant. He was fed up with the public relations blitz conducted against the administration and was determined to bring the matter to an end. The United We Stand Resolution had outlived its purpose and it was time for the General Assembly to adjourn. The good news was that with the expiration of the resolution, the threat of sanctions against Israel would also come to an end.

Abba Eban and his team of diplomats met with the Americans to compose the speech in veiled diplomatic language that would include the terms and conditions for the deal. Golda would announce Israel's prompt withdrawal from Gaza and the Straits of Tiran. In return the United States provided Israel with two commitments: first, there would be a strong UN presence in Gaza to guarantee that the territory no longer served as a base for terrorist harassment of Israel; second, the Straits of Tiran would remain open to free navigation for all including Israel. Dulles did not, however, want Israel to announce these terms. Instead they agreed that Golda's speech would refer to them merely as "assumptions and expectations."[34]

In addition to feeling defeated by the end result, Golda must have been humiliated as a result of the process by which it came about. The lion's share of the negotiations had occurred behind her back. Dulles felt more comfortable dealing with Eban, and Ben-Gurion was satisfied with Eban's services. Dulles, Eban, and their teams were busy crafting the speech and Golda was reduced to the position of a messenger, a voice announcing a "deal" couched in legalistic terms to which she was a stranger. The position of "minister of foreign affairs" proved to be empty, all words and no action. It was precisely the kind of role for which she had always said she had little respect.

Golda's gender again proved to be an impediment. In the world of international diplomacy she was surrounded by men who resisted interacting with a woman in power. Most diplomats were cold or unfriendly toward her, and Dag Hammarskjöld was perhaps the coldest. Not only did he fiercely reject any gesture of goodwill toward Israel prior to withdrawal but he also seemed particularly irritated by Golda. In his universe, women were honored in their private roles. It was not their place to disrupt the realm of international affairs. The hostility between the two was unconcealed.

Dulles understood that Hammarskjöld, who was also compelled to compromise under the proposed terms of the Aide-Memoire, might decide to "throw a spanner [wrench] into the machinery." Several delegates from other countries, led by the French delegation, volunteered to implore the secretary-general to stay away from the General Assembly while Golda spoke. He indicated he would and there was some hope that a showdown might be averted.

Perfidy, March 1, 1957

Two hours past midnight, long after the Jewish Sabbath had descended, Golda finished reviewing the speech that Dulles and Eban had crafted, which she was set to deliver to the UN General Assembly the following day. The legal terms of the withdrawal were both face-saving and operationally critical and Golda hoped to emphasize the meager gains Israel retained. Shortly before dawn, she requested that the speech be printed and placed on the desks of the assembly's delegates before the beginning of the meeting. But printing was no easy task in the late 1950s, let alone during the small hours of the night. The consulate employee told her it could not be done. Already on edge, Golda yelled: "I know that in New York anything can be done. Anything!" Proving their boss right in this instance, her staff succeeded in locating a printing service that was able to complete the job. But Golda knew not everything could be done in New York. If the president of the United States had decided on a course of action, a tiny country was powerless to dissuade him.[35]

Golda must have felt like a lamb being marched to the slaughter as she arrived at the United Nations headquarters and entered the General Assembly. Throughout the morning, members of her team knocked on the doors of the U.S. delegation. The U.S. ambassador to the UN, Henry Cabot Lodge Jr., was scheduled to follow Golda and affirm the terms agreed upon with Dulles, and the Israelis requested to see the text of his speech. The American delegation stalled. The speech, they said, was not yet ready. Golda was anxious. Would the United States keep its promise?

At 3:35 P.M., Golda slowly walked to the podium and stood before a packed General Assembly composed almost entirely of men. She could feel the schadenfreude radiating from many of the delegates and was determined not to disclose her feelings of devastation. Projecting as much dignity and steadiness as she could muster, she stated calmly: "The government of Israel is now in a position to announce its plans for full and prompt withdrawal from the Sharm el-Sheikh Area and the Gaza Strip, in accordance with [the] General Assembly's resolution."[36] As per their agreement, after Golda's speech, Henry Cabot Lodge Jr. made his way to the podium, and Golda anxiously waited for him to declare that these "assumptions and expectations" were "reasonable and legitimate."[37]

With regard to the status of the Straits of Tiran, Lodge kept his end of the bargain. He declared that the right to free navigation was an international right for all to enjoy. But then, he shifted to an unfamiliar tune. He hailed the General Assembly's legitimate role in resolving crises and denounced aggressive nations that violated the UN Charter (i.e., Israel).[38] The Israeli delegation listened in dismay as Lodge announced the terms Eban and Dulles had laboriously negotiated as "hopes and expectations which seem to us not unreasonable." Lodge had transformed "assumptions" into "hopes" and "reasonable" into "not unreasonable." The term "legitimate" was omitted altogether and he offered no hint whatsoever that there was any deal concerning Gaza. His speech implied that while Israel was free to nurture "hopes and expectations," the United States was under no obligation to assist it in fulfilling these wishes. There was no escaping the conclusion that the United States had reneged on the terms of the deal.

To add insult to injury, Lodge concluded his speech by applauding Egypt for acting "with commendable forbearance on the issues with which we are confronted today" and by heaping praise on Dag Hammarskjöld, who was "a patient statesman as well as a great intellect." Neither Israel nor Golda received a whiff of recognition. Had Lodge's speech been made available to Golda before the meeting, she most certainly would not have delivered the speech Eban and Dulles had prepared for her.[39] These were not the terms of the deal to which the parties had agreed. To Golda, as well as to most Israelis, this was betrayal, plain and simple. Before turning to the aftermath of this miserable episode, it is worth taking a moment to reflect on the ending of Golda's speech.

The Search for Tikkun, Golda's Cadenza

Unbeknownst to members of her team, Golda decided to conclude her speech with two paragraphs of her own. The mechanical reading of a dry legal text needed a personal touch she decided and Golda was eager to end the speech on an upbeat note that would counterbalance the image of Israel as a belligerent state. In the first paragraph she emphasized commonality:

> Now may I add these few words to the states in the Middle East area, and more specifically to the neighbors of Israel. We all come from an area which is a very ancient one. The hills and the valleys of the region have been witnesses to many wars and many conflicts. But that is not the only thing which characterizes that part of the world from which we come. It is also a part of the world which is of an ancient culture. It is that part of the world which has given to humanity three great religions. It is also that part of the world which has given a code of ethics to all humanity. In our countries, in the entire region, all our peoples are anxious for and in need of a higher standard of living, of great programs of development and progress.[40]

In this paragraph Golda draws attention to the collective identity of the "neighborhood." Their common history, she points out, has been not only one of war and violence but a noble message of universal values, and the time has come to cultivate the better moral side of this shared identity. In outlining the common aspirations of the peoples of the region—improved living standards and economic development—she called on the countries to unite in order to advance these goals. The second paragraph offered a commitment to do so:

> Can we, from now on—all of us—turn a new leaf and, instead of fighting with each other, can we all, united, fight poverty and disease and illiteracy? Is it possible for us to put all our efforts and all our energy into one single purpose, the betterment, and progress and development of all our lands and all our peoples? I can here pledge the Government of Israel and the people of Israel to do their part in this united effort. There is no limit to what we are prepared to contribute so that all of us, together, can live to see a day of happiness for our peoples and see again, from that region a great contribution to peace and happiness for all humanity.[41]

This was a reformulation of the best and most noble ideas of utopian Zionism, the register in which Golda felt most comfortable. It was a

remarkable message. She identified the problems that turned "t[]
neighborhood" into a backward swamp, called for a united effort []
eradicate them, and hinted that she had the knowledge and wherewith[]
to restore the region to its erstwhile glory. Her final note was an appea[]
to the better side of humanity, to cooperation and unity. Golda thus
returned full circle to the first steps taken by the General Assembly in
November of 1956. When Dulles and Hammarskjöld engineered the
United We Stand Resolution, the nations of the world united in their
resolve to vindicate international law by forcing the three belligerents
into full withdrawal. Unity served to restore the status quo, which itself
was fraught with violence and ill will. Golda's cadenza offered a different
vision of unity: unity harnessed to eradicate poverty, illiteracy, and
disease.

She knew that one precondition would be hard to swallow and yet
she hoped it could be accepted: "the neighborhood" had to "turn a new
leaf." That meant ignoring the violent events surrounding the birth of
the State of Israel and accepting the legitimacy of Israel's existence. It
was a vision based on planning for the future and letting go of the past.
More than half a century later it remains the key to peace in the Middle
East.

Golda's cadenza also demonstrated a link between the advice Dulles
had given Golda on December 29 and the project on which she would
embark the following year—bringing progress to Africa. Dulles urged
Golda to think of means to integrate Israel into the Middle East so that
Arabs would not view it as an invasive species. Her conclusion signaled
to Dulles that she had heard his message. For the next few years she
invested tremendous energy in offering Israeli aid to African states.[42] It
may well be that in her heart she felt anguish for her role in facilitating
wars and was yearning for what Jewish heritage calls "tikkun" (amends).

The noble dream that Golda outlined in her closing remarks evaporated once Lodge offered his version of the deal. The brutality of realpolitik felt like a physical assault. In the neighborhood of politics there
were no friends, only wolves baring their teeth at one another. In her
memoirs Golda recalled that she sat there "biting her lip, not even
able to look at the handsome Mr. Cabot Lodge," and feeling utterly

helpless.[43] Throughout her life Golda dreaded the loss of personal agency. These moments at the United Nations must have been some of her worst.

A Posttraumatic Stress Disorder?

The next morning when asked by one of her aides how she was doing, Golda replied: "I washed my underwear all night, to keep at least something in my environment clean."[44] The response is well known in the literature on posttraumatic stress disorder in rape victims. Having experienced utter helplessness, sexual assault victims develop an obsession to keep themselves clean. Did Golda feel as if she had been victimized by a group of men more powerful and cunning than she? The tendency to engage in repetitive acts in order to reaffirm one's sense of normalcy is also common. Golda had always emphasized hygiene and cleanliness and had always washed her underwear by herself. But telling a stranger that she had been washing underwear "all night" appears to confirm posttraumatic behavior. Did Golda suffer pain akin to that felt by victims of sexual assault, even rape? She concluded this part of her memoir on a note of profound understatement: "It was not one of the finest moments of my life."[45]

March 17, Golda Loses Her Temper

Golda was already seething from what she termed "Dulles' dupery" when she arrived back at her hotel. But matters were soon made worse: Mossad informed Golda that Hammarskjöld was already discussing with Nasser Egypt's return to Gaza upon Israel's withdrawal. She was now boiling with anger and frustration. She blamed herself for not being more vigilant and having agreed to speak without seeing Lodge's speech in advance. Better to face sanctions, she thought, than be forced to withdraw without any gain. Given Dulles's dupery, Golda believed that Israel was entitled to renege on its commitment to withdraw and her gut told her that she should recommend to Ben-Gurion that Israel call off the deal with the United States.

She asked Eban and his deputy, Gideon Rafael, to come to her hotel suite.[46] The pretense of mutual respect was abandoned and Golda's bitterness toward Eban came spilling out. It was as if Golda were again a rebellious teenager talking back to her parents in Milwaukee. There is only one fairly muted description of the confrontation, written by Rafael, yet even this demonstrates the wrath Golda unleashed on Eban. According to his account, Golda began by requesting that Eban send a cable to Ben-Gurion advising that Israel should not withdraw and that the orders for Israel's evacuation from Gaza be canceled. Eban responded in a lawyerly fashion. The deal had been signed and delivered. It could not be undone. Golda's "advice," he predicted, would be met with fierce U.S. retaliation in the form of sanctions, and Israel's position in world public opinion would be "demolished."

Eban did not hesitate to use a bit of chutzpah, a Yiddish term he once translated into "effrontery": "He suggested Golda herself warn Dulles that Israel is about to turn its back on the deal." Golda could take no more. She erupted like a geyser: "Now you want me to repair the mess," she yelled, "after you have confronted me with a *fait accompli*." She suspected that Eban had been working behind her back during these four long months, which culminated in her humiliation on the global stage. She had not been properly consulted nor brought into the negotiations, and then was told to read a speech that she did not write and with which she did not entirely agree. As the result of sacrificing her dignity, Israel found itself in the very same situation it had been before the war—the Egyptians would be back in Gaza, terrorists would infiltrate the border, and America might or might not guarantee free shipping in the Straits of Tiran. Further war and violence waited on the horizon and she had been made a fool by giving this deal the imprimatur of her state.

Rafael reports laconically that he had never before witnessed such a scene. As a forty-four-year-old high-ranking diplomat he was accustomed to fastidious manners and decorum. Eban too must have been let down and worried. He had found Lodge's speech disappointing, but not so alarming, and felt that withdrawal was imperative. Moreover, Golda had given her consent to the "deal" and should accept responsibility for the outcome. He told Golda that if she wanted she should send a cable to Ben-Gurion. From Rafael's description it appears that Golda had arrived at the end of her rope. She threatened that if Eban did not comply she would jump out of the window, which happened to be located twenty-six floors above street level. Rafael recalled that she "raised her voice from demand to command level." Eban marched out of the room and slammed the door behind him. After Eban left, Golda calmed down. She offered Rafael coffee and said they needed to work on a cable to Ben-Gurion. Rafael gently advised that Ben-Gurion already had the relevant information and it would be better to let sleeping dogs lie. By now Golda had returned to her senses. "Forget it," Rafael remembered her saying.

Golda never forgave Eban. They worked together until the end of her life, and when she was the prime minister he would serve as her minister of foreign affairs. But the barbs never ceased. He dismissed her as an ignorant woman suffering from "personal rancor in the general system of her thought and emotion." She reciprocated by placing political obstacles in his way. She enjoyed telling her friends that when he came to her following her retirement to announce that he was running for prime minister, she responded sarcastically: "Of which country?" Rather than attribute Golda's disapproval to their myriad policy differences or even to their different personalities and backgrounds, he attributed it to the fact that Golda was a woman. It appears that even the rational, urbane Eban resorted to the evil female stereotype when he discussed Golda with his children. One day when Eban's daughter returned home from art class, she presented him with a ceramic dish engraved with the ancient symbol of a blue eye, which she said was "to protect you from Golda's evil eye, Daddy."[47]

Aftermath and Assessment of the Diplomatic Campaign

Golda emerged from the diplomatic battle a battered woman. She had worked so hard to persuade the public, the press, members of Congress, public intellectuals, and leaders of the Jewish community that Israel had good reasons for going to war and should therefore be allowed to keep its territorial gains. In this quest she had endured so many unpleasant

experiences, all of which had taken their toll: the hostility of the delegates at the UN, the antagonism of Dag Hammarskjöld, the betrayal of
John Foster Dulles, and the secrecy between Ben-Gurion and Eban. She
felt very lonely. At the same time, however, she became a celebrity in
the United States. She gained national recognition, scored high approval
ratings in public opinion polls, and earned admiration among American
Jews. Golda was on her way to becoming an icon, the mother (or grandmother) of the Jewish people.

Despite Golda's intense disappointment, the results of this episode
were not as bleak as she feared. As Abba Eban later argued in his brilliant book *Modern Diplomacy*, their diplomatic campaign in New York
represents a clear example of the superiority of diplomacy over war.[48]
The work done by John Foster Dulles and other allies behind the scenes
provided Israel with ten years of peace. The Straits of Tiran indeed reopened to free navigation. Egypt retained a symbolic presence in Gaza,
but Nasser ensured that the Fedayeen did not return. And the United
Nations Emergency Force (UNEF) preserved the Sinai Desert as a buf-
fer between Egypt and Israel.

Golda should have been satisfied with her performance. She was new
to the job and surrounded by skeptical or downright hostile actors, yet
she successfully steered "this crazy ship through the wicked waves of a
stormy sea towards the safe harbor" and ushered in a decade of relative
calm from 1957 to 1967.[49] Even if Golda did not deserve all the credit for
this outcome, she certainly deserved some.

CHAPTER 18

THE AFRICAN CONNECTION

IN THE UNITED NATION's General Assembly Israel was an "odd member," disliked and misunderstood by most delegates. Golda had a plan to improve this situation: Israel would support development projects in African nations and lend them expertise in nation-building. From her perspective as a woman Golda craved social relations with other nations and thought her "African projects" would make Israelis feel that they were not friendless among nations. Moreover, as she often explained, she saw similarities between the Jewish and African history of otherization and discrimination and wished to help Africans recover their equal place in the world. Between 1957 and the Six-Day War in 1967 Golda's development projects in Africa were highly successful, nurturing feelings of goodwill and satisfaction on both sides.

A Dancing Minister of Foreign Affairs

Golda fell in love with African women, and they loved her in return. She laughed with them, dressed like them, and danced with them. Their spontaneous warmth and enthusiasm awoke her proletarian spirit, her down-to-earth sensibility, and made her feel comfortable in her skin.

Many in Israel ridiculed her projects and diminished her efforts as "woman's work." Michael Bar-Zohar, a biographer of David Ben-Gurion and Shimon Peres, argued that her success at building bridges between

Israel and Africa was a mere illusion, a trompe l'oeil: "While she spoke and toured, attended independence ceremonies and danced with the women of the liberated countries of Africa, or was photographed dressed in their colorful garments—Peres signed agreements with governments, sent there experts and equipment, formed paramilitary units on the ground and brought to Israel officers, ministers and senior leaders."[1] In this analysis Bar-Zohar falls back on a stereotypical gendered division of labor: Peres, the director general of the Ministry of Defense, did the (serious) male work, while Golda performed the (fluffy) female tasks of dressing colorfully, dancing, and appearing in group photos.

Bar-Zohar's dismissal of Golda's work ignores a crucial fact: the photos of Golda dancing with African women received considerable publicity and enhanced Israel's reputation in a world awakening to the emergence of developing countries. Menachem Meir, Golda's son, described his mother dancing at a gala farewell party given in her honor in Ghana: the orchestra began playing the hora, the traditional Israeli folk dance, and

> there was mother, leading the Israeli delegates and some of the Africans. . . . The waiters stopped in their tracks, the Europeans looked shocked, and reporters reached for their pads. But soon some of the cabinet ministers and tribal chiefs [joined, and the dancing went on] . . . and Golda almost sixty years old, continued to twirl as if there were no tomorrow.[2]

Golda felt at home in the African milieu. She loved folk music and folk dance and relished the opportunity to interact with those who shared those joys. Indeed, in a different context, she observed that "to dance means to embrace people and offer them a cultural-humane touch."[3] This was diplomacy with a woman's touch.

Golda was mindful of realpolitik. Through her visits she sought to consolidate Israel's influence in Africa and thereby gain support for Israel on the world stage. But she also valued the unpretentious manners of Africans and the absence of stuffiness associated with the highly educated European diplomatic corps. It appears that the Africans, too, felt she was "one of them," at least for a few years.

Golda's Progressive Vision for the Women of Africa

On Mount Carmel in the Israeli city of Haifa, Golda established an "international training center" where women from developing countries could acquire leadership and organizational skills. Golda's vision was to develop agency among African women and prove "to them that they could become surgeons, pilots, citrus growers, community workers . . . and that technical ability was not—as they had been made to believe for so many decades—the permanent prerogative of the white race."[4] This vision, at once feminist and antiracist, harks back to her observation thirty years earlier concerning her work with Pioneer Women. Hard work, she had noted, was required to break free from traditional gender stereotypes and integrate women into all walks of life. Her vision for Africa aimed to advance that goal. But Golda also understood the unique disadvantages suffered by all people of color on account of race, and she often denounced racism.

Golda loved her work on the African continent because it revived her connection to the ideals of social justice. Having been involved in Israeli nation-building for over thirty years, she felt confident about the measures needed to improve an emerging country and she relished seeing results on the ground. The International Center in Haifa, which now carries Golda's name, is still active today and benefits scores of women from developing countries. It is a living monument to her vision and her commitment to benefit the disadvantaged. (See part II in this volume.)

End of an Era

Golda served at the Ministry of Foreign Affairs for almost a decade. She not only handled Israel's foreign affairs during the Suez War but also saw the country through the international crisis surrounding the capture of Adolf Eichmann from Argentina, tension with the United States over Israel's emerging nuclear capabilities, and rumors that German scientists were helping Egypt build lethal weapons to destroy Israel. While she talked at length about the desire for peace with Israel's neighbors, she never developed the "long-term vision" for the country that

Ben-Gurion judged to be an essential characteristic of a good minister of foreign affairs. For the most part she reacted to crises as they came along and retained a pessimistic view of her Arab neighbors' willingness to accept Israel as a bona fide part of the region.

Even though her health was quite precarious after leaving the ministry, Golda continued to be involved in domestic affairs. She engineered an earth-shattering break with her erstwhile idol Ben-Gurion, a break that split Mapai in two. Her public "J'accuse" speech against him at the Central Committee of Mapai stunned the public and was dubbed "Golda's poisonous speech" by Ben-Gurion.[5] It was indeed a sharp attack on his politics, which she saw as undermining the country and the party. A new party named Rafi, led by Ben-Gurion and his lieutenants, would target her as the mother of all evil, branding her "Mrs. Divisiveness."[6] Golda conceded in her memoirs that, as much as she had adored Ben-Gurion and hailed his pivotal role in founding the state, during the 1960s she underwent a fundamental change and "opposed him strongly."

Ben-Gurion was no longer the heroic figure of yesteryear. From the early 1960s the great leader had deteriorated: he was losing his acute political capabilities and was increasingly under the influence of his young advisers such as Shimon Peres and Moshe Dayan. Golda and her comrades suspected that Ben-Gurion and those "young" politicians sought to wrest political power from her generation. Thus her break with Ben-Gurion, the man she had followed almost blindly for decades, may have been motivated as much by self-preservation as by her conviction that the spreading political chaos might harm Israeli society. She decided to back Ben-Gurion's political rival, Levy Eshkol, the prime minister at the time. Even though Golda saw no other option, tearing herself away from Ben-Gurion left her distraught and feeling very guilty.

Her gender now became an easy target for both praise and attack. Her supporters, first and foremost Eshkol, referred to her as "Die Malkae" [Yiddish for "the queen"]. Although when Golda made him unhappy, he also referred to her as "die mechashefa" [Yiddish for "the witch"]. Her detractors in Rafi's camp claimed that she possessed the "capacity to hate as only a woman can."[7] The vitriol directed at Golda would only increase during the period leading to the Six-Day War.

PART IV

1964–1978

CHAPTER 19

ASCENDANCE
Madam Prime Minister

Out of Retirement and on to the Top Job

On March 9, 1969, Israel's president, Zalman Shazar, invited Golda to form a coalition cabinet and serve as prime minister. Eight days later a resounding majority of the Knesset approved her nomination. At the age of seventy Golda had added a new entry to her long list of firsts—the first woman to serve as prime minister in Israel. She was also only the third woman worldwide to occupy the position.

Photos of Golda and Israel's president, her former lover, must have amused those in the know. One photo shows Golda looking at him almost bashfully, her eyes lowered, while Shazar looks at her directly and affectionately, his palm wrapped around hers as if saying: "You have come a long way, Goldinyu," his term of endearment for her in the 1940s. His young lover was now an old lady poised to hold the reins of power while he had "merely" achieved the ceremonial position of head of state. Regardless of how much Golda's relationship with Shazar had benefited her early in her career, her final ascent to the pinnacle of government served as the ultimate proof that her success could not be attributed to intimate relations with the powerful men whom she had long surpassed.

The public was barely aware of the politics at play behind Golda's selection. By and large the media presented her as a stopgap—a

Figure 8. Golda Meir with President Zalman Shazar at her side, announcing the formation of Israel's fourteenth government, with her as prime minister. Courtesy of Israel Government Press Office.

Figure 9. Golda and her first cabinet, all men. Next to president Shazar is seated his wife, Rachel Katznelson-Shazar, a founder of Israeli feminism. Courtesy of Israel Government Press Office. Credit: Moshe Milner.

candidate promoted to avoid a showdown between two military heroes, Yigal Allon and Moshe Dayan. Some expected that Golda would serve only temporarily until the elections scheduled for the end of that year. None of this was accurate. The party bosses had known about Prime Minister Eshkol's spreading cancer for some time and had given serious consideration to neither Allon nor Dayan. Allon lacked charisma and many doubted his leadership skills, while Dayan was suspected of disloyalty to the party's old guard as well as to its values.

From the perspective of the party's leadership, Golda was the best choice. She was not only flesh of their flesh but also experienced in both domestic politics and foreign affairs, highly capable of running a tight ship, and well known and connected at home and abroad. The fact that only 3 percent of Israelis favored her candidacy did not matter. There is little doubt that those who catapulted her to the top expected her to continue as prime minister beyond the upcoming elections.[1]

How did Golda feel at this moment? Throughout her life she had cultivated a posture of humility, expressing gratitude for any opportunity to serve and sharing self-doubts about her capacity to perform the job under consideration. This self-effacing identity, a deliberate construction, had become part of the very fabric of her being such that she may no longer have been consciously aware of her overwhelming drive to succeed. Golda understood from an early age that it was dangerous for a woman to display ambition lest she be perceived as arrogant and pushy, qualities unwelcome in the company of men. Better to confess self-doubt and gratitude.

Upon retirement from the ministry of foreign affairs in 1964, all Golda wanted was to spend more time with her family. When Eshkol died, a reporter informed her, "Everyone says that 'Golda must come back,'" to which she snapped, "I don't know what you are talking about . . . please please please go away."[2] Of course she knew very well what he was talking about. She did, however, consult her children before accepting the offer. Asking for their consent was both a reflection of her genuine desire to bring them on board with the decision and a shrewd cultivation of her public image as a loving family woman, willing to forgo ambition for the sake of her children. Her children, either because they knew better than to stand in their mother's way or because they believed that her services were indispensable, gave her the green light. Golda was ready.[3]

Public praise arrived with a touch of misogyny. Rumors spread that Eshkol, aware of the search for his successor, irritably complained in Yiddish that, "That bitch" (*klaftae*) could not wait to occupy his seat. The fact that she had been his ally and confidante for decades did not prevent him from exercising knee-jerk misogyny in response to an ambitious woman.

During the Knesset's deliberation and confirmation process little doubt was cast on Golda's qualifications. One modern Orthodox religious minister compared Golda to the biblical prophetess Deborah, thereby legitimating her appointment as a matter of Jewish heritage. Others extolled her hawkish views and international reputation. Only two members voiced deep disagreement, but their critique would reverberate in the coming months as criticism of Golda grew louder. The ultra-Orthodox political leader Rabbi Yitzhak Meir Levin, leader of the Ger Hassidic dynasty, opened the debate by questioning the very idea of a female prime minister: "I have nothing personal against Golda," he began, "and recognize her talents and value." But, he continued, there were 133 countries in the world and only India and Sri Lanka had appointed a woman as prime minister. Israel he thought would be well served to stick with the vast majority. He also suggested that the appointment was poorly timed, since the Arab "savages" are "out to get us" and the appointment of a woman might be interpreted as a sign of weakness. This argument was a classic misogynist ploy: while the esteemed rabbi and his fellow Jews had no problem with a female leader, the presence of others—savage and uncultivated—demanded that a macho leader was needed. Levin's final argument, however, appealed directly to Jewish law. Maimonides, the great tenth-century sage "says explicitly [that] a woman is not eligible to rule because [the Bible] speaks of the anointment of a king, not a queen." Jewish law, therefore, denies women eligibility for all positions of public service, making Golda ineligible for the top job.[4]

Uri Avnery, a staunch secularist at the other extreme of the political spectrum, rejected Golda's nomination on different grounds. Golda, he said, represented the old generation. She was a conformist who was deaf to fresh ideas. Avnery, a Knesset member representing a new party called New Power, was the publisher of a political magazine *Ha-Olam Ha-Zae* known for its attacks on the establishment. The magazine combined fiery political commentary with rampant misogyny, including photos of half-naked young women in the style of *Playboy* magazine. Eleven days prior to this speech, in an article titled "A Woman Skilled in Hating," Avnery wrote, "There is a consensus that [Golda] is a woman driven by hatred [which] often leads her to lose self-control. Golda hates everyone who disagrees with her, and thereby brings a clear feminine quality to political life." Avnery's commitment to nonconformism apparently did not extend to gender stereotypes. Hating, he lectured his readers as if discussing the law of gravity, was a "typical feminine quality" that Golda would bring to governance.[5]

The Knesset and the [In]visible Code of Misogyny

The Knesset appeared festive and supportive, yet there was little recognition or celebration of the fact that Israel had elected its first woman to serve as prime minister. None of the nine women in the Knesset (less than 10 percent of the nation's representatives) came to the podium to address Golda's nomination. And none of the male speakers noted the relationship between the historic event and Zionism's commitment to gender equality or reflected upon the status of Israeli women. The deliberations centered exclusively on matters of defense and foreign affairs, typically male subjects, as if to divert attention from the issue of gender. They also referenced the term prime minister in the male form, despite the fact that they were discussing a woman for the position. This practice followed Golda's earlier decision to use the male conjugation (sar) when she was appointed minister of labor. (See chapter 13 in this volume.)

During the parliamentary debate no one asked whether other women would serve in Golda's cabinet and Golda conveniently ignored the issue. The health, education, and labor ministries—all traditionally connected with women's interests—could have been filled by women without casting doubt on the patriarchal division of labor. Golda could have discreetly instructed the various ministers to see if there were eligible women for senior positions. Instead, she signaled that business would continue as usual by staffing her cabinet entirely with men.

The public also had reservations about a woman leading the country. In one political cartoon, for instance, a middle-aged man points to a poster of Golda and quips: "At long last, a man as prime minister." People reconciled themselves with the fact that a woman was in charge by almost obsessively referring to her as the "only man in the cabinet." They were yearning for a strong leader to replace the late prime minister, who had been perceived as weak and indecisive, and they could not imagine a woman possessing these qualities. Better to think of Golda as a man.

Brief Assessment of Golda's Prime Ministership

Golda suffered from two major impediments as she assumed the reins of power: her health and the volatility of political events in the early 1970s. She entered the prime minister's office as an ill woman suffering from blood disorders and malignancies. Her habit of smoking nonstop and drinking numerous cups of coffee every day did not help matters. She also entered office confronting a war with Egypt (the War of Attrition); Palestinian Liberation Organization terrorist attacks on Israeli targets around the globe; intensifying animosity from the Soviet Union; and an American administration prevailing upon Israel to withdraw from conquered territories. At home Israelis were beginning to benefit from prosperity and were eager to join Western consumer culture. They expected stability and security. Yet Israel was also seeing serious faults in the foundation of its social structure, even if these were only visible to the discerning eye. The gap between the rich (mostly Ashkenazi) and the poor (mostly Mizrahi) was widening; messianic passions nursed an appetite to annex the West Bank; and the younger generation was ready to replace the old guard.

In the beginning Golda performed splendidly. While only 3 percent of the public thought of her as an adequate candidate for prime minister in early 1969, later that year she led her party to its greatest victory ever, a gain of fifty-six seats in the Knesset. Still one wonders, had she known what the future held would she have still taken the job?

Golda Confronts Israel's Black Panthers

Golda was fortunate to inherit a growing economy. The ranks of Israel's middle class were swelling and the country's standard of living was rising. Unemployment was low and the gross national product was high. Nevertheless, every fourth Israeli still lived in poverty or on the verge of it. To make matters worse, the population afflicted by economic hardship comprised mostly Mizrahi Jews, who had arrived in Israel in the early 1950s primarily from Morocco. Israel's poor had many children to feed but lacked adequate housing, education, and the social networks necessary to help them improve their lot. They were ignored by the government, and they felt it.[6]

Golda was aware of the problems. She allocated substantial sums in the national budget to social welfare and established a high-level commission to study children and youth in distress. The composition of the commission, however, reflected the social consciousness of yesteryear. Well-known leaders and academics were included but they were mostly men. Even though the idea for the commission came from her daughter-in-law Aya Meir, and even though matters of welfare had historically been women's turf, Golda's commission marginalized women as decision makers. Of the seventeen members who served on its steering committee, only two were women; of the seventy-one members on the commission, only sixteen were women. Consciously or not Golda maintained the integrity of the glass ceiling. This decision should partly be attributed to her conception of agency—women should fight for their place in government rather than be promoted by the prime minister—but not entirely. Her yearning to avoid criticism and maintain stability even at the price of perpetuating the status quo cannot be overestimated.

While Golda was implementing measures to mitigate the problems of social injustice, a group of young Mizrahi men from a Jerusalem slum burst onto the scene with a furious condemnation of the government and blaming it for decades of systematic discrimination against Mizrahi Jews. They called themselves the Black Panthers, adopting the name of the revolutionary organization in the United States. Assisted by politicians and academics they released a public declaration of grievances and demands for social justice reform. Their demonstrations were a threat to law and order and triggered a robust public debate. Golda was concerned both by miserable conditions of life in the slums and by the challenge to her leadership. Since her childhood days in Pinsk when social unrest heralded the Russian Revolution, she had appreciated that violence in the streets could lead to unpredictable results. She also feared that provocateurs might use the unrest to undermine her party's hegemony, tar her government as racist, and accelerate the replacement of the old guard.

"They Are Not Nice"

Following a particularly violent demonstration in Jerusalem, the leader of the Moroccan Immigrants Association declared that despite public perceptions the Panthers were "nice" guys. By expressing this judgment he may have hoped to elicit empathy—to remind Golda that these young rebels, poor, uneducated, and dark skinned, were not that different from "nice" middle-class Ashkenazi youth—and thereby defuse the tension. But the preceding demonstration, which had involved Molotov cocktails hurled at the police, convinced Golda that this was no time for reconciliation. In response Golda quipped, "People who throw Molotov cocktails at the Jewish police are not nice guys." In collective memory, however, the phrase that would linger and serve as proof that she was out of touch and even racist was "they are not nice." Although Golda meant to condemn the violent perpetrators rather than Mizrahi Jews in general, her statement was experienced as a "verbal" Molotov cocktail thrown by the prime minister at Mizrahi Jews. To many, her statement betrayed a lack of empathy and deafness to the cries of the downtrodden. Golda was widely denounced as coldhearted and callous. Six years later, Mizrahi Jews, feeling unappreciated by the founding generation, crossed the aisle and made Menachem Begin prime minister.[7]

The tension between Golda and the Panthers escalated following her statement. In August 1971, more violence erupted and the Panthers burned an effigy of Golda in the center of town. The effigy depicted Golda naked and flat chested, with a long phallic nose. Golda was an old witch, reminiscent of the Brothers Grimm, a representation that demonstrated the depths of male animosity to women in general and to this powerful woman in particular. In interviews, the Panthers blamed the incident on unaffiliated provocateurs.[8]

Whatever Golda felt inside, she responded with bravado and instructed the police to crush the demonstrations with an iron fist. She feared that being perceived as "weak" would erode her political support particularly because a large portion of the public did not trust a woman to stand tall in the face of conflict. This may be the reason that she adopted "tough" positions in matters of defense as well.

"The Merry Wives of Windsor"

In the months before Golda became the prime minister, questions about national security occupied center stage. Golda was ready to assume political power, but was the public ready to accept that a woman could handle matters of defense?

As the sense of an imminent Arab attack slowly suffocated Israeli society, public pressure mounted to name Moshe Dayan, the military hero of the 1950s, as minister of defense. Dayan exuded masculinity and audacity. A known womanizer, he wore a black patch over his left eye due to an old war injury and represented the popular yearning for a strong leader. Both Golda and Eshkol were confident that Israel was superbly prepared for war and did not need Dayan to secure victory. Nevertheless, after resisting for a few weeks, they ultimately felt compelled to appoint him as minister of defense. This incident, one aspect of it in particular, would shape Golda's security policy in the years to come.[9]

On June 1, 1967, five days before the Six-Day War began, a demonstration of one hundred women gathered below Golda's office at Mapai's headquarters to protest her resistance to appointing Dayan to the cabinet. They held signs depicting Golda as the ultimate villain, an irrational woman driven by hatred and standing in the way of the military "savior." Eshkol dismissed the protest as frivolous and nicknamed the women "the merry wives of Windsor."

Golda and Eshkol assumed that Rafi, the new political party, had organized the protest as it was orchestrating a countrywide push for an immediate overhaul of the cabinet. Rafi was Mapai's rival and its two leaders, Shimon Peres and Moshe Dayan, were the most hostile critics of the old leadership. Despite seeing itself as the face of change, Rafi was not known for progressive views about gender equality, and its deployment of women demonstrators under Golda's office confirmed the old patriarchal division of labor: women and children were vulnerable, especially during war. Golda, the woman at the top of Mapai's leadership, was pitted against the multitude of Israeli women who signaled that only a man could save them.

Golda described the campaign against her as vicious, complaining that people even called on "her driver and her son, demanding that they [physically] prevent her from leaving home," so as to preclude her from fulfilling her official duties as Mapai's general secretary.[10] Rafi's public relations campaign to appoint Dayan accompanied by vile stereotyping of Golda had a significant impact on public opinion. In her memoirs Golda commented: "There was a growing pressure for the appointment of a new minister of defense, someone bolder and much more charismatic. Thousands of Israelis were looking to Moshe Dayan to express the national determination to endure and to prevail."[11] While Golda did not identify with these Israelis, she understood the political and social dynamics of the crisis. Women had rarely taken an active role in defense matters so it was only natural for people to see men as possessing the virtues necessary to defend the nation. It was also natural for people to long for a relatively young charismatic leader at the helm. In 1967 Dayan was the people's choice.

As Golda became prime minister she knew that public perceptions about matters of defense left her vulnerable and so she appointed Dayan and other decorated generals to her cabinet. Throughout Golda's tenure as prime minister, Dayan and other male advisers shaped Israel's defense policy. By and large, Golda deferred to their judgment. She consciously cultivated her image as a true hawk, sometimes even more hawkish than Dayan himself, and she generally avoided meddling in matters of defense. Dayan reciprocated by signaling his approval of her leadership.[12]

Fearing a torrent of popular disapproval similar to what she had experienced leading up to the Six-Day War, Golda also adjusted her practice of governance. She turned herself into the spokeswoman for Israel's military needs, the "housewife" who went to Washington and returned home with shopping bags full of sophisticated weapons.[13] She also tolerated Dayan and his generals' growing hubris and conceit, perhaps persuading herself "to let boys be boys." When the Yom Kippur assault arrived, however, she realized that she had given them too much rope and that as prime minister it was her duty to maintain oversight of their actions. But by then it was already too late.

Golda's Gaze

To mask her fear of popular disapproval, Golda developed governing techniques meant to project her image as a strong leader, a person with full control over government business. One such technique mentioned often by those in attendance was "the gaze"—a piercing, threatening look that would freeze the onlooker in his shoes. That gaze, some observed, made the onlooker "feel small" and diminished his willingness to stand by his view or challenge hers. One is reminded of Medusa, the monstrous gorgon from Greek mythology whose gaze would turn men into stone. Whether or not consciously deployed, that gaze performed an important function. It transformed Golda from an object to be looked at by the men around the cabinet table into a subject projecting agency and control. The practice, it appears, was quite effective.

Secrecy and Other Techniques of Governance

Secrecy was another technique Golda used to consolidate power and cover up her vulnerability. According to Golda's former cabinet spokesperson and biographer, Meron Medzini, "keeping information tightly protected and limiting the right to know to very few were her means to combat leaking." In terms of her governance he pointed out that secrecy

had severe consequences. It limited and often prevented healthy deliberations. "The absence of arguments, particularly in matters of security,
meant that fundamental issues and even some actions and secret negotiations were not discussed in a structured way. Alternatives were not
explored and if mistakes were made there was no process to evaluate
them and derive lessons."[14] Keeping information under a tight lid provided Golda with the protection she desired. From the time that she
had her sister's letters sent to a friend's address when she was a teenager,
Golda understood that knowledge was power and preferred to keep it
tightly guarded.

More generally, Golda's fear of being exposed by ill-wishers made her
reticent to trust anyone beyond a tight circle of friends and advisers and
she built protective walls around herself: a small body of trusted
ministers—nicknamed "Golda's kitchen"—made most of the crucial
governing decisions in the privacy of her own home. During these
"kitchen cabinet" meetings, the group assembled was duly declared "the
ministerial committee for matters of defense," thereby making its content confidential and subject to military censorship. Golda let it be
known that she was serving coffee and cake to the assembled ministers,
in her expectation that the amiable appearance would justify the fact
that matters of life and death were being decided without the required
deliberative procedures or proper oversight.[15]

It is hard to tell the extent to which these practices should be attributed to the intensity of the political climate and to what extent they
should be attributed to her ailing body, her age, and her lack of confidence in her ability to do the job. But Golda was certainly conscious of
the negative stereotypes that accompanied being "an older woman" and
she understood the need to always display tough, masculine leadership.
Both of these facts played an important role in shaping her style of governance, a style heavy in rhetoric and sarcasm and laced with proud
deference to military experts.

Four years after her ascent to office, the Yom Kippur War arrived like
a bolt of lightning. The Agranat Commission, which studied the factors
leading to the war, strongly criticized Golda's mode of governance and
insisted that the government install a more structured process of decision making, including the creation of a national security council.[16] The

commission unanimously concluded that Golda erred in part because of her tunnel vision, the result of a process that rarely welcomed open argument or considered alternative points of view.

Public Opinion and Responsible Leadership

Golda's approach to governing was also informed by her earlier experience with those "merry wives of Windsor," women who did not trust their own gender to lead. During the weeks preceding the Six-Day War their protests and demonstrations relentlessly criticized Golda's "deficiencies"—her age, her irrationality, her lack of education. For the most part, Golda was unmoved by the demonstrations. With Ben-Gurion she believed that leadership should not be a pawn in the hands of public opinion. Her considered judgment was that the public panic was politically engineered and must not be allowed to determine policy decisions

Nevertheless, Dayan's appointment as minister of defense left a mark. Responsible leadership was one thing and staying in power quite another. By 1969 it was clear that a majority of Israelis wished to keep the conquered territories—the Sinai, the Golan Heights, and the West Bank—if not forever, then at least until Israel received a satisfactory deal from the Arab states. As prime minister, Golda tried to abide by this public wish. As she always had, she desired peace with Israel's Arab neighbors, which she knew would not arrive without fundamental compromises, but she treaded carefully so as not to contradict the people's will. As a result, her legacy came to be associated with loyalty to the status quo: keep the territories, reject suggestions of full Israeli withdrawal, and call for a peace based on direct negotiations and an expectation that some of the territories would remain in Israeli hands—conditions she well knew the Arabs would find hard to accept.

Behind the scenes, Golda examined several options to launch negotiations with the Arabs, particularly with Egypt's president Anwar Sadat.[17] Perhaps had circumstances been different—had she been healthier and more confident in her leadership, or at least less burdened by continual international and domestic crises—she might have succeeded. Instead she presided over one of Israel's most traumatic wars for which the public never forgave her.[18]

CHAPTER 20

GOLDA AS AN OBJECT OF HUMILIATION

BY THE TIME GOLDA assumed the highest office in the land, the tectonic plates under Israeli society had already begun to shift. Intergenerational tensions within Mapai as well as in the country at large had been increasing for years. Golda concluded that David Ben-Gurion, her former ally turned nemesis, had been nurturing and promoting a group of young politicians whom he hoped would replace the old guard. Led by Moshe Dayan and Shimon Peres, these young men believed it was their turn to govern. Their new party, Rafi, aggressively promoted the idea that it was time for the young to take over.[1] Although not particularly young (these were middle-aged men with a long list of accomplishments behind them), they represented a new generation. The founders of the country had been born in Eastern Europe, spoke with thick accents, and led an austere, ascetic lifestyle. The young spoke native Hebrew, were somewhat arrogant, and preferred a more relaxed, fun-loving lifestyle. Golda was well aware of the rising tensions as she took office and, seeking balance and adjustment, she included both Dayan and Peres in her cabinet.

Less familiar to Golda were the voices coming from further below signaling a cultural change. Young university students, artists, and writers felt increasingly alienated from the conventional political views of their society as well as from the political leadership. They were shocked by the carnage of the Six-Day War and the casualties from the War of

Attrition. They wanted the government to actively seek a compromise with Israel's Arab neighbors, resented the price they were expected to pay as soldiers, and rejected the calls to keep occupied territories. In contrast to their young opponents on the right who possessed a Messianic worldview, they were drawn to cosmopolitanism. They felt a sense of camaraderie with the young generations of Europe and the United States whose call to "make love not war" resonated in their hearts. These young people heralded a movement that challenged the sacred ideological pillars of Zionism, which would later come to be known as "post-Zionism." At the birth of this movement in the early 1970s, their attacks appeared utterly shocking to mainstream society.[2]

Queen of a Bathtub

I roared like a lioness who had lost her cubs. Because I was pained by the lie . . . one must be a villain or blind to turn everything so dear to us into excrement and urine.

—A FEMALE VIEWER DESCRIBING HER REVULSION
TO QUEEN OF A BATHTUB, JUNE 1970

In April 1970, just as Golda was celebrating her first anniversary in office, the budding playwright Hanoch Levin was invited to stage his satirical review *Queen of a Bathtub: Fraternity in the Shadow of Guns* at the prestigious Cameri Theatre in Tel Aviv.[3] Writing in a style falling somewhere between *Saturday Night Live* and Lenny Bruce, the skinny twenty-seven-year-old hurled mud at the pillars of the Zionist edifice: the professed yearning for peace coupled with an obvious desire for war; the consensus that constant death and maiming in battle were inevitable parts of being Israeli; the veneration of the pioneering spirit as the epitome of the noble foundations of Zionist society; and the attachment to the West Bank as the "cradle of our forefathers." Rather than represent Israelis as honorable, enlightened kibbutzniks, Levin's satire brought to the stage a narrow-minded, avaricious, and self-centered petite bourgeoisie befitting a Balzac novel. He captured the narrow horizons of the working poor, which were inescapably shaped by the climate of nationalism, want, and neglect. Instead of the noble Israeli superego, the satire depicted the Israeli id. The body replaced the mind, while excrement, urine, and flatulence saturated the dialogue.[4]

Later in his life Levin would be recognized as one of Israel's greatest playwrights. Some even insisted he was a genius. But when *Queen of a Bathtub* first appeared on stage, people were traumatized by the depiction of a fallen son singing to his grieving father while being laid to rest: "Dear father: Do not say that you made a sacrifice, because the one who sacrificed was I . . . as you watch me being buried, ask for my forgiveness, father."[5] Golda was appalled. To a father who had lost his son in battle and protested the play, Golda responded that she shared his "revulsion and sadness" but maintained that "it is not in my power to censor the work."[6]

Golda had more reason than most to feel appalled. *Queen of a Bathtub* first introduced her in a skit titled Cabinet Meeting. The skit portrayed Golda opening the cabinet meeting with a self-absorbed speech basking in her own perfection. She then called upon the minister of foreign affairs to deliver "a speech to the United Nations." The minister, Abba Eban, repeatedly attempted to present the "fundamental foreign policy principles of Israel," only to be rudely interrupted by Golda. Each time he attempted to make a dovish statement Golda would thrust her hand underneath the table and grab his balls.

The skit after which the show was titled, "Queen of a Bathtub," went even further in its ridicule and vulgar representation of Golda. In previous years, Prime Minister Levy Eshkol, speaking Yiddish, displayed his ambivalence about Golda by calling her alternately "Die Malkae" (the queen) or "die mechashefa" (the witch). Levin inverted Golda's royal status by turning her into the ultimate Israeli petite bourgeoise. The scene, set in a working-class neighborhood, focuses on a family of four— mother, father, son, and daughter—sharing a very small apartment with a tenant, the husband's male cousin. The five share a single bathroom consisting of a bathtub and a toilet.

Golda is presented as a narrow-minded, self-centered, rude "balabusta" (Yiddish for housewife; the ultimate stereotype of the petite bourgeoisie).[7] She openly disdains the tenant-cousin and wishes he would disappear. She monopolizes the bathroom, making sure that only members of her immediate family are allowed to take hot showers. She also bars the tenant from using the toilet. At one point in the skit the tenant begs her to let him use the bathroom. She refuses and, helpless, he ends up urinating in his pants. The husband addresses the audience: "We were sure that this time he would declare defeat or leave the apartment. Never mind not being able to shower. But pee pee is not something you can argue with. And nevertheless he did not break down." The thinly veiled reference to the Palestinians, stubbornly refusing to let go of the land, as well as the depiction of the dire living conditions that prevailed in Israel, would have been evident to any Israeli. Near the end of the sketch, Golda sits on the toilet as if it were her throne, declares herself "queen of the bathtub kingdom," and delivers a vacuous speech about "our desire for peace."[8]

If in Levin's initial portrayal of Golda she was the emasculator in chief, this skit portrayed her as a middle-aged woman hungry for sex:

HUSBAND: "Look, you cannot speak this way" [to my cousin].
WOMAN: "Oh yes? All right then, why don't you run the household . . . I shall lie on the couch and entertain sexual phantasies about the minister of transportation."[9]

Israelis were shocked and disgusted by Levin's show. They were not used to viewing themselves in this light and they resented the attack on their credo. Their collective consciousness had been shaped by Zionist ideology and was carefully protected by the government's censorship of plays and films. Narratives deviating from the prevailing ideology were for the most part excluded before they could reach the public. The fact that the censors decided to ask for modification of the production of *Queen of a Bathtub* rather than block it in full was itself proof that times were changing and that the liberal principle of freedom of expression was taking root. The production was nevertheless shut down after only nineteen performances, primarily because the public controversy kept intensifying and the theater management decided it had had enough.[10]

The media's response to the play focused primarily on its sacrilegious attack on national values, in particular Levin's attack on the venerable place accorded to the military and Israel's image of itself as David going up against Goliath. Very little public attention was given to the debasement of women or general misogyny permeating the show. Silence on this matter can partly be explained by the puritanism of the Israeli public. Israelis and their media felt awkward about discussing sex or bodily functions in the public sphere. They preferred that respect for Golda as prime minister and a grandmother be accompanied by respect for sexual taboos. Referring to the prime minister as a sexual abuser and as someone who indulged in sexual fantasies violated their conservative sensibilities.

And yet the misogyny in the play deserves further attention. In reality Golda did not conform to the conventional stereotype of the feminine woman—weak, delicate, and sensitive. Her depiction on the stage as aggressive and abrasive conveyed a dark yet pervasive image of Golda in Israeli and Jewish culture. Beneath the facade of the loving, self-sacrificing Jewish mother stood a monstrous, emasculating, sex-hungry woman. Moreover, Levin's play cleverly inverted common gender stereotypes. In the skit with Abba Eban, Golda was presented as the uncivilized aggressor and Eban as the soft-spoken minister. Israelis' fondness for calling Golda "the only man with balls in the cabinet" was, among other things, their way of soothing their anxiety about the fact that a woman was navigating the ship of state. Here, however, the balls took center stage. Not only was the woman sexually assaulting a man, she was interrupting him and preventing him from making his points, both common male behaviors toward women. Herein lay the ultimate inversion: the man, not the woman, fell silent. That attack on Israeli masculinity must have been hard to swallow regardless of whether or not one agreed with Eban's dovish approach.

The central skit, "Queen of a Bathtub," presented an even more humiliating portrayal of Golda as an abrasive, coarse, and domineering woman. Devoid of moral compass, the central character possessed no empathy for the weak and needy, an unattractive portrait of a nation's leader. Levin's inversion of gender stereotypes was also on display in this skit. As a scion of an Orthodox family and well versed in religious sources, Levin was certainly aware of the religious explanation for the exclusion of women from the public sphere: men would not be able to control their sexual fantasies if they encountered women in public. Levin reversed the stereotype by making Golda's namesake, the "powerful queen of the bathtub," indulge in sexual fantasies.[11] The object of the queen's fantasies, the minister of transportation, is also telling. At the time, the minister of transportation was Ezer Weizman, the legendary chief of Israel's air force during the Six-Day War. A tall mustachioed war hero, Weizman was the epitome of aggressive masculinity and known for inventing the slogan "the best (men) to the air force and the best (women) to the pilots." Portraying Weizman as the object of Golda's sexual fantasies fortified the image of her as emasculating and power hungry.[12]

The genius in Levin's work was his ability to capture the collective Israeli subconscious. His obsession with "phallic women" was no mere individual fancy.[13] Misogyny ran deep in Israeli society from the top echelons to the underclass. Consciousness-raising about the role of women in society had not yet crossed the ocean and most Israelis lived in peace with the contradiction between their public ideals and its practices. On one hand, they placed Israel's commitment to gender equality on a pedestal and took pride in having a woman as prime minister; on the other hand, they valued "men with balls" and expected most women to conform to traditional feminine stereotypes. This widely shared state of mind may explain why the media ignored the misogyny of Levin's play and focused instead on its attack on Israeli nationalism.[14]

Unsurprisingly, Golda was very critical of *Queen of a Bathtub*. In discussion with senior newspaper editors she expressed fear that the show would undermine the public morale necessary during the ongoing War of Attrition. She suggested that the press should urge people to avoid the show and thereby force the theater to shut it down. She even asked the minister in charge of the broadcasting agency, "How many times shall we be obliged to listen to the pearls of 'queen of [a] bathtub' on the radio?" During a cabinet meeting she denounced the satire, asking "Is this art? Progress? A liberal point of view?" rhetorically implying that it was culturally worthless.[15] But she never explicitly raised the issue of misogyny.

Rise of the Intergenerational Divide

She could have and did attribute the unsavory discourse to the emerging zeitgeist that appeared in many different elements of youth culture of which Golda disapproved. As the curtain was rising on *Queen of a Bathtub*, fifty-six high school students in Jerusalem wrote a letter to Golda in which they protested the prospects of continuous war. They were eager to see Israel's government make efforts to achieve peace and feared what they perceived as a stubborn fidelity to the status quo.[16] Similarly, waves of "new music" such as that of the Beatles swept the land and galvanized young Israelis. To Golda's ears this "cacophony" was unworthy of the term *music* and was "only good to give you a headache."[17] Despite the fact that her own grandchildren were fond of Beatles music and imitated their long hair and jeans, Golda could not accept that times were changing.[18] She found the fashion of miniskirts particularly irksome: "[Their] fashions irritate me. . . . Why that long hair, those short skirts? I hate fashions . . . somebody in Paris decides for some reason that women should wear miniskirts, and here they all are in miniskirts: long legs, short legs, skinny legs, fat legs, ugly legs." Golda's real fear, however, did not concern passing fashions, but rather her losing control and being left behind:

> What I condemn in [the young] is their presumption in saying,
> "Everything you have done is wrong so we'll redo it all from the beginning." Well, if they were to do it all over again better, I wouldn't even mind, but in many cases they're no better than us old people and can even be worse.[19]

She perceived herself as the custodian of the grand Zionist narrative and was determined to protect it from the growing chorus of detractors. In particular Golda directed her wrath against Shulamit Aloni, a rising star in politics who was rapidly becoming her nemesis.[20]

FROM BATHTUB TO PEDESTAL

An Interview with Oriana Fallaci

BY THE TIME the Italian journalist Oriana Fallaci approached Golda for an interview, both women were world famous. Known for her commitment to exposing abuses of power, fearless war coverage around the globe, and penetrating interviews with the great and the mighty, Fallaci had been dubbed by *Rolling Stone* magazine as "the greatest political interviewer of modern times." Her interview with Golda stands among her greatest achievements and is featured in nearly every retrospective of her work.[1]

Fallaci told an intriguing story about her interview with Golda. After conducting the initial interview she returned to Rome where her tapes mysteriously went missing from her hotel room. She had to repeat the entire interview and recounted Golda's gracious willingness to interrupt her busy schedule for a second interview.[2] Golda had enjoyed meeting Fallaci and did not wish to disappoint her, but the decision to sit for a second interview went beyond mere graciousness: Golda recognized this as an extraordinary media opportunity at a time when her country was licking its wounds following the massacre of eleven Israeli athletes in Munich, with the Mossad already ferociously hunting down the terrorists seeking not only deterrence but also revenge.[3]

Golda was pleased with the results. The two women had chemistry, perhaps a deep solidarity of sisterhood, and in this atmosphere Fallaci was able to elicit rare insights into Golda's approach to feminism.[4]

"The Only Man in the Cabinet," an Irritant

Fallaci deftly put Golda at ease by asking about her early history and her political views concerning the Arab–Israeli conflict.[5] Despite the fact that referring to women using the prefix "Ms." was quickly becoming standard practice (*Ms.* magazine had been launched in the United States ten months prior), Fallaci addressed Golda as Mrs. Meir, thereby appealing to Golda's conservative sensibility. In the final third of the interview after Golda had happily confessed her enthusiasm for America, Fallaci said: "Okay, we finally come to the figure of Golda Meir. So shall we talk about the woman Ben-Gurion called 'the ablest man in my cabinet'?" Fallaci had planned the interview, carefully postponing the question until an opportune moment. Moreover, despite Fallaci's reputation as a tough interviewer, throughout the interview she was neither aggressive nor provocative. One feels that she studied Golda carefully and avoided language that might have irritated her. Referring to Golda as the "ablest man in my cabinet," for example, was the gentlest, kindest version of the statement attributed to Ben-Gurion. More sexual versions included the statement that Golda was "the only man with balls in the cabinet" or "the only man with iron balls in the cabinet." Golda, who generally ignored the famous statement, answered: "That's one of the legends that's grown up around me. It's also a legend I've always found irritating, though men use it as a great compliment."[6]

Golda proceeded to offer a sharp analysis of the "legend," showing that she both understood its poisonous nature and resented it, even if she generally kept that resentment locked inside: "Because what does it really mean? That it is better to be a man than a woman, a principle on which I don't agree at all. So, here's what I'd like to say: And what if Ben-Gurion had said, 'The men in my cabinet are as able as women?'" Maybe Golda had never read Hegel or Marx but she could certainly turn a question on its head. Under the patriarchal sun, being as able as a woman could never be a compliment, a fact that both she and the men who kept her company understood. "Men always feel so superior," she said, ending her train of thought. They were willing to concede her talents but only at the price of denying her womanhood. "It's a good thing I have a sense of humor," she concluded, sublimating the irritation into humor. She well knew that if she allowed her irritation to morph into aggression, her career would suffer. Men would not tolerate it. Golda had internalized the cultural reality of male superiority and decided it was best to look the other way rather than confront it headlong and pay the price.

Golda's Views on the Women's Liberation Movement

Fallaci seized the opening. Well aware of the tension between Golda and the American leaders of the Women's Liberation Movement, Fallaci suggested that Golda's insights into Ben-Gurion's statement would be embraced by feminists. Off guard, Golda took the bait and launched a scathing attack on the women's movement:

O. F.: The Women's Liberation Movement will like that, Mrs. Meir.

G. M.: Do you mean those crazy women who burn their bras and go around all disheveled and hate men? They're crazy. Crazy. But how can one accept such crazy women who think it's a misfortune to get pregnant and a disaster to bring children into the world?

Feminists as Crazy Bra Burners

Golda had forgotten her own history. When she had discovered that she was pregnant soon after her marriage in the early 1920s, she had viewed the pregnancy as a "misfortune" and sought an illegal abortion. More generally, Golda understood as well as anyone that the obligations imposed by young children prevented many young mothers from seeking self-fulfillment. (See parts I and II in this volume.) Golda was making a convenient U-turn. Having just offered a thoughtful analysis of why men find it hard to accept powerful women, she stereotyped feminists as misguided rebels.[7] In the course of three sentences she branded them "crazy," that is, beyond the pale of reason, and presented them as a sad caricature, disheveled bra burners who rejected motherhood.

As Golda well knew, these were unfair and gross generalizations. Ruth Bader Ginsburg, a leader in the women's movement, working to address the rampant gender discrimination in the United States, was impeccably dressed, organized, and happily married with two children. At home in Israel, Shulamit Aloni, an outspoken advocate for women's rights, was well dressed and married with three sons. Had Golda wished to be thoughtful or balanced she would have discussed these women in her response. But she preferred mockery. One possible explanation is that, confronted with her earlier statement, she realized that she had put herself at a risk of backlash and felt the need to deny her association with feminism. She may have imagined the disappointment of so many Israelis who found that "legend" poignant or predicted that the conservative Israeli press would accuse her of being a feminist. Or perhaps her reaction was driven by her general perception that hippies and feminists shared the anti-Israeli policies of the New Left. More personally, perhaps she worried that the feminist movement might revive the conflicts she had known during the 1930s at the Women Workers Council. That was a Pandora's box Golda knew not to open.

Golda preferred to present herself as Exhibit A of gender equality in Israel, a depiction that also communicated a course of action to ambitious Israeli women: deny the existence of gender-based discrimination and take care to avoid alienating men. As she told Fallaci, "I've lived and worked among men all my life, and yet to me the fact of being a woman has never, never I say, been an obstacle. It's never made me uncomfortable or given me an inferiority complex. Men have always been good to me." The facts of her life, of course, belie this claim. Did she not run away from home because her parents refused to let her go to high school? Would the comrades in the Kibbutz have denied her application for membership if she hadn't been an American girl? Would the rabbis have opposed her ascent to power with the same vehemence had she been a man?

Fallaci knew that she was getting under Golda's skin and pushed back gently: "Are you saying you prefer [men] to women?"

Confronted with the idea that she preferred men to women, Golda again reversed course.[8] While she continued to emphasize that her life experience was blessed with supportive men, she conceded that the Women's Liberation Movement had a point: "To be successful, a woman has to be much more capable than a man . . . it's ridiculous that towards women there still exist so many reservations, so many injustices." But she immediately qualified her statement by asking, "But is it all the fault of men? Wouldn't it be, at least partially, the fault of women too?"

Fallaci followed with another gentle question: "[Is it] perhaps more difficult to be a woman than a man?" "Yes, of course," Golda agreed, "for biological reasons, I'd say."[9] Golda elaborated that women were expected to raise the children, to keep house, and if they also wanted to "be somebody" they faced conditions that are "hard, hard, hard."

"I Stooped Enough and That's Bad"

Golda may not have been familiar with Betty Friedan's *The Feminine Mystique* or other contemporary feminist writings, but she certainly was familiar with the analysis of the great Zionist feminists as well as the American Pioneer Women, both groups having denounced tradition and the idea that conventional gender roles were somehow natural and immutable. But Golda as Israel's leader had political reasons to refrain from alienating the conservative camp, which included members of the religious parties who were the lynchpins of her cabinet.

Near the end of the interview, Golda stated: "When you are doing the job I am doing you always have to stoop to compromises, you can never let yourself remain one hundred percent faithful to your ideas. . . . I stooped enough and that's bad."[10] Golda was well aware of the compromises she had been forced to make to reach the top. Basking in Fallaci's admiration, she was able to put her finger on the technique she had chosen to pursue success—stooping—and to identify the price she had paid for doing so.

CHAPTER 22

GOLDA AND HER NEMESIS

Shulamit Aloni and the Question of Who Is a Jew

Intergenerational Struggle

In 1965, as Golda stepped into the powerful position of Mapai's secretary general, a mid-level politician in her late thirties, Shulamit Aloni, joined the Knesset as a junior member of Golda's party.[1]

Aloni was a good-looking, outspoken woman, well connected and passionately committed to social and political reform. Her gospel was that Israel should be a polity imbued with civic virtue where citizens possessed rights as well as duties. After the long decades of collectivist hegemony, which neglected civil and political rights in favor of statism, her claim that Israel should respect the citizen sounded fresh and timely. She also developed a feminist agenda that rejected the gendered division of labor and insisted that women be treated as "human beings" rather than as "objectified others."[2] She spoke in a secular Jewish voice according to which the universal values underlying Judaism, such as justice, trumped rabbinic rules embedded in Jewish law (Halacha).[3] While she emphasized her deep roots in the biblical tradition, she rejected the rabbinical imposition of halachic rules on Israelis, an imposition that she called "clericalism."

Like all great progressive leaders, Aloni located her forward-looking ideas in a common past and appealed directly to Israel's

Declaration of Independence. The declaration promised equal protection of the laws, a democratic system of government, and the free exercise of religion. It also promised a constitution. The crown jewel of a constitution, she believed, must be a bill of rights that grants each citizen particular freedoms, and she was determined to lead a popular movement on behalf of this idea. Aloni argued that with the adoption of a Bill of Rights Israel would finally take the rights of Israeli women seriously and guarantee gender equality in all areas of life, including in family matters. Indeed this last point had been the Achilles' heel of Israel's legal system since its beginning. The rabbinical courts where Orthodox men enjoyed a monopoly applied a set of rules to family life that was out of touch with modern sensibilities and secular Zionism.[4]

Like John F. Kennedy, Aloni felt that the torch had been passed to a new generation, and she saw herself as its bearer. Her first appearance in the Knesset confirmed that a new era had indeed arrived. She appeared in a sleeveless dress, well-coiffed and radiant. A better image of "youth" could not be imagined: flesh and femininity were displayed in a blatant challenge to conservative mores. The sight, so unfamiliar in the somber legislature, startled the (mostly male) Knesset members. To members of the religious parties accustomed to female modesty, her appearance was an outright provocation. Every fiber in her being was demanding change: the old generation had to go.

Golda was not amused. Like most senior members of the government she did not feel old, nor did she think that her values were outdated.[5] In Aloni's call to pass the torch, Golda heard the sound of the broom sweeping her and her comrades off the stage. To the great detriment of Israel's struggle for gender equality this personal resentment Golda felt toward Aloni fed the feud between these two women. But politics also played its part. Golda was no longer the same woman who had entered into heated debates with religious cabinet ministers in the early 1950s. She had learned to reduce her expectations, temper her criticisms, and accept the support of the religious camp in matters of security and foreign affairs. Letting the rabbis prevail in personal matters, she calculated pragmatically, was a price worth paying.

When she joined the Knesset, Aloni was thirty-eight years old, twenty-nine years younger than Golda and the same age as Golda's daughter, Sarah. Despite this difference in age Golda and Aloni had a great deal in common. Both were fiercely ambitious, charismatic, and possessed the qualities of a natural leader. Like Golda, Aloni was a captivating public speaker unafraid to speak truth to power, for which she earned many devoted fans. Both women pursued a career despite having young children and understood firsthand the dilemma of satisfying the competing needs of family and work. Both were also from working-class backgrounds and had complex relationships with their parents. Regarding policy, they shared the belief that a regulated market best supported the ideal of social progress.[6] Concerning personal relationships, both sought the company of strong intellectual men.

There were significant differences as well. Perhaps most important, Aloni arrived at the Knesset armed with liberal principles and a legal education. Golda was by then a senior matriarch in possession of the party's power and determined to keep it even if this meant maintaining an alliance with the religious camp and bending principles in favor of expediency.

Aloni Denied a Knesset Seat

A ferocious struggle between the two women followed. Aloni was often very vocal while Golda used her power quietly behind the scenes. During this struggle another fundamental difference between the two emerged: temperament. Golda was patient and careful not to alienate potential allies even if it meant change would come more slowly. Aloni by contrast had little patience. Throughout her tenure in the Sixth Knesset she clashed with both the party's old guard and the religious camp. Golda concluded that Aloni did more harm than good and decided to exclude her from the next Knesset.

The structure of Israel's electoral system based on proportionality rather than personal representation made this task easy to accomplish.[7] Each party submits a list of nominees drawn up and ordered by the party's nominating committee, and the voters decide not which individuals they wished to represent them but rather which list they preferred. The more seats a party wins the farther down the list its candidates are selected. In 1965 Aloni was placed as the thirty-second nominee on Maipa's list while Golda was number four. Mapai won forty-five seats so Aloni entered parliament. In the 1969 elections Golda was first on the list and Aloni was assigned the sixty-fourth seat, thereby sealing her fate. Golda did not blink when she told a reporter that sixty-four was a perfectly likely number to win a seat, but she could sleep well at night as she had little doubt that this political firebrand would be kept out of the Knesset. Mapai won fifty-six seats, an impressive showing but, as expected, Aloni did not make the cut.

Israel's advocates of women's rights saw this as an alarming déjà vu. Israel's founding feminist, Ada Fishman Maimon, chair of the Women Workers Council in the 1920s, was defeated via an identical process. In party meetings Maimon insisted on open elections to the party list. She pointed out that while women were allowed to vote, the party bosses included very few women on the list. Ada was ignored as women's interests were low on the party's agenda.[8] In 1955 David Ben-Gurion decided that he had had enough of Ada's belligerent insistence on women's rights and her calls for the separation of church and state. She was demoted to the bottom of the party list and inevitably failed to be elected to the Third Knesset. As a result she all but faded away from politics. Golda, herself a party boss at the time, presumably did not object and was handsomely rewarded for her nonobjection with the prestigious position of minister of foreign affairs.[9] The history of the first wave of feminism in Israel was barely known to second-wave activists like Aloni who were destined to repeat its most painful lessons.

Hurt and humiliated, Aloni increased her attacks on Golda. She never tired of emphasizing that Golda, deaf to the music of the age, was a self-centered politician skilled in promoting special interests at the expense of the public good. In many ways Aloni echoed the portrayal of Golda in *Queen of a Bathtub*. Despite no longer being in the Knesset, Aloni remained active in party politics, expanded her public support, and hoped to be included on the list of candidates by the time of the next elections. She tried to work within the system by campaigning and lobbying party members. Nevertheless, when the list was formed, Golda again prevailed. After this second defeat, Aloni decided to form her own party (Ratz, Hebrew for running, later renamed Meretz), on whose ticket she ran and won.[10]

Golda was aware that she was dealing with a ticking time bomb. In 1965 when Aloni was first elected, the Knesset consisted of 120 members, representing all parties, but had only 10 women. As had been the case since the founding of the country, Israeli politics was dominated by men. In 1969, as Golda rose to the position of prime minister and the feisty Aloni was excluded from Mapai's party list, only eight women served in the Knesset. The low and declining number of women in politics was not sustainable in a country in which women composed roughly 50 percent of the population. Golda tried to recruit women candidates to her own party and prevailed upon a few to accept the party's nomination. But Golda wanted control over those "chosen" and promoted only women who, while talented, were acquiescent and nonthreatening.[11] Charismatic or opinionated women like Golda were not considered.

Aloni's Temporary Triumph after the Yom Kippur War

Aloni and Golda continued to spar for the next several years. In May 1974, after Golda's resignation and the formation of a cabinet by Prime Minister Yitzhak Rabin, the question arose whether Aloni's new civil rights party (Meretz) would join the coalition. Her inclusion would strengthen the cabinet and appeal to the secular electorate and Aloni was eager to join. Golda had already resigned her position but was poised for one last fight. She dressed her opposition in meritorious political reasons claiming that she had "nothing against her" and even agreed that including Aloni would serve the Party's interests. Nevertheless she insisted that Aloni should be excluded from the coalition.

The recent war, however, had left Israelis eager to clean house. Deserted by many of her supporters, Golda was a sinking ship. The promise of change invigorated the people, and Rabin, the military hero of the Six-Day War and first Israeli-born prime minister, had declared that his cabinet signaled the "turning of a new leaf." As a cabinet member, Aloni would be emblematic of that change.

At the final party meeting convened to approve the next cabinet, the now retired Golda presented a motion to exclude Aloni from the cabinet. The party's secretary-general chairing the meeting ignored Golda's motion and insisted that by doing so he was simply following common procedure. A year earlier his head would have rolled for giving such an excuse. This was a poignant indication of Golda's fall from power. She rose in a fit of rage, hurried out the door, and slammed it behind her.[12] Publicly losing to her nemesis must have felt even worse than the chemotherapy she was undergoing at the time for her cancer. A deep sense of humiliation overwhelmed her as she realized that she had become irrelevant.

In her darkest nightmares, Golda could not imagine that her departure from the party that had been her home for a half century would be accompanied by a loss to her political nemesis. This was the nadir of Golda's career, and the horrors of the Yom Kippur War continued to torment her. In particular, the accusation that she was responsible for the devastation and loss of so many young lives caused her immense distress. Her insecurity and her sense of worthlessness always present beneath the surface were taking over. Powerless, despised, and rejected, she slammed the door noisily just as she had as a teenager when she left her sister Sheyna's home. She was once again homeless and alone.

Do not imagine, however, that this moment ushered in a glorious new chapter in the history of Israeli women. For a short while Aloni celebrated her victory and felt hopeful about what her appointment meant for her progressive agenda. She joined the Rabin cabinet as a minister without a portfolio and instructed her office and the media to refer to her as sara, the feminine construction of sar (a male minister)—a rebuke to Golda's preference for the male designation. A woman, Aloni proudly announced, was a female minister and should not hide her gender.

But soon enough the opposition began to publicly challenge her universalist agenda, her insistence on the principle of the separation of church and state, and her barbed comments. Now that Golda was out of the way, the arrow of misogyny was trained squarely on Aloni. She was increasingly referred to as "that woman," and not only in religious circles, although they remained her harshest critics. Israelis were used to seeing women in power as the source of trouble and they were comfortable blaming Aloni rather than Golda for their current malaise. With Rabin's support Aloni remained in the cabinet, held various ministries, and even led her party to capture twelve seats in the 1992 elections. She tried to make Israeli society more tolerant of "the other" and open to Western ideals, including the norm of diversity. Some accused her of mindlessly imitating American trends. When she brought a bill to outlaw violence against women, members of the Knesset reacted with giggles and ridicule. The same reaction accompanied her suggestion that the criminalization of homosexual relations be repealed. In her words, she became "a victim of power struggles, [of] brute and arrogant male machoism."[13] Slowly she came to understand that being a woman made her an easy target. She never admitted, however that that same fire she directed towards Golda was now deployed by others to burn her. As she observed in her memoirs: "when you create hysteria around a person, especially a woman, and a woman who has opinions and positions, then you turn her into a lightning rod for the entire cabinet you wish to topple.... Even if I kept silent they would have done the same. My personality and everything I represented were like a red cloth."[14]

Ambitious men who were attracted to her rising political power joined the party that she founded and then, she believed, pushed her out in order to advance themselves. Ultimately she was replaced by Yossi Sarid, a well-known politician whom she accused of having undermined her every step of the way. The moment of her demise, not so different from Golda's, arrived at a party meeting convened to demand her capitulation. She knew that the procedure used to dethrone her was faulty, yet she acquiesced. When she decided to resign her position as minister of education, she was wrongly informed that unless she did so the coalition would fall, and she felt that this would be too high a price for the state to pay. In her own words, she said:

> I broke down out of shame, humiliation, under pressure from people who should have supported me and instead trapped me. Of course, I should have been stronger, and I am sorry that my husband ... was not next to me ... he died in 1988 ... he always gave me feelings of empowerment and the ability to withstand difficult conditions.

Her shame, humiliation, and a yearning for the support of a strong man, as we will see in the following chapters, makes the moment echo Golda's remembrance of David Remez at her last cabinet meeting as she announced her resignation. (See chapter 26 in this volume.)

A Counterfactual Ending

It is difficult to resist fantasizing about a counterfactual history in which Golda had decided to take Aloni under her wing and mentor her. Golda could have explained to her why she had decided to live with the offensive epigram that Israelis so enjoyed repeating—that she was the "only man in the cabinet"—and could have instructed Aloni on how best to navigate the game of politics, including when to speak and when to keep quiet.

Golda made many mistakes in her treatment of Aloni, but Aloni was far from blameless for their fractious relationship. Golda was not an "ignorant woman," as Aloni relentlessly repeated. By the 1970s Golda possessed an unparalleled trove of experience. She may not have held a university degree, but she could have taught a graduate-level seminar on the art of politics and governance. Aloni could have learned so much from Golda, perhaps even enough to remain in power and effect the changes her followers desired.

Sadly, none of this came to pass. Instead Aloni's career, like Golda's, ended on a bitter note. As Aloni later reflected: "I was hoping to retire in a different way. I did not think that I would be a victim of power struggles and of arrogant, rude male chauvinism. . . . I left with a broken heart."[15]

CHAPTER 23

WHO IS A JEW?

Individual Rights, Jewish Law, the Expediency of Politics, and the "Foreign Woman"

"WHO IS A JEW?" This question about Jewish identity has long been a source of intense conflict in Israel because its answer carries important legal ramifications. The question was also a factor in one of the most significant confrontations between Golda and Aloni.

The Shalit Case

Benjamin Shalit, a native Israeli Jew, served as an officer in the Israeli army. While pursuing doctoral studies abroad he met Anne Geddes and the two fell in love.[1] As an Israeli, Shalit felt unburdened by the yoke of Jewish history and the demands of Jewish law and he was unconcerned by the fact that Anne was not Jewish. He asked only that Anne agree to settle in Israel and adopt the Israeli way of life, by which he meant speak Hebrew, celebrate the Jewish holidays as Israelis celebrate them, and adapt to the local Israeli culture. Being Zionists both believed that in modern Israel, national identity was shaped by the emerging secular culture rather than by rabbinical norms. There was thus no need for Anne to convert to Judaism.[2]

Under Jewish law, only a child born to a Jewish mother is Jewish. When Shalit arrived at the Ministry of the Interior to register their children, he was told that the children could not be registered as Jews because Anne was not Jewish. From the ministry's perspective, Jewish law, rather than the desire of the parents, defined the identity of his children. Under the secular Israeli Statute of Registration, two categories would be completed by the registrar: nationality and religion. Shalit was told that Israeli law incorporated Orthodox religious law in the definitions of both categories, so if the children's mother was not Jewish they could not be registered as Jewish either as a matter of religion or as a matter of nationality.[3] The decision deeply offended Shalit. He was raising his children as Israelis, in keeping with the promised national revival embedded in Zionist ideology. In order to avoid Orthodox law, he proposed registering his children as "Hebrew" or "Israeli" rather than "Jewish." The official at the Ministry of the Interior rejected this alternative. As a matter of law, Shalit was informed, there was no such thing as Israeli or Hebrew people. The only category that existed under Jewish law was "Jewish," and the children were not Jewish. In 1968, feeling rejected by his society, Shalit decided to petition the High Court of Justice and challenge the ruling.

The shadow of the Six-Day War loomed over Israeli society, and people on both sides of the question felt that the war vindicated their position. Young secular Israelis like Shalit, whose valiance and sacrifice contributed to the victory, sought confirmation of the "new Israel" as envisioned by secular Zionism. Freedom from the shackles of an outdated religion remained at the very heart of this vision. Conversely, in the eyes of the religious camp, victory in the Six-Day War was proof of divine intervention in human affairs, thereby making evident the state's messianic origins. The definition of a Jew in accordance with Jewish law, they held, was not amendable by secular norms.

In a 5–4 opinion, Israel's High Court of Justice ruled in favor of Shalit and the power of self-determination.[4] Aware of the issue's volatility, the majority relied on a very technical mode of reasoning: a government official had no authority to inquire whether Mrs. Shalit was

Jewish or not, but rather must accept Shalit's good faith declaration and register his children accordingly.[5] The Court cautioned that Israeli law was complex and that if the children were to come before the rabbinical courts, which retained exclusive jurisdiction in matters of marriage and divorce, Jewish law would prevail. Thus, the rabbinical courts had authority to refuse to marry a person registered as "Jewish" if their independent investigation showed that the person did not meet the Orthodox criteria. Such were the contradictions of Israeli law. However the High Court said these issues were not before the court at this moment.[6] The only question at issue concerned whether a government official had the power to cast doubt on a bona fide declaration of a father that his child was Jewish, to which the court declared that the official did not.

Almost overnight, Israeli society became polarized around the ruling. Liberals hailed the opinion as a vindication of Theodor Herzl's vision of a Zionist state in which the church was kept out of the public sphere and the court was embraced as a beacon of the rule of law. Religious Israelis reacted with alarm, warning that Jewish law was the ultimate guarantor of the survival of the Jewish people, and blamed the court for "playing politics" by condoning mixed marriages and putting Israel on the road to spiritual self-destruction. The chief rabbis insisted that the court's decision should be ignored. It was an open challenge to the rule of law, similar to the reactions in the United States to the desegregation decrees of *Brown v. Board of Education* and *Cooper v. Aaron*.[7]

Enter Golda

Golda was annoyed. She had been hoping that the court would allow her to avoid this political hot potato and she worried about the stability of her cabinet in the wake of the decision. If the court's ruling prevailed, the religious parties would leave the coalition government and her party might lose power. On its face the case concerned the mere registration of children, but a much more significant issue was implicated by the decision: the Law of Return. That law, proudly considered by Israelis as the fundamental raison d'être of the state, promised every Jew the right to enter Israel and become a citizen. But if the category of "Jew" was restricted only to those who met the strict Orthodox definition, then many victims of the Holocaust and countless other members of the contemporary Jewish Diaspora would not qualify. Neither Reform nor Conservative Jews in America, nor assimilated Jews in the Soviet Union, would officially count as Jews. The Law of Return would be transformed into a hollow promise.

Golda was well aware that the crisis was receiving intense attention in American Jewish circles, and the international dimension of the case dominated her concern. Tensions between Israel and the United States were already beginning to boil over. Israel was in the midst of the diffi-cult War of Attrition with Egypt, and its strongholds along the Suez Canal were regularly bombarded. In retaliation Israel conducted air raids deep into Egyptian territory, a move that risked provoking the Soviet Union to come to the rescue of its client state. Such a response would not only give the then USSR a firmer foothold in the Middle East but also jeopardize the recent détente pursued by President Richard Nixon and Secretary of State Henry Kissinger. Nixon, unhappy with Israel's recent actions, was signaling that the United States might halt the shipment of new Phantom jets if Israel failed to moderate its bel-ligerence. Golda also feared that any tensions between the United States and Israel would increase the likelihood that the global community would blame Israel for triggering an international crisis. The question of "Who is a Jew," given the international political climate, presented a major threat to Israel's national security.[8]

The timing moreover could not have been worse. Golda was ill with cancer and undergoing chemotherapy. She needed peace and quiet on the domestic front and she dreaded the possibility of becoming mired in a culture war. But many members of her party were avid secularists and they were pleased to see the rabbinical yoke somewhat eased by the Court's decision. She knew that if the matter was put to a vote they would opt for self-determination.

The minister of justice, a savvy Mapai stalwart, immediately went to work to mollify the religious ministers. He knew that the only solution was to amend the law, thereby rendering the High Court's ruling inapplicable in future cases. At the cabinet meeting of January 25, 1970, he proposed two amendments to the current law. The first would allow the Ministry of the Interior to register people in accordance with the strict norms of Jewish law; the second amended the Law of Return by defining a "Jew" as one who is "born of a Jewish mother and is not a member of another religion or one who converted." To appease the secular camp, the amendment provided that any Jew who met this definition would be entitled to bring along his or her immediate family, even if they were not Halachically Jewish.[9]

Central to Shalit's case was the identity of his wife, Anne Geddes Shalit. By all rights she should have been at the center of the controversy since she was the one who had been made an "other" under Israeli law for refusing to convert. Her willingness to embrace Israeli culture, while avoiding the anachronistic procedures of conversion that violated her secular conscience, was deemed irrelevant and ignored.

The biblical Book of Ruth tells the story of a Moabite woman who decided to join the Jewish people and marry a Jew. Despite not meeting any of the criteria for conversion, Ruth is given the distinct honor of being the matriarch of the mythical King David. A subsequent rabbinic tradition, however, held that Jews should be suspicious of "foreign women," and emphasized their alterity, or otherness. Women's agency and good faith became irrelevant. In eastern Europe, the cradle of the Israeli and Zionist elite, a non-Jewish woman was known in Yiddish as a "shiksa"—a temptress who would lead the naive Jewish man astray. In the quest to protect young Jewish men from gentile sexual temptation, Ruth the Moabite was altogether forgotten. But secular Israelis like Shalit rejected the Eastern European stereotype as a relic of the past. They believed that what mattered was one's willingness to live on Israel's soil, speak Hebrew, and embrace the local culture. The rabbis, on the other hand, adhered to the letter of Jewish law. Thus, Anne Shalit was left to bear the brunt of being made an "other" in the land she called home.[10]

The "Foreign Woman" as a Subject in the Cabinet's Deliberations

Golda was alone in expressing concern for Anne Shalit's predicament. Opening the cabinet meeting to discuss the issue she said:

> It is enough that a foreign woman decides—a grave decision for her—to follow her husband, to leave her country, her environment, her family . . . to bring her children with her, knowing that here they will be Jewish, will be educated as Jews. And she accepts this decision . . . but goes further . . . she thinks that for the children she has to take another step—to accept Judaism. We have a duty, for her, as a matter of fairness to her, certainly for the family and for us, to make it easier for her and not to burden her. Today [she faces] a terrible burden. . . . We must make conversion simpler, civilize the requirements, turn [conversion] into a civilized process.[11]

Golda's introduction revealed deep empathy for this "foreign woman." She understood her plight and hoped that if she could soften the hearts of the religious ministers they might share in her empathy. Golda also said she wished Anne would convert because she knew that without this step no political deal could materialize, but Anne refused to take this step. In return for the amendments to the law articulated by the minister of justice, Golda hoped for the adoption of a more civilized conversion ritual, one fitting with modern sensibilities.[12] She was familiar with such procedures among the Reform and Conservative Jewish denominations and believed these could be adopted in Israel as well. In opening the meeting with this reflection, perhaps she hoped a majority of her cabinet would heed her plea and join her in urging the rabbis to display more flexibility and adjust Halachic norms to the modern age.

Golda was the only woman in the room (except for the stenographer). The protocol of the cabinet meeting, an eighty-page document (recording four hours of deliberations), suggests that the ministers, all men, were not listening. They launched into a discussion of various hypotheticals that centered on men who, because of their non-Jewish mothers, were deprived of "legal" Jewish status. Women, however, remained invisible. Most telling was the story by Yisrael Barzilai, a senior member of the left-wing Mapam Party, whose brother-in-law had been killed in battle. The young widow, the minister's sister, had to drag her dead husband's younger brother, a traumatized teenager, before a rabbinical court to participate in the archaic ritual of freeing her to remarry (a ritual recounted in the Book of Ruth). Barzilai emphasized the pain of a young man being forced to participate in this ritual while mourning his brother. The plight of Barzilai's own sister, however, was not mentioned. The ministers only empathized with the Halachic consequences of intermarriage for men. It is easy to imagine that the deliberation would have gone differently if Golda had included more women in her cabinet.

Golda was restless. She respected the process of deliberation but she was hoping for an efficient meeting and a vote in favor of the amendment. As smoking was not permitted in the cabinet room, Golda stood by the open door to the room finishing cigarette after cigarette as she listened to the irksome deliberations.[13] The ministers understood how they were expected to vote, yet they enjoyed the opportunity to share their experiences, philosophize about the relationship between Zionism and religion, and offer their impressions of the various Jewish denominations in America. Shalit's case was barely mentioned, and Anne Shalit was ignored altogether. The cabinet focused instead on the Diasporic Jewish communities in America and the Soviet Union. Soviet Jews were described as hostages—prisoners, as Golda called them. American Jews were addressed mostly as Reform Jews. The ministers were both attracted to and repelled by Reform practices such as driving on Shabbat, which they could only comprehend as a violation of Jewish law rather than a practical accommodation meant to encourage suburban Jews to attend religious services. Some of the ministers went so far as to cast doubt on the loyalty of American Jews to Zionism and Israel because of their "outlandish" religious practices.

Golda periodically intervened in defense of Reform Jews, such as an anecdote about the Sears, Roebuck magnate Bill Rosenwald, a Reform Jew and a great supporter of Israel. When the debate finally came to an end and she took the floor she avoided mentioning the "foreign" woman or the anachronistic conversion procedures prevailing in Israel. She understood that the ministers were not interested and that raising the issue might further alienate the religious ministers. Instead she used the conventional argument that the unity of the Jewish people was in jeopardy. All Jews, she emphasized, whether Reform, Conservative, or Orthodox, were entitled to equal treatment. She had traveled a long way from her starting point. Consciously or not, she allowed herself and her audience to turn a blind eye to the plight of Anne Shalit.

The Knesset Amends the Law

Two weeks later Golda arrived before the Knesset to defend the amendment. This time she did not begin with the "foreign woman" and her plight. Rather she talked about her own credo: "The most important principle, more important than the state of Israel, more important than Zionism, is the survival of the Jewish people. The second—is love of the Jewish people, all Jewish people."[14] She paused and in a brief aside attacked the religious Knesset members: "I suspect," she said sardonically, "that you love religious Jews more than you love non-religious Jews."[15] With this approach Golda was articulating a principle that many of Israel's founders preferred to keep vague: that between the State of Israel and the Jewish people, priority should be given to the latter.

After defending the amendment by an appeal based on other grounds, Golda did, however, address the "foreign woman," perhaps strategically making it the final order of business. The Knesset protocol reads:

> As for conversion, I can imagine that there are non-Jewish women who do not find it pleasant. I do understand it. But members of the Knesset [7 women plus Golda and 112 men], a non-Jewish woman: a) marries a Jewish man, b) goes with him to live her life in the Jewish state. She leaves her family, her neighborhood, her relatives, her language, her religious belief—if she had one—and comes to live among Jews. She knows that her children will be Jewish. As Jews they will

fulfill all the duties of Jews. I think that she makes a great sacrifice . . . there is no doubt that she is making a sacrifice.

Call from the Floor, in Violation of Her Conscience?

Golda promptly deviated from her formal statement. Turning to the requirement of conversion she offered the following rationale:

> She needs to make another sacrifice. I do not know a normal mother, who will stop short of making a sacrifice for her children. . . . [This woman had already given a lot] but now she must do one more thing. I am not saying it is simple. But those who are now shocked because [they see] her conscience violated . . . they must know of other cases in which [conversion] was performed. And if other women converted [even if, in doing so, they compromised their conscience], why is it immoral and a violation of conscience for others. [*sic*]

Golda was sacrificing women's autonomy on the altar of patriarchy. She now referred to Anne Shalit, the person for whom she had displayed so much empathy in the cabinet meeting, as "not a normal mother." Golda was eager to be done with this irritating matter, and her insistence that conversion was not a violation of conscience was rooted in pragmatism. Her argument that many women proceed with conversion even if it goes against their conscience amounted to a confirmation that the formal process of conversion was empty: it failed to reflect a bona fide desire to abide by Jewish law. She must have known that this was a poor argument and, moreover, that it was an outcome feared by Orthodox rabbis.[16] Perhaps this was why she felt compelled to claim, in her next breath, "I am not ashamed of pushing the amendment in such a rush."

Years earlier, as a young mother eager to engage in political work, Golda insisted that her right to pursue her calling must be respected even if it proved that she was not a "normal mother."[17] As she spoke to the members of the Knesset and placed the "normal mother" on a pedestal, did Golda feel shame?[18] Or had she simply traveled so far in her life that she had forgotten what it was like to be in Anne's place? As she observed in her interview with Oriana Fallaci, in politics one needs to stoop.[19] When Golda told Fallaci that she had "stooped enough and that's bad," she might have had this moment in mind.

There is another way to look at Golda's defense of conversion, however. Being Jewish always mattered to her. Her disagreement with the rabbis was about the process, not the substance of conversion. In her view, the progressive American approach to conversion could and should have been adopted in Israel. She believed that law had the capacity to modernize to meet society's needs and she knew from her American experience that it could be done in the case of Jewish law as well. In other words, she did not think that the Halacha should monopolize the definition of a "Jew" and she believed that Reform or Conservative conversions were just as meaningful. Indeed the amendment to the law remained ambiguous on that question.[20]

While Golda was willing to bend the rules related to process, she was never willing to compromise when the existence of the Jewish people was at stake. As a testament to this commitment, consider a small scrap of paper from the Archives of the Labor Party, on which Golda had written to her intimate friend and mentor David Remez: "I once said to my children that if, God forbid, one of them marries a goy [gentile], I shall commit suicide."[21]

Aftermath

Golda expected that if members were allowed to vote their conscience the new law would fail. Eager to avoid this outcome, Golda's party informed its members the day before the vote that they were not permitted to oppose the amendment. Party discipline prevailed and the statute was enacted into law on March 10, 1971, with 51 votes in favor, 14 opposed, and 9 abstentions. Thirty-eight percent of the legislative body decided not take a part in one of the defining moments of Israel's raison d'être.

Israel's High Court of Justice quickly became a political target. Many thought that the justices should have invoked the "political question doctrine" in order to avoid ruling on the case. Once the Court had ordered the Ministry of the Interior to register Shalit's children as Jewish and the rabbis had urged defiance of the decree, there was no way to avoid a constitutional crisis. The minister of justice, a conservative man, protested that the Court was meddling in politics and believed that the court should have deferred to the Ministry of the Interior. The secular camp hailed the Court for defending freedom of conscience and for being committed to the rule of law. The liberals said that the Court was the noble institution that defended the individual against executive transgressions.

That issue revealed a fundamental disagreement between Golda and Aloni. Aloni thought the Court had correctly and faithfully applied Israeli administrative law to Shalit's petition. The practice of the ministry, imposing religious norms on the applicants, lacked transparency and turned the state bureaucracy into servants of the religious establishment. Aloni insisted that no mere regulation, certainly not an internal classified regulation, could impose religious norms on the public. In her view, only a statute could impose such a requirement and, at the time of the Court decision, no such statute existed. Golda, on the other hand, cared less about the principles underlying the decision. She was result-oriented. All she wanted was to resolve the crisis and keep her coalition intact.

Golda, Aloni, and the Rule of Law

In her memoirs Aloni recalled that whenever she and Golda were in a heated argument, Golda would ask, "Do you think that just because you are a jurist you have a blank check to act as you wish?"[22] A lawyer by training and temperament, Aloni was dedicated to improving society through legal reform and she tirelessly expounded the importance of the rule of law. She dreamed of passing an Israeli Bill of Rights similar to the one appended to the U.S. Constitution that would guarantee the right to the free exercise of religion.

Golda had other things to worry about. Her worldview was forged in the crucible of the fight for a Jewish state and the advancement of the working class. The most important element of law, she believed, was legislation that would translate social policy into statutes, the kind of work she performed as minister of labor. Like her party comrades, she eyed "pure" or "neutral" principles of law, limitations on majority rule, entrenched individual rights, and even transparency in governance as legalistic hurdles that might stand in the way of promoting good outcomes. Her experience taught her that "the best was the enemy of the good": in order to achieve results, one must compromise, rather than demand perfection.

Competing Views from America

Golda and Aloni both looked to America as a political model but they had different understandings of what Israelis should learn from the American example. Golda considered herself an expert on the subject because she had grown up there and was familiar with the American mechanisms of federal governance, foreign affairs, and fundraising. She had a firm grasp on the respective powers of the House of Representatives and the Senate of the United States vis-à-vis the presidency. By contrast, Aloni had been exposed to the America of the 1960s through attending meetings organized between young Israeli and American intellectuals. The America she fell in love with was the America of the civil rights movement, the Warren Court, and the countercultural call to "question authority." Her imagination was ignited by the promise of equal protection of the laws, the separation of powers, minority rights, and consumer protection. She admired American intellectuals who openly criticized their government's policy and offered elaborate arguments for reform.[23] In an interview with Idith Zertal, she said:

> When you come to Washington you see there the palaces of democracy, the documents of Jefferson, and the constitution. . . . In the United States everyone speaks about their constitutional rights from childhood—for them it is the superior value. We do not have palaces for democracy. We do not educate that the sovereign must exercise self-restraint and care for the minority and for the other . . . we just learn that because we were victims, we can do no wrong.[24]

In interviews Aloni did not mention the Warren Court, but it is clear that had she been asked she would have elaborated on its blessed contribution to American culture.

Herein lay the fundamental difference between Golda and Aloni. Golda grew up in America during the turn of the twentieth century. The Supreme Court of the United States during this era was overtly hostile to organized labor and other social rights, so Golda saw the courts as a potential obstacle to progress. Moreover, in her mind judicial decisions simply depended on the numbers rather than on any impartial legal principles. The 5–4 Shalit opinion would have ended in her favor had one judge crossed the aisle and joined the dissent, thereby transforming it into a majority. Letting the Knesset make the decision, she thought, was more democratic.[25] Thus competing interpretations of American political and legal history served as another source of ammunition for the confrontation between the two leaders.

The Constitutional Establishment of Religion in the Jewish State

While Golda justified the amendment to the Law of Return as necessary for the "protection of the Jewish people from destruction by interfaith marriages," Aloni denounced the amendment as a violation of Zionist ideology and Israeli law. During this disagreement Aloni was no longer a member of the Knesset, having recently been excluded from the party list by Golda, but she was widely popular in progressive circles.

Aloni appealed to David Ben-Gurion, the elderly founder known for his staunch support of the separation of church and state, to protest the pending amendments. She presented him with people whose devotion to Israel was unequivocal but who could not be recognized as members of the community because they did not meet the Halachic definition of a Jew. As expected, the old man dispatched letters to Golda demanding clarifications and redress. While Golda could not have been fond of Aloni for going behind her back, Golda's actions reflected her general approach to the matter: resolve issues ad hoc by having a sympathetic rabbi address the grievance and avoid a generalized policy based on any single principle. She feared that the choice of one principle (religion or liberty) would only polarize the country further, an outcome she was determined to avoid.[26]

At the time of the amendments Aloni was working on a book titled *The Deal*, to be published later that year.[27] The title alluded to the unsavory political arrangements that tilted Israel toward the establishment of religion. The book comprised three parts: first, a collection of quite distasteful incidents in which people were denied Jewish status; second, a manifesto of the basic values of Zionism embedded in the Declaration of Independence, chief among them the equal protection of the laws, which she tied to both the explicit language in the Declaration and the Jewish tradition of "accepting the foreigner"; and third, a detailed analysis of relevant Israeli administrative law arguing that only Knesset legislation could authorize the denial of Jewish status to Shalit's children. Because there was no such statute, Aloni argued the regulations applied to Shalit's case were null and void. The book positioned her as a defender of the rule of law as well as the utopian Israel envisioned by the founders of Zionism.

On February 5, five days before the bill to amend the law was set for Knesset deliberations, Aloni penned an "open letter" to Golda, which was published in the popular daily newspaper, *Ma'ariv*. The headline asked: "What Is Distinct about the Labor Party?" Addressed to "Comrade Golda Meir," the letter was facetious at best. Tell us, it urged Golda, how your support of the pending amendment to the Law of Return squares with the noble principles of the Labor Party. Explain why the young should support the Labor Party if it abandons these principles. Aloni reminded Golda that she herself had repeatedly declared the party's commitment to the "construction of a new society, better, liberated, committed to liberty and dignity, one that advances socialism." I am confused, she feigned, about how your practice (imposing Orthodox religious rules to define one's legal status) is compatible with these noble principles. Moreover, she continued in her "confused" schoolchild tone, how should she, Aloni, explain these developments to the younger generation? She warned that Golda's actions created an alliance between the Labor Party and the clergy, thereby taking the country back to the dark ages of clerical rule in violation of the cardinal principles of social democracy.

The most stinging paragraph came near the end of the letter: "you would be wrong if you hope to pacify the young with quotations from the movement's founders." These platitudes, Aloni taunted, have grown stale and are now "museum pieces that unfortunately have no echo in our daily lives." In casting such aspersions, Aloni underscored the intergenerational divide and portrayed Golda as old and out of touch.

Golda was too savvy to take the bait. She ignored Aloni, and told a reporter that she had no intention of responding. Her silence was rooted neither in pain nor humiliation but rather in cold political calculation. Aloni wanted Golda to twist and turn in public as she defended her position. Why give Aloni the satisfaction? The truth is that Golda was not particularly happy with the solution that she herself was advocating. While she did not say so openly, she approved of the Conservative and Reform innovations in Jewish law and wished her society would take such a kinder, gentler approach to the issue. Yet she needed the support of the Orthodox camp and felt it was better to keep quiet. She had a coalition to keep.

The next day the editor in chief of *Davar*, the Labor Party's powerful daily, published a response. Y. Guthalf, a highly educated intellectual, rejected Aloni's arguments. He charged that the principle of the separation of church and state as understood by Aloni was antiquated. Contemporary social democratic movements he observed chose to accommodate religion. World War II and Nazism, he wrote, showed "what people can do if there is no God in their hearts." He concluded his rebuttal with a call for practicality. The new amendment, he argued, would validate Reform and Conservative conversions, thereby bringing more progress to Israel (a predication it is worth noting, that ultimately proved false).

While the rebuttal conveniently ignored the commitment of the Declaration of Independence to the separation of church and state, it foresaw the future more clearly than Aloni did. In Israel as well as in the United States an alliance between government and religion was in the early stages of being formed and liberal principles were slowly losing support. From this perspective, it was Aloni who was out of touch with the zeitgeist.[28]

The argument between Golda and Aloni could not have been more profound. For Golda, the ideal of the rule of law was an abstract value. She was prepared to fight for concrete cases but not for an abstract notion of citizens' rights. She knew that ad hoc solutions were sometimes best, even if they did not satisfy the juridical mind. Deeper still, Golda did not conceive of the Zionist project as one creating a new "Hebrew nation." For her, Jews were one people, whether in Israel or in the Diaspora. The reinvention of the "New Hebrew person" or the "Israeli" was never a part of her vision. Jewish law was the glue that had bonded Jews for millennia and, although she sought to see it reformed to meet contemporary expectations, she felt it deserved an important place in the nation's pantheon. A pragmatist, she believed that synthesis between progress and Jewish law could be worked out incrementally.

Both Golda and Aloni empathized with the indignity inflicted upon the Shalits. They simply had radically different ideas about how their plight should be addressed. With the passage of the amendments Golda won the peace and quiet that she needed. Many religious people in Israel and abroad applauded her staunch stand for Jewish unity through Jewish law. This episode fortified the stereotype of Golda held by the public, particularly by religious Jews in Israel and abroad: she was the doting grandmother of the Jewish people, the female version of Tevye from *Fiddler on the Roof*, waxing eloquent about tradition. The secular camp saw her as Beethoven near the end of his career, deaf to the music of the age.

Postscript: Women and the Wounds of Aging

As she grew older, Aloni experienced the particular discomfort that many women feel as they age. Golda had made peace with her looks and even turned it to her advantage by embracing the grandmother persona. She deliberately avoided cosmetic efforts to improve her appearance, and if she used makeup she did so very discreetly. Aloni found her physical decline more difficult to manage, perhaps because the expectations of her generation were less ascetic. As she aged she colored her hair and applied cosmetics heavily. Her interviews on television showed her once beautiful face distorted by facelifts and liposuction.[29] Both Golda and Aloni thereby came to represent the woman's predicament. As an old woman, Golda accepted the otherization associated with age, whereas Aloni used every tool in the box to keep a youthful appearance. Both experienced the truth that no matter what a woman does, old age is harder on women than men.

But there was one major difference between the two: as Aloni grew older, she stepped into another role that distinguished her from Golda—she was recognized as a pillar of the women's movement. It may well be that Aloni's vocal insistence on women's liberation, or as she called it "women as human beings," prompted Golda to distance herself farther from the movement. This proved to be a tragic outcome for all women in Israel.

CHAPTER 24

GOLDA AND THE REVIVAL OF FEMINISM

"But Can She Type?"

In September 1969, amid the publicity surrounding her first visit to the Nixon White House, Prime Minister Golda Meir graced the cover of the September 19 issue of *Time* magazine. By any measure it was an extraordinary coup. During the course of that year the prestigious magazine featured forty-six men and only four women. Two of the women were movie stars and the third was Ethel Kennedy, the well-known widow of Robert F. Kennedy.[1] The men included mighty figures such as the German chancellor Willy Brandt and the symbol of American manhood, actor John Wayne. Golda was among formidable company. A halo of the Star of David appeared in the background of her portrait as if to confirm her iconic status.

The cover inspired activists in the women's movement looking for imaginative ways to raise the average American woman's consciousness. To these women, Golda symbolized just how far women could go past stereotypes of housewives and secretaries. As part of this spirited campaign, the activists designed a poster that featured Golda's picture along with a question that became a battle cry for the feminist struggle: "But can she type?"[2] On the poster Golda was presented as the old woman that she was. Dressed in black attire with her gray hair pulled back, she looked plain and humble. With her hands clasped together on the table in front of her and a look of concentration and confidence on her face, she projected no "niceness." Here was a political leader ably handling the business of state.

The poster implied that there was only one answer to the rhetorical question it posed: Golda did not need to type because typing, long associated with women's work, was neither required nor helpful in the political big leagues. Indeed merely posing the question to a high-level politician revealed its absurdity. In Golda's particular case it may well have been that she made a conscious decision not to acquire typing skills. When she was a teenager her parents, opposed to higher education, offered her a compromise: she could enroll in secretarial school instead of a teachers' college as her best friend Regina Hamburger had decided to do. In 1922, when Golda and Regina arrived in Palestine, Regina's skills helped her find a comfortable job in Jerusalem while Golda struggled to make a living by giving English lessons. Indeed, Regina rose to the highest levels in Israel's administrative structure. During the 1920s, she was even financially comfortable enough to assist Golda, who was then toiling as a laundress to support her family. Although typing skills were convenient and useful, Golda may have understood that they would also be a dead end for a politically ambitious woman.[3]

In her memoirs Golda recalled vehemently rejecting her parents' arguments in favor of secretarial school: "Besides, I sobbed, I would rather die than spend my life—or even part of it—hunched over a typewriter in some dingy office."[4] The typewriter symbolized precisely what the women's movement protested: a suffocating patriarchal environment in which women were subordinate to men. Considering that Golda dictated her memoirs to a secretary, it stands to reason that her statement reflected not only what she thought at the age of fourteen but also what she had observed since that time. In hindsight there was a lot for Golda to identify with in the simple rhetorical question on the poster. Despite this, her honeymoon with the nascent women's movement came to a rather abrupt ending.

One of Golda's favorite reactions to the activism of American feminists was to condemn them as "bra burners" who "denounced motherhood." She also frequently labeled the activists as "men haters." To these verbal assaults Golda would add that she had never been discriminated against as a woman nor had she ever been a member of a women's movement.[5] These statements contained significantly more hyperbole than truth.[6] The breadcrumbs of gender discrimination were visible throughout her long journey to the top, from her parents' initial refusal to let her become a teacher to the misogynistic attacks she suffered as prime minister. Golda had represented feminist interests as a member of the Women Workers Council and Pioneer Women in the 1920s and 1930s. More importantly, her gross generalizations about "American feminists" ignored the most important voices of the American women's movement, including the leaders of the National Organization for Women (NOW) and Betty Friedan, one of the leaders of the movement.

To Golda, the encounter with second wave feminism provided a sense of déjà vu. The American rabble-rousers reminded her of the young female kibbutzniks she encountered upon her arrival in Merhavia in 1922 and the militant feminists in the Women Workers Council in the late 1920s. (See part II in this volume.) Nevertheless, the tension between Golda and second-wave feminism is in some ways difficult to understand. Golda cared about women and could easily have identified with the substance of Betty Friedan's well-known book *The Feminine Mystique*. Like many feminists, both American and Israeli, she would often complain that "she needed a wife."[7] Why then the tirade against feminism?

Politics, Family Values, and Women's Liberation

There is no direct evidence to explain Golda's motives, but there is plenty of circumstantial evidence. First and foremost, there is the fact that Golda occupied a position of leadership. As prime minister and head of the largest party in her country, her public statements could not stray too far from the Israeli consensus. During the 1970s, gender discrimination was not a central concern for most Israelis. The myth of women's equality was deeply rooted in social consciousness and, moreover, that myth served Golda well. Wasn't she herself proof of the opportunities open to Israeli women? That myth, later referred to as the "Golda syndrome," served to cover up the status of Israeli women as the second sex.[8] Israeli culture marching to the music of militarism reaffirmed patriarchal values while paying lip service to gender equality. Thus Golda might have concluded that she would pay a significant political cost if she expressed sympathy toward the women's movement.

The international dimension of the issue perhaps played an even greater role in shaping Golda's response. As the prime minister of a small country surrounded by enemies Golda's most important political objective was to cultivate the support of that juggernaut on the world stage—America. Eager to solidify and strengthen U.S. support for Israel, Golda was hesitant to express public sympathy for the women's movement, even if she agreed with its premises. American public opinion, including Jewish public opinion, was only beginning to digest the ideas of feminism. Golda's sharp political instincts may have told her that now was not the time to embrace the controversial cause of women's liberation.

A Friendship with Billy Graham

Golda's relationship with the Reverend Billy Graham presents a particularly striking example of the constraints she faced as a political actor in the United States. Golda had cultivated a connection with the noted evangelical minister in the late 1950s. Graham was a close friend of Richard Nixon's and instrumental in Golda's campaign to convince Nixon to support Israel generally and to approve shipments of sophisticated weapons to Israel in particular. In one letter from March 1970, Golda implored Graham to urge the administration to reach a "positive decision" before "terrible effects" visited Israel. "We would feel abandoned and alone," Golda warned. A sophisticated student of realpolitik, she reminded Graham that "a strong Israel is an American asset." At this moment the United States was reassessing its policy of supplying arms to Israel in the context of its effort to reignite the peace process between Israel and Egypt, and Golda feared that Israel would permanently lose access to the arms it needed to defend itself.[9] A cable from Yitzhak Rabin, Israel's ambassador in Washington, DC, informed Golda that Graham had assured Rabin that he would approach the matter "through an intermediary" and that "you will not be abandoned."

At the very same time that Graham was working behind the scenes to persuade Nixon to revoke his decision to suspend arms sales to Israel, he was also thinking about the status of American women. In December of that year, the immensely popular magazine *Ladies' Home Journal* published an article by Graham titled "Jesus and the Liberated Woman."[10] In the article Graham elaborated his theory that the essence of "woman" was best reflected in her roles as wife, mother, and homemaker. Women, he asserted, could be fulfilled and fulfill God's will only if they performed their traditional roles. Work outside the home was permissible but a woman's primary responsibility was always to her family.[11] From Golda's article "Borrowed Mothers," we know that she had little sympathy for Graham's familiar thesis, a thesis shared by Israel's rabbinical establishment. (See part II in this volume.) Indeed Golda's entire personal history stood in defiance of Graham's thesis. And yet so much was at stake. If she challenged Graham's view she risked alienating him as an ally, thereby putting Israel's security at risk. Realpolitik dictated that she tread carefully.

The women's liberation movement was not making her life any easier. Graham's article in the *Ladies' Home Journal* appeared after "two hundred feminists showed up unannounced at the *Journal*'s offices to protest the magazine's editorial content" and the magazine responded by hosting feminists in a section titled "The New Feminism."[12] Graham was trying to rebut the feminists. Under different circumstances, Golda would have been unlikely to curry favor with Graham, and it is possible that she might have embraced the "new feminism." But beyond the imperative of staying in Graham's good graces there remained questions about the politics of the women's movement itself.

Golda and the Emergence of the New Left

In its early years of mobilization the feminist movement resorted to grassroots politics—rallies, marches, fists raised in the air to protest patriarchy. Golda recognized the strategy because her early career had been rooted in street politics. In Milwaukee, for instance, she organized a demonstration in 1917 to protest the antisemitic pogroms perpetuated by the Ukrainian leader Symon Petliura. As Golda later recalled, a leader in the Jewish Community suggested to her that the demonstration was a bad idea but she defiantly stood her ground: "I told him I was sure that by showing how we felt . . . we would earn the respect and sympathy of the rest of the city."[13] Golda was proud of speaking truth to power, as she frequently did throughout the Zionist struggle against the British in Palestine.

On August 26, 1970, four months before Billy Graham published "Jesus and the Liberated Woman," ten thousand women linked arms and marched on New York City's Fifth Avenue. They called for gender equality, chanting, "I am not a Barbie doll." The march also protested the war in Vietnam with women carrying signs that read, "I am no breeder for man's war" and "Sisterhood is powerful, end the war." The march must have given Golda every reason to feel uncomfortable. Whatever she thought about the war in Vietnam, she knew well to avoid voicing any reservations. More important, it was becoming evident that some feminist activists had ties to the New Left and that the New Left was increasingly critical of Israel and pro-Palestine.[14] Golda undoubtedly perceived the drift of the women's liberation movement toward the New Left as a threat to the generally favorable place that Israel held in mainstream American public opinion. She also may have feared the movement's influence on Israel's younger generations. At that time, Shulamit Aloni was writing a book titled *Women as Human Beings,* and she was emerging as a voice for Israeli feminism and vocal critic of the Arab–Israeli conflict.[15] Seen in this light, Golda's negative reaction to the women's liberation movement had less to do with the substance of their agenda and more to do with complex political calculations.

In her memoirs Golda distanced herself from contemporary feminism by drawing a forced and false distinction between the contributions of Israeli and American feminists.

The "women of the Yishuv [her generation of founding mothers]," she wrote, were proving that it was possible to function as wives, mothers, and comrades in arms, enduring constant danger and hardship without complaining, but with a sense of enormous fulfillment, and it seemed to me that [they] were doing more—without the benefit of publicity—to further the cause of our sex than even the most militant of suffragists in the United States or England.[16]

The passage is choked with platitudes—idealizing those good "wives and mothers," thereby paying homage to family values—but its central complaint is that U.S. and English suffragists "resorted to publicity." Golda contrasted the noble silence of those who made progress "without complaining" to those women who went public with their grievances. The feminists who marched on Fifth Avenue on August 26 certainly sought publicity, and were convinced that the policy of not complaining was unlikely to get them anywhere.[17] Better to avoid such tactics, Golda was telling Israeli women, and therefore to avoid the women's liberation movement.

The Myth and Reality of the Status of Women in Israel

Golda's attack on the women's liberation movement is one of the factors that delayed women's equality in Israel. Her criticisms spared men the need to reconsider the traditional division of labor in the family and society. It signaled to women that it was acceptable to distance themselves from this "evil" ideology, and many Israeli women throughout the 1970s and 1980s loudly declared that they were not feminists.[18] According to Hanna Safran, a historian of women's liberation in Israel: "So deep was the belief that women are equal to men, that any challenge to this fact [sic] was met with criticism and a charge that these ideas are 'foreign import' ungrounded in Israeli reality."[19] Because consciousness-raising was discouraged, few women could even perceive the glass ceilings under which they labored. The facts that Israeli women served in the military, enjoyed the protection of the labor laws Golda enacted in the 1950s, and held part-time jobs was taken as proof that Israeli women were already liberated.

To examine this myth, Golda only needed to look at the Knesset, an institution with which she was intimately familiar. In 1949 with all the fanfare accompanying the emerging state and its commitment to gender equality, only twelve women served in the Knesset—one-tenth of the legislative body. By 1969 when Golda became prime minister, the situation was even worse: only eight women served as Knesset members. Similarly there were large numbers of able women in lower positions in every governmental ministry but none at the top; at Hebrew University, just a few miles from Golda's office, only 4 percent of women reached the position of full professor, while bright and able women filled the ranks of assistants and doctoral students. No woman had ever served as a justice on Israel's Supreme Court and, according to a widely known rumor, one senior justice had stated that a woman would only be appointed "over his dead body."[20] Catharine MacKinnon had not yet invented the term "sexual harassment," but Golda would have immediately recognized it as ubiquitous, particularly in Israel's military.[21]

In Golda's defense, she was preoccupied with other domestic and international problems. During this time she was struggling to keep her political coalition from unraveling, managing the War of Attrition, and dealing with her failing health—she had little time left to sit back and observe the shifting cultural attitudes or to welcome the new dawn of women's liberation. The fact that she was surrounded by men added to her myopia. Very few of Israel's top-level policymakers were women, and those few were careful to "act nice." A few Israeli women were beginning to challenge the system, but Golda likely identified them with her nemesis, Aloni, which would have been enough to chill her enthusiasm for their projects.

Golda was accustomed to thinking about policy in terms of the electorate. The pertinent question in her mind was always: Who would vote for what agenda? Thus, when presented with a copy of a book by the mother of Israeli feminism, Ada Fishman Maimon, she asked "Could you tell me how many women readers of this book will also adopt Ada's ideas and way of life?" For Golda, women's liberation was a lovely idea but it lacked political support. For the foreseeable future at least, the glass ceiling was there to stay. This attitude more than anything else explained her decision to ignore the new voices calling for gender equality.[22]

The Sisterhood Crashing the Gates and the Poison Pill of "Zionism Is Racism"

Jewish members of the American feminist movement meanwhile were beginning to turn a critical eye toward Israel. Examining the practices of Jewish life in the United States, they quickly realized the breadth of gender discrimination in the synagogue.[23] They also understood that such discrimination was officially sanctioned by Israel's government as part of its compromise with the rabbinate.[24] In December 1972 an article in Ms. magazine "gave" Golda a Torah scroll for Hanukkah. Subtly alluding to Virginia Woolf's groundbreaking feminist essay "A Room of One's Own," the article stated: "For Golda Meir, who, under Jewish law, is not allowed to touch the Torah, even as chief of state, a Torah of her own."[25]

Despite this joke at Golda's expense, American Jewish feminists earnestly believed in solidarity and global sisterhood. When the United Nations declared an International Decade for Women in the years spanning from 1975 to 1985 and held its first feminist conference in Mexico City, feminists felt the world had finally come to recognize the significance of gender equality. During the conference, however, they were shocked to witness the agenda taken over by various special interest groups. Supporters of the Palestinian cause in the Palestine Liberation Organization (PLO) managed to pass a resolution known as "Zionism Is Racism." Feminists like Letty Cottin Pogrebin were traumatized. "I could not believe that supposed feminists who had been entrusted with the inauguration of a ten-year commitment to improving the status of all the world's women . . . could allow their agenda to be hijacked on behalf of this unspeakable PLO slogan."[26] She condemned the Palestinian movement for having "cynically co-opted a feminist event for anti-Israel activity."[27] For the first time, she and her Jewish sisters experienced blatant antisemitism.[28]

When the conference ended, some disappointed feminists tried to comfort themselves with the observation that the resolution was inconsequential, just a piece of paper. In New York attending a reception in her honor given by the Commission on the Status of Women for Human Rights, Golda offered a different view. Asked about the resolution, she lashed out, going so far as to invoke patriarchal stereotypes: "If women can pass resolutions of that kind without knowing what they are doing, on what do they base their claim to equal rights and opportunities? If they're so—excuse me, stupid—then let them stay home."[29] She must have felt that the sisterhood was naive and starry eyed in believing that women coming together could address women's monumental problems in an environment insulated from politics. Her angry riposte also disclosed her conviction that the new feminism linked to the New Left would be a poor ally to Israel. Tormented by the Yom Kippur War and its aftermath, Golda was concerned that the PLO was winning the hearts and minds of young Americans, Jews included. Blinded by this fear she could not muster the patience to listen to the women, understand their agenda, and realize how much they had in common.

As Pogrebin tells it, the Mexico Conference brought a rapprochement between the women's movement and Israel. Under the leadership of Golda's successor, Yitzhak Rabin, Israel slowly opened to concerns about gender equality, and a visit by a delegation of American Jewish feminists was arranged. The women arrived eager to observe, discuss, and puncture the myth of gender equality in Israel about which they had heard so much. Each time Israeli women, confused and defensive, tried to use Golda as proof of gender equality, their American visitors challenged them. At times they snickered impatiently. The American delegation expected a genuine discussion of the status of women in Israel accompanied by the admission that gender equality was indeed a myth. They felt that "Golda's example" was merely a cover-up for the complex problems of gender inequality in Israel. Ultimately the Israeli women abandoned their mention of Golda as an example.[30] Perhaps it was too difficult for the Israeli women, who were conditioned to defend Israel as a land of gender equality, to see the reality through the lens of their visitors.

The Americans did, however, secure a breakfast meeting with Golda. She arrived looking regal and matronly wearing a simple dress and "the coiffeur of a Lower East Side landlady." When Pogrebin asked her, "Why, do you think, in all your years in power you never inspired more women to follow in your footsteps?" Golda reacted defensively: "I am not to blame for that. . . . But our women have been active; nothing is done in this country without our women. Maybe they don't want to be elected."[31] Golda indeed tried to recruit more women to run for the Knesset but she also vetted the candidates and excluded women who had independent voices, as she did to Aloni. Golda was a courageous woman but she did not have the energy or perhaps commitment to confront the challenge. It was left to the younger generation of feminists to nurture the bonds between Israeli women and the next generation of American Jewish women. Golda was too old, too ill, and above all, devastated by the Yom Kippur War.

CHAPTER 25

NIGHTMARE

The Yom Kippur War

I will never again be the person I was before the Yom Kippur War.

—GOLDA MEIR

The Perils of Arrogance

The stunning victory of the 1967 war six years earlier had left Israel confident of its military superiority; the economy was humming, and America was friendlier than ever before. The general elections were set for the end of October about three weeks after Yom Kippur, and Golda, atop the list of the Labor Party's candidates, felt supremely confident.[1]

On September 19, a fortnight before Yom Kippur, the Labor Party distributed an election poster it called "The Bar-Lev Line." It referred to the reputed series of fortifications along the Suez Canal that the army insisted made war impossible. The poster hailed Golda's government for "judicious, bold and far-sighted policies."[2] Military hubris trickled down to the people and Golda did nothing to question its intoxicating charm.

Yom Kippur, the holiest day in the Jewish calendar, fell on October 6, 1973, a Saturday, the Sabbath. From the perspective of Jewish culture it was endowed with a double sacred meaning. The majority of Israelis had no idea about the calamity soon to be unleashed. At 2:05 P.M. that day, however, Syria (from the north) and Egypt (from the south) launched a simultaneous attack against Israel. Over the next three weeks the Israeli people experienced a protracted frightening roller coaster of a conflict; by its end, more than 2,500 Israeli soldiers lay dead, with an-other 7,500 wounded, a staggering number for a nation of 3 million people.[3] During the first week in particular, Israelis felt like they were walking in the valley of death: it was as if the deep subconscious Jewish fear of annihilation harking back to the historic trauma of the destruc-tion of the First Temple was coming true.[4]

Deciding to Avoid a Preemptive Strike

Leading up to October 5, dreadful news kept piling up. Golda canceled her plans to spend Yom Kippur at her daughter's kibbutz and stayed in Tel Aviv. She asked Henry Kissinger to inform Egypt and Syria that Israel was not about to start a war, a message she hoped would lead them to cancel their planned attack. On October 10, the secular Golda, who neither fasted nor attended synagogue, summoned the U.S. ambassador to her office and enlisted the Lord in her appeal: "God is my witness, and you are my witness: we did not decide to start a war."[5]

At 8:00 A.M. the next day, Yom Kippur, the cabinet met to discuss whether Israel should launch a preemptive strike. Golda hesitated, em-phasizing that the United States had often warned Israel that it should not be the first to attack. If Israel defied the United States, American help might be withheld and Israel would risk losing the war, diplomatic support at the United Nations, and life-saving military aid.

Should the Reserves Be Mobilized?

Golda also had to decide whether to accept the chief of staff's recom-mendation to mobilize the entire military reserves, or to follow Moshe Dayan's recommendation to approve only partial mobilization. Dayan believed that full mobilization was unnecessary insofar as the enlisted army would be able to withstand the attack. He also remembered the previous mobilization a few months earlier, which had gravely damaged the country's economy. The chief of staff disagreed. Using her pragmatic common sense, Golda split the difference and called for a partial mobi-lization, a decision that somewhat softened the awful blow to come.

Figure 10. Golda visiting the troops in the Sinai desert during Yom Kippur War, 1973.
Courtesy of Israel Government Press Office. Credit: Tsion Yehuda.

Both she and Dayan were confident that Israel's military would defeat
any invasion in a matter of days.[6] In hindsight, this decision to mobilize
the reserves, unlike the decision to avoid a preemptive strike, was enthu-
siastically received by the public.

At 2:00 P.M. the warning sirens began to wail; Egypt and Syria had
begun their attack. In the following days, Israeli despair deepened. The
number of dead and wounded climbed by the hour. Scores of Israeli
tanks lay burned in the desert, airplanes were destroyed, and the stock-
piles of ammunition were dwindling. Golda's assessment that it would
be very difficult to get American support was soon confirmed. Nixon
and Kissinger either were confident that Israel would defeat the invasion
or were hoping that a weakened Israel would be more motivated to offer
concessions. To make matters worse the American planes sent to re-
plenish Israel's air force had to land and refuel midway through their
journey. European allies, however, were reluctant to cooperate, fearful
that Arab wrath could result in higher oil prices.

A Woman of Sorrows

A few hours after the start of the war Israel's position was desperate. The tide began to turn only when massive American military aid began to arrive by airlift. In keeping with military doctrine, Israel's aim was to contain the progress of the invading forces and shift the battle to enemy territory. In the north, Israeli troops approached the outskirts of Syria's capital, Damascus; in the south, the Israeli Defense Forces crossed the Suez Canal heading toward Egypt's capital, Cairo. Israel did not intend to occupy these cities but rather wished to demonstrate its military might. Most significantly, Israel's army trapped and threatened to destroy the Third Egyptian Division comprising twenty thousand men. The international crisis quickly escalated as Sadat appealed for Soviet help and both Moscow and Washington signaled their expectation that Israel make concessions. Golda was disheartened. Israel's military success meant not only sweet revenge and a vindication of Israeli superiority on the battlefield but also the chance to send a message about the dire consequences for any future Arab attack.

Under immense duress, Sadat agreed to enter face-to-face negotiations with Israel. This was a historic event as no Arab leader had ever publicly agreed to enter direct negotiations with Israel. The negotiations led to a ceasefire, which culminated in the 1979 peace treaty with Egypt. By then, however, the Labor Party had been ousted from power, Menachem Begin's Likud led the government, and Dayan had crossed party lines to join Begin's cabinet as minister of foreign affairs. Golda died before the peace treaty between Israel and Egypt was signed, but she did live long enough to witness Sadat's historic visit to Israel and to hear his speech to Israel's Knesset, developments Golda had previously firmly predicted would never happen.

The Only Female Amputee among the Wounded

Anat Yahalom, a young female soldier, served as a secretary to a battalion commander stationed on the banks of the Suez. Observing orders of high alert, Anat exercised her authority and sent the other women soldiers home, but she decided to stay with her unit.[7] Shortly thereafter, she heard the deafening sound of Egyptian artillery, felt the desert shake powerfully under her feet, and caught a glimpse of Soviet-made Egyptian planes releasing their bombs "like drops of salt." With a bang, the walls of her modest office collapsed, crushing her lower body. She was covered in blood. "I want to live," she remembered thinking; "I don't want my parents to bury me." Anat suffered multiple injuries, ultimately losing one of her legs.

Three days after Anat Yahalom was wounded, Rachel Shalev (the widowed mother of her battalion commander Lieutenant Colonel Shaul Shalev) received news that her only son had been killed in battle. In Jerusalem, ashen-faced, Shaul's wife Gabriela and their two children, Narkis and Eran, seven and three, would slowly comprehend the devastating reality of a home without a father. Across the country Israeli lives were shattered. Gabriela Shalev and Anat Yahalom were the pride of the Zionist dream. They represented the best among Israeli women: resilient, resourceful, patriotic, and ready to sacrifice.[8] Yet women were largely taken for granted as the war raged. Attention was focused on men in combat positions.

In her office Golda smoked cigarette after cigarette, urging herself to keep calm and focus on the problems at hand. For ten days she avoided interviews, perhaps too busy to meet the press or perhaps hoping to avoid embarrassing questions. She knew that public anger was building up. As the reality of the calamity sank in, Golda began a round of hospital visits. She wanted to connect with the soldiers and their families as well as to show the people that she cared. Golda stood next to the beds of the amputated and the burned, and men with crushed jaws, bones, and internal organs. She cried uncontrollably, putting her emotions on full display.

Anat Yahalom remembered Golda visiting her hospital bed "all wet with tears," and her saying to her prime minister, "You must be strong," and "We shall overcome." The severely injured soldier comforted the weeping head of state who looked like her grandmother. Despite their vastly different stations they had something in common: both were women in a sea of men, struggling with serious injuries, their lives forever shattered by the war.

Can She Be Both an "Emotional Old Woman" and a Competent Head of State?

The ethos of the sabra was that of a tough, unsentimental man born and raised on the soil of the homeland and free of the complexities of the (feminized) Jew in exile. A sabra was honor bound to display restraint and withhold his feelings. He was certainly not expected to weep in public.[9] Golda was neither a sabra nor a man and although reputed to be a very tough woman, she allowed herself to weep in public. The media had mixed reactions. Some leading newspapers refrained from displaying the weeping prime minister on their front pages, and pundits suggested that she was too emotional to carry out the responsibilities of a leader. A rational, emotionless man would be preferable and more compatible with the heroic ethos of Israel's military.[10]

Golda, like the biblical Rachel mourning for her sons, decided not to hide her womanhood. Her public message was genuine and spontaneous. At these moments, just as she had expected Israeli soldiers to show courage, she displayed the courage to be herself. It was a signal to everyone, both men and women, that mourning was acceptable because the calamity was so horrible. Despite the patriarchal anxieties that her emotions might prevent her from thinking clearly and rationally, it appears that she remained in full charge of the developments. Moshe Dayan, who spent endless hours with Golda throughout the war, later said: "I cannot imagine a more attentive ear, open mind and courageous heart than Golda's. . . . I have known Golda for many years and *saw her more than once shed tears, but not at war.*"[11] Avner Shalev, assistant to the chief of staff during the war, said in 2010: "Golda was extraordinary during the war—sharp and determined, a true leader. Very strong, truly made of steel. Always lucid."[12]

Critics embraced the Israeli conception of the "woman" as an "other" and therefore viewed her as unfit for the imperative of defending the land. This masculine militarism embedded in Israeli culture also explains why of the 2,500 fallen soldiers, only one woman was killed; why of the more than 7,000 wounded, only one woman was wounded seriously; and why of the 556 Medals of Honor awarded, only three were given to women, all for supportive roles rather than for action in combat. Golda did not try to challenge the othering of women but she did fall victim to this otherization, unjustly judged as unfit to engage in the complex decision making called for during the war.

Israeli Women and the Yom Kippur War, an Excursus

According to the sociologist Hanna Herzog, the Israeli euphoria after the Six-Day War fortified the myth that gender equality prevailed in Israel. Women failed to notice that their integration into the labor force depended on their acceptance of a gendered division of labor. Women occupied feminine, secondary roles, had minimal political representation, and accepted the reality that women would not be involved in political or economic policymaking, Golda being the notable exception.[13]

The Yom Kippur War, by contrast, served as a mirror reflecting the inferior state of Israeli women. As soon as the war began, the economy came to a halt because it depended on men to sustain it. Bus driving, for example, was an occupation restricted to men. Once the war erupted and the men were sent to the front, public transportation was discontinued and women found it hard to go to work. Schools, on the other hand, were the traditional domain of women and therefore reopened by the second week of the war.[14] Herzog explains: "Because of the social structure prevailing prior to the war, the war itself became a powerful mechanism to reproduce the traditional division of labor in Israeli society." The patriarchy asserted its hegemony and in doing so perpetuated the status of women as "other."[15]

Even if she was considered the "only man in the cabinet," Golda could not escape the female stereotype. Israeli media was also a prisoner to gender stereotypes. Its depiction of Golda as "Rachel weeping for her children" perpetuated conventional norms. In the upheaval of the first days of the war, Golda likely failed to notice or was unable to process the fact that her great rival, the mother of Israeli feminism, Ada Fishman Maimon, had passed away. Ada had always insisted that Zionism was about the liberation of both Jewish man and woman. Tragically, events during the war made it evident that her decades-old campaign had failed.[16]

IN THE COMPANY OF MEN

Phase 1, Pre-war Diplomacy

After the war, both Golda and Dayan were accused of having failed to pursue various diplomatic options to prevent the eruption of hostilities. This failure, critics insisted, led to the horrifying war. The literature on this question is voluminous and contested. Thanks to the declassification of additional archival material, the debate has grown detailed and extensive. The main arguments as they relate to Golda's actions from the early 1970s to October 1973 can be briefly summarized.

There seems to be a consensus that until the beginning of 1973, relations between Egypt and Israel amounted to a stalemate. When Richard Nixon assumed office his secretary of state, William Rogers, issued the Rogers Plan. The plan envisioned Israeli withdrawal from the Sinai accompanied by security measures to prevent future conflagrations and conduct peace negotiations.[1] In public Nixon gave the plan his blessing but private records show that he "surreptitiously . . . undertook to sabotage it."[2] Golda persistently opposed the plan. She did not hide her government's intention to keep large parts of the Sinai (as well as other occupied territories) and expressed reluctance to tie any agreement to a resolution of the Palestinian question.[3] In addition, Israel insisted on direct negotiations accompanied by a full Arab recognition of the Jewish state. Golda thought that these were "reasonable expectations." She believed, and members of her cabinet concurred, that the stalemate should continue until Egypt acquiesced to Israel's demands. Golda's position also shielded the ruling Labor Party from right-wing attacks.

Golda continuously consulted with senior members of her cabinet whose collective consensus reflected the judgment of the Knesset as well as Israeli public opinion. Israelis were united in their opposition to any agreement that would require full withdrawal from territories seized in 1967.[4] Only in hindsight did they begin to suggest that a territorial compromise should have been energetically pursued.

Meanwhile, the Egyptian president, Anwar Sadat, who had been in power since Nasser's death in 1970, considered the stalemate intolerable and kept searching for ways to break it. Sadat focused on Egypt's honor. From his perspective, that honor was badly wounded and could only be healed through repossession of the lost land. His national security adviser Hafez Ismail came to Washington armed with various plans to reignite the process but none of these proposals sparked Israeli interest.

Scholars disagree about what followed. The historian Hagai Tsoref, head of the Documentation and Commemoration Department at the State of Israel's Archives, insists that after 1971 Golda's cabinet made several attempts to begin a diplomatic process that would break the stalemate. Based on documents in Israel's State Archives, Tsoref concludes that Golda favored a partial agreement that would make incremental progress and pave the way for a future peace treaty. Egypt preferred full Israeli withdrawal.[5] Others, such as the historian Yigal Kipnis detect a change in Washington's policy starting in 1973. Nixon and Kissinger, worried about the eruption of war, urged Golda to offer substantial concessions. According to Kipnis, Golda's "kitchen cabinet" concluded that war was preferable to the proposed concessions.[6] Of course, none of them imagined that war would prove so catastrophic.[7]

Phase 2, Golda's Deference to the Military Experts

According to Meron Medzini, who served as Golda's cabinet press secretary during the war, Golda complained about the recommendations offered by her military advisers: "Except for me, all were men experienced in the business of war . . . and I, the civilian who did not know precisely what a military division was, had to decide. This matter torments me to this day." As Medzini, who also wrote a fine biography of Golda, noted, this was one of the very rare instances in her long career in which Golda invoked the fact that she was "the only woman in the room." He also observed that "she trusted the minister of defense and the generals."[8] Golda was reluctant to argue with highly decorated generals lest she be seen as "stupid" or "the hysterical old woman."[9]

Medzini rejected Golda's complaint that she was ill-informed. In his view, Golda had wasted a precious five years during which she could have developed the expertise necessary to make independent and informed decisions about mobilization and preemption. The validity of this critique, however, rests upon the answer to an underlying question: Why did Golda not familiarize herself with military matters?

From the beginning of her career, Golda was known as one who took her responsibilities seriously. She carefully studied every organization of which she was a part. Why did she not do the same with the military? One answer might point to the presence of Minister of Defense Moshe Dayan, a walking military legend and the prototype of Israeli masculinity.[10] In 1967 public pressure propelled him to the position of Minister of Defense, an appointment Golda had opposed vehemently but eventually accepted, understanding that people identified him with the security of the state.[11] With Dayan on her side Golda must have assumed that public support for military issues would be forthcoming. Their informal pact reflected a division of labor: she would be in charge of foreign relations and he defense; each was careful not to trespass on the other's turf. Dayan was, moreover, closely associated with Shimon Peres, Ben-Gurion's right hand in the Ministry of Defense when Golda served as minister of foreign affairs.[12] Dayan and Peres presented themselves as spokesmen of the "young generation" and projected authority in matters of defense.[13] Golda trusted that these men were reliable and therefore probably assumed that her intervention in the field of defense was at least unnecessary and perhaps even counterproductive.[14]

This interpretation is only the tip of the iceberg, however. The iceberg itself, which Dayan both embodied and handsomely contributed to, was the culture of militarism that permeated Israeli society. Militarism— understood as the primacy of the military in nation-building, the construction of citizenship, and society—functioned as a tool to maintain and perpetuate patriarchy.[15] Ben-Gurion understood this from the beginning. While he was too old to fight in any of Israel's wars, he joined the famed Jewish Legion formed in 1917 to assist the British Empire in conquering Palestine. He proudly displayed his photo in military uniform to promote his military credentials. In Milwaukee in 1917 Golda also tried to join the Jewish Legion but was turned down. Women were not admitted and thus, unlike Ben-Gurion, Golda could not display a photo of herself in uniform.[16]

Along with most Israeli women, Golda internalized the sense that military affairs were the business of men. Had she included other women in her cabinet or had she searched for women with knowledge of military affairs, she might have been able to dislodge the dangerous groupthink of her military experts, which prevented them from reading the writing on the wall.[17] We know that before the war erupted Golda was consumed with worries. According to Medzini, "Her heart told her that Israel was rapidly moving towards war. Her brain told her that there was nothing to worry about."[18] Golda intuited that something was wrong; when her military secretary woke her at 4:00 A.M. to tell her "a war will start today," she responded "I knew it."[19]

Phase 3, Golda Asserts Agency and Leadership

Deference was Golda's modus operandi prior to the war and during its first hours. Yet, as soon as she witnessed Dayan melt down and speak of defeat, she understood that it had fallen to her to lead. Golda realized that her initial intuitions about the situation had been correct, or at least not as misguided as the cerebral approach taken by her military experts, and she drew upon her inner strength to provide the leadership necessary to get the country out of harm's way.[20]

In recent years theorists have argued that men and women tend to take different approaches to decision making—women tend toward an intuitive, emotional approach compared to a more deliberative, rational approach typical of men—and that the rational, male mode of thinking is not inherently superior. But throughout Golda's lifetime, rational approaches were dominant. While Golda did not always embrace this mode of decision making, she respected it when it came to matters of defense. She took the reins after the initial attack only because no one else stepped up to the plate. She performed well because she possessed high-level decision-making skills including courage and, most important, because she understood that survival was at stake.

Only Woman in the Room? Homage to the Support Staff

Golda was initially puzzled by the wailing sirens. "It appears that the war started," the cabinet stenographer volunteered. The stenographer dutifully transcribed Golda's reaction: "Nur dos felt mir oys" she uttered in Yiddish (*This is the last thing I needed*), and then added in English, "They will be sorry for it."[21] The claim that Golda was the only woman in the room is only well-known because like the biblical wife of Noah, stenographers typically have no name or place in history. But thanks to that stenographer, we know that under immense stress Golda did not think in Hebrew. Underneath the garb of the "Israeli" identity was a Jewish girl thinking in Yiddish and English, a girl shaped by czarist Russia and the American Midwest.

Golda Relies on Her Feelings

On October 9, 1973, as the army was running out of tanks, airplanes, and ammunition, Golda said to her cabinet:

> I have a *crazy idea*. What if, secretly, I . . . fly to Washington for 24 hours? . . . We can send other people, but now, just like in 1948 [Israel's war of independence] I imagine, just like I said to Ben-Gurion, that I can do it. *I have a feeling* that this is a moment when I *feel* that I need to speak to him *and a feeling* that he will understand. . . . *I have the impression* that a conversation between us is essential now.[22]

In these moments of crisis Golda relied on her emotional intelligence, and the cabinet went along with her plan. Kissinger and Nixon were not enthusiastic about supporting Israel but they acquiesced to her wishes and ultimately overruled the Pentagon. As the massive airlift materialized, Israel's army gained the tools necessary to implement the counteroffensive. These were also the moments in which Golda disclosed her long-held philosophy about the Jewish predicament: the world has never liked Jews she said and "would throw us to the dogs." "If we do not show our strength, we shall be lost."[23]

Golda Changes Course as the War Comes to an End

At the end of the Israeli counteroffensive, the Third Egyptian Army of twenty thousand men was trapped by Israel's forces and threatened with annihilation. Sadat felt he had no choice but to accept the conditions Golda insisted on all along: face to face negotiations between Israel and Egypt, with no preconditions attached. The negotiations between the Egyptian and Israeli chiefs of staff ended with a historic agreement between the two enemies. Israel agreed to begin an incremental withdrawal from the Sinai Peninsula and Sadat sent a letter to Golda (another historic first from an Arab leader to Israel's head of government) announcing that "when I threatened war I meant it, now when I speak of peace I mean it . . . let us speak to each other, and then the connection between us will never be broken." Golda is reported to have been very moved by this message and she increasingly displayed a willingness to make territorial concessions. Hagai Tsoref, author of *Golda Meir, The Fourth Prime Minister* summarized Golda's state of mind: "Golda was not the same Golda of the days that preceded the war. The heavy toll of the war made clear to her, as it did to Sadat, that power had its limits and that a compromise was essential . . . the war and the extensive frustrations that accompanied it exhausted her. Her status in the eyes of public opinion was deteriorating and she was determined to prevent any renewal of the fighting. All of these resulted in a modification of her positions and a willingness to compromise."[24]

Golda tried to deflect attention from her leadership before the war by focusing on what transpired after the war had begun. True, she insisted, the number of casualties was staggering but more would have died had Israel launched a preemptive strike, thereby forfeiting the good will of the United States. She flagged her pivotal role in persuading the Nixon administration to provide Israel with the airlift that enabled it to fight back. Her leadership saved lives and restored Israel's position of strength. This response was part apologia for not foreseeing the war in the first place, part atonement for the awful losses, and part rationalization.

She also somewhat reluctantly put into motion a commission of inquiry tasked with reviewing the events of the first few days of the war and making recommendations concerning the performance of the leadership.

The Agranat Commission of Inquiry

Five men formed the Agranat Commission, all selected by Israel's chief justice, Simon Agranat, who also chaired the commission.[25] None of the very few women who served in any position of power at this time could claim military expertise (the Israeli Defense Forces never encouraged women to acquire any such expertise) so the fact that the committee was exclusively male is hardly surprising. Argranat's choice confirmed the conventional wisdom that dominated Golda's milieu: women had little understanding of the business of war. In a report that remained mostly classified for decades, the commission recommended that several high officers, including the chief of staff, be relieved of their duties. But the commission distinguished between personal and political responsibility and concluded that neither Dayan nor Golda was personally responsible for the mishap. In a democracy, the commission advised, any political malfeasance by the leadership, however grave, should be subjected to the people's judgment and not to the judgment of any appointed commission.[26]

The commission unanimously praised Golda's performance during the war as wise and judicious: "The Prime Minister made the right use of her decisional powers. . . . Using her healthy intuitions, she wisely and speedily moved to mobilize the reserves, notwithstanding the heavy political arguments against mobilization, and her action contributed mightily to the defense of the state."[27] Critics were bitterly disappointed. Many focused on Golda's alleged assertion that "she was only a woman" and mocked her for cynically seizing on her gender as a way to avoid responsibility. People often taunted her publicly, using a high-pitched voice (despite the fact that her voice was anything but) as they repeated her exculpatory statements. Where was the concern about her gender before the war, people asked angrily, when did she ever complain that "she was only a woman"?

Was Golda using her gender to exonerate herself? One should begin by interpreting her words. The statement she repeated frequently was, "Except for me, all were men trained in military affairs, but no one thought differently . . . and I, the civilian, who did not know exactly what a military division was, had to decide." Her words imply that as the lone civilian among military experts she was unfairly required to make military decisions. The sociologist Pierre Bourdieu coined the term "habitus" to denote a set of ingrained norms that shape individuals' experiences and expectations. Golda's habitus was dominated by security considerations that assigned priority to military practices and needs.[28] Her habitus was gendered, a habitus shaped, developed, and perpetuated by men.

On the morning of Yom Kippur, when Dayan and the chief of staff disagreed about whether two or four divisions should be mobilized, Golda was perplexed. "What do you want from me?" the protocols show her exclaiming, "how can I [make] such a decision?" She did not even know how many men or tanks made up one division, let alone the significance that two additional divisions would make. These military experts feared the consequences of their decisions and preferred someone else to take responsibility. Other experts, however, continued to reinforce the norms of male domination. For example, when Golda was fretting about the "finding" that the probability of war was "lower than low," Haim Bar-Lev, the minister of commerce and architect of the "the Bar-Lev Line" said to her: "I know what is a third level of alert. You don't." It was statements like this that "put her in her place" and established her as ignorant in matters of war, a judgment that Golda accepted.[29] She testified before the commission that she did not dare face the experts and suggest something that [they] . . . did not say. Take me as an example: what would have happened to me? They would have thought that she is dumb. Well, to a large degree this is also true. But what would have happened to me had I said what I felt then, it would not have been good for me. I could not stand my ground in a confrontation with the head of intelligence or the chief of staff.[30]

Golda felt awkward before those self-confident men speaking military language. She was haunted by the fear that if they judged her to be "dumb" it would erode her authority. Deep in her psyche vibrated the faint echo of her father's warning to her when she was fourteen: "Men do not like smart girls." Had she not harbored so much self-doubt about her intelligence, she might have taken the generals to task, perhaps overruling them and deploying the necessary measures to confront an attack.

Should one believe her or dismiss her argument as self-serving excuses? Was this a feminine way to avoid responsibility and encourage the commission to have pity on her, an old woman, or was it a valid justification given the patriarchal environment in which she governed? Here one sees the notion of "patriarchal equilibrium" working in full force. Golda had reached the top of the political pyramid; she was feared by many members of her cabinet and was able to make crucial decisions on a wide range of questions. Nevertheless the power to make decisions in matters of war remained in the hands of men.

At the same time, one should not ignore the harsh criticism the commission directed at Golda with respect to matters of proper governance. Instead of consulting the larger cabinet that the law vested with power to make crucial decisions, Golda handpicked a subset of ministers to decide what to do, both before and during the initial phases of the war. The larger cabinet was not invited to deliberate on crucial matters. She also abused her power by keeping relevant information classified and thus inaccessible to the cabinet as well as to the appropriate Knesset bodies in charge of oversight. Furthermore, despite her familiarity with the American model of governance, she failed to empower institutions that would check and challenge the military command. She neither invited nor called for a second opinion that might have brought nuance to the picture of the conflict presented by the monolithic military bloc.[31] Had she heard from a larger spectrum of opinions, she perhaps would have found support for her gut-level intuitions, which could have helped her overcome the fear of appearing "dumb." Such is the wisdom of hindsight.

The Critics on the "Old Woman" Factor

Some members of the press ascribed at least part of the calamity to Golda's gender. In a book hastily put together and published immediately after the war, seven journalists—all men—offered their insights into the most traumatic mishap in Israeli history. One chapter, "The Writing on the Wall," reviewed Golda's policies before the war. The author accused her of failing to follow the national interest by allowing personal predilections to influence critical political appointments and by focusing on the war on terrorism while neglecting "other fateful issues," such as relations between Egypt and Israel. Moreover, he attributed all these shortcomings to the fact that Golda was a woman:

> The appointments process under a woman like Golda are not done in accordance with the qualities of the appointees or the requirements of the job. As an emotional woman Golda's public actions follow her private loves and hatreds. . . . In the Palestinian matter, as in other matters, Golda did not examine matters substantively. She decided in accordance with her hatreds and loves.[32]

The book's jacket displayed a photo of Golda's face artificially enlarged, sending the message that Golda personified the war. In the photo Golda was disembarking from a military airplane with Israeli prisoners of war (POWs) returning from Syria. Golda fought like a tigress to bring these POWs home and thought of them as her sons. Her face on the cover was a distillation of pure pain, her skin sagging, eyes shut, eyebrows furrowed, and lips tight. Under different circumstances the photo might have appealed to viewers' empathy, but on the cover of this book, expected to be a best seller, it conveyed Golda's incompetence.

Disaffection with Golda as a leader reverberates among Israel's public intellectuals to this day as does the implication that her gender was part of the problem. Seventeen years after the war, Michael Bar-Zohar, a historian, published a book about political developments from the Yom Kippur War to the Intifada of 1987. Bar-Zohar argued that since Ben-Gurion's departure from office, Israel had experienced a crisis of leadership. In the chapter devoted to Golda, "The Iron Lady," he wrote, "I am convinced that Israel began its deterioration under the charismatic leadership of Golda Meir." Calling her time in service "tragic," he opened the chapter with praise: "It appears that Golda was blessed with all the characteristics—uncompromising nature, strong will, total identification with her people, blunt indifference to what people may think of her, full confidence that her path was the right one and magnetic presence." He followed this praise with a string of highly personal gendered attacks: "She was far from good looking, her taste in clothes was pathetic, she did not read books, and her vocabulary was limited." Bar-Zohar understood that given his readership, focusing on Golda's "feminine" attributes would help vindicate his conclusion: Golda was bad for Israel. "As a leader," he concluded, "she lacked all political imagination and the insights of a statesman." The word "statesman" was written in the masculine even though Hebrew translation contains a feminine equivalent. While there was a grain of truth to Bar-Zohar's analysis, the focus on Golda's gender sent the message that women did not belong in the realm of public affairs.[33]

Even more recently, in 2017 the retired senior political columnist of *Haaretz*, then Israel's leading daily newspaper, offered his own version of this sexist analysis: "Everyone said she was the only man in the cabinet. . . . I said . . . to the contrary . . . with her hostilities, her jealousies, she is the ultimate woman. A woman with all her negative attributes."[34] The portrayal of Golda in a recent Israeli television documentary series dedicated to Israel's prime ministers echoes the same theme. The series focused on Golda's lovers and illnesses and summarized her performance during the war as "emotional." The underlying message: here was a woman reputed to be strong but who in fact crumbled under the pressures of war.[35]

These unflattering opinions rooted in misogyny reflect the pain Israelis felt and still feel about the Yom Kippur War. Perhaps the explanation lies in the psychology of denial: instead of facing up to their own support for Israeli's refusal to pursue territorial compromise, which played a central role in the events that led to the war, the Israeli public preferred to blame the "old woman." Some Israelis acknowledge that public opinion supported Golda's policies but hasten to add that had she been a great leader she would have bucked public opinion and steered the ship of state in a different direction. They often quote Ben-Gurion, who said more than once that he would not do what the people want but rather what was good for them. Indeed, Golda was no Ben-Gurion. Her sensibilities were more democratic. She wished to stay in power and therefore went along with public opinion. When she stated that she "would never be the same person she had been before the war," perhaps she meant that she was too uncritical in her pursuit of the "people's will." Public opinion was no substitute for independent thinking.

A Final Duel with Shulamit Aloni

Because of the war the general elections, originally set for October 31, 1973, were postponed to the last day of the calendar year. Early on the morning of January 1, Golda learned that her Labor Party had won, again. The voters hesitated to change horses so soon after disaster had struck.[36] Despite this victory, Golda's political power eroded rapidly. The members of her cabinet, fuming, blamed her for abusing the constitutional procedures of cabinet decision making. The many Knesset deliberations dedicated to the war painted Golda and Dayan as fallen heroes.

The political strain took its toll on Golda's physical health. She was bedridden with shingles and in excruciating pain. Evidently her immune system, already beaten by excessive smoking, a history of illnesses, chemotherapy, and natural aging had reached its limit. Golda's people fought valiantly but her own body was giving in.

Aloni, whom Golda exiled from the party list, ran on an independent ticket and won three seats in the Knesset. It was a formidable achievement, supported by the burgeoning women's movement.[37] According to the scholar Hanna Herzog, there was a tight connection between the experience of the male-centered war and the awakening of women to their entitlement to full citizenship: women moved to assert their rights precisely because they were so badly ignored during the war.[38] During this period Golda did not do much for Israeli women. She was literally and metaphorically ill and tired, and her attention was consumed by the Separation of Forces agreements negotiated between Israel, Syria, and Egypt. The other seven female Knesset members who represented the Labor Party, all vetted by Golda, were good, intelligent women but none had Aloni's charisma or passion for reform and transformation. Golda's new cabinet, presented to the Knesset on March 10, 1974, was made up of twenty-two male ministers and Golda at the helm, once again the only woman in the room.

Nor did Golda, in her speech to the Knesset presenting her new cabinet's policies, address women's issues as central to Israeli society. Rather, she offered her familiar vision of social justice. In one sentence, she mentioned in passing the need to create national day-care centers to help mothers, but she went no further. Golda may have thought that the gravity of the situation precluded attention to the "luxury" of gender equality. Or she may have been angry about the support Aloni was receiving from women as well as the criticism being directed her way, thus deciding to ignore women's issues.[39] In all likelihood Golda's thoughts during this period centered on survival: the survival of the state, the survival of the party, and the survival of herself.

Later that day Aloni mounted the podium to deliver her maiden speech to Israel's legislative body. To many people's surprise, her speech did not address women's issues. Instead, the forty-six-year-old rebel offered a scathing critique of Golda, whom she referred to as "the big mother," a thinly veiled attack on Golda's age. Aloni told the Knesset that Golda had been reconfirmed as prime minister only because her cabinet had lost all sense of shame. They should have resigned. Because shame was dead, she continued sarcastically, shame should be given a funeral with large crowds and great pomp.[40] The 110 male members of the Knesset were treated to a bizarre spectacle—two women, each formidable in her own way, crossing swords. To many this must have been seen as a confirmation that women were too emotional—and too consumed by their personal hatreds and petty impulses—to govern. Did Aloni pause to consider that she was fortifying stereotypes that would return to bite her?

Golda's Resignation

Golda resigned as prime minister on April 4, 1974, one day after the Passover holiday, as the final report of the Agranat Commission was being placed on her desk. In her final cabinet meeting she told the ministers that she was sorry that they too had to resign, but it was required by law. The ministers proceeded to analyze the Agranat Commission's recommendations and the following exchange took place:

> MINISTER OF POLICE: "I would like to recount a story from the days when I was young . . ."
> MINISTER OF TREASURY: "Were you too once young?"
> GOLDA: "Remez used to say that old age is the problem of the young."[41]

Ageism, although not explicitly mentioned, was the elephant in the room. People considered Golda too old, out of touch with the public and its needs. Golda's true nemesis was neither Shulamit Aloni nor the young generation she claimed to represent, it was simply time. At that precise moment as she was contemplating the problem of age, David Remez—her old mentor, dear friend, and former lover, the one man who more than anyone else coached her and facilitated her ascent— came to her mind. Remez, who had passed away twenty years earlier, had been practically forgotten by all, and yet she summoned him to stand by her side as her cabinet deliberated for the last time. Was she wondering what his advice would be? Did she remember his warning in the late 1940s that the hawkish policy she and Ben-Gurion were following would "smash the hopes of the Jewish people?"[42] Or did his appearance reflect a more intimate longing? Lonely and dejected, she must have yearned to be in his arms.

In letters to Golda's lifelong friend Marie Syrkin, Lou Kaddar wrote that Golda's mood was "awful" and that she "did not view with pleasure [Syrkin's suggestion] that she retires from office." Of course, Syrkin's suggestion was offered because the public as well as Golda's own party wanted her and her government out of office. "As a matter of cold fact," Kaddar wrote, "she didn't take it [the decision to resign], it was pushed down her throat, and not too gently either."[43] Golda tendered her resignation bitter and heartbroken. Like many leaders she stayed in power too long, having failed to realize when it was time to leave. But many Israelis saw her poor performance as a confirmation of their sexist prejudices. No woman has since been elected prime minister of Israel.

CHAPTER 27

THE END

"The Book"

In retirement Golda first concentrated on preparing her memoirs for publication. Not much of a writer herself, she hired the journalist Rinna Samuel to ghostwrite it. Perhaps Golda felt more comfortable telling her life story to a woman or thought that a woman would convey a woman's voice more effectively. Golda recorded her recollections, which Rinna turned into text, and Golda expected Rinna to rely primarily on these recollections along with a few documents submitted by her staff. She did not want Rinna to interview people or draw on other external sources. Rinna was not a biographer attempting to bring an outsider's critical perspective to the narrative, and Golda was not eager to experience an outsider's gaze in the creation of her own story. "The Book," as her staff called it, was her book, intended to reflect her personal perspective. Appropriately titled *My Life*, it was by her and about her. She identified so intimately with its creation that she did not even include an acknowledgments page or otherwise list those involved in its gestation. Indeed, her life reflected the grand narratives of Israel and Zionism but no one could mistake the personal tone.

My Life was a great success. It remained on the *New York Times* bestseller list for nine weeks, received mostly favorable reviews, and was translated into a wide variety of languages.[1] The book did so well in part because it conveyed Golda's personal voice. Golda's friend the evangelical leader Billy Graham called it "the greatest book I have ever read," perhaps momentarily letting his awe overshadow the special place the Bible occupied in his life.[2]

A Broadway Play

The acclaimed playwright William Gibson, known for *The Miracle Worker* and other Broadway works, approached Golda to suggest the production of a Broadway play about her life. Although at first uncomfortable, she agreed and even collaborated on the project. Gibson hired the renowned actress Anne Bancroft to play Golda, and Bancroft visited Israel to familiarize herself with Golda's body language and persona.

Inviting such attention was uncharacteristic of Golda. Throughout her life she deliberately turned herself into a subject, a mover and a shaker, but she was always careful to downplay any ownership of her accomplishments. Why did she collaborate on this dramatization of her life? When a journalist posed this question, Golda deflected attention from herself saying that the success of her autobiography made her think that the play "would be a big thing for Israel."[3] In reality several factors likely motivated Golda's decision. One imagines, for instance, that she yearned for redemption and hoped to present the Yom Kippur War in ways that would exonerate the decisions she had made. The play offered an opportunity to focus on what everyone agreed was her extraordinary leadership once the war began, rather than on what had transpired under her stewardship during the years preceding the war. Moreover, a successful Broadway play could serve as an antidote to the vicious satirical presentation of her in *Queen of a Bathtub*, which was staged in 1970.[4] It would also put to shame the many critics who denounced her as being out of touch and deaf to the rhythm of the times.[5] She must have been hoping that the play would show her in her full splendor partaking in the creation of the state of Israel at every turn, perhaps with the implication that "Israel" could not have happened without her.

As attested by Lou Kaddar's letters, Golda was often depressed during this period of her life. Could it be that, feeling so low, she needed a boost to snap her out of this mood? Did she hope to find in America the affection and approval that she once had in Israel but no longer did? Kaddar captured the high expectations when she wrote only half jokingly, "Of course it would be lovely if the play is a success, otherwise a general suicide might be contemplated."[6] Golda was so pleased when the play was read to her in the company of her family in the summer of 1977 that she decided to invite a large group of family and friends to the Broadway premiere. She must have thought it would be fun to bring them all together to bask in the warm welcome America would surely offer. After all, her family was also wounded by the relentless attacks on her character and leadership and they, too, deserved a break.

The premiere was a debacle and the show closed within a few weeks. The *New York Times* called it "an artistic and financial failure."[7] The more Golda watched Bancroft play her on the stage the more shocked she became. She is reported to have sat through the performance stony-faced, not displaying a hint of emotion. On the stage she did not see the "fantastic living woman" as the theater had advertised, but a stooped, limping, somewhat lethargic old lady. The character perhaps looked like her mother but it certainly did not resemble the way Golda imagined herself. She denied that she walked with her head down or that she had a limp. Bancroft maintained, however, that both attributes were vintage Golda: "Golda was never able to lift her head and she does walk with a limp, which is something she doesn't recognize." Golda's subjective self-image was in serious conflict with Bancroft's Golda. An experienced and gifted actress, Bancroft defended her art: "[Golda] is a woman with a certain amount of vanity. When I was in Israel visiting her, I would look at her photographs and say, 'Look at that dress,' she would say 'Look how fat I am!' That was very womanly. Most women do say, 'How terrible I look!' I like to show normal human vanity."[8]

As Israel's leader on the world stage Golda imagined herself as embodying fortitude and stamina, not as a weak and fragile lady. Bancroft pointed out that in fact the performances brought standing ovations, but for Golda the experience brought only shame and reminded her of the afflictions she had already experienced, from the misogyny and widespread denunciations in the media to the catastrophes of the war

Figure 11. Golda Meir with President of Egypt Anwar El-Sadat, 1977, upon Sadat's historic visit to Israel. Minister of Defense Shimon Peres is to Sadat's left. Courtesy of Israel Government Press Office. Credit: Sa'ar Ya'acov.

and the miserable way in which she left office. Hopes for redemption vanished. Years later, after Golda's death, Gibson rewrote the play. With Tovah Feldshuh in the title role, *Golda's Balcony* became the longest-running one-woman show in Broadway history.[9]

Meeting President Anwar al-Sadat

Golda was still smarting from her disappointment when astonishing news arrived from Israel. The government of Prime Minister Begin had invited Egypt's president Anwar al-Sadat to Jerusalem and Sadat had accepted. The news added insult to injury. Begin, the Likud leader and now prime minister, had been Golda's political nemesis since the 1930s. Golda, along with her successor Yitzhak Rabin, had developed the framework for the Israeli–Egyptian rapprochement, a framework that now bore the fruit of the historic visit. Golda felt that the seeds of the peace treaty with Egypt had been planted under her leadership and that she deserved some credit for the historic developments.

When she received a formal invitation to attend the ceremonies surrounding Sadat's visit she immediately cut short her trip to New York.
She canceled meetings and appearances, hurriedly packed, and boarded
a plane to Paris. In Paris an El Al jetliner was held for three hours until
she arrived from New York. The woman who had discussed war and
peace with King Abdullah of Jordan a quarter of a century earlier was
now flying to Tel Aviv to greet the president of Egypt. The next day she
stood in line at the airport, the only woman in a sea of men waiting to
greet her erstwhile enemy. Sadat had made it clear that he wanted to see
Golda, and his broad smile and warm handshake confirmed that she was
very much still a "somebody" in his eyes. At the Knesset she headed the
opposition's delegation addressing Sadat on matters of war and peace.
Her speech was vintage Golda—exuding excitement, certitude, and
self-confidence. At the end of her address she raised the issue of her
gender. Turning to Sadat who was seated next to her she said "I am an
old lady." Chuckles were heard from the audience. She paused, deftly
timing her performance, and then repeated with a smile somewhat mis-
chievously: "You called me an old lady." Everyone broke out laughing,
including Sadat and Shimon Peres, the current chairman of the Labor
Party. The two men in their fifties looked somewhat boyish as if their
hands had been caught in the cookie jar. Sadat turned to Peres and could
be heard saying: "I called her that frequently." They both knew how often
they had used the "old woman" stereotype to damage her reputation.[10]

In the aftermath of the failed Broadway show, the reality of being an
old woman was very much on Golda's mind. It is difficult to know
whether her offhand comment to Sadat was premeditated or a Freudian
slip. But her performance proved that, old or not, Golda could still grab
the limelight. It was as a message to Anne Bancroft in New York: "This
is who I am. This is how both friend and foe see me."

Golda's Final Months

Golda had suffered from lymphoma for more than a decade but for the
most part she had successfully kept her condition out of the public eye.
She knew that bad news about her health would only exacerbate worries
that she was too old for the job. Meron Medzini recalled that people in

the prime minister's office could tell whenever Golda visited the hospital for chemotherapy by the Band-Aid on her arm, but she never spoke a word about it.

In addition to cancer, Golda suffered from rheumatism, a frozen shoulder, and other minor ailments. She was in constant pain and spent the last fifteen weeks of her life in the hematology department at Hadassah Medical Center. "Her legs were swollen from the hips down," which forced her to walk with a cane until even this became too difficult. At one point, she said to a nurse "even steel weakens." Her son recalled that his heart sank when "she stopped smoking and drinking coffee." He knew the end was near.[11]

One night shortly before she died, doctors called the family to say that nothing more could be done. Lou Kaddar reported that one member of Golda's family "made a scene," insisting that they call her personal physicians immediately. Although they knew that the end was near, a fact so hard to face, her family still saw it as their duty to prolong her life. Indeed a last-minute medical intervention gained Golda a few more days. However, Golda was too ill to have a will of her own and one wonders if, although she never tired of emphasizing the value of life, she would have preferred to refuse the medical efforts and simply let go. Following this intervention, Kaddar described Golda's condition: "She can't move alone in bed, refuses to eat and drink, sleeps a lot, and has no pain for hours. She talks normally, listens with pleasure to my reading her letters, etc. Still, it is the end."[12]

Golda Meir died at Hadassah Medical Center in Jerusalem on December 8, 1978. She was eighty years old. Lou Kaddar's letter describes Golda's physical deterioration, sadness, and depression in her final days.[13] After leaving office in April 1974 she was unable to find peace. She experienced the pain of no longer being at the center of the maelstrom, and the media's relentless criticism for the catastrophic war felt like torture.

Golda passed away at 4:30 P.M. on a Friday afternoon when, in accordance with Jewish law and tradition, the Sabbath descends upon the land. The news of her death spread quickly. Only Moscow's media remained silent. Perhaps they remembered her powerful impact on Soviet Jews when she was an emissary in Moscow and feared another emotional wave.

Although Golda grew up in a religious family and was familiar with the tropes of traditional Jewish life, she was a secular woman. She valued Shabbat as a pillar of Jewish cultural existence and as a day of rest for laborers, but she did not hold it sacred. At every turn in her career, she ignored the rules concerning the sanctity of Shabbat—as minister of labor she legalized permits for work on the Sabbath; as minister of foreign affairs she delivered a crucial speech before the United Nations General Assembly on the Sabbath; and as prime minister she held emergency meetings with her staff and cabinet during the dreadful start of the Yom Kippur War, which fell on the Sabbath. Now she lay dead and a rival political party was in power, a party more sympathetic to religious rules. The Likud leader Menachem Begin was in Oslo waiting to receive the Nobel Peace Prize when Golda died. He instructed his cabinet to wait until the Sabbath was over and then hold a special meeting in her honor.

Golda did not specify where she would like to be buried so the cabinet decided to bury her at the National Cemetery on Mount Herzl alongside Israel's most important leaders. In death as in life Golda was an only woman in the company of male leaders. Rachel Katznelson, the matriarch of the Israeli women's movement was also buried there, but only because she was President Zalman Shazar's wife. Other wives are buried there too but to this day Golda is the only woman buried in Israel's National Cemetery because she had been one of the nation's great leaders.

Golda's Will

In Golda's will, composed in 1967, she wrote: "I forbid any eulogies and naming anything after me. I further repeat and emphasize this request to [my] Party. I am sure that my request will be honored." It wasn't. Numerous eulogies were written. While those given by her erstwhile political enemies may have been insincere, most were genuine and full of admiration and respect.

Golda's instruction that nothing be named after her likely reflects her lifelong insecurity. She may have feared that she was not "worthy" of such an honor or that any initiative to name something after her might meet with reluctance and thereby tarnish her name. She always felt the sting of criticism much more intensely than she felt the glow of praise. But the letters and cables coming from near and far proved how much she meant to so many, as did the movements to remember her through sites and monuments. In Tel Aviv, her first destination as a young immigrant to Palestine as well as the town where she raised her children and launched her brilliant career, Israelis now listen to opera and see Shakespeare's plays at the majestic Center for the Performing Arts, known to all as the Golda Center. In Jerusalem, where she held political power for twenty-five years, a major highway is named Golda Meir Interchange. You cannot drive in and out of the state's capital without experiencing its continuous, boisterous traffic. Streets and roads, schools and libraries, parks and hospitals are named after her throughout the land. Stamps, gold coins, and banknotes bear her image. The University of Wisconsin in Milwaukee named its library after Golda and hosts a Golda-related archive. Although Golda never graduated as she had hoped from Wisconsin's State Normal School for teachers, hundreds of students sit in the library named for her every day, building their future through reading and study.

The Israeli people have also come to express their fondness for Golda. Restaurants, shops, and even items of food are sometimes advertised as "Golda" this or that—little did she ever expect her name to have market value. In death something inexplicable happened. Throughout her career Golda was the target of relentless misogyny and criticism. Israelis could not transcend gender-based stereotypes and often attributed Golda's mistakes and failures to the fact that she was a woman. The expressions of love following her death reflected a different, equally meaningful and equally deep sentiment. After poking fun at her appearance, her simple prose, her being at once a tough man and an old woman, the Israeli people felt she stood for something bigger than life—the power to face adversity, remain resilient, and be oneself.

The Funeral

The weather on the day of her funeral was bitter cold, as only Jerusalem can be, and everyone was chilled to the bone. "Simple, thick, continuous and sad" rain was falling.[14] Her coffin, covered by the flags of Israel and plastic sheets to protect it from the rain, stood in the Knesset Square. People came by droves and stood under their umbrellas patiently waiting for their turn to pay their respects.

The funeral was planned in accordance with the traditional gender-based segregation. As usual, there were male rabbis and military personnel—the two pillars of Israeli existence. Young male cadets stood guard, followed by fifty young women soldiers carrying wreaths. Displaying once again the gap between myth and reality when it came to gender equality, male soldiers at the funeral held guns while the female soldiers carried flowers. This was the "natural order of things," emblematic of Golda's Israel since she had arrived in 1922.

Golda admired the Zionist leader Henrietta Szold, another great woman and fellow American, so she may have known that Henrietta insisted on reciting the kaddish for her father. Had Golda paid attention to this issue, what would she have preferred? Golda's parents had three daughters, but no son. Would she have liked her own daughter Sarah to take part in the final ritual? After all, she always treated both her son and daughter with equal care and respect. As it happened, only Menachem, Golda's son, recited the kaddish. Sarah and the other women members of the family—her sister Tzikpe-Clara, daughter-in-law Aya Meir, granddaughter Naomi Rahabi, oldest friend Regina Hamburger-Medzini, assistant and confidant Lou Kaddar, biographer and friend Marie Syrkin, and many more women—were sidelined, as men who were not nearly as close to her stood by the grave.

And then it was over, and the family returned to Ramat Aviv to sit Shiva.

Marie Syrkin's Poem

After Golda's death, Marie Syrkin, her lifelong friend and biographer, published a poem in her memory. Syrkin had known Golda since childhood and had published several admiring books about her as a great leader. Her last poem about Golda brought to life the young Golda: beautiful, slim, and sought after by many men. It was an important reminder that while Golda became internationally famous as an old lady in the final decades of her life, she was not always the heavy-legged, sexless, "grandmother of the Jewish people." She was a human being, a woman who was sexually attractive, who loved men, and was loved in return. That Golda was also worthy of remembrance.

For Golda

Because you became a great woman
With strong features
Big nose
And heavy legs,
None will believe how beautiful you were,
Gray-eyed and slim ankled
The men who loved you are dead,
So I speak for the record.
Indeed you were lovely among maidens
Once
In Milwaukee and Merhavia
And sometimes in Jerusalem.[15]

Golda's Message

In the 1930s, as Golda was working day and night to climb the political ladder and smoking like a chimney, her mother is reported to have frequently asked: "Golda, what will be your end?"[16] Bluma Mabowitz feared that her daughter was drifting, not devoting the proper energy to her children, and pouring her heart and soul into some insubstantial Zionist project that only few believed would succeed. This could not end well, her mother implied. But the young Golda persisted in her activism and to calm herself continued smoking.

She had had the good luck to taste a wide variety of life experiences, some very sweet and others exceedingly bitter. She had children— something most women of her generation dearly wanted—more romantic relationships than the ordinary person, and excitement and fulfillment in the world of politics. Had Golda known then the heights she would reach she could have responded with frank honesty, "Mother, this is not such a bad end."

In an era when most women were trained to tame their inner drive and instead "sacrifice" for the sake of conventional values, Golda steadfastly followed her desires and found the satisfaction she longed for. She had the gift of knowing what she truly wanted, not what convention or tradition dictated, and she dared pursue it even when it brought pain to those dear to her. Beyond love for family and nation, Golda considered the dignity of labor to be an essential part of her life and work to be a vehicle of self-fulfillment. She made many mistakes and, as she had told Oriana Fallaci, made perhaps too many compromises, but she also decided for herself where she would compromise and where she would not. In a speech delivered in 1952 as minister of labor, she said: "For the state, for the economy but *first and foremost for the fifty percent* residents of this country, the women . . . it is essential that we restore *the feeling of an inner need, of a drive to go to work and stay at work.*"[17]

Twenty-five years later, a year before she died, she looked back on her life and said:

> I was involved [in my jobs] one hundred percent . . . I didn't take on work that I didn't really want. Yes, of course, I loved my work. I loved what I was doing. *I never see myself as having sacrificed anything.* Sure, you have to give up things. You can't have everything. But you choose what you think is important and you do it. So, it's no sacrifice.[18]

ACKNOWLEDGMENTS

DEREK PENSLAR was the first to suggest the title "The Only Woman in the Room." It immediately ignited my imagination because it not only described Golda's existence in politics, mostly alone among men in the endless meetings she participated in, but echoes David Ben-Gurion's famous saying that Golda "was the only man in the cabinet." The book's title turns this mostly pejorative statement on its head by arguing that in fact she was "the only woman" in the cabinet and in meeting rooms in general. In many conversations with me about this biography, Derek Penslar, a true friend, challenged and questioned my premises and helped me clarify ideas. I cannot thank him enough. In time, his wife Robin Penslar also joined my circle of friends and helped me during critical moments of bringing the manuscript to its destination.

In 2008 while I was a fellow at the center of advanced studies at the Hebrew University in Jerusalem, I hired Rivka Brot as a research assistant to help me collect archival materials about Golda. She did a splendid job. Rivka has also become a good friend and I thank her for her help and support as I worked on this book. Many other research assistants helped me over the year, chief among them is Omer Aloni. I am afraid that they are too many to list here, but Elizabeth Nagel, Gabriela Morales, Caleb French, Eitan Rom, Brian Hayes, Arielle Kristan, Noa Roth, Ariela Rivkin, and Jacob Palmer deserve particular thanks.

Special thanks go to Peter Bernstein, my formidable book agent, to Fred Appel my capable editor at Princeton University Press, to James Collier, Fred's assistant, to Therese Malhame, the careful copyeditor, and the team at Princeton University Press whose superb skills awed me and contributed immensely to this book. Most especially, Thomas

LeBien, my developmental editor, worked his magic and turned the book into a more coherent, fluent, and better structured volume. Over the course of editing, he has taught me a great deal about writing in general and book editing, and I shall always treasure his contribution. Rachel Brenner, a good friend and wise literary critic, was one of the early readers of this manuscript and provided valuable comments. Her untimely death last year pained me and prevents me from presenting this book to her, but her fingerprints are everywhere. At Princeton University Press, I also thank an anonymous reader who offered excellent comments and suggestions.

While writing this book I was heartened by the support of many who agreed to read some chapters and otherwise provide feedback, and I regret that I cannot mention them all. Standing out is Gabriela Shalev, my contract professor at Hebrew University more than fifty years ago, who became a dear friend. Professor Shalev was the first woman in Israeli history to be appointed to the esteemed position of Israel's ambassador to the United Nations. I cherish our conversations and her insights. David Kretzmer, Leora Bilsky, Assaf Likhovsky, Ron Harris, Hannah Herzog, Doreen Lustig, Esther Carmel Hakim, Natan Aridan, Abigail Gillman, and Yael Zerubavel warmed my heart and strengthened my spirit with advice and support. For several years I was a member of a small group of legal biographers who met during the annual conference of the American Society for Legal History. Among them were Tomiko Brown-Nagin, Jane De Hart, Felice Batlan, Barbara Allen Babcock of blessed memory, Marlene Trestman, Serena Mayeri and Leandra Zarnow. The vibrant force of this group was the judicial biographer Constance Backhouse, who energetically organized the seminars and tirelessly provided excellent feedback on our manuscripts. Constance earned the eternal admiration and gratitude of us all and I am particularly grateful to her. My dear and close friend Laura Kalman, a great legal historian, did not attend these seminars regularly but remained interested in our work and over the years provided immense support and friendship. A fortunate outcome of the activity of our group is my friendship with Jane De Hart, the author of an excellent biography of Supreme Court Justice Ruth Bader Ginsburg.

The leadership at Boston University School of Law (BUSL), Maureen O'Rourke, Angela Onwuachi-Willig, Stacey Dogan, and Anna di Robilant offered support and assistance, and to them I send my heartfelt thanks.

So too I wish to thank members of the BUSL staff. Ken Westhassel served as my secretary from 1978 until his recent retirement. By now he is practically a member of my family. Ken applied his superb skills to checking footnotes carefully and reviewing the manuscript more than once. Ken: I couldn't have done it without you and, again, I acknowledge my debt to you. Kristen Queenan and Linda Skinner also helped enormously. Heather N. Hayes graciously agreed to continue the work and provided excellent assistance as I was nearing the completion of the work. She, along with Ben Morgan, deserve enormous thanks.

The skill, efficiency, and energy of the Fineman and Pappas Libraries at Boston University School of Law proved, as usual, to be outstanding, and made the research, which can often be so demanding, an easy chore to manage. My heartfelt thanks to Kelly Johnson and Amelia Landenberger and all the librarians who assisted me in bringing this project to fruition.

Several Israeli compatriots who took an interest in this book and provided generous and invaluable help are Hagai Tsoref, head of the Department of Archives and Documentation at Israel State Archives and the editor of *Golda Meir: The Fourth Prime Minister*; Meron Medzini, author of *Golda Meir: A Political Biography*; Nahum Karlinsky of the Department of Israeli History at Beer Sheva University; and Orit Rozin of the Department of Jewish History at Tel Aviv University. My interviews with the professors Yechiam Weitz of Haifa University, Zach Levey, and Zaki Shalom were also an important source of enlightenment. Gideon Meir and Shaul Rahabi, Golda's grandsons (children of Menachem and Sarah, respectively), generously contributed their deep knowledge and insights. I learned an enormous amount from each. Of course, any remaining errors are mine alone.

Last but most essential to my life and welfare, my children Alexandra D. Lahav and Absalom J. Lahav provided love, encouragement, and abundant care without which I could not have handled the work. I never fail to be amazed and gratified by their brilliance and goodwill. My daughter Alexandra, an accomplished jurist and intellectual, was always willing to pause her busy schedule and lend me her ear. My son Absalom, an accomplished artist, has always been my best photographer and provided my photo for the book jacket. Absalom and my daughter-in-law Nora Lynn Leech were always there for technical support and insights into the various artistic aspects associated with the manuscript. Nora's background in the state of Wisconsin, where Golda grew up, created a special and extra bond between us and enriched my understanding of the culture from which Golda drew her backbone and friendly attitude. It took many years and a village to complete this manuscript, and if I have forgotten to mention all those who have helped me, I offer them my apologies along with sincere thanks.

NOTES

Introduction

1. Yotam Reuveny, "The Journalist Who Witnessed Israel's Entire History," *Haaretz*, November 30, 2017, https://www.haaretz.com/israel-news/.premium.MAGAZINE-the-journalist-who-witnessed-israel-s-entire-history-1.5627383.

2. Interview with Gideon Meir, Golda's grandson, a musician, May 25, 2019, Tel Aviv.

3. Ralph G. Martin, *Golda Meir: The Romantic Years* (New York: Charles Scribner's, 1988), 49.

4. Avi Shlaim, "Review of Elinor Burkett, *Golda: The Face That Launched a Thousand MiGs*," *The Guardian*, August 15, 2008.

5. Michael Bar-Zohar, *Facing a Cruel Mirror: Israel's Moment of Truth* (New York: Charles Scribner's, 1990), 45.

6. Letty Cottin Pogrebin, *Deborah, Golda, and Me* (New York: Crown, 1991), 175; Oriana Fallaci, "Golda Meir," *Interview with History* (Boston: Houghton Mifflin Harcourt, 1976).

7. Anita Shapira, "Golda: Femininity and Feminism," in Shapira, *Jews, Zionists and In Between* (Tel Aviv-Yafo: Am Oved, 2007), 197 (Hebrew). All translations from Hebrew and Yiddish are by the author.

8. Surely the "institution" of the Jewish mother was central in the larger Jewish Mizrahi communities as well. However, in the United States where Eastern European Jewish culture was dominant, the public identified with the Yiddishe Mamma.

9. Letter from W. J. Covell to Golda Meir, August 14, 1971, Israel State Archives.

10. Fallaci, "Golda Meir," 112.

11. Golda Meir, *My Life* (New York: Dell, 1976), 37.

12. Ruth Halperin-Kaddari, *Women in Israel: A State of Their Own* (Philadelphia: University of Pennsylvania Press, 2004), 16–29. The equal rights law proclaimed gender equality but attached significant exceptions to it.

13. These episodes involving Rabbi Yitzhak Meir Levin are discussed in part III, ch. 19.

14. Reuveny, "Journalist Who Witnessed"; see also Uri Avnery's comments in part IV, ch. 19, and Isaac Remba's comments in part III, ch. 16 in this volume. These individuals were all male journalists, speaking at different times and from different angles of the political spectrum. Another slogan popular among children at the time was "Boys for soccer, girls to the trash can."

15. Fallaci, "Golda Meir," 113.

16. Hagai Tsoref, ed., *Golda Meir: The Fourth Prime Minister, Selected Documents, 1898–1978* (Jerusalem: Israel State Archives, 2016) (Hebrew), 626.

17. This dilemma is known in the scholarship as intersectionality.

18. Meir, *My Life*, 61.

19. Fallaci, "Golda Meir," 119.

20. Fallaci, "Golda Meir," 119.

21. Part IV, ch. 25 in this volume.

22. She would also remain prime minister during the War of Attrition fought against Egypt between 1967 and 1970.

23. The most recent scholarly book on this topic is Yoav Gelber, *Hubris: Israel's Road to the Yom Kippur War* (Tel Aviv: Kinneret, Zmora, Dvir, 2021) (Hebrew.) See also Tsoref, *Golda Meir: The Fourth Prime Minister* (597–601, 621), (Hebrew) and references in chapters 25 and 26 in this volume. Tsoref recounts that on October 31, 1973, as she was presented with a proposal to separate Israeli and Egyptian military forces, she retorted: "this we could have achieved without war," thereby referring to earlier Israeli proposals for territorial compromises (599).

24. Michal Kremer Asaf, *Golda Meir's Foreign Decision-Making Process* (Newcastle upon Tyne: Cambridge Scholars, 2018). Rumors that Golda contemplated suicide in the case of a disastrous defeat were never corroborated but not refuted either.

25. But the Agranat Commission appointed to examine the events that led to the war did not find her performance blameworthy. See part IV, ch. 29.

26. Y. Ben-Porat et al., *Ha-Mechdal* (*The Mishap*) ("Special edition" is listed as the publisher. Tel Aviv, 1973) (Hebrew). It appears that the book was hastily put together at the end of the war. Golda is described on p. 151, Yariv is described on p. 150.

27. Therese Huston, *How Women Decide* (New York: Houghton Mifflin Harcourt, 2016), 211.

Chapter One: In Imperial Russia

1. Sheyna Korngold, *Zichronot* (Tel Aviv: ID Press, 1968) (Hebrew).

2. Golda Meir, *My Father's House* (Tel Aviv: Hakibbutz Hameuchad, 1972), 15 (Hebrew).

3. Steven J. Zipperstein, *Pogrom: Kishinev and the Tilt of History* (New York: W. W. Norton, 2018), 15.

4. Meir, *My Father's House*.

5. In the academic literature, the condition of experiencing two separate sets of discrimination is known as intersectionality.

6. Korngold, *Zichronot*, 18.

7. Eliyana R. Adler, *In Her Hands: The Education of Jewish Girls in Tsarist Russia* (Detroit: Wayne State University Press, 2011). The author notes that education did not go beyond elementary school.

8. Korngold, *Zichronot*, 37.

9. Korngold, *Zichronot*, 15.

10. Korngold, *Zichronot*, 24–27. Janovsky's first name is not mentioned, perhaps indicating the class distance between Golda's family and that of her employer.

11. I thank Gideon Meir, Golda's grandson, for this information (see figure 1).

Chapter Two: To America

1. Golda Meir, *My Life* (New York: Dell, 1976), 57.

2. Meir, *My Life*, 25–29.

3. Golda Meir, *My Father's House* (Tel Aviv: Hakibbutz Hameuchad, 1972), 29–30 (Hebrew).

4. Meir, *My Life*, 29.

5. Meir, *My Life*, 35.

6. "On the Hearth," or "Oifen Pripitchick" in Yiddish, a song capturing the painful life of a Jewish boy in the Pale of Settlement.

7. Original Yiddish manuscript by Sheyna Korngold (Tel Aviv: ID Press, 1968) at 107.

8. Meir, *My Life*, 37.

9. This is an interesting contrast to Russia, where married women experienced no constraints on pursuing the teaching profession. The U.S. legal prohibition was probably meant to encourage a bourgeois lifestyle for a woman. A woman with children was expected to provide a home for her family by staying at home. Work and motherhood were not considered compatible.

10. Meir, *My Life*, 37.

11. Korngold, *Zichronot*.

12. Meir, *My Life*, 39.

13. Meir, *My Life*, 39.

14. Meir, *My Life*, parts III and IV.

15. Meir, *My Life*, 45.

16. Meir, *My Life*, 46.

17. Meir, *My Life*, 47.

18. See, for example, Golda's testimony before the Agranat Commission, discussed in greater detail in part IV.

19. Meir, *My Life*, 47.

20. Meir, *My Life*, 47.

21. Meron Medzini, the son of her best friend Regina, recalled the many times Golda would send a chauffeur to fetch Regina late at night so that they could talk. Golda's need for company was well known.

Chapter Three: Goldie and Morris Get Married

1. Golda Meir, *My Life* (New York: Dell, 1976), 48.

2. Rachel Rojanski, *Conflicting Identities: Poalei Zion in America, 1905–1931* (Beersheba: Ben-Gurion University, 2004), 18–20.

3. Letter from Morris, October 19, 1915, Israel State Archives.

4. Meir, *My Life*, 54.

5. Letter from Morris, October 19, 1915, Israel State Archives.

6. Her biographer and the son of her best friend Regina observed: "This marriage was a failure before the couple stood under the canopy." Meron Medzini, *Golda Meir: A Political Biography* (Tel Aviv: Yediot Ahronot, Sifre Hemed, 2008), 45 (Hebrew).

7. Letter from Clara, quoted in Meir, *My Life*, 41; letter to Golda Meir from Regina Hamburger Medzini, located in Israel State Archives.

8. Letter from Morris, September 3, 1915 Israel State Archives.

9. Letter from Sheyna Korngold, Golda's personal letter GM/106.04/1886/29. April 7, 1918. Israel State Archives. Sheyna's letter is dated less than four months after Golda's wedding, and the abortion could have taken place before her marriage. See also Francine Klagsbrun, *Lioness: Golda Meir and the Nation of Israel* (New York: Schocken, 2017), 72–73.

10. Klagsbrun, *Lioness*. Abortion only became legal in Wisconsin after *Roe v. Wade*, decided in January 1973. At that time, Golda was already Israel's prime minister. It is quite likely that she would have approved of the landmark U.S. Supreme Court opinion. In Israel at the time, abortions were available by decree of the attorney general.

11. E-Mail from Professor Lilach Rosenberg, July 23, 2013, on file with the author. The e-mail refers to a 1976 statement by Mr. Warhaftig, located in Ben-Gurion Archives.

12. Klagsbrun, *Lioness*, 46.

13. Meir, *My Life*, 61.

14. Meir, *My Life*, 61; Rabbinical Courts Act, Marriage and Divorce, 1953.

15. Chapter 27 in this volume.

Chapter Four: Finding Her Vocation

1. Golda Meir, *My Life* (New York: Dell, 1976), 63.

2. Oriana Fallaci, "Golda Meir," *Interview with History* (Boston: Houghton Mifflin, 1976), 115.

3. Rachel Rojanski, "At the Center or on the Fringes of the Public Arena: Esther Mintz-Aberson and the Status of Women in American Poalei Zion, 1905–35," *Journal of Israeli History: Politics, Society, Culture* 21, no. 1–2 (Spring 2002): 27.

4. Rojanski, "At the Center," 54.

5. Sara Feder, Golda's childhood friend, later became an accomplished sociologist and activist in the suffragist movement; see https://jwa.org/encyclopedia/article/feder-keyfitz-sara-rivka.

6. Rojanski, "At the Center," 54.

7. Meir, *My Life*, 54.

8. Meron Medzini, *Golda Meir: A Political Biography* (Tel Aviv: Yediot Ahronot, Sifre Hemed, 2008), 280.

9. Francine Klagsbrun, *Lioness: Golda Meir and the Nation of Israel* (New York: Schocken, 2017), 55.

10. Meir, *My Life*, 57.

11. For the history of Yiddish in Palestine and then Israel, see Rachel Rojanski, *Yiddish in Israel: A History* (Bloomington: Indiana University Press, 2020). Golda did have Mizrahi Jews in her family (most notably her son-in-law, Zecharya Rahabi, of Yemenite origin), but it is probably true that she felt most natural and spontaneous speaking Yiddish. In a letter to Ruth Shabtai on July 26, 1971, she wrote: "I never thought . . . that one who does not know Yiddish is not Jewish . . . [but] we here should and must preserve the [European Jewish] heritage . . . that was largely transmitted in Yiddish. . . . I shall insist that my children learn Yiddish and it is inconceivable that our children will not know their parents' language," Hagai Tsoref, ed., *Golda Meir: The Fourth Prime Minister, Selected Documents, 1898–1978* (Jerusalem: Israel State Archives, 2016) (Hebrew), 369.

12. Milwaukee rabbis were not too happy with the decidedly secular curriculum because it did not prepare pupils for a Bar Mitzvah. Louis J. Swichkow and Lloyd P. Gartner, *The History of the Jews of Milwaukee* (Philadelphia: Jewish Publication Society of America, 1963), 324.

13. Ralph G. Martin, *Golda Meir: The Romantic Years* (New York: Charles Scribner's, 1988), 89; and Zosa Szajkowski, *Jews, Wars, and Communism* (New York: Ktav, 1972), 3–217.

14. Robert A. Hess, interview, 1965, TR-643, The Jacob Rader Marcus Center of the American Jewish Archives (AJA), Cincinnati.

15. Martin, *Golda Meir*, 90.

16. *The Role of Women in Librarianship, 1876–1976: The Entry Advancement, and Struggle for Equalization in One Profession*, ed. Kathleen Weibel and Kathleen M. Heim (Phoenix, AZ: Oryx Press, 1979), 204. Goldie did prove to be a successful librarian and was encouraged to stay and could likely rise up in the ranks of the profession even without formal education. It was a good, solid job that was perfectly suitable for a young woman who wanted to raise a family and work in an intellectual environment. But it was not an exciting job, and the quiet of the reading or cataloging room did not appeal to her. She needed to talk, even talk loudly, and certainly not whisper. She needed to push people to action, not to gently introduce them to the world of culture and middle-class values.

17. Thea Keren wrote: "The movement's goals, the establishment of a Jewish workers' commonwealth, would solve all social problems, including the inferior status of women." Thea Keren, *Sophie Udin: A Portrait of a Pioneer* (Jerusalem: Old City Press, 1984), 33. The party accepted gender discrimination as a part of the state of nature. Historically, two women members were recorded at the beginning of the twentieth century: Esther Mintz Aberson and Bella Fevzner. They were "history" by the time Golda joined the party. "Poalei Zion believed women belonged to the fringes of public life, not at its center." Rojanski, "At the Center," 27, 39.

18. Also, Golda's childhood friend, Sarah Feder, was a suffragette. She earned a PhD in sociology and became an academic and a labor activist. The two taught together at the Yiddishe Folks Schule; a photo shows them standing as two bookends between several men teachers at the school. Medzini, *Golda Meir*, 19.

19. Meir, *My Life*, 53.

20. Meir, *My Life*, 53.

21. Genevieve G. McBride, *On Wisconsin Women: Working on Their Rights from Settlement to Suffrage* (Madison: University of Wisconsin Press, 1993), 213.

22. See Melissa R. Klapper, "Suffrage in the United States in the Shalvi," *Hyman Encyclopedia of Jewish Women,* Jewish Women Archives, https://jwa.org/encyclopedia/article/suffrage-in -the-united-states#pid-11331.

23. Elinor Lerner, "Jewish Involvement in the New York City Woman Suffrage Movement," *American Jewish History* 70, no. 4 (June 1981): 461.

24. The conservative women's movement fighting socialist ideas grew stronger on the heels of the passage of the Nineteenth Amendment, and women were designated as particularly vulnerable to the socialist message. By then, Golda was already in Palestine. See Kirsten Marie Delegard, *Battling Miss Bolsheviki* (Philadelphia: University of Pennsylvania Press, 2012), ch. 2.

25. Meir, *My Life,* 42. World War I started in Europe in 1914. The Russian Revolution was launched in 1917, and that same year the United States entered the war alongside England and France against Germany.

26. Meir, *My Life,* 62. Until the war broke out the Central Committee of Poalei Zion was either supporting Germany or advocating neutrality.

27. Woodrow Wilson, State of the Union Address, December 7, 1915, National Archives. http://www.let.rug.nl/usa/presidents/woodrow-wilson/state-of-the-union-1915.php.

28. Emerson Hough, *The Web: History of the American Protective League* (Chicago: Reilly and Lee, 1919).

29. As part of the campaign to purge "disloyalty" and dissent, Milwaukee Jews were urged to march together in the Liberty Parade, and the restaurants on Walnut Street (Goldie's neighborhood) "were pressed to join in the weekly 'dairy days,' a very expensive request for a kosher meat restaurant" (which could not sell or prepare dairy products). When they resisted, they were denounced as "slackers." The *Wochenblat*, the conservative Yiddish newspaper in Milwaukee "'fulminated' . . . if they [the restaurants] will not become patriotic on Walnut Street and provide blintzes, knishes fired in butter, dairy kreplakh, and similar foods for the public— something is going to happen . . . the names of the slacker restaurateurs will be printed." Swichkow and Gartner, *History of the Jews in Milwaukee,* 278.

30. Felice Batlan, "Déjà vu and the Gendered Origins of the Practice of Immigration Law: The Immigrants' Protective League, 1907–40," *Law and History Review* 34, no. 4 (2018): 755–56.

31. Signed M.F.E., dated 1919 (letter written on War Department and Navy Department stationary). Golda Meir's personal letter's GM/106.04/1886/29, Israel State Archives. The "exploitation of the masses by the Wall Street few" was a well-known antiwar Marxist slogan during World War I. The letter mentioned the socialist leader Eugene V. Debs several times. In his memoirs Menachem Meir, Golda's son, mentions that Golda "tremendously admired" Rosa Luxemburg. As an adult Golda diligently stood away from the famous socialist leaders. Menachem Meir, *My Mother, Golda Meir: A Son's Evocation of Life with Golda Meir* (New York: Arbor House, 1983), 171.

32. Jonathan Sarna, *American Judaism: A History* (New Haven, CT: Yale University Press, 2004), 210–11. The umbrella organization became known as the "Joint." For the lot of Jewish immigrants during the war years, see Joseph Rappaport, *Hands across the Sea* (Lanham, MD: Hamilton Books, 2005).

33. Meir, *My Life,* 58.

34. Letter from Regina Hamburger to Golda Meir, Golda's personal letter GM/106.04/1886/29, May 10, 1919. Israel State Archives. See also Szajkowski, *Jews, Wars, and Communism.*

35. As a popular Zionist song of the period stated, "we come to our homeland to build and be rebuilt." Golda knew that not everyone in the American Poalei Zion agreed with her views.

36. Medzini, *Golda Meir,* 42.

Chapter Five: The USS *Pocahontas*

1. Golda Meir, *My Life* (New York: Dell, 1976), 41; Sheyna Korngold, *Zichronot* (Tel Aviv: ID Press, 1968) (Hebrew); and Marie Syrkin, *Golda Meir: Israel's Leader* (New York: G. P. Putnam's, 1969).

2. Syrkin, *Golda Meir,* 65.

3. Ralph G. Martin, *Golda Meir: The Romantic Years* (New York: Charles Scribner's, 1988), 105.

4. Korngold, *Zichronot*; and Syrkin, *Golda Meir.*

Chapter Six: A Sojourn in Tel Aviv

1. Golda Meir, *My Life* (New York: Dell, 1976), 73.

2. Anat Helman, *Young Tel Aviv: A Tale of Two Cities* (Boston: Brandeis University Press, 2010), 84, quoting a letter from 1933.

3. Meir, *My Life,* 75.

4. Helman, *Young Tel Aviv,* 78.

5. Meir, *My Life,* 76.

Chapter Seven: Comrade Golda and Comrade Morris in Kibbutz Merhavia

1. Psalms 118:5.

2. Golda Meir, *My Life* (New York: Dell, 1976), 83.

3. Meir, *My Life,* 83.

4. Meir, *My Life,* 83.

5. Orit Kamir, *Israeli Honor and Dignity: Social Norms, Gender Politics and the Law* (Carmel, CA: Carmel Press, 2005), ch. 2.

6. Anat Helman, "Kibbutz Dress in the 1950s: Utopian Equality, Anti-Fashion, and Change," *Fashion Theory* 12, no. 3 (2015): 313.

7. Meron Medzini, *Golda Meir: A Political Biography* (Tel Aviv: Yediot Ahronot, Sifre Hemed, 2008) (Hebrew).

8. Recorded Minutes, Merhavia Archives, 2017, 30.

Chapter Eight: Love and Marriage

1. "Two poetesses at the height of their beauty," *Haaretz*, August 15, 2017. According to Medzini, Golda thought of joining Kibbutz Ein Charod in 1927. Meron Medzini, *Golda Meir: A Political Biography* (Tel Aviv: Yediot Ahronot, Sifre Hemed, 2008) (Hebrew).

2. Medzini, *Golda Meir*.

3. Medzini, *Golda Meir*, 57.

4. Medzini, *Golda Meir*, 66.

5. Golda Meir, *My Life* (New York: Dell, 1976), 97.

6. Elena Ferrante, *The Story of the Lost Child* (New York: Europa Editions, 2015), 62–65.

7. Golda Meir letters to David Remez, the Pinchas Lavon Institute for Labour Movement Research, Lavon Institute, Tel Aviv. Hagai Tsoref, *Golda Meir, The Fourth Prime Minister, Selected Documents, 1898–1978* (Jerusalem: Israel State Archives, 2016), 51–52 (Hebrew).

8. Correspondence from Liuba Remez to David Remez, undated, IV-104-113, file no. 8, Lavon Archives, Tel Aviv.

9. Margalit Shilo, *Girls of Liberty: The Struggle for Suffrage in Mandatory Palestine* (Lebanon, NH: Brandeis University Press/University Press of New England, 2016), 104.

10. Medzini, *Golda Meir*.

11. Ralph G. Martin, *Golda Meir: The Romantic Years* (New York: Charles Scribner's, 1988), 162.

12. Tamar Schechter, *Conquering the Heart: The Story of Rachel Katznelson-Shazar* (Jerusalem: Yad Yitzhak Ben Zvi, 2011) (Hebrew). Rachel Katznelson-Shazar's quote is integrated into the title.

13. Zalman Shazar, the Third President, Israel State Archives, Selected Documents, 2007 (Hebrew), 274.

14. Martin, *Golda Meir*, 89.

15. On the illegitimate children of Israeli celebrities, see https://www.makorrishon.co.il/nrg/online/55/ART2/538/650.html (Hebrew). The German-born Gusta Schtrumpf was also a close friend of Shazar's and one of the few women who reached high positions in the Histadrut.

16. Menachem Meir, *My Mother, Golda Meir: A Son's Evocation of Life with Golda Meir* (New York: Arbor House, 1983), 39.

17. Oriana Fallaci, *Interview with History* (Boston: Houghton Mifflin Harcourt, 1976), 115.

18. Selim Nassib, *The Palestinian Lover* (New York: Europa Editions, 2007).

19. Jackie Circle, "Golda Meir's Arab Lover," *NRG*, September, 19, 2004, http://www.nrg.co.il/online/1/ART/784/523.html.

20. Yossi Goldstein, Golda's biographer who worked with extensive archival materials, opined that the story was fictional. Yossi Goldstein, *Golda: A Biography* (Beersheba: Ben-Gurion University Press, 2012), 62, 68.

21. Selim Nassib, *The Palestinian Lover* (New York: Europa Editions, 2007), 68.

22. Nassib, *Palestinian Lover*, 70.

23. Goldstein, *Golda*, 251. Goldstein also points out that while shaken, Golda was firm in her belief that those who had left should not be allowed to return. The creation of a Jewish majority, in her mind, was imperative for the survival of the nascent Jewish state.

24. Nassib, *Palestinian Lover*, 161.

25. In this context, it is worthwhile to reflect on the violent protests against the Israeli establishment (of which Golda was a leader) orchestrated by Jewish immigrants of Moroccan descent in Haifa in 1959. The Mizrahi immigrants were associated with "Arabness," a stereotype that

facilitated discrimination against them. Social prejudice against the Mizrahi Jews was not dissimilar to the prejudice against Palestinian Arabs. Yfaat Weiss, *A Confiscated Memory: Wadi Salib and Haifa's Lost Heritage* (New York: Columbia University Press, 2011). Weiss aptly compares the creation of the Haifa Palestinian refugee crisis in 1948 with the creation, a few years later, of the Haifa slums populated by Jews of Mizrahi descent.

26. BBC interview with Golda Meir, 1970. https://youtu.be/w3FGvAMvYpc.

27. Golda could and should have distinguished between the formality of issuing passports by the Mandate government and the culture of nationhood developing on the ground. In addition, she could have recognized a historical process through which nationhood is crystallized, in parallel to the crystallization of Jewish nationhood under Zionism. For her softened statement about a Palestinian entity, see Golda's speech at the Labor Party Secretariat, December 4, 1973, quoted in Medzini, *Golda Meir*, 509.

Chapter Nine: The Attraction of Socialist Politics

1. See generally, Jacob Metzer, *The Divided Economy of Mandatory Palestine* (Cambridge: Cambridge University Press, 1998) and the references there; and Nahum Karlinsky, "Beyond Post-Zionism," *Israel Studies* 9 (2004): 169. At the time, the population of Jewish Palestine, the "old Yishuv," and members of the first Aliya were mostly farmers with conservative values.

2. In Israeli historiography, this wave of immigration is called "the second Aliya."

3. Bat-Sheva Margalit Stern, *Redemption in Chains* (Jerusalem: Yad Ben-Zvi, 2006), 55 (Hebrew).

4. The socialist organization was not the only organization established to promote the rights of women. Dafna Izraeli et al., *Sex Gender Politics: Women in Israel* (Tel Aviv: Hakibbutz Hameuchad, 1999).

5. David Ben-Gurion, *Memoirs* (Cleveland: World, 1970), 214.

6. The Histadrut did wish to count wives as Histadrut members as it thereby enabled the organization to present a wider membership. Ada Maimon (Fishman), *Fifty Years of the Women Workers' Movement: 1904–1954* (Tel Aviv: Ayanot, 1955), 183 (Hebrew). Another illustration of the deep-seated gender discrimination is the policy of the Jewish National Fund to list only the male heads of the household as owners of property. The woman could not be considered an owner. That policy was discontinued only after a long campaign by the council. See Maimon, *Fifty Years of the Women Workers' Movement*, 245; and Bat-Sheva Margalit Stern, *The Revolutionary: Ada Fishman Maimon* (Beersheba: Ben-Gurion University Press, 2018).

7. Golda Meir, *My Life* (New York: Dell, 1976), 97.

8. Meir, *My Life*, 97.

9. Meir, *My Life*, 95: "I did not come to Palestine to spread American culture."

10. Meir, *My Life*, 106.

11. Oriana Fallaci, "Golda Meir," *Interview with History* (Boston: Houghton Mifflin, 1976), 112.

12. She is also known as Ada Fishman Maimon, but in this work will be referred to as Ada Maimon.

13. Stern, *Revolutionary* (Jerusalem: Yad Ben-Zvi, 2006).

14. On this issue, see Aviva Halamish, *The Exodus Affair: Holocaust Survivors and the Struggle for Palestine* (United Kingdom: Vallentine Mitchell, 1998); and Stern, *Revolutionary*.

15. The most salient component of this compact was the retention of rabbinical control over marriage and divorce, thereby perpetuating the inferior status of women. Izraeli, *Sex Gender Politics*.

16. Margalit Stern, *The Revolutionary*.

17. Maimon was affiliated with Hapoel Hatzair and Meir was associated with Ahdut Ha'avoda.

18. I heard about this nickname from the historian Aviva Halamish, who heard it from her mother.

19. Bat-Sheva Margalit Stern, "They Have Wings but No Strength to Fly: The Women Workers Movement between 'Feminine' Control and 'Masculine' Dominance," in *Jewish Women in Pre-State Israel*, ed. M. Shilo, R. Kark, and G. Hasan-Rokem (Boston: Brandeis University Press, 2008), 292–314.

20. In the first quarter of the twentieth century Berlin was a center of Zionist activity. Shazar had studied in Berlin before arriving in Palestine. Martin, *Golda Meir*, 164.

21. Meir, *My Life*, 112.

22. Interview with Meron Medzini, November 10, 2016, Jerusalem.

23. Meir, *My Life*, 112.

24. The epigraph following the subheading is from Golda Meir, "Borrowed Mothers," in *The Plough Woman: Memoirs of the Pioneer Women of Palestine*, ed. Rachel Katznelson-Shazar, 165, (New York: Herzl Press, 1932); Meir, *My Life*, 112.

25. Eshkol said about her that she was always "injecting herself."

26. Menachem Meir, *My Mother Golda Meir: A Son's Evocation of Life with Golda Meir* (New York: Arbor House, 1983), 26.

27. See Golda's letter to her sister Sheyna: "Before I left the doctor assured me that Sarale's health permits of my going, and I have made adequate arrangements for Menachem." Meir, *My Mother Golda Meir*, 27.

28. Billie Moscone Lerman, "Golda: Flesh and Blood," *Ma'ariv*, February 26, 1988.

29. Lerman, "Golda."

30. Golda's letters from Israel State Archives, on file with the author.

31. The description of Morris is from Meron Medzini, *Golda Meir: A Political Biography* (Tel Aviv: Yediot Ahronot, Sifre Hemed, 2008), 72 (Hebrew).

32. Meir, *My Mother Golda Meir*, 27. Meir does not mention the name of the kibbutz her letter referred to. Meron Medzini, her biographer, does: it was Kibbutz Ein Charod, significant in the context of the Zionist feminist theory concerning home and work. Medzini, *Golda Meir*, 86. Another biographer, Yossi Goldstein, noted that the kibbutz did not accept her. The kibbutz was not interested in too many needy people knocking on its doors. Yossi Goldstein, *Golda: A Biography* (Beersheba: Ben-Gurion University Press, 2012) (Hebrew).

33. Meir, "Borrowed Mothers," 207.

34. Katznelson-Shazar, *Plough Woman*, 207.

35. Meir, "Borrowed Mothers," 78.

36. Katznelson-Shazar, *Plough Woman*, 206. These insights were presented as a series of rhetorical questions: "Can we today measure devotion to husband and children by our indifference to everything else? Is it not often true that the woman who has given up all the external world for her husband and her children has done it not out of a sense of duty, out of devotion and love, but out of incapacity? Because her soul is not able to take into itself the many sidedness of life."

37. Sheyna Korngold, *Zichronot* (Tel Aviv: ID Press, 1968), 18 (Hebrew).

38. Katznelson-Shazar, *Plough Woman*, 206.

39. Katznelson-Shazar, *Plough Woman*, 206.

40. Meir, *My Life*, 97.

41. This information is based on an interview with Gideon Meir, Golda's grandson, the son of Menachem, December 19, 2017, Tel Aviv. For Meira's mother's version of events, see Francine Klagsbrun, *Lioness: Golda Meir and the Nation of Israel* (New York: Schocken, 2017), 389–90.

Chapter Ten: Pioneer Women

1. For an elaboration, see Pnina Lahav, "A Great Episode in the History of Jewish Womanhood: Golda Meir, the Women Workers Council, Pioneer Women, and the Struggle for Gender Equality," *Israel Studies* 23, no. 1 (2018): 1. The first emissary to the United States was Rachel Yanait Ben-Zvi, a noted feminist who established the girls training farm in Jerusalem.

2. See Oryan Chaplin, *Four Hours A Day* (Tel Aviv: Hakibutz Hameuchad, 2020) (Hebrew); and Amia Libliech, "One Hundred Years of Childhood, Parenthood and Family in the Kibbutz," *Israel* 17, no. 1 (2010): 1–24 (Hebrew) and the references there.

3. Golda Meir, *My Life* (New York: Dell, 1976).

4. Meir, *My Life*, 224.

5. Golda Meir, Rishmey Massa (impressions of travel) *Davar*, May 25, 1932 (Hebrew).

6. The familiar contemporary feminist terminology was not available to Golda but her description fits the building blocks of feminist theory.

7. Golda Meir, Rishmey Massa (impressions of travel) *Davar*.

8. Meir, *My Life*, (New York: Dell, 1975) 222.

9. Meir, *My Life*, 222.

10. Meir, *My Life*, 223.

11. Yitzhak Greenberg, *Pinchas Sapir: A Political and Economic Biography* (Tel Aviv: Ressling, 2011).

12. Note the metaphor, based on agriculture (a cardinal theme in Zionist revival) and its connection to the title of the volume published by the Women Workers Council with the help of Pioneer Women. Rachel Katznelson-Shazar, ed., *The Plough Woman: Memoirs of the Pioneer Women of Palestine* (New York: Herzl Press, 1932), 206.

13. The question "And now what?" did appear in the middle of the article.

14. Meir, *My Life*, 222.

15. However, Golda had been a member of the council since 1924.

16. Meir, Massa (impressions of travel) *Davar*.

17. See the description in Meron Medzini, *Golda Meir: A Political Biography* (Tel Aviv: Yediot Ahronot, Sifre Hemed, 2008), 45 (Hebrew).

18. At the time, Shazar had not yet Hebraized his name and was known by his original name, Rubashov.

19. Tamar Schechter, *Conquering the Heart: The Story of Rachel Katznelson-Shazar* (Jerusalem: Yad Yitzhak Ben Zvi, 2011) (Hebrew).

20. Surely, discussions with the members of Pioneer Women contributed handsomely, but it stands to reason that Golda discussed the conflicts between Pioneer Women and the leadership of Poalei Zion in the United States with Shazar and that these discussions included deliberations on the merits of feminism.

21. Immigration certificates were given to heads of households—generally men. Women fortunate enough to be members of the household were eligible as well. But single women without a proven way to support themselves were rejected. A. Halamish, "Aliyah I Accordance to Criteria of Economic Absorption," *Iyunim BiTkumat Yisrael* (2003), 216 (Hebrew).

22. Many women workers were tempted to get married and stay home. As she observed, women were dominated by false consciousness and what is called "the ideology of role conflicts," in Dafna Izraeli et al., *Sex Gender Politics: Women in Israel* (Tel Aviv: Hakibbutz Hameuchad, 1999), 73.

23. She did maintain certain aspects of the private–public distinction. Some of her best friends were women: first and foremost Regina Hamburger Medzini, to whom she was attached her entire life. See also her letter to Bebba Idelson in 1933 alluding to "such treatment from the [comrades] back home." Hagai Tsoref, ed., *Golda Meir: The Fourth Prime Minister, Selected Documents, 1898–1978* (Jerusalem: Israel State Archives, 2016), 23 (Hebrew).

24. Yossi Goldstein, *Golda: A Biography* (Beersheba: Ben-Gurion University Press, 2012), 62. The Histadrut payroll department was asked to give Golda a stipend for childcare, but its internal regulations did not permit that and therefore it was decided to name the stipend "care for a sick child," Goldstein, *Golda*, 62. Bat-Sheva Margalit Stern states that at the same time Ada Fishman Maimon, the senior leader of the council received the sum of 7.5 pounds per month as also did Golda's husband Morris Myerson when he was employed. Bat-Sheva Margalit Stern, *The Revolutionary: Ada Fishman Maimon* (Beersheba: Ben-Gurion University Press, 2018), 134. Y. Greenberg, *Pinchas Sapir, A Political and Economic Biography* (Tel Aviv: Ressling, 2011), 71 (Hebrew).

25. She rejected the Pioneer Women's offer to stay on as general secretary. Greenberg, *Pinchas Sapir*, 71.

26. The all-powerful board had sixty-one members. David Ben-Gurion served as chairman, and was followed in 1935 by David Remez. See Avi Bareli, *Authority and Participation in a New Democracy: Political Struggles in Mapai, Israel's Ruling Party, 1948–1953* (Boston: Academic Studies Press, 2007), ch. 1. The position was equivalent to that of a cabinet minister.

27. Greenberg, *Pinchas Sapir*, 73.

Chapter Eleven: World War II

1. Interview with Chaim Weizmann, *Manchester Guardian*, May 23, 1936.

2. The phrase "the ground is burning" is Ben-Gurion's. Shabtai Teveth, *Ben-Gurion: The Burning Ground, 1886–1948* (Boston: Houghton Mifflin Harcourt, 1987).

3. Ute Frevert discussed the event of Kristallnacht at Boston University, as part of the Elie Wiesel Memorial Lecture, October 22, 2018.

4. Golda Meir, personal letters. GM/106.04/1886/29 Israel State Archives.

5. "I am an orphan: lucky me" opened the celebrated Yiddish author Sholem Aleichem's story, "Motl, the Cantor's Son." The story tells of a boy whose father dies and leaves his family in economic ruins but the boy feels lucky that no one will insist that he observe Jewish law and social expectations. Sholem Aleichem, *The Letters of Menakhem-Mendl and Sheyne-Sheyndl and Motl, the Cantor's Son*, trans. Hillel Halkin (New Haven, CT: Yale University Press, 2002). Another example of Golda's sarcasm appears in her memoirs. The Yishuv leadership decided to launch a hunger strike in protest against the British refusal to permit immigration. Here is the exchange between Golda and a British officer: "Mrs. Myerson, do you think for one minute that his Majesty's Government would change its policy because you are not going to eat?" Golda replies: "No, I have no such illusions. If the death of six million did not change the government policy, I do not expect that my not eating will do so. But it will at least be a mark of solidarity." Golda Meir, *My Life* (New York: Dell, 1976), 186.

6. Compare her analysis with Ben-Gurion's analytical approach: "This is not a denial of Jewish rights as there was in Russia; these are not the pogroms of the Czar's Day . . . [Rather] this is a state policy whose ambition, to be achieved by totalitarian, absolutist methods, is dispossession, destruction, and eviction on a massive scale." Teveth, *Ben-Gurion*, 641.

7. Golda Meir Archive, postcards and personal letters in English, GM/106.04/1886/29, Israel State Archives.

8. Yossi Goldstein, *Golda: A Biography* (Beersheba: Ben-Gurion University Press, 2012), 190.

9. Goldstein, *Golda*, 191.

10. Goldstein, *Golda*, 197.

11. Ezra Danin, *Zioni B'chol Tnai* [A Zionist in Every Condition] (Jerusalem: Kidum, 1987), 194 (Hebrew).

12. Goldstein, *Golda*.

13. Interview of Golda Meir on the television program *This Is Your Life*. Kan 11, Formerly Israel Broadcasting Agency, 1977.

14. Meir, *My Life*, 212.

15. Abigail Adams, wife of John Adams, soon to be President of the United States, famously urged her husband to "remember the ladies" and codify laws that free women from the control of their fathers and husbands. Letter from Abigail Adams to John Adams, March 31, 1776. Cokie Roberts, *Founding Mothers* (New York: William Morrow, 2004), 72.

16. Kagan remembered the dire security conditions and refugees, but she also made sure to emphasize the achievement as one pertaining to women. On file with the author, original in Jacob Rader Marcus Center of the American Jewish Archives, Cincinnati.

Chapter Twelve: From Israel's First Emissary to the Soviet Union to Minister of Labor

1. Meron Medzini, *Golda Meir: A Political Biography* (Tel Aviv: Yediot Ahronot, Sifre Hemed, 2008), 203–6 (Hebrew).

2. Golda's biographer Yossi Goldstein writes that Sharett had a history of conflict with Golda, and "sending" her to Moscow was his way of neutralizing her political influence in Israel. By 1956 Golda had replaced Sharett as minister of foreign affairs. Yossi Goldstein, *Golda: A Biography* (Beersheba: Ben-Gurion University Press, 2012), 246–47 (Hebrew). See also Avi Bareli, *Mapai in Israel's Early Independence 1948-1953* (Yad Ben-Zvi Press: Jerusalem 2007), 80–91 (Hebrew).

3. This woman was Esther Herlitz, who was appointed as an ambassador to Denmark in 1966.

4. "It appears that I committed a very grave sin that [justified] keeping me out of Israel at this time . . . you have no idea how difficult it is to be away when the country is at war [1948 War of Independence]." Golda Meir, *Under the Banner of Labor* (Tel Aviv: Am Oved, 1972), 239 (Hebrew).

5. Marie Syrkin, *Golda Meir: Israel's Leader* (New York: G. P. Putnam's, 1969), 212–13.

6. Knesset debates, response to Member of Knesset Wilenska of the Communist Party, reprinted in Meir, *Under the Banner of Labor*, 311.

7. Golda Meir, *My Life* (New York: Dell, 1976).

8. Meir, *My Life*.

9. Interview with Lou Kaddar, http://www.goldameir.org.il/index.php?dir=site&page =content&cs=307&langpage=heb. Drora Beit-Or, interview with Lou Kaddar, July 10, 1986, on file with the Golda Meir Institute.

10. Medzini, *Golda Meir*, 218.

11. See the image at https://images.app.goo.gl/n7B9iLjYY36LPBLf9, accessed August 22, 2021.

Chapter Thirteen: In Israel's First Cabinet

I wish to thank Dr. Rivka Brot for research assistance on the history of the Women's Employment Law.

1. In keeping with the promise in the Declaration of Independence, the elections were for a "constituent assembly" but upon convening the assembly changed its name to "the Knesset." Golda was the sixth member on Mapai's list of candidates, a fact that confirms her senior status. See Israel Democracy Institute, https://www.idi.org.il/policy/parties-and-elections/elections /1949/.

2. Yossi Goldstein, *Golda: A Biography* (Beersheba: Ben-Gurion University Press, 2012), 276–77 (Hebrew).

3. See Anita Shapira, *Israel: A History* (Waltham, MA: Brandeis University Press, 2012), ch. 10, "The Great Aliya: Mass Immigration," and the selected bibliography there. See also Sammy Smooha, "Class, Ethnic, and National Cleavages and Democracy in Israel," in *Israeli Democracy under Stress*, ed. L. Diamond and E. Sprinzak, (Boulder, CO: Lynn Rienner, 1993), 146–82; M. Lissak, *Mass Immigration in the Fifties: The Failure of the Melting Pot Policy* (Jerusalem: Bialik Institute, 1999) (Hebrew).

4. Hagai Tsoref, "The Policy of Golda Myerson (Meir) in the Ministry of Labor: 1949–1956 in the Light of her Socio-Economic Worldview" (PhD diss., Haifa University, 2010) (Hebrew).

5. The source of the epigraph preceding this section is Dafna N. Izraeli, "Gender in the Workplace," in *Sex, Gender, Politics: Women in Israel* (Tel Aviv: Hakibbutz Hameuchad, 1999), 177.

6. There were select females in the Knesset: Member of Knesset Shoshana Persitz of the General Zionists (the mainstream liberal party). Like Golda, Persitz was born in Kiev, Ukraine. Her parents were the founders of the Hebrew school system Tarbut and she herself was a graduate of Moscow State University and the Sorbonne in Paris. Her expertise was in education, and this is what she pursued in her political career. She was wealthy. Hanna Lamdan was a member of the left-wing Mapam party and in the first Knesset she served as deputy to the Speaker. The sole judge was Eugenia Vinogradov.

7. Amalia Saar, "Masculine Talk: On the Subconscious Use of the Masculine Linguistic Forms among Hebrew-and-Arabic-speaking Women in Israel," *Signs: Journal of Women in Culture and Society* 32, no. 2. (2007), 405–29.

8. Saar, "Masculine Talk."

9. In the twenty-first century, when her grandsons established the Golda Meir Institute, the Hebrew female term "Roshat Ha-memshala" was already a part of the mainstream and used by the institute to designate a Golda Prize. It would seem that Golda would have felt comfortable with this change.

10. The discussion of labor codification in this section is based primarily on Frances Raday's "On Equality: Judicial Profiles," *Mishpatim (Israel Law Review)* 35 (2003): 380 (Hebrew); Ruth Ben Israel, *Equality of Opportunity and Prohibitions of Discrimination in Employment* (Ra'anana: Open University, 1998) (Hebrew); and Ruth Halperin-Kaddari, *Women in Israel: A State of Their Own* (Philadelphia: University of Pennsylvania Press, 2004).The epigraph is from Golda Meir's introduction of the social security bill in the Knesset, Hagai Tsoref, ed., *Golda Meir: The Fourth Prime Minister, Selected Documents, 1898–1978* (Jerusalem: Israel State Archives, 2016), 98 and see generally 96–100 (Hebrew).

11. These were Yitzhak Kanev, Giora Lotan, Zvi Bar-Niv, and Zvi Berinson; see Dan Giladi, "Social Security and Social Welfare Legislation," in *Golda: The Growth of a Leader (1921–1956)*, ed. M. Avi Zohar et al. (Tel Aviv: Am Oved, 1994), 368–69.

12. The statutes were, in the order of enactment: Hours of Work and Rest Law (1951); Prohibition of Night Work Law (1951); Annual Leave Law (1951); National Insurance Law (1952); Youth Labor Law (1952); Apprenticeship (vocational training) Law (1952); Employment of Women Law (1952); Labor Insurance (Organization) Law (1954); Collective Agreements Law (1955); and Settlement of Labor Disputes Law (1956). Some of the legislation reflected regulations already in place under the Mandate government but expanded further to reflect the progressive spirit of the new state.

13. Tsoref, *Golda Meir*, 97.

14. Tsoref, *Golda Meir*, 97.

15. See Giladi, "Social Security" 3; Tsoref, *Golda Meir*, 96–100, and the references there; and Tsoref, "The Policy of Golda Myerson," 15.

16. Kirstin Downey, *The Woman Behind the New Deal: The Life and Legacy of Frances Perkins—Social Security, Unemployment Insurance, and the Minimum Wage* (New York: Anchor, 2010).

17. Golda Meir, *My Life* (New York: Dell, 1976).

18. Golda Meir's speech reproduced in *D'var Ha-Poelet* 8 (1952): 137. (Hebrew).

19. Statement of the minister of labor, recorded in *Divrei Haknesset* [Knesset Plenary Records], May 23, 1949, 12. Some of these data were provided by the International Labor Organization (Hebrew).

20. See Sharon Geva, *Women in the State of Israel* (Jerusalem: Magnes Press, 2020), documenting the campaign conducted by the Israeli press to construct women as primarily fit for traditional gender-based roles.

21. *The Plough Woman, A Critical Edition*, Mark A. Raider and Miriam B. Raider eds. (London: Brandeis University Press, 2002), 164–65.

22. Golda Meir's speech reproduced in *D'var Ha-Poelet* 8 (1952): 137 (Hebrew).

23. Golda Meir's speech in *D'var Ha-Poelet* 8 (1952): 137.

24. Meir, *My Life*, 302: "We had to think how to shape a law that won't be so good as to exclude women 6-100 statute."

25. Orit Kamir, *Israeli Honor and Dignity: Social Norms, Gender Politics and the Law* (Carmel, CA: Carmel Press, 2005).

Chapter Fourteen: Golda's Conception of the Family

1. *Divrei Haknesset* [Knesset Plenary Records], thirty-third session of the First Knesset, May 23, 1954, 12.

2. For an excellent review of the influence of Israel's media on the conception of gendered roles in Israel see Sharon Geva, *Women in the State of Israel, the Early Years* (Jerusalem: Magnes Press, 2020) (Hebrew). On planting flowers as an attribute of the American character, see Lee Somerville, *Vintage Wisconsin Gardens: A History of Home Gardening* (Madison: Wisconsin Historical Society Press, 2011), 45.

3. *Divrei Haknesset*, May 24, 1954, 313–14 (Hebrew).

4. Workers engaged in hard labor had a different plan: sixty-two for men and fifty-seven for women. The five-year difference reflected an expectation that women generally marry men five years older than themselves and that it would be good for the woman to retire when her husband does. National Insurance Law, 1954.

5. A few decades later, Ruth Bader Ginsburg, then a law professor and later a U.S. Supreme Court Justice, led the revolution that applied equal treatment to both men and women. See Jane Sherron De Hart, *Ruth Bader Ginsburg: A Life* (New York: Knopf, 2018).

6. But Wisconsin law prohibited the practice and Golda was soon sent back to school. See part I in this volume.

7. Golda Meir, *My Life* (New York: Dell, 1976). But we do not know if she was aware that the Supreme Court of the United States had declared the federal child labor law unconstitutional.

8. *Divrei Haknesset*, July 21, 1952.

9. Meir, *My Life*, 295.

10. Meir, *My Life*, 295. Golda was referring to domestic workers, but as boys. Later in her rebuttal she did mention girls. She said, "As long as boys and girls have to go to work let the working conditions be as structured as possible." But this was an exception in a speech centered on "boys" and "lads" that merely implied girls.

11. There was a fierce fight in the cabinet and in the Knesset about the creation and extent of "national insurance," known in the United States as Social Security. The National Insurance Law was passed in several successive phases and only in its final form included the obligation to pay for maternity leave.

12. *Divrei Haknesset* , February 5, 1952, 5.

13. *Divrei Haknesset*, May 24, 1954, 5.

14. *Divrei Haknesset*, May 24, 1954, 308.

15. *Divrei Haknesset*, May 24, 1954, 308.

16. Knesset deliberations, *Divrei Haknesset*, May 24, 1954, 309–10. It is worth quoting the rest of this passage: "We must make sure that pregnancy is not a reason for firing, but that pregnancy will serve as a barricade behind which one is powerless to act—this is not reasonable. I am not willing to hold that there is certainty in all cases and of course [the minister of labor] may make a mistake. But there are various means to investigate the case and decide accordingly. But it is impossible to insist on something that is not reasonable."

17. Knesset deliberations, *Divrei Haknesset*, May 24, 1954, 309–10.

18. *Divrei Haknesset*, December 29, 1952, 305.

Chapter Fifteen: Enter the "Other Woman"

Source of the epigraph: Minister of Welfare, Rabbi Yitzhak Meir Levin, member of the United Religious Front, recorded in *Divrei Haknesset* [Knesset Plenary Records], August 10, 1950, 2590 (Hebrew).

1. Derek Penslar, *Theodor Herzl: A Charismatic Leader* (New Haven, CT: Yale University Press, 2019).

2. Anita Shapira, "The Religious Motifs of the Labor Movement," in *Zionism and Religion*, ed. Smuel Almog, Jehuda Reinharz, and Anita Shapira (Waltham, MA: Brandeis University Press, 1998), 251.

3. For an insightful analysis, see Alexander Kaye, *The Invention of Jewish Theocracy* (Oxford: Oxford University Press, 2020).

4. Ada Maimon had extensive general as well as Jewish education and believed that Jewish law should adjust itself to the idea of gender equality, based on the biblical statement that God created men and woman as equal partners.

5. Levin's father, Chanoch Zvi Ha-Cohen Levin, was a noted Hasidic rabbi in Poland, and his mother, Feiga, was the daughter of another leader of the Ger Hasidic dynasty, Avraham Mordechai Alter.

6. Guy Ben-Porat, *Between State and Synagogue: The Secularization of Contemporary Israel* (Cambridge: Cambridge University Press, 2013).

7. Francine Klagsbrun, *The Fourth Commandment: Remember the Sabbath Day* (New York: Harmony Books, 2002), 136.

8. See generally, Abraham Joshua Heschel, *The Sabbath* (New York: Farrar, Straus and Giroux, 1951). Note that coincidentally Heschel was working on his theory at the same time that the Israelis were struggling with the passage of the Day of Rest law; Heschel notes that the concept of the Sabbath is of a bride, betrothed to the people of Israel in Mount Sinai. Heschel

does warn the reader not to attribute "personification" to the Sabbath, but the historical con-
ceptualization of the Sabbath as a bride implies the "maleness" of the Jewish people, as if only
men were standing at Sinai. The objectification of women and the referral to the Sabbath as "a
gift of God" go hand in hand to reinforce a consciousness that starkly divides the masculine
from the feminine. See also Reuven Kimmelman, *The Mystical Meaning of Lekhah Dodi and
Kabbalat Shabbat* (Jerusalem: Magnes Press, 2003), 1–9 (Hebrew). Kimmelman traces the
"feminization" of the Shabbat to the Zohar and discusses in detail the analogy of the Sabbath
to a bride and a queen. The implication is that the ritual of welcoming the Sabbath was invented
by the male imagination and was male centered. Women, the 50 percent of the population who
were also present at Mount Sinai, have been marginalized and ignored. See also Judith Plaskow,
Standing Again in Sinai: Judaism from a Feminist Perspective (San Francisco: Harper One, 1991).

9. For an insightful analysis of the meaning of Shabbat in Jewish law and culture see
F. Klagsbrun, *The Fourth Commandment*, supra n.7.

10. Ahad Ha'am, "Shabat and Zionism," *Ha-Shiloach* 3, no. 6 (1898) (Hebrew). The statement
was later adopted by the leaders of the United Religious Front in their campaign to sanctify the
Sabbath in the State of Israel.

11. Babylonian Talmud, Tractate Shabbat. "Redemption will come if Jews observe the rule
of Shabbat two Saturdays in a row."

12. The bill gave members of other religions the right to opt for a different day of rest, in
accordance with their religion.

13. The agreement reached in 1947 committed the state to observe certain cardinal principles
of Jewish law and is still valid today. The secular camp agreed to honor practices such as the
closure of businesses during the Sabbath and the laws of Kashrut. See Shuki Friedman, "The
Shabbat Wars: A Guide for the Perplexed on the 'Status Quo,'" Israel Democracy Institute,
https://en.idi.org.il/articles/14015.

14. Earlier Golda also noted that one of the religious ministers, Moshe Shapira, was present at
the Knesset Labor Committee and did not raise any objections. Apparently, he changed his mind,
perhaps as a result of pressure from religious circles. *Divrei Haknesset*, November 28, 1950, 75–76.

15. Hours of Work and Rest Law (1951), section 7.

16. Hours of Work and Rest Law (1951), section 7.

17. Hours of Work and Rest Law (1951), section 12(A). The United Religious Front opposed
this formulation as well, but the new version passed in the Knesset.

18. During the cabinet deliberations, the religious ministers refrained from raising another
woman's name—Ada Maimon, a noted labor feminist and sister of the minister of religions,
Rabbi Leib Fishman Maimon. In the Knesset deliberation, the sister's name did come up, in
addition to Kagan's, as a justification to oppose the idea that permits would be issued subsequent to consultations between the minister of labor and the minister of religions. Members
feared the possibility of Ada Maimon's serving as minister of religions.

19. Numbers, 15:32–36.

20. Reuven Shari was a member of the Mapai Party and the Knesset Labor Committee.

21. *Divrei Haknesset*, November 28, 1950, 362.

22. Avraham Rekanti, in *Divrei Haknesset*, November 28, 1950, 368.

23. *Divrei Haknesset*, November 28, 1950, 360.

24. *Divrei Haknesset*, November 28, 1950, 360.

25. "Israel Rounds Up Fanatics in Plot: 42 Religious Zealots Arrested in Alleged 'Scare-Bomb' Attempt on Parliament," *New York Times*, May 16, 1951, 13. They called it "operation bride"—to protect Shabbat, and also the young women who would be drafted into the military.

26. Part IV, ch. 27 in this volume.

27. Golda Meir, *My Life* (New York: Dell, 1976), 270. Here, too, Golda exploded in frustration and anger: "In the land of Israel, where there has always been an honorable place for the woman . . . In this country . . . the woman, our daughter, our sister, partakes in activity and work, and . . . settlement, in standing guard, in the war of independence; in this country where women gave their life for aliyah (immigration) against the British authorities, in this country of Hanna Senesh, in 1955, the eighth year of Israel's independence, they dare raise anew the dark-ages argumentation that there is no equal right to the woman . . . the same persons . . . sit alongside women in the Knesset . . . in the cabinet . . . voted for women in the cabinet several times . . . in the Jewish Agency and in the National Council, and we cannot take [their opposition to a woman] seriously but see it as yet another bargaining point"; quoted in Eran Eldar, "The First Case of Segregating Women in Israel: Golda Meir vs. The Religious Parties in the Tel Aviv Municipality," *Kivunim Hadashim* 26 (2012): 260.

28. Meir, *My Life*, 245.

Chapter Sixteen: Golda's Appointment as Minister of Foreign Affairs, 1956

This chapter is based largely on State of Israel, Israel State Archives, Documents on the Foreign Policy of Israel, vol. 11 (2008), 498; see also Motti Golani, "There Will Be War Next Summer . . . The Road to the Sinai War" (Ministry of Defense, Israel, 1997) (Hebrew). For a survey of Israeli foreign policy, see Uri Bialer, *Israeli Foreign Policy: A People Shall Not Dwell Alone* (Bloomington: Indiana University Press, 2020); and Anita Shapira, *Israel: A History* (Waltham, MA: Brandeis University Press, 2012), 281–85 and the bibliographies there.

Source of the epigraph: David Ben-Gurion, reflecting on Golda's appointment as minister of foreign affairs, quoted in Rina Sharett and Moshe Sharett, eds., *A Statesman Assessed: Views and Viewpoints about Moshe Sharett* (Tel Aviv: Moshe Sharett Heritage Society, 2008), 95 (Hebrew).

1. Painful concessions, namely on three primary issues: borders, refugees, and recognition of a Palestinian state.

2. See generally Ury Bialer, *Israeli Foreign Policy: A People Shall Not Dwell Alone* (Bloomington: Indiana University Press, 2020).

3. However, the majority of ministers siding with Sharett represented other parties in the coalition, not the ruling party Mapai. In his diary, Sharett expressed discomfort about this situation.

4. Orit Rozin, *The Conflict and Israel's Emotional Regime 1949–1967* (in preparation).

5. Israel has always operated as a coalition government. The cabinet was made up of several representatives of parties with different ideologies and expectations. Mapai's ministers were

generally supportive of Ben-Gurion whereas other ministers, members of other parties, and those forming a majority, sided with Sharett. Tom Segev, *A State at Any Cost: The Life of David Ben-Gurion* (New York: Farrar, Straus and Giroux, 2019), 528–40.

6. Michael Bar-Zohar, *Ben-Gurion: A Biography*, vol. 2 (New York: Delacorte Press, 1979), 1192.

7. Speech delivered by Ben-Gurion on January 18, 1957, at Kibbutz Givaa't Chaim, reprinted in *Davar*, January 20, 1957. The speech continued: "Because of that we could implement our policy not . . . by following . . . protocol, and not through regular channels, and these unorthodox efforts bore fruit. We managed to get the minimal amount of weapons that was essential to our survival."

8. Meron Medzini, *The Proud Jewess: Golda Meir and the Vision of Israel* (Jerusalem: Idanim, 1990), 4 (quotation from Sharett's diary).

9. Bar-Zohar, *Ben-Gurion*, 1196.

10. Isaac Remba, "Madam Minister of Foreign Affairs," *Haboker*, June 22, 1956.

11. Walter Eytan, *The First Ten Years: A Diplomatic History of Israel* (New York: Simon and Schuster, 1958), 221.

12. Golda Meir, *My Life* (New York: Dell, 1976), 281.

Chapter Seventeen: Golda's First International Crisis

1. Nasser did not dispute the contractual entitlements of the canal company. Israel had some stake in the crisis because the canal had been closed to Israeli shipping, but was only marginally considered a factor in the crisis.

2. See Golda's speeches at Mapai's Central Committee, September–October 1956. The Moshe Sharett Archives of the Labor Party, Beit Berl, files related to the Sinai Campaign, IL-BBRL-001 (Hebrew).

3. Golda Meir, *My Life* (New York: Dell, 1976), 285.

4. On the table was the question of a preventive war, illegal under the United Nations Charter. This was the reason England and France insisted that Israel be the one to attack first and that they appear to be "coming to the rescue" to "restore the peace." Neither Ben-Gurion (who ultimately acquiesced) nor Golda was happy with that instrumental deployment of Israel as the aggressor.

5. Mordechai Bar-On, *Challenge and Quarrel: The Road to Sinai—1956* (Beersheba: Ben-Gurion University, 1991), 206 (Hebrew).

6. Be that as it may, Golda came to be portrayed as an obtuse politician. Michael Bar-Zohar, the biographer of both Shimon Peres and David Ben-Gurion, discussed Golda's ambivalence, but instead of addressing the merits of her objections, he concocted a stereotype of Golda, the country bumpkin: "The truth (about Golda's reasons) was simpler and crueler. Golda Meir simply did not comprehend the subject matter and did not get what a colossal achievement this conference was for the small eight-year-old Israel," Michael Bar-Zohar, *Phoenix: Shimon Peres and the Secret History of Israel* (Tel Aviv: Magal Books, 2016), 205. The stereotype of Golda as limited and unsophisticated, harking back to Sharett's description of her the previous year, united left and right in denouncing her as a woman incapable of making sophisticated decisions in foreign affairs.

7. For the Treaty of Sèvres, see Avi Shlaim, "The Protocol of Sèvres, 1956: Anatomy of a War Plot," *International Affairs* 73, no. 3 (1997): 509.

8. *Divrei Haknesset* [Knesset Plenary Records], October 28, 1956, analyzed more thoroughly in Pnina Lahav, "A Small Nation Goes to War: Israel's Cabinet Authorization of the 1956 War," *Israel Studies* 25, no. 3 (Fall 2010): 61–86.

9. Cabinet Protocols authorizing the invasion, file in the author's archives. See also Lahav, "A Small Nation Goes to War."

10. Foreign Affairs and Defense Committee Report, 1957. Israel State Archives.

11. The United States halted oil shipments to both countries (winter was imminent) and manipulated the pound sterling. London was facing a crushing financial crisis. For an instructive discussion of Israeli foreign affairs in the United States, based on extensive archival documentation, and a discussion of the Suez War, see Natan Aridan, *Advocating for Israel: Diplomats and Lobbyists from Truman to Nixon* (Lanham, MD: Lexington Books, 2017).

12. For the language of this resolution and the ones following and discussed in this section, see Dietrich Rauschning, Katja Wiesbrock, and Martin Lailach, *Key Resolutions of the United Nations General Assembly 1946–1996* (Cambridge: Cambridge University Press, 1998). It was a somewhat strange development, as it displayed an unexpected harmony of minds between the United States and the Soviet Union at precisely the time that the Soviet Union was crushing the Hungarian rebellion. But Hammarskjöld and Dulles were focused on the Sinai, not on Budapest, and held their noses as they collaborated with the Soviet Union.

13. "Foreign Office," Israel State Archives, November 27, 1956. On file with the author.

14. Letter from Israeli Consul, January 24, 1957. On file with the author.

15. On January 24, 1957, Teddy Kollek, then director general of the prime minister's office, wrote to Israel's consul general in New York: "For proletarian reasons [Golda] decided to come to the United States by herself. Maybe when she takes her next trip she will take with her an experienced secretary." Letter from Teddy Kollek to Israel's consul general in the United States, January 24, 1957. On file with the author.

16. Esther Herlitz, *Esther: How Far Could a Woman Go?* (Tel Aviv: Ministry of Defense, 1994) (Hebrew).

17. Menachem Meir, *My Mother, Golda Meir: A Son's Evocation of Life with Golda Meir* (New York: Arbor House, 1983).

18. Stephanie Coontz, *A Strange Stirring: The Feminine Mystique and American Women at the Dawn of the 1960s* (New York: Basic Books, 2011); and Gail Collins, *When Everything Changed* (New York: Little, Brown, 2009), ch. 1.

19. Also at stake was the validity of the armistice agreement signed in 1949. Indeed, Israel's invasion of Egypt did violate these agreements, but Egypt did not recognize the validity of the agreements and therefore could not fault Israel for their violation. Golda was calling for a more rigorous implementation of the agreements by Egypt before a withdrawal followed.

20. Suzy Eban, *A Sense of Purpose: Recollections* (London: Halban, 2009).

21. Herlitz, *How Far Could a Woman Go?*, 109.

22. Herlitz, *How Far Could a Woman Go?*, 111.

23. Of all the supporters, Golda singled out Clare Boothe Luce in her testimony before the Knesset Foreign Affairs and Security Committee in March 1957.

24. Senator William Knowland, the Senate Republican minority leader, an isolationist, staunch anticommunist, and anti–New Deal man, was a member of the U.S. delegation to the UN during the fall and winter of 1956/1957. He complained bitterly of the administration's selective enforcement of international law, condemning Israel but failing to condemn the Soviet Union for its brutal invasion of Hungary. At one point he even threatened to resign his membership in the UN delegation as a protest against Eisenhower's "double standard" policy toward Israel. Isaac Alteras, *Eisenhower and Israel: U.S.–Israel Relations, 1953–1960* (Gainesville: University Press of Florida, 1993), 265.

25. Alteras, *Eisenhower and Israel*, 246–315.

26. "Dulles Formulated and Conducted U.S. Foreign Policy for More Than Six Years," Obituary, *New York Times*, May 25, 1959.

27. Member of Knesset Itzhak Ben-Aharon, Protocols, Knesset Committee on Foreign Affairs and Security, Israel State Archives, February 19, 1957.

28. For more information on Dulles and his daughter, see Stephen Kinzer, *The Brothers: John Foster Dulles, Allen Dulles, and Their Secret World War* (New York: Times Books, 2013), 46. For more information on Sullivan and Cromwell's sex discrimination, see Elizabeth Schneider and Stephanie M. Wildman, *Women and the Law: Stories* (New York: Foundation Press, 2010). For information on sex discrimination in the U.S. State Department, see Eleanor Lansing Dulles, *Chances of a Lifetime: A Memoir* (Englewood Cliffs, NJ: Prentice Hall Direct, 1980), ch. 18.

29. The first minister of foreign affairs in twentieth-century history was Ana Pauker of Romania; even if Dulles had met her, he would have had little interaction with her.

30. Lansing Dulles, *Chances of a Lifetime*, 228–29, 239.

31. Lansing Dulles, *Chances of a Lifetime*, 238.

32. An aide-memoire is an informal diplomatic message. For the language of this aide memoire and other documents submitted by the United States Department of State to Israel's government see Ambassador Abba Eban: *The Diplomatic Campaign in the United Nations and in the United States Following the Sinai Campaign*, October 1956–March 1957, Washington, June 1957, internal report, 199. The report was originally classified top secret but has since been declassified. Israel State Archives and on file with the author. See also *Documents on the Foreign Policy of Israel*, Volume 11 January–October 1956, Baruch Gilad ed. (Jerusalem: Israel State Archives, 2008) (Hebrew). See also Abba Eban, *The New Diplomacy, International Affairs in the Modern Age* (London: Widenfeld and Nicholson) 394–401.

33. Eban's classified report, February 21, 1957, 237. Israel State Archives.

34. Eban's classified report, February 21, 1957, 237.

35. Herlitz, *How Far Could a Woman Go?*, 113.

36. Golda Meir's speech, U.N. GAOR, 11th Sess., 666th plen. Mtg. at 1275, U.N. Doc. A/PV.666 (Mar. 1, 1957).

37. Ambassador Henry Cabot Lodge Jr. speech, U.N. GAOR, 11th Sess., 666th plen. mtg. at 1277, U.N. Doc. A/PV.666 (Mar. 1, 1957). As previously agreed with the Americans, Golda began with the Straits of Tiran. Dulles developed the legal doctrine that the straits were "international waters" and therefore she declared that the legal principle of "free and innocent passage" applied to them under international law. This was quite a major gain for Israel and an unmistakable fruit of her diplomatic campaign. She then announced the stick that the United States handed Israel:

she would regard any interference with Israel's rights to free and innocent passage as an act of war, legally recognizing her right of self-defense. The second and more contentious part of the speech was related to Gaza and was drafted by the French. Israel's withdrawal was not unconditional as the assembly had insisted. It rested on three "assumptions and expectations," a term that Christian Pineau, the French minister of foreign affairs, offered as a euphemism for "conditions": first, Gaza will be "exclusively" administered, militarily and administratively, by the United Nations; second, the UNEF will serve as the local government in charge; and third, the United Nations will stay in Gaza until peace is achieved between Israel and Egypt. The first condition was termed an "assumption" and the remaining two were termed "expectations." Thus, Gaza would not go back to Egypt as Dag Hammarskjöld had insisted.

38. This was done through mentioning the various assembly resolutions adopted in this matter, thereby giving them legitimacy as legal sources. In addition, Lodge invoked the armistice agreement that had earlier been declared null and void by Ben-Gurion and later by Golda.

39. Golda Meir's speech, U.N. GAOR (Mar. 1, 1957). Did Lodge take instructions from Dulles, who may have wanted to show America's Arab friends that it was not doing Israel's bidding? Was he speaking for Eisenhower, his direct boss, who may have preferred a nuanced message not to be aired? Was Lodge influenced at the last minute by the fuming Hammarskjöld, who felt that the "deal" destroyed the efficacy and moral base of the United Nations and sent the world into pre–World War II chaos? Did Lodge fear that Hammarskjöld might resign? Perhaps.

40. Meir, *My Life*, 296.

41. Meir, *My Life*, 296.

42. Zach Levey, *Israel in Africa 1956–1976* (Dordrecht: Republic of Letters Publishing, 2012).

43. Meir, *My Life*, 296.

44. Meron Medzini, *Golda Meir: A Political Biography* (Tel Aviv: Yediot Ahronot, Sifre Hemed, 2008), 314 (Hebrew).

45. Meir, *My Life*, 296.

46. The following description is based on Rafael's memoir, *Destination Peace*, 64–67.

47. Asaf Siniver, *Abba Eban: A Biography* (New York: Abrams Books, 2015), 289–90.

48. Abba Eban, *The New Diplomacy: International Affairs in the Modern Age* (New York: Random House, 1983).

49. In a letter to Herzl Berger, Ben-Gurion specified the qualifications required of a minister of foreign affairs: "a substantial capacity to foresee the future, courage and a deep understanding of the factors and actual circumstances of foreign affairs." Yaakov Sharett and Rina Sharett, eds., *A Statesman Assessed: Views and Viewpoints about Moshe Sharett* (Tel Aviv: Sharett Heritage Society, 2008), 95 (Hebrew).

Chapter Eighteen: The African Connection

1. Michael Bar-Zohar, *Shimon Peres: The Biography* (New York: Random House, 2006), 289. Bar-Zohar concedes that as the energetic director general of the ministry of defense, Peres was relentless in usurping Golda's governmental responsibilities. Golda's complaints to Ben-Gurion were mostly ignored.

2. For a more nuanced look and photos of Golda dancing, see https://quod.lib.umich.edu /cgi/p/pod/dod-idx/when-golda-meir-was-in-africa.pdf?c=fia;idno=11879367.2015 .008;format=pdf, accessed August 22, 2021.

3. Meir Chazan, "Golda Meir: A Female Leader, Chairwoman of the Party," *Iyunim Bitkumat Yisrael* 20 (2010): 259 (Hebrew). Menachem Meir, *My Mother, Golda Meir: A Son's Evocation of Life with Golda Meir* (New York: Arbor House, 1983), 163–64.

4. Golda Meir, *My Life* (New York: Dell, 1976), 315. For more information on Golda's anti-racist legacy, see Hagai Tsoref, ed., *Golda Meir: The Fourth Prime Minister, Selected Documents, 1898–1978* (Jerusalem: Israel State Archives, 2016), 243–49 (Hebrew).

5. Ben-Gurion was keeping company with the "young" rising politicians, later members of his Rafi party. He did not hide his expectation that they would take over the reins of power soon. One can imagine that this prediction did not please Golda. She was also unhappy about his obsession with the mysterious Lavon affair that had taken place a few years back and had recently been reignited. Anita Shapira, *Israel: A History* (Waltham, MA: Brandeis University Press, 2012), 202–5; and Yossi Goldstein, *Golda: A Biography* (Beersheba: Ben-Gurion University Press, 2012), 410–26 (Hebrew).

6. Chazan, "Golda Meir," 249, 256. For the background to the split, see Meron Medzini, *Golda Meir: A Political Biography* (Tel Aviv: Yediot Ahronot, Sifre Hemed, 2008), 378–406 (Hebrew).

7. Medzini, *Golda Meir*, 397–400; and Chazan, "Golda Meir," 262.

Chapter Nineteen: Ascendance

1. Yitzhak Greenberg, *Pinchas Sapir: A Political and Economic Biography* (Tel Aviv: Ressling, 2011), 352–57 (Hebrew).

2. Golda Meir, *My Life* (New York: Dell, 1976), 365.

3. Meir, *My Life*, 363.

4. *Divrei Haknesset* [Knesset Plenary Records], March 17, 1969, 1958–59 (Hebrew).

5. *Divrei Haknesset*, March 17, 1969, 1958–59 (Member of Knesset Levin) and 1972 (Member of Knesset Avenry). Avnery's description of Golda as a woman skilled in hating appeared in his magazine, *Ha-Olam Ha-Zae* [This World], March 3, 1969 (Hebrew).

6. One of their grievances was the lavish packages offered to Soviet Jewish immigrants as compared to the dearth of resources offered Mizrahi Jews.

7. Hagai Tsoref, ed., *Golda Meir: The Fourth Prime Minister, Selected Documents, 1898–1978* (Jerusalem: Israel State Archives, 2016), 362–65 (Hebrew); and Deborah Bernstein, "Conflicts and Protest in Society: The Case of the Black Panthers in Israel," *Youth and Society* 16 (1984): 129–52.

8. *Ha-Olam Ha-Zae*, August 7, 1971 (Hebrew). The magazine placed the naked Golda poster on its front cover. This attests to its bad taste, male chauvinism, and wish to make a profit. One wonders whether it would have done the same had the poster portrayed an elderly male leader.

9. For an excellent discussion, see Arye Naor, "An Anatomy of Yearning for a Savior," in *Crossroads of Decisions in Israel*, ed. Dvora Hacohen and Moshe Lissak (Jerusalem: Ben-Gurion Research Institute, 2010), 454.

10. Quoted in Tom Segev, *1967: Israel, the War, and the Year that Transformed the Middle East* (New York: Metropolitan Books, 2007), 329.

11. Meir, *My Life*, 349–50.

12. Mordechai Bar-On, *Moshe Dayan: Israel's Controversial Hero* (New Haven, CT: Yale University Press, 2012), 267.

13. Dalia Gavriely Nuri, *Israeli Culture on the Road to the Yom Kippur War* (New York: Israel Academic Press, 2014) (Hebrew).

14. Meron Medzini, *Golda Meir: A Political Biography* (Tel Aviv: Yediot Ahronot, Sifre Hemed, 2008), 471 (Hebrew).

15. Medzini, *Golda Meir*, 474.

16. *The Agranat Commission Report* (Tel Aviv: Am Oved, 1975), 27 (Hebrew).

17. Hagai Tsoref, "The Golda Meir Government Prior to the Yom Kippur War: Reply to Yigal Kipnis," *Iyunim Bitkumat Israel* 28 (2017): 7. This article responds to Kipnis's description of Golda Meir's policy as obstructing all initiatives to peace, in Yigal Kipnis, *1973: The Road to War* (Charlottesville, VA: Just World Books, 2013).

18. In the last few years, more in-depth archival research shows that in fact Golda and her cabinet did pursue various options of accommodating the demands of Israel's Arab neighbors but that these efforts did not yield the desired fruit. See Tsoref, *Golda Meir, The Fourth Prime Minister*, 459–571 and Hagai Tsoref, "Golda Meir's Leadership in the Yom Kippur War," *Israel Studies* 23, no. 1 (2018): 50; and exchange between H. Tsoref and Y. Kipnis fn 17 in this book. As this book goes to press another important book by one of Israel's leading military historians, based on extensive archival research is published, Yoav Gelber, *Rahav* (Tel Aviv: Kinneret, Zmora, Dvir, 2021) (Hebrew). Gelber's book confirms Hagai Tsoref's findings above, however its content is not incorporated into the research presented herewith.

Chapter Twenty: Golda as an Object of Humiliation

1. Meir Chazan, "Golda Meir: A Female Leader, Chairwoman of the Party," *Iyunim Bitkumat Yisrael* 20 (2010): 259 (Hebrew).

2. Uri Ram, *Israeli Nationalism: Social Conflicts and Politics of Knowledge* (New York: Routledge, 2011).

3. The epigraph following the subheading is from Hanoch Levin, *What Does the Bird Care?* (Tel Aviv: Siman Keria and Hakibbutz Hame'uchad, 1987), 92 (Hebrew).

4. For an analysis of the genre, see Susanna Morton Braund and Barbara K. Gold, "Introduction," *Arerthusa* 31, no. 3 (1998): 247.

5. Levin, *What Does the Bird Care?*, 92. This skit was cut by the Israeli censor. The entire play (*Queen of a Bathtub*) is printed in this volume.

6. Ofer Aderet, "What Miri Regev Should Learn from *Queen of a Bathtub*," *Haaretz*, August 3, 2016.

7. A *balabusta* in Yiddish culture is an accomplished housewife. Perhaps unbeknownst to Levin, here was the unhappy side of the role Golda's mother wanted her daughter to assume. See parts I and II in this volume.

8. The double entendre was clear to any Israeli. On the one hand, the scene depicted the dire living conditions in Israel since independence (prosperity following the Six-Day War was only beginning), and on the other hand, the scene stood for the dark side of the Israeli–Palestinian conflict. While Jews and Palestinians (cousins) were sharing the crumbled dwelling, the Jews were aggressively pushing their Palestinian cousins out while their prime minister piously repeated Israel's desire for peace.

9. Levin, *What Does the Bird Care?*, 93, 97.

10. Itzhak Laor, *Hanoch Levin* (Tel Aviv: Ha-Kibbutz Ha-Meuchad, 2010), 21–25 (Hebrew).

11. For a fascinating analysis of how men project their sexual fantasies onto women (under cover of safeguarding women's modesty), see Tova Hartman, *Feminism Encounters Traditional Judaism* (Waltham, MA: Brandeis University Press, 2007), 45–61.

12. Weizman refused to consider the concept of gender stereotypes. As president of Israel in 1993, when a young woman petitioned to the High Court of Justice to be trained as a combat pilot (until then closed to female candidates), Weizman confronted her: "Listen Meydele [little girl in Yiddish], have you ever seen a man knit socks? Seen a woman surgeon or orchestra conductor? Women cannot withstand the pressures experienced by combat pilots." Smadar Shmueli, "Little Girl, Have You Ever Seen a Man Knit Socks?" *Yediot Acharonot*, July 2, 2000.

13. For a discussion of Levin's misogyny, see Laor, *Hanoch Levin*, 195.

14. Both *Haaretz* and *Ma'ariv* protested the obscene language in the play, but did not address its misogynistic aspects. Haim Gamzu, "*Queen of the Bathtub*, the End," *Haaretz*, May 22, 1970, Yaacov Ha-Elyon, "Whistles and Scourge at 'Queen of Bathtub'," *Ma'ariv*, April 1970 (Hebrew); and Reuven Yanai, *Ma'ariv*, April 19, 1970.

15. Hagai Tsoref, ed., *Golda Meir: The Fourth Prime Minister, Selected Documents, 1898–1978* (Jerusalem: Israel State Archives, 2016), 329–37 (Hebrew).

16. Tsoref, *Golda Meir*, 330.

17. Francine Klagsbrun, *Lioness: Golda Meir and the Nation of Israel* (New York: Schocken, 2017), 547; and Oriana Fallaci, "Golda Meir," *Interview with History* (Boston: Houghton Mifflin Harcourt, 1976), 121.

18. Interviews with Gideon Meir and Shaul Rahabi, December 19, 2017, Tel Aviv.

19. Fallaci, "Golda Meir," 121.

20. See chapter 22 in this volume.

Chapter Twenty-One: From Bathtub to Pedestal

1. Oriana Fallaci, "Golda Meir," *Interview with History* (Boston: Houghton Mifflin Harcourt, 1976), 88.

2. Fallaci, "Golda Meir," 90–93.

3. Simon Reeve, *One Day in September* (New York: Arcade, 2018).

4. On Fallaci, see Margaret Talbot, "The Agitator," *New Yorker*, June 5, 2006; and Cristina de Stefano, *Oriana Fallaci* (New York: Other Press, 2017).

5. The epigraph to this section is from Fallaci, "Golda Meir," 112.

6. Fallaci, "Golda Meir," 112.

7. Susan Faludi, *Backlash: The Undercover War against American Women* (New York: Crown, 1991); Jane Sherron De Hart, *Ruth Bader Ginsburg: A Life* (New York: Knopf, 2018); and Dafna Izraeli et al., *Sex Gender Politics: Women in Israel* (Tel Aviv: Hakibbutz Hameuchad, 1999).

8. Compare Golda's zigzagging on the woman question to her report on Pioneer Women, 1932, part II. Golda Meir, *Impressions on Travel to America*, Davar, 5.25.1932 (Hebrew).

9. Fallaci, "Golda Meir," 113.

10. Fallaci, "Golda Meir," 119.

Chapter Twenty-Two: Golda and Her Nemesis

1. Anita Shapira, in her insightful short essay on Golda, situates her in the context of the rising intergenerational divide rocking Israel in the 1960s and 1970s. Anita Shapira, "Golda: Femininity and Feminism," in *American Jewish Women and the Zionist Enterprise*, ed. Shulamit Reinharz and Mark A. Raider (Lebanon, NH: Brandeis University Press/University Press of New England, 2004), 306–7. For an analysis of Golda's role in the late 1960s, as Aloni entered politics and the intergenerational divide intensified, see Meir Chazan, "Golda Meir: A Female Leader, Chairwoman of the Party," *Iyunim Bitkumat Yisrael* 20 (2010): 249 (Hebrew). For an analysis of Israeli women in politics, see the comprehensive study, Hanna Herzog, *Gendering Politics: Women in Israel* (Ann Arbor: University of Michigan Press, 1999). Much of the information in this chapter appears in Aloni's interviews with the historian Idith Zertal. Shulamit Aloni, *I Can Do No Other* (Tel Aviv: Maariv Book Guild, 1997) (Hebrew).

2. Shulamit Aloni, *Women as Human Beings* [Nashim k-vnei Adam] (Jerusalem: Keter, 1976) (Hebrew). She was also a well-known and widely popular consumer advocate.

3. For a good discussion of family matters in Israel, see Ruth Halperin-Kaddari, *Women in Israel: A State of Their Own* (Philadelphia: University of Pennsylvania Press, 2004).

4. Aloni, *Women as Human Beings*. Among the many aspects of gender discrimination, she flagged the monopoly of the rabbinical courts, populated only by male rabbis, over matters of marriage and divorce and the many ancient practices affirming the patriarchy.

5. Julia Twigg, *Fashion and Age: Dress, the Body and Later Life* (New York: Bloomsbury Academic, 2013).

6. "At the First Labor Session, Staffing Committees Began," *Ma'ariv*, June 5, 1974, 3 (Hebrew).

7. The electoral system has since changed to incorporate primaries.

8. Bat-Sheva Margalit Stern, *Redemption in Chains* (Jerusalem: Yad Ben-Zvi, 2006) (Hebrew).

9. Bat-Sheva Margalit Stern, *The Revolutionary: Ada Fishman Maimon* (Beersheba: Ben-Gurion University Press, 2018), 479–80. While Golda appeared as fourth on the list of Mapai's candidates to the Third Knesset, Ada was pushed to the back of the list and had no chance of being reelected.

10. Aloni ran on this ticket in 1974, following the Yom Kippur War. The party won three seats, which was quite an achievement. This party still exists under the name Meretz, indicating its sturdy place in the Israeli political landscape.

11. See interviews with Zina Harman in the Milwaukee Golda Meir Archives. See also Esther Herlitz, *Esther: How Far Could a Woman Go?* (Tel Aviv: Ministry of Defense, 1994) (Hebrew). All these women were talented, but they did not have the fire in the belly that drove Aloni.

12. "Golda Meir Left the Labor Party's Meeting in Rage," *Ma'ariv*, May 10, 1974, 2 (Hebrew). Two women members, Beba Idelson and Shoshana Arbeli-Almozlino, opposed Aloni's cabinet post as well.

13. Golda Meir, *My Life* (New York: Dell, 1976), 64, 103, 117.

14. Aloni, *I Can Do No Other*, 104.

15. Aloni, *I Can Do No Other*, 117.

Chapter Twenty-Three: Who Is a Jew?

This chapter was presented at the Anita Shapira Forum, Tel Aviv University Department of Jewish History. I thank Professor Orit Rozin for inviting me, reading my chapter and providing insightful comments and to Professors Ron Harris and Hanna Herzog for offering excellent reviews of my paper. Thanks too to Professor Danny Gutwein for his instructive comments and to other members of the workshop who participated in the discussion. I benefited enormously from all.

1. Anne was the granddaughter of Sir Patrick Geddes, a well-known Scottish town planner who also worked for the British government in Palestine.

2. Secular Zionists trusted that life in the Jewish state would construct an independent "Israeli identity," unencumbered by the exilic Jewish past and rabbinical law. It is interesting that at the same time, prominent rabbis also paid attention to the developing Jewish identity in the sovereign state of Israel. Arye Edrei, "Secularism and Nationalism: The Modern Halakhic Discourse on the Identity and Boundaries of the Jewish Community," in *Secularism in Question: Jews and Judaism in Modern Times*, ed. Ari Joskowicz and Ethan Katz (Philadelphia: University of Pennsylvania Press, 2015), 232, 249–57.

3. They could be registered either as "British" or "without nationality." Similarly, they could be registered either as "Christian" or as "having no religion."

4. See Pnina Lahav, *Judgment in Jerusalem: Chief Justice Simon Agranat and the Zionist Century* (Berkeley: University of California Press, 1997). This was the first time Israel's High Court sat in a panel of nine justices.

5. The majority did concede this was a technical matter that did not affect the power of the rabbinical courts to inquire into the children's Jewishness, if and when they desired to get married in Israel.

6. Lahav, *Judgment in Jerusalem*, 196–220.

7. Brown v. Board of Education of Topeka, 347 U.S. 483 (1954); and Cooper v. Aaron, 358 U.S. 1 (1958).

8. Hagai Tsoref, ed., *Golda Meir: The Fourth Prime Minister, Selected Documents, 1898–1978* (Jerusalem: Israel State Archives, 2016), 320 (Hebrew); and Yoav Gelber, *Attrition: The Forgotten War* (Modiin: Kineret Zmora Dvir, 2017), 474–77 (Hebrew).

9. The amendment did not require that the relatives accompany the one who meets the statutory definition of a Jew or even that the one who met the statutory definition be alive.

10. For an interesting analysis of the way in which the rabbinical authorities handle the issue of conversion in Israel, see Michal Kravel-Tovi, *When the State Winks: The Performance of Jewish Conversion in Israel Religion, Culture, and Public Life* (New York: Columbia University Press, 2017).

11. "Cabinet Meeting," Fifteenth Israel's Cabinet, January 1, 1970, 15 (Hebrew).

12. The Orthodox attitude toward candidates for conversion is generally negative, based on the suspicion that one could not possibly be sincere in the wish to join the Jewish people. The candidate is expected to display intense knowledge of Jewish law, prove that she is following all the rules (which secular Jews typically are neither familiar with nor follow), and during the conversion submit to ritual immersion in the mikvah (ritual bath) in the presence of three rabbis (men) who together form the converting court. Converting men must go through the ritual of circumcision. The Reform and Conservative process performed in the United States embraces the converting candidate, thereby displaying a positive attitude toward someone's decision to become a Jew. It does not require intense learning of Jewish law and is more respectful of the dignity of the converting candidate. See Kravel-Tovi, *When the State Winks*.

13. I thank Meron Medzini for sharing this information with me.

14. "Law of Return," *Divrei Haknesset*, February 10, 1970, 770.

15. *Divrei Haknesset*, April 4, 1972, 133. All quotations in the text are derived from the Knesset records .

16. See Kravel-Tovi, *When the State Winks*.

17. Golda Meyerson, "Borrowed Mothers," in *The Plough Woman: Records of the Pioneer Women of Palestine, A Critical Edition*, ed. Mark Raider and Miriam B. Raider-Roth (Boston: Brandeis University Press, 2002), 164–65.

18. Myerson (Meir), "Borrowed Mothers."

19. Oriana Fallaci, "Golda Meir," *Interview with History* (Boston: Houghton Mifflin Harcourt, 1976).

20. The Law of Return, 5710 (1950). The relevant text is reproduced below. Section 4B of the amended law provided that "For the purposes of this Law, 'Jew' means a person who was born of a Jewish mother or has become converted to Judaism and who is not a member of another religion." (The religious parties demanded that the words "in accordance to Halacha" be added to the sentence after "converted to Judaism." But this did not come to pass and has been a subject of controversy ever since.) To extend protection to family members who did not meet the Halachic criteria, section 4A of the law provided: "(a) The rights of a Jew under this Law and the rights of an Oleh under the Nationality Law, 5712-1952, as well as the rights of an Oleh under any other enactment, are also vested in a child and a grandchild of a Jew, the spouse of a Jew, the spouse of a child of a Jew and the spouse of a grandchild of a Jew, except for a person who has been a Jew and has voluntarily changed his religion." Golda continued to criticize the rabbinical establishment throughout the following year. In 1972 she criticized the rabbis for ignoring the plight of the non-Jew: "A bit of a humane attitude to the personal suffering—is certainly lacking." Golda's speech at the Central Labor Assembly, *Divrei Haknesset*, April 4, 1972, 133.

21. This note is undated, but was probably written in the 1930s. It contains a misspelling (Golda's Hebrew was still weak) and ends with "and nevertheless I disagree with you." It is not clear what the disagreement was about.

22. Shulamit Aloni, *I Can Do No Other* (Tel Aviv: Maariv Book Guild, 1997), 50.

23. Aloni, *I Can Do No Other*, 40.

24. Aloni, *I Can Do No Other*, 136.

25. And if the majority were coerced into following the party line through the mechanism of party discipline, that was acceptable too, as an exception to the rule under special circumstances.

26. On Golda's preference for compromise over absolute principles see Tsoref, ed., *Golda Meir: The Fourth Prime Minister, Selected Documents 1898–1978* (Jerusalem, Israel State Archives, 2016, 130–31 and State Document 41 there, Hebrew).

27. Shulamit Aloni, *Ha-Hesder: From the Rule of Law to the Rule of Halacha* (Jerusaem: Otpaz, 1970) (Hebrew).

28. Aloni's response was published on February 9, 1970. She repeated her arguments that Israeli law did not permit the introduction of Jewish law into the registration documents.

29. See documentary by Anat Saragusti, Citizen Aloni, https://youtu.be/teOnGBmfBK8.

Chapter Twenty-Four: Golda and the Revival of Feminism

1. The movie stars were Mia Farrow and Raquel Welch. Farrow appeared alongside film star Dustin Hoffman with her face below his (February 7, 1969), and Welch appeared in a bikini (November 28, 1969).

2. "But Can She Type? [Golda Meir]," Seattle-King County National Organization for Women, 1970.

3. Regina worked for the World Zionist Organization, and from there moved to the Jewish Agency and then to the Israeli Ministry of Foreign Affairs. Like many able women of her generation who chose to work while raising a family, she reached the top of the administrative and bureaucratic hierarchy (one expects that a little help from Golda, already in high positions of power, could not have hurt).

4. Golda Meir, *My Life* (New York: Dell, 1976), 37.

5. Oriana Fallaci, "Golda Meir," *Interview with History* (Boston: Houghton Mifflin Harcourt, 1976) and Meir, *My Life*, 108–9. Note her description of her feelings when she accepted the lot of a homemaker in Jerusalem: "I was sort of a prisoner . . . I was filled with a bitter resentment against my lot in life. Was this what it was all about—poverty, drudgery and worry?" (97).

6. Bra burning happened only once and was not typical of the feminist protests. Golda herself was a member of the feminist Women Workers Council, participated in their decision-making meetings, and served as their representative on many occasions. On the myth of bra burning see Dorothy Sue Cobble, Linda Gordon, and Astrid Henry, *Feminism Unfinished* (New York: Liveright Publishing, 2014), 64, 69. This book also reviews the history of the American women's movement and its connection to the New Left.

7. Menachem Meir, *My Mother, Golda Meir: A Son's Evocation of Life with Golda Meir* (New York: Arbor House, 1983), 36.

8. Dafna N. Izraeli, "Gender in the Workplace," *Sex, Gender, Politics: Women in Israel* (Tel Aviv: Hakibbutz Hameuchad, 1999); and Letty Cottin Pogrebin, *Deborah, Golda, and Me* (New York: Crown, 1991).

9. Henry Kissinger, *White House Years* (Boston: Little, Brown, 1979), 564–67. A similar handwritten letter from Golda was delivered to Richard Nixon at the same time (568).

10. The first article was published in May 1969. Billy Graham, "Vocation of Honor," *Ladies' Home Journal* (May 1969), 14.

11. Graham, "Vocation of Honor"; Billy Graham, "Jesus and the Liberated Woman," *Ladies' Home Journal* (December 1970), 42. See also Ellen Ott Marshall, "A Matter of Pride: A Feminist Response to Billy Graham," in *The Legacy of Billy Graham*, ed. Michael G. Long (Louisville, KY: Westminster John Knox Press, 2008), 91, 89. At that time, the *Ladies' Home Journal* had a circulation of 6.8 million and was therefore a major player in the field of public opinion.

12. "The New Feminism," *Ladies' Home Journal* (August 1970). Graham, "Jesus and the Liberated Woman" was published in December 1970.

13. Meir, *My Life*, 58.

14. Gail Collins, *When Everything Changed: The Amazing Journey of American Women from 1960 to the Present* (New York: Little Brown, 2009); Ruth Rosen, *The World Split Open: How the Modern Women's Movement Changed America* (New York: Penguin Books, 2000). In 1969 Leila Khaled, a Palestinian member of the Popular Front for the Liberation of Palestine, participated in the hijacking of TWA flight 840 from Tel Aviv. She was the first woman to hijack an airplane and was widely admired in New Left feminist circles. Student protests during Golda's visits to American campuses flagged Khaled's act of terrorism as a heroic act and embraced the Palestinian Struggle.

15. Shulamit Aloni, *Women as Human Beings* [*Nashim k-vnei Adam*] (Jerusalem: Keter, 1976) (Hebrew).

16. Meir, *My Life*, 53.

17. See Betty Friedan's enthusiastic description of this event when she visited in Israel: Betty Friedan, "Women and Jews: The Quest for Selfhood," in *Woman as Jew, Jew as Woman: An Urgent Inquiry*, American Jewish Congress, *Congress Monthly* 52, no. 2 (March, 1985): 7.

18. In my experience, the statement was generally accompanied by the insistence that "women never helped me," whereas men did offer assistance. Note Joanne Yaron, founder of the Tel Aviv Rape Crisis Center, speaking at the American Jewish Congress Dialogue: "We should . . . stop starting every sentence with 'I believe in women's rights but I am not a feminist.'" *Woman as Jew, Jew as Woman*, 18.

19. Hannah Safran, *Don't Wanna Be Nice Girls: The Struggle for Suffrage and the New Feminism in Israel* (Haifa: Pardes, 2006), 70.

20. The argument against Ben-Porat was that she was "difficult to get along with," implying that a woman should be nice and accommodating, Miriam Ben-Porat, *Through the Robe* (Jerusalem: Keter, 2005), 89–90, 122 (Hebrew).

21. Orna Sasson-Levy, *Identities in Uniform: Masculinities and Femininities in the Israeli Military* (Jerusalem: Magnes, 2006) (Hebrew). Catharine MacKinnon, *Sexual Harassment of Working Women* (New Haven, CT: Yale University Press, 1979).

22. Rina Dotan, "Golda and the Next Generation of the Women Worker's Movement," *Golda: A Memorial Collection* (Tel Aviv: Am Oved, 1981), 99, 100.

23. Aviva Cantor, *Jewish Women/Jewish Men: The Legacy of Patriarchy in Jewish Life* (San Francisco: Harper One, 1995).

24. Aloni, *Women as Human Beings*.

25. *Ms.* 1 (1972): 43.

26. Pogrebin, *Deborah, Golda, and Me*, 154.

27. Pogrebin, *Deborah, Golda, and Me*, 167; see also Joyce Antler, *Jewish Radical Feminism: Voices from the Women's Liberation Movement* (New York: New York University Press, 2018).

28. Pogrebin, *Deborah, Golda, and Me*, 30.

29. Patricia Burstein, "It's Get Up and Go Go for a 77-year-old Granny Named Golda Meir" *People*, January 26, 1976.

30. Pogrebin describes her wonder at a gathering where Israeli women expressed unawareness of gender discrimination, insisting women did not wish for equality, and asking rhetorically: "Where were the feminists?" She also described a luncheon given by the Israeli Commission on the Status of Women, at which the Americans "snickered when one of the Commissioners said, as if she'd invented the idea, 'Golda Meir proved that it can be done.'" Pogrebin, *Deborah, Golda, and Me*, 173.

31. Pogrebin, *Deborah, Golda, and Me*, 175.

Chapter Twenty-Five: Nightmare

The epigraph is from Golda Meir, *My Life* (New York: Dell, 1976), 410. There is a vast literature on the war, and not all the sources consulted can be included herein. For a sober, authoritative, and documented analysis and review, see Shimon Golan, "War on Yom Kippur: Decision-Making in the Israel High Command in Yom Kippur War," *Ma'arachot* (2013) (Hebrew). Golan is chief of strategic research in the Department of History of the Israel Defense Forces and his book relies on extensive documentation (not all declassified). Another valuable source is Hagai Tsoref, ed., *Golda Meir: The Fourth Prime Minister, Selected Documents, 1898–1978* (Jerusalem: Israel State Archives, 2016), ch. 18 (Hebrew). And most recently, Yoav Gelber, *Rahav (Hubris)*, (Tel Aviv: Dvir, 2021) (Hebrew). Gelber's book is based on the most updated archival research. The book was published as this manuscript goes to press and most of its findings and discussion are not covered herewith.

1. For an insightful analysis, see Dalia Gavrieli-Nuri, *Israeli Culture on the Road to the Yom Kippur War* (Israel Academic Press: 2014) (Hebrew).

2. Akiva Eldar, "Border Control," *Haaretz*, October 11, 2011 (Hebrew).

3. Syria lost an estimated 3,500 dead, and 21,000 wounded. Egypt had an estimated 15,000 killed and 30,000 wounded. Iraqi casualties were 125 killed and 260 wounded.

4. Dayan famously stated that the military situation amounts to "the destruction of the Third Temple." Tsoref, *Golda Meir*, 520. Golda instructed the Israeli ambassador to the United States to call Kissinger immediately, "I don't care what is the time," and tell him Israel was being defeated. The U.S. Secretary of Defense James Schlesinger recalled that "as Israel began to fall apart, Henry began to fall apart." Walter Isaacson, *Kissinger: A Biography* (New York: Simon and Schuster, 1992), 521. It should be added that it appears that Sadat's war plan was to stop short of invading the green line. Rather, he planned to get back Egyptian territory conquered in 1967. Meron Medzini, *Golda Meir: A Political Biography* (Tel Aviv: Yediot Ahronot, Sifre Hemed, 2008) (Hebrew).

5. Medzini, *Golda Meir*, 515.

6. Medzini, *Golda Meir*, 547. Mordechai Bar-On, *Moshe Dayan* (Tel Aviv: Am Oved, 2014), 278–79 (Hebrew).

7. High alert was activated a few days earlier in view of the military maneuvers on the front. The military command took the necessary precautions, but doubted any attack was imminent. https://anatyahalom.co.il/about-anat-yahalom/ (Hebrew).

8. Of course, many found no consolation and would never overcome the shattering loss.

9. Oz Almog, *The Sabra: The Creation of the New Jew* (Tel Aviv: Am Oved, 2000), 334–35.

10. Y. Ben-Porat et al., *Ha-Mechdal* (*The Mishap*) ("Special edition" is listed as the publisher. Tel Aviv, 1973) (Hebrew). It appears that the book was hastily put together at the end of the war. The book characterized Golda as "an emotional woman who follows her personal predilections while ignoring the public interest" (151) and also that "Golda did not understand the complex interrelationship between the various intelligence organs and that therefore . . . one could not expect her to distinguish between top secret messages, reliable and unreliable sources or intelligence reports" (70).

11. Moshe Dayan, *Milestones* [Avney Derech] (Jerusalem: Dvir, 1976), 609.

12. Eli Ashkenazi, "Dayan Had Ups and Downs," *Haaretz*, October 5, 2010 (Hebrew); and Dayan, *Milestones*.

13. Hanna Herzog, "Women in Politics and the Politics of Women," in *Sex Gender Politics*, ed. Dafna N. Izraeli (Tel Aviv: Hakibbutz Hameuchad, 1999), 338–40 (Hebrew).

14. Herzog, "Women in Politics," 338–40.

15. Herzog, "Women in Politics," 338–40.

16. Bat-Sheva Margalit Stern, *The Revolutionary; Ada Fishman Maimon* (Beersheba: Ben-Gurion University Press, 2018). Ada Fishman Maimon died on October 10, 1973.

Chapter Twenty-Six: In the Company of Men

1. Natan Aridan, *Advocating for Israel: Diplomats and Lobbyists from Truman to Nixon* (Lanham, MD: Lexington Books, 2017), 259–60, and the references there. The plan generally envisioned overall withdrawal accompanied by peace agreements.

2. Aridan, *Advocating for Israel*, 260.

3. Boaz Ventick and Zaki Shalom, *The Yom Kippur War: The War That Could Have Been Prevented* (Tel Aviv: Resling Books, 2010), 259 (Hebrew).

4. Negotiations for a partial Israeli withdrawal from the Suez Canal took place throughout 1971, but ended in deepening the stalemate. Ventick and Shalom, *Yom Kippur War*, 153–62.

5. Hagai Tsoref, "Golda Meir's Cabinet before the Yom Kippur War—A Reply to Yigal Kipnis," *Iyunim Bi-Tkumat Yisrael* 28 (2017): 7 (Hebrew).

6. Yigal Kipnis, "The Turning Point in Studying the Circumstances of the Outbreak of the Yom Kippur War," *Iyunim Bi-Tkumat Yisrael* 26 (2016): 41 (Hebrew). See also Yigal Kipnis, *1973: The Way to War* (Or-Yehuda: Kinneret, 2012) (Hebrew). Still, even if the cabinet thought war was preferable, it is quite likely that they did not anticipate the catastrophic war that was to come. For a rebuttal of Kipnis's narrative, see Tsoref, "Golda Meir's Cabinet before the Yom Kippur War," 7.

7. For the Israeli cultural arrogance in expecting a preordained victory in any war, see Uri S. Cohen, *Security Style and the Hebrew Culture of War* (Jerusalem: Bialik Institute, 2017) (Hebrew), and Dalia Gavriely Nuri, *Israeli Culture on the Road to the Yom Kippur War* (New York: Israel Academic Press, 2014) (Hebrew).

8. Meron Medzini, *Golda Meir: A Political Biography* (Tel Aviv: Yediot Ahronot, Sifre Hemed, 2008), 547–48 (Hebrew).

9. See Golda's testimony before the Agranat Commission following the Yom Kippur War, Israel Ministry of Defense Archive. https://www.mod.gov.il/Memorial_Legacy/articles/Pages /21.1.21.aspx (Hebrew). She often referred to herself as stupid, a mark of her deep insecurity.

10. Mordechai Bar-On, *Moshe Dayan* (Tel Aviv: Am Oved, 2014), and Oz Almog, *The Sabra: The Creation of the New Jew* (Tel Aviv: Am Oved, 2000), describing the archetypical image of the Israeli warrior.

11. In fact, it was Yitzhak Rabin, the chief of staff during 1967, who prepared the army for the victory.

12. Michael Bar-Zohar, *Phoenix: Shimon Peres* (Yediot Ahronot: 2006), 241 (Hebrew).

13. Meir Chazan, "Golda Meir: A Female Leader, Chairwoman of the Party," *Iyunim Bi-Tkumat Yisrael* 20 (2010): 249 (Hebrew).

14. Dayan and Peres had left Mapai together with Ben-Gurion and formed Rafi, an independent party that did not do so well in the elections. In time, they rejoined Mapai, but Golda always suspected them for being disloyal to Mapai.

15. Orna Sasson-Levy, *Identities in Uniform: Masculinities and Femininities in the Israeli Military* (Jerusalem: Magnes, 2006), 18–32 (Hebrew). This highlights Israeli as well as international research into the connection between militarism and patriarchy. See also Ury Ben-Eliezer, *War over Peace: One Hundred Years of Israel's Militaristic Nationalism* (Oakland: University of California Press, 2019).

16. See part I in this volume; Tom Segev, *A State at Any Cost: The Life of David Ben-Gurion* (New York: Farrar, Straus and Giroux, 2019).

17. For example, the Israeli cabinet operated under the assumption that Egypt and Syria wished to annihilate Israel. Sadat, however, stated that he planned to stop the advance of his troops long before they arrived at the 1967 border. The head of the Mossad did point out this fact to the cabinet on October 10, 1973. Hagai Tsoref, ed., *Golda Meir: The Fourth Prime Minister, Selected Documents, 1898–1978* (Jerusalem: Israel State Archives, 2016), 534 (Hebrew).

18. Medzini, *Golda Meir*.

19. Tsoref, *Golda Meir*.

20. This chapter does not address the so-called war of the generals during the Yom Kippur War or Golda's role in that context. For an analysis, see Zaki Shalom, "The War of the Generals," 24 *Strategic Assessment*, Occasional papers of the Institute for National Security Studies (INNS), July 2021.

21. Medzini, *Golda Meir*, 548. It is not clear whether the cabinet secretary, Shulamit Yafe, recorded this phrase or whether the stenographer did. The name of the stenographer is unknown. I thank Meron Medzini for sharing the secretary's name with me.

22. Tsoref, *Golda Meir*, 531; emphasis added.

23. Tsoref, *Golda Meir*, 534.

24. Tsoref, *Golda Meir*, 599. During the negotiations, when Golda reviewed the proposed separation of forces she said "we could have reached this result without war." By then she was ready for compromises.

25. Two former chiefs of staff, two senior Supreme Court justices, and the state comptroller. For a discussion of the significance of the commission, a statutory body, and an analysis of its findings, see Pnina Lahav, *Judgment in Jerusalem: Chief Justice Simon Agranat and the Zionist Century* (Berkeley: University of California Press, 1997).

26. Many criticized this decision vehemently, feeling that the distinction was whitewashing, meant to exonerate the cabinet. For a discussion of the commission's reasoning, see Lahav, *Judgment in Jerusalem*.

27. *Agranat Commission Report*, 50 (Hebrew).

28. Pierre Bourdieu, *Outline of a Theory of Practice* (Cambridge: Cambridge University Press, 1977).

29. The *Agranat Commission Report* described Zeira as an arrogant man who thinks he "knows better than anyone." *Agranat Commission Report*, 56.

30. *Agranat Commission Report*, 56.

31. *Agranat Commission Report*, 25–28.

32. Y. Ben-Porat et al., *Ha-Mechdal* (*The Mishap*) ("Special edition" is listed as the publisher. Tel Aviv, 1973) (Hebrew).

33. Michael Bar-Zohar, *Facing a Cruel Mirror: Israel's Moment of Truth* (New York: Charles Scribner's, 1990), 45–47. As late as 2001, the celebrity poet Yehonatan Geffen published a book of gossip about the life of noted celebrities in Tel Aviv and placed Golda's photo on the cover, her hair bleached and a cigarette her mouth. The book's title *Chomer tov* (*Good stuff*) probably alluded to marijuana. Yehonatan Geffen, *Chomer Tov* (Tel Aviv: Kinneret Zmora Dvir, 2001) (Hebrew). The author and publisher (Kinneret Zmora-Dvir) evidently expected Golda's photo to increase sales.

34. Yotam Reuveny, "The Journalist Who Witnessed Israel's Entire History," *Haaretz*, November 30, 2017, https://www.haaretz.com/israel-news/.premium.MAGAZINE-the-journalist -who-witnessed-israel-s-entire-history-1.5627383.

35. Tsoref, *Golda Meir* (rejoinder).

36. Labor got fifty-six mandates or 46.2 percent of the popular vote. The rival Likud got thirty-nine mandates or 30.2 percent of the vote. The change came in the next election in 1977, where Likud got 33.4 percent of the vote and Labor plummeted to 24.6 percent of the vote.

37. Aloni called her party the Civil Rights Party and emphasized the ties between citizenship and rights.

38. Hanna Herzog, "Women in Politics and the Politics of Women," in *Sex Gender Politics*, ed. Dafna Izraeli et al. (Tel Aviv: Hakibbutz Ha-Meuchad, 1999), 342 (Hebrew).

39. Her coalition government gave strong representation to the national religious party, with an explicit agreement to examine the Halachic issue of "who is a Jew." She saw this issue as problematic only because she worried about the reaction of American Jewry, mostly Reform and Conservative. The issue of women was ignored.

40. *Divrei Haknesset* [Knesset Plenary Records], March 10, 1974 (Hebrew).

41. Cabinet Meeting, April 11, 1974, Israel State Archives (Hebrew).

42. Medzini, *Golda Meir*, 184, quoting Golda.

43. Correspondence from Lou Kaddar to Marie Syrkin, May 7, 1974, American Jewish Archives, Cincinnati, Ohio.

Chapter Twenty-Seven: The End

1. Laurie Johnson, "Notes on People, Broadway Play," *New York Times*, April 6, 1976, 29.

2. Billy Graham's blurb on the jacket of Golda Meir, *My Life*, 1st ed. (New York: Dell, 1975).

3. Golda quoted in an interview, Margaret Croyden, "When the Telephone Rang, Did You Know It Meant War?" *New York Times*, August 14, 1977, 67.

4. Hagai Tsoref, ed., *Golda Meir: The Fourth Prime Minister, Selected Documents, 1898–1978* (Jerusalem: Israel State Archives, 2016) (Hebrew).

5. Indeed, at that time Golda tried to correct public misapprehensions of her legacy. For example, she insisted on the publication of correct information related to the recommendations of the committee to investigate youth in distress and also on truthful depiction of the context of her remarks about the Black Panthers. Tsoref, *Golda Meir*, 632.

6. Correspondence from Lou Kaddar to Marie Syrkin, September 5, 1977, American Jewish Archives, Cincinnati, Ohio.

7. Mel Gussow, "How and Why 'Golda' Sank," *New York Times*, March 1, 1978, C23.

8. Gussow, "How and Why 'Golda' Sank"; and Meron Medzini, *Golda Meir: A Political Biography* (Tel Aviv: Yediot Ahronot, Sifre Hemed, 2008), 632 (Hebrew).

9. Stephanie Merry, "Tovah Feldshuh Brings Broadway Hit 'Golda's Balcony' to Theater J," *Washington Post*, April 10, 2014.

10. Ronald Koven, "Sadat Jokes, Laughs with Golda," *Washington Post*, November 22, 1977.

11. Menachem Meir, *My Mother, Golda Meir: A Son's Evocation of Life with Golda Meir* (New York: Arbor House, 1983), 240.

12. Correspondence from Lou Kaddar to Marie Syrkin, November 26, 1978, American Jewish Archives, Cincinnati, Ohio; correspondence from Shulamit Nardi to Marie Syrkin, October 2, 1987, American Jewish Archives, Cincinnati, Ohio.

13. Letter from Lou Kaddar to Marie Syrkin, November 26, 1978, American Jewish Archives, Cincinnati, Ohio.

14. Yisrael Eldad, "Golda," *Yediot Ahronot*, December 15, 1978.

15. Carole S. Kessner, *Marie Syrkin: Values beyond the Self* (Lebanon, NH: Brandeis University Press/University Press of New England, 2008), 440.

16. Meir, *My Mother*.

17. From Golda Myerson's speech printed in *D'var Hapoelet*, July 27, 1952 (Hebrew); emphasis added.

18. Quoted in Croyden, "When the Telephone Rang"; emphasis added.

INDEX

Page numbers in *italics* refer to photographs and their captions